COLLECTED ESSAYS IN LAW

Beyond Law in Context

Collected Essays in Law Series
General Editor: Tom D. Campbell

Legal Rules and Legal Reasoning

Larry Alexander

ISBN: 978 0 7546 2004 4

Dispute Processing and Conflict Resolution

Carrie Menkel-Meadow

ISBN: 978 0 7546 2305 2

Objectivity in Ethics and Law

Michael Moore

ISBN: 978 0 7546 2329 8

Crime, Compliance and Control

Doreen McBarnet

ISBN: 978 0 7546 2349 6

Democracy Through Law

Johan Steyn

ISBN: 978 0 7546 2404 2

Legal Reasoning, Legal Theory and Rights

Martin P. Golding

ISBN: 978 0 7546 2669 5

Meaning, Mind and Law

Dennis Patterson

ISBN: 978 0 7546 2749 4

Law as Resistance:
Modernism, Imperialism, Legalism

Peter Fitzpatrick

ISBN: 978 0 7546 2685 5

David Nelken

Beyond Law in Context

Developing a Sociological Understanding of Law

ASHGATE

Published by
Ashgate Publishing Limited
Wey Court East
Union Road
Farnham
Surrey GU9 7PT
England

Ashgate Publishing Company
Suite 420
101 Cherry Street
Burlington, VT 05401-4405
USA

Ashgate website: http://www.ashgate.com

British Library Cataloguing in Publication Data
Nelken, David
 Beyond law in context : developing a sociological
 understanding of law. - (Collected essays in law)
 1. Sociological jurisprudence
 I. Title
 340.1'15

Library of Congress Cataloging-in-Publication Data
Beyond law in context : developing a sociological understanding of law / [edited] by
 David Nelken.
  p. cm. – (Collected essays in law)
 Includes bibliographical references and index.
 ISBN 978-0-7546-2802-6 (alk paper)
 1. Sociological jurisprudence. I. Nelken, David.

 K376.B49 2008
 340'.115–dc22

2008026246

ISBN 978 0 7546 2802 6

Mixed Sources
Product group from well-managed
forests and other controlled sources
www.fsc.org Cert no. SGS-COC-2482
© 1996 Forest Stewardship Council
FSC

Printed and bound in Great Britain by
TJ International Ltd, Padstow, Cornwall

Contents

Acknowledgements

The author and publishers wish to thank the following for permission to use copyright material.

Blackwell Publishing; Cambridge University Press; De Gruyter Rechtswissenschaften Verlags-GmbH; Israel Law Review; Sweet and Maxwell; Taylor and Francis; Windsor Yearbook of Access to Justice.

David Nelken graduated from Trinity College, Cambridge with degrees in history, law and criminology. He then taught philosophy of law and sociology of law at Edinburgh University (1976–1984) and at University College, London (1984–1990). He is currently Distinguished Professor of Legal Institutions and Social Change in the University of Macerata in Italy. He is also Distinguished Research Professor of Law at Cardiff University, and Honorary Visiting Professor of Law at the London School of Economics. His areas of interest lie in law and social theory (as reflected in this volume), as well as in empirical sociology of law, criminal justice, criminology (in 1985 he was awarded an American Sociological Association Distinguished Scholar Award in this field) and comparative Law (especially the study of legal culture).

Married to an Italian judge, with four children and one grandchild, he keeps up a demanding travel schedule so as to teach and learn more about differences in legal culture in a variety of countries.

In 2007–2008 he held the Wiarda Chair at the Willem Pompe Institute of Criminal Law at the University of Utrecht, and, in 2008–2009, will be the S.T. Lee Professor at the Institute of Advanced Studies of London University. David Nelken is an active member of the Law and Social Theory academic community: he has been a Trustee of the (USA) Law and Society Association, Vice-President of the Research Committee of Sociology of Law (International Sociological Association), and Member of the Governing Board of the Onati International Institute of Sociology of Law.

Series Editor's Preface

Collected Essays in Law makes available some of the most important work of scholars who have made a major contribution to the study of law. Each volume brings together a selection of writings by a leading authority on a particular subject. The series gives authors an opportunity to present and comment on what they regard as their most important work in a specific area. Within their chosen subject area, the collections aim to give a comprehensive coverage of the authors' research. Care is taken to include essays and articles which are less readily accessible and to give the reader a picture of the development of the authors' work and an indication of research in progress.

Introduction

This volume gathers together some of my papers which deal with the relationship between law, society and social theory. Some of these essays are reasonably well known. Others, in keeping with the motive for this series, have been rescued from relative obscurity (it is for the reader to judge whether this was always justified!). One way of describing this collection could be as some sort of response to the late Herbert Hart's invitation many years ago to write a book on the subject of sociology of law for the Clarendon Oxford University Press series, for which he was the general editor. Hart's strong advice to me was not to write 'a book about books' but instead to develop my own theory. What he explicitly warned me against was the type of encyclopaedic books written by Julius Stone. But, as Nicola Lacey's biography (*Herbert Hart: An Intellectual Biography*, Oxford University Press, 2004) makes clear, my upbringing – with its emphasis on the reverential studying of texts – may have had more in common with that of Stone than Hart. On the other hand, Hart himself dedicated the latter part of his life to working on Bentham manuscripts. Not having anything like his abilities, however, the best I could do was to try to do this by smaller steps. I thought then – and still do now – that one way of writing such a book would be to consider the various ideas social theorists have had about the 'fit' between law and its social context – as well to ask how far it could be possible to get beyond that paradigm.

I have therefore put together here those of my papers that converge on this common theme. This brief introduction will first say something about where I stand on the issues of context, fit and legal specificity. It will then go on to summarize the individual chapters so as to show how they contribute to the overall argument and how my views have evolved over time. Although this means that there is also some small overlap amongst the chapters this may itself be helpful at showing the unexpected continuities in arguments about subjects that are not always seen as related. The value of social theorizing for studying law will be illustrated with reference to a range of issues and will include reference to specific developments in substantive areas such as housing law, tort law, the law of evidence and criminal law. But this volume is also most certainly – notwithstanding Hart's advice – in large measure a book about books. Hopefully, the range of insights generated by the authors discussed – who include Boyd-White, Cotterrell, Ehrlich, Fish, Habermas,

Legrand, Luhmann, Pound, Teubner and Watson, will do something to justify this.[1]

Context, 'Fit' and the Specificity of 'the Legal'

The goal of relating 'law' to 'society' – by examining the social sources and effects of legal rules and ideas and the way law is shaped by and helps shape its historical and social setting – is a central aspect of social theorizing about law. Our concern here, however, is with the relevance of such enquiry for legal education and legal practice. The title of this volume makes explicit reference to a highly successful (and still lively) book series called *The Law in Context* that was making its mark at the time I began teaching sociology of law at Edinburgh University in 1976. Building on the heritage of the American Legal Realists,[2] this series successfully set out to transform law teaching in the UK.[3] But numerous other books and essays about law, especially those published in other common law countries such as the US, Canada and Australia, have some reference to context in their titles.

The general aim of such work is to get beyond the study of leading cases decided in the higher courts so as to examine law from the standpoint and perspective of a variety of social actors. The analysis of 'mandarin' decision-making provides little insight into what goes on in lower-level courts and tribunals, in the world of the police, in lawyers' offices; it misses most of what is important about the activities of arbitrators and others involved in alternative dispute processing; and it tells us little or nothing about the demands, experiences and consciousnesses of those who use law or are subjected to it. For the contextualizers, law is treated less as a self-sufficient body of doctrine than as part of the wider human sciences, something that can be understood with the aid of a variety of different intellectual disciplines such as economics, sociology and psychology (in the US this is also known as the 'law and' type of research). Law in context means learning to think of law in terms of larger processes – bringing out, for example, the similarities between decision-making in legal and other settings. It suggests that we configure law as one stage, aspect, or method, of dealing with wider processes of disputing or social

---

1   My ideas have also benefited from exchanges with many colleagues and students in teaching law and social theory at Edinburgh and London. I would especially like to thank Neil McCormick, Zenon Bankowski and Roger Cotterrell.

2   See e.g. Patricia Ewick, Robert A. Kagan, and Austin Sarat (1999), 'Legacies of Legal Realism: Social Science, Social Policy, and the Law', in Patricia Ewick, Robert A. Kagan, and Austin Sarat (eds), *Social Science, Social Policy, and the Law*, Russell Sage, pp. 1–38.

3   A series first published by Butterworths and now by Cambridge University Press.

regulation, and that we treat these processes as related in some way to the needs, (social) problems and conflicts of social groups. Especially in earlier contributions to the series, law often comes to be analyzed as just one policy tool that can help, alongside others, in regulating such matters as the provision of housing and employment, or the protection of the environment.

The originators of the law in context approach were deliberately light on theory and claimed not to be making rigid prescriptions about what could be meant by the term.[4] There was no pretence to be offering a new philosophical or sociological 'theory' of law, and their slogan – 'to broaden the study of law from within' – mainly targeted other academic lawyers rather than social scientists. Despite their ecumenism, however, there is no doubt that those advocating this kind of approach do have some shared theoretical assumptions. Most obviously, any disagreements about how law relates to society rest on agreement that such a relationship exists[5] and that it is cognizable. And it is the prior separation of 'law' from 'the social' that provides the occasion and the necessity for 'law-in-context' or 'law-in-society'.[6]

There is also much shared ground in the normative agenda pursued by these scholars, whether this concerns 'external' critiques that seek to show how law does not achieve what it claims to do, or 'internal' critiques which concentrate more on deconstructing the coherence of the claims themselves. The past (and future) of law in context work is closely related to the search for both the actual and the ideal 'fit' between 'law' (in all of its forms) and 'society' (in all its possible articulations). As much as some scholars try and show that law depends on and 'fits' given conditions, other scholars – or the same scholars for different purposes – also seek to show that law can, and should, rise above 'false necessity'.[7] Thus the project of seeking to show a given 'fit' also involves

---

4   As William Twining, one of the founders of the law in context approach, has always insisted.

5   This has not gone unchallenged. According to the legal historian Alan Watson (1990) whose many books about the growth of law via legal transplants include one entitled appropriately *Law out of Context*, University of Georgia Press, the details of legal doctrine can only be deciphered by finding their roots in the societies from which they have been borrowed (or which have imposed them) and the interests of sacred cliques of lawyers or priests as interpreters of such complexities. But even he would admit that issues of context and fit would be relevant (by definition) to the way such rules are actually used (or not used) in a given society.

6   See Christopher Tomlins (2007), 'How Autonomous is Law?' *Annual Review of Law and Social Science*, **3**, pp. 45–6.

7   See e.g. Roberto Mungabeira Unger (1987), *False Necessity*, Cambridge University Press. According to Philip Selznick *Law in context; fidelity to context* (2002, Centre for jsp repositories .edlib.org/csls/ fwp/2). 'Law is disciplined by context and contexts are transcended by more comprehensive principles and ideals' (p. 1). What Selznick

– by implication – the necessity to theorize the 'relative autonomy' of law[8] (as compared to all social, political, economic or cultural reductionisms). By understanding the specificity of 'the legal' it becomes possible to see how and why law may be able to transcend given contexts.

The literature on social theory and law[9] – on which law in context writers largely rely – offers a variety of ways in which claims of a 'fit' between law and society can been explored. At the macro-social level types of law may be connected (reciprocally) to types of society, as in arguments about the move from 'status to contract'[10] (and back again), or changes in forms of 'social solidarity'[11] (and the challenge) of finding out what new form of solidarity (and conflict) are being created through globalization. There are also classical analyses of the intimate connection between the 'form' of law and the society it helps create, as in suggestions of an intimate relationship between capital exchange and 'equivalence' in legal notions of rights.[12] Descriptions and analyses of micro-social connections between law(s) and interest or status groups, and between decisions by legal actors and their social locations or political preferences are legion.

This is far from exhausting the possible occasions in which writers speak of context and 'fit'. Such concepts are regularly (increasingly?) marshalled in debates about social and legal change. How far does law need to 'fit' its context to be effective? (especially as law is often used in an attempt to change contexts).[13] Does it make sense for China to import American styles of administrative law, or does this type of law presuppose a certain type of society?[14] Do the prospects for implanting the rule of law in ex-communist

---

terms 'fidelity to context' means that 'Law must be adapted to make sense of and deal with distinctive problems of whatever special context we think should be governed by law and should redeem, in its own way, the ideals we associate with the rule of law'... concepts of growth, freedom, rationality, caring, fairness, and justice are among the criteria by which we *judge* contexts and make proposals for their reconstruction (id. 3).

8   Tomlins, op. cit.

9   It should be borne in mind that the relationship between what is meant by 'social theory and law' and 'sociology of law' (considered as a specific sub-discipline of sociology) is controversial. I shall use the former broader term wherever possible in this introduction. But it should not be assumed that the use of this category avoids the need to face the limits or boundaries of its perspective.

10   Sir Henry Maine (1917 [1861]), *Ancient Law* J.M. Dent and Sons.

11   Emile Durkheim (1984), *The Division of Labour in Society*, trans. W.D. Hall Macmillan.

12   Eugene Pashukanis (1983), *Law and Marxism: A General Theory*, Pluto Press.

13   David Nelken and Johannes Feest (eds) (2001), *Adapting Legal Cultures*, Hart.

14   Edward Rubin (2000), 'Administrative Law and the Complexity of Culture', in A. Seidman, R. Seidman and J. Payne (eds), *Legislative Drafting for Market Reform:*

countries depend on the extent to which people there come to form a 'society of non-intimates connected by market exchanges and lubricated by civility'?[15] The idea of context is also employed in seeking to understand writers in their own historical and geographical time and place, and the way their work is applied in different or later contexts. Or again, context is crucial in explaining where legal or alternative types of decision-making rationalities are most likely to prevail in clashes between law and science.

Given that the law in context series has been going strong for almost 40 years it is hardly surprising that the sense of what context means has changed in that time.[16] And, in fact, earlier mainstream work by socio-legal scholars has been challenged in a number of ways. Some structuralist, critical legal scholars and post-modern theorists claim that we should abandon the effort to determine the functional or instrumental links between law and society in favour of trying to show how law plays a 'constitutive' role.[17] If constitutive theories suggest that it is law which makes society possible, Luhmann's social system theory claims that law cannot see its social context but instead filters its environment according to its own communicative code.[18] Other theorists argue that law and the social sciences must be treated as rival discourses, or that we should think about law as literature – as a means of world-making, rather than as a type of social policy. Their interest in deconstructing texts brings their methods nearer to those of doctrinal scholars than to those used by empirical social scientists studying the 'law in action'.

Beyond this, however, more attention needs to be given to the significance of the idea of context itself. As shown by Peter Burke, the historian of ideas, the notion of context itself has a history – or context. It was actually the Renaissance and Reformation which conceived knowledge as contextual; the Enlightenment period, by contrast, made it possible to think of de-contextualized knowledge.[19] An appeal to a given context is usually directed against some alternative. Typically, law in context books seek to distinguish themselves from the easily stigmatized 'formalist' or 'conceptualist' way of interpreting law or what is called, in England especially, 'black-letter' law

---

Some Lessons from China, Macmillan, pp. 88–108.

15   Martin Krygier (1990), 'Marxism and the Rule of Law: Reflections after the Collapse of Communism', *Law and Social Inquiry*, **15**, p. 633.

16   It is enough to compare Patrick Atiyah's *Accidents, Compensation and the Law* (first published in 1970, published in its 7th edition in 2006), with Marie Dembour's *Who believes in Human Rights?* published in 2006.

17   See e.g. Alan Hunt (1993), *Explorations in Law and Society: Toward a Constitutive Theory of Law*, Routledge.

18   Gunther Teubner (1993), *Law as an Autopoietic System*, Blackwell.

19   Peter Burke (2002), 'Context in Context', *Common Knowledge*, **8**, pp. 152–77.

teaching. The call for more law in context in the post-world-war period thus itself needs to be contextualized, perhaps as part of a modernizing project which, taking a left-liberal political viewpoint, sought to use law as a form of social engineering.[20] Law can be placed in a variety of linguistic, literary, ideological, social, psychological, political, cultural, and material contexts. But the choice to prioritize one or other of these is itself a significant step that requires justification, which is often not provided.

We can also ask whether the underlying metaphor of 'fit' is a satisfactory one. (Does it 'fit' the relationship between law and society?) In an earlier effort to sum up my thinking on this subject[21] I distinguished between three uses of the term: 'context as environment' – the claim that law 'fits' in some way its historical and spatial location; 'context as contingency' – the claim to show the dependency of law on extra-legal political economic and other constraints; and 'context as assumptions' – the claim that we can get at the presuppositions that guide our interpretative choices. I argued then that moves to put law into context can also lead to infinite regress – for example in the (vain) attempt to draw a line between text and context. More than this, the attempt to put the law 'in context' often only succeeds in actually getting it out of context. Even for social scientists, it is heuristic to treat law's lack of awareness, or selective awareness, of its context as an intrinsic, if changing, feature of its social reproduction, rather than as simply the origin of corrigible errors to be excized by the expert or political activist.[22] Although there are many excellent studies of how law transforms, avoids or represses alternative ways of describing and judging social reality[23] what is missing is a theory of why, how and when given social insights it should be made relevant to different kinds of legal proceedings.

---

20   As I wrote in 1996, 'The more recent trend away from centralised intervention and regulation in Britain and America has provided fertile ground for the rediscovery that, criminal law, for example, is both more and less than an instrument for reducing the crime problem and that tort law is not merely a supposedly efficient means of responding to accidents. From our present vantage point it now seems as if the utility of social science perspectives on law is bound up with the advocacy of a particular role for law.' (David Nelken (id.) (1996), 'Getting the Law "out of Context"', in *Socio-Legal Newsletter*, **19**, pp. 12–13; reprinted in *South African Newsletter of Law Libraries*, 1997.)

21   Nelken, 1996 id.

22   Some have argued that the specificity of legal thinking is actually its ability to abstract from context, as in the well known saying by Thomas R. Powell (quoted in Lawrence Rosen (2006), *Law as Culture*, Princeton University Press, p. xi) 'if you think that you can think about a thing, inextricably attached to something else, without thinking of the thing it is attached to, then you have a legal mind'.

23   See e.g. Alan Norrie (2001), *Crime, Reason and History*, 2nd ed., Butterworth.

The argument should not be overstated. Looking at law's relationships to society is obviously of value if our task is to understand its sociological role. More than this, in a range of different settings – such as the university, or courts, tribunals or regulatory policy-making bodies – and at various stages of legal and administrative processes, those who take or influence decisions may have their ideas informed by education, policy discussions, political action or activism, legal advocacy, lobbying or media reports. Present or future legal and other decision-makers will often be informed by, presuppose or actually seek out assistance in obtaining such insights. But at the same time we need to be aware of (and seek to identify) the limits of such influence. Expertize itself has its own range of relevant practical contexts. In the 1970s and 1980s the legal publisher Sweet and Maxwell sent free copies to law lecturers in the UK of what they called *The Students' Law Reporter*. This contained commentary on leading cases but it also added supposedly 'relevant' opinions by non-legal experts familiar with the area of social life being adjudicated, under such headings as 'a Planner writes'. Almost inevitably the expert would be unhappy with the legal decision. I was puzzled about the educational point of these commentaries – and the credibility of the criticisms they contained, given that such experts would likely have disagreed with other types of experts (or even amongst themselves). It is not obvious that sociological, psychological or other such insights are always relevant for legal self-understanding and self-reproduction. The issue has been given some discussion by those engaged in 'economics and law' and 'law and psychology', the areas where social science has made its largest inroads. It is also a matter of controversy in the law of evidence (especially because of the difficulty of reconciling what experts may see as the soundest approach to weighing probabilities with the need for remain in touch with lay understanding). But the preoccupation with so-called 'junk science' often obscures the larger question of the relevance of even sound science. And there may be good reasons why law does not or, at least, should not, always adopt more 'scientific' approaches.[24]

The reason for calling this volume 'Beyond the Law in Context' is thus to draw attention to the need to interrogate the broader foundational presuppositions of these sorts of enquiry. To critique some examples offered by the founders of the law in context approach, the *differences* between what is involved in judges and parents settling disputes, or criminals and husbands confessing, may be as important as what they have in common. Throughout the chapters the focus is on the following questions. What is gained (and what may be lost) by putting law in context? What attempts have been made to go beyond this approach? What are their (necessary) limits? Can law be seen as anything other than in

---

24   See e.g. Laurence H. Tribe (1970), 'Trial by Mathematics: Precision and Ritual in the Legal Process', *Harvard Law Review*, **84**, p. 1329.

some way both separate from and related to 'the social?'. What else could it be related to? [25]

The difference between the way law reaches closure, and social science approaches advance their agendas, does not mean that social insights, ideas or facts do not (or should not) enter the reproduction of legal cognition. But each attempt to contextualize law or to approach it from some sort of external perspective is itself in need of contextualization. This has various implications. Not least, the fact that if social theorizing about law (or any other disciplinary approach to law) is to count as a contribution to its own discipline it is bound to reveal only those aspects of law that are possible for it to fathom by following the assumptions, protocols and methods of its own knowledge-practices. Because any way of seeing (and doing) is also a way of not seeing [26] – and not doing,[27] such approaches can risk missing (valuable) aspects of legal ways of seeing (and not seeing) – even, or perhaps especially – where they succeed in transforming legal practices.

What is distinctive about my approach to social theorizing about law therefore is the effort to keep in tension two claims. The first of these is the argument that social theorizing about legal practices is vitally important in understanding the connections between legal and social structures and revealing what law means and does for (and to) various social actors. It brings to our notice matters that legal actors themselves cannot or will not see. The second point is that it does not follow that what we learn in this way can, without further argument, be assumed to be necessarily relevant to (re)shaping legal practices. My position seeks to go beyond those who see the 'broadening' of perspectives offered

---

25   Tomlins, 2007 op. cit. has recently suggested that law's 'other' should be 'justice' and 'memory'. But it is hard to see how this can be given substance in practice without it involving some sort of contextualizing social enquiry.

26   Alain Pottage and Martha Mundy (2004) in their introduction to *Law, Anthropology and the Constitution of the Social*, Cambridge University Press, summarize a chapter by Bruno Latour called 'Scientific Objects and Legal Objectivity' by suggesting (at p. 23) that 'law on the other hand produces objectivity by knowing as little as possible about the object'. See also Tim Murphy (1997) *The Oldest Social Science? Configurations of Law and Modernity*, Oxford University Press.

27   This does not exhaust the problems of understanding the relationships of contextualizing knowledges in and to law. For example, (pace Luhmann) law is more obviously subject to the play of political calculation which, as in the sphere of criminal law and criminal justice, often leads to choices that are more concerned with what the public believe, expect and want, than what experts advise. Also, as anticipated in the law in context approaches' stress on the importance of 'standpoint', theorists cannot put themselves in the place of practitioners without distorting the experience they seek to evoke; see Pierre Bourdieu (1977), *Outline of a Theory of Practice*, Cambridge University Press.

by social theorizing as necessarily helping lawyers and other legal actors to do a better job,[28] and those, on the other hand, who argue that any given interpretation can never be 'broader' or 'better' than any another but only different from it.[29] In any given case we should rather ask whether the expert analysis we are impressed by will involve us introducing, for example, more bureaucratic, managerial or technocratic rationalities (or even just increasing the weight given to such considerations) into legal operations. Insofar as it does, it may sometimes be 'out of place' or otherwise inappropriate.[30] On the other hand, acknowledging the difficulties that legal practices may have in taking on board insights from social science does not necessarily mean that law should always be left to do what it does autonomously. We might choose instead just to circumscribe the areas of public life we seek to regulate through law and use other rationalities.

Outline of the Chapters

I have divided this collection of essays into three parts. The first part – entitled 'Only Connect'[31] – includes papers which sought to offer variations on the major theme of social theorizing about law, the effort to connect 'law' and 'society'. By contrast, the second part, called 'Changing the Questions' – deals with attempts to break with this paradigm. The last part – 'Finding the Limits' – then examines the limits faced by work which seeks to get beyond the mainstream framework if it is to pursue something recognizable as social theorizing about law.

Can social theorizing about law be true to itself whilst at the same time offer insights that can be of value to legal practice? Unusually in the panorama of writing on this topic, the essays in this collection focus *both* on how the attempt by social theorizing to understand law may have deleterious effects on its own disciplinary progress, and, conversely, on how its reformulations of legal issues for its own purposes may have unfortunate consequences for law. The opening essay of the first part, (Chapter 1) comments on the oft-

---

28 See e.g. Roger Cotterrell (1998), 'Why Must Legal Ideas be Interpreted Sociologically?' *Journal of Law and Society*, **25**, pp. 171–92.
29 See e.g. Stanley Fish (1989), *Doing What Comes Naturally*, Oxford University Press; Stanley Fish (1991), 'The Law Wishes to have a Formal Existence', in Austin Sarat and Thomas Kearns (eds), *The Fate of Law*, University of Michigan Press, p. 159.
30 The very real difficulties in finding a meta-theory, (distinct from law or a contextualizing expertise) able to guide us in making such choices are discussed in Nelken 1990 and in part two of this collection.
31 See e.g. Robert Kidder (1983), *Connecting Law to Society*, Prentice Hall.

repeated warning that sociology of law can only progress by being true to its own concepts and methodological protocols and will lose its way in trying to deal with questions posed by and for legal institutions and the purposes of law reform. In the 1970s this issue was captured in a key contrast between the contrasting enquiries of socio-legal studies and sociology of law.[32] Whereas socio-legal studies was seen as starting from un-theoretical, legally- or policy-driven agendas, which 'took' their problems ready-made from legal institutions and policy-makers, sociology of law was seen as interested in 'making' its problems so as to illuminate the larger place of law in the social structure, thus linking up to wider theoretical developments in sociology as a discipline.

As against this I argued that it was neither possible nor desirable to erase practical concerns so as to pursue a purely theoretical agenda. In a contribution to a journal whose title announced its commitment to legal reform, I pointed out that theoretical and applied works were not so easy to distinguish *a priori* and that it would be more helpful to seek to contrast good and bad research. As an illustration I took perhaps the most criticized of socio-legal approaches, the so called 'gap problem' with its repeated discovery of disjuncture between that which law mandates and what actually takes place.[33] After providing a historical review of how this approach had evolved over time I went on to show how it could be reformulated in a theoretically fruitful way so that claims about what law was supposed to do and what it actually did could themselves become the objects of research.

Chapter 2, (first presented at the IVR international conference on philosophy of law in Helsinki) offers an exegesis of the work of Roscoe Pound and Eugene Ehrlich. But its purpose was more ambitious than this. As the subtitle 'back to the beginning in sociology of law' suggests, these writers' ideas are often taken as the founders of the modern discipline of empirical sociology of law. This article seeks to show that, without denying the argument of the previous paper, some starting points can indeed be more fruitful than others in developing the subject. In particular, I sought to extricate Ehrlich from the (re-)presentation of his ideas made by Pound. Making sense of the different concerns of these two different authors involved placing them in the 'context' of the time and place in which they lived and the role they therefore envisaged for state law and judicial intervention. For Pound rapid social change and social disorganization had left a vacuum which had to be filled by law as a new form of 'social control'; hence law had to be defined and improved in terms of its 'effectiveness'. Ehrlich, on

---

32   Social theorists continued and continue to give advice against these dangers, see e.g. Austin Sarat and Susan Silbey (1988), 'The Pull of the Policy Audience', *Law and Policy*, **10**, p. 98.

33   For further discussion of 'the gap' problem see Brian Z. Tamanaha (1999), *Realistic Socio-Legal Theory: Pragmatism and a Social Theory of Law*.

the other hand, thought that law under ordinary conditions (of peaceful social relations) should be thought of more as a result of social processes than as a tool of intervention – which was only the role of legislative acts and 'norms for decision' to be used by judges in cases of dispute.

Pound's concerns – his invitation to study the 'law in action', the need to adjust the law to meet changing social conditions, to treat law as in large part a matter of institutional design and social engineering, have become today's orthodoxies, especially in common law countries. (They were also an important inspiration of the publishing enterprise of the 'law in context'.) But by the 1970s it was widely felt that these ideas had led to something of a dead end for the purpose of sociological enquiry. To get over this impasse I explained why Pound's famous distinction between 'law in books' and 'law in action' (the origin of the focus on the 'gap' problem) did not correspond, as it was widely assumed to do, to Ehrlich's older contrast between 'norms for decision' and 'living law'. I argued that the concept of living law was a more interesting, if challenging, starting point for research because it was more open to mainstream sociological concerns. Less geared to the problem of legal effectiveness it led instead to research on legal pluralism and the sociology of normative life.[34] In a final footnote I also argued provocatively that those most keen to use law to protect the environment often neglected to consider that the operation of (legal) norms too had to be conceived ecologically.

Chapter 3, 'Is there a crisis in law and legal ideology?' continues the theme of how law must be understood as being both more and less than as an instrument of social engineering. It begins by identifying the task of macro-social theorizing about law as examining the connection between 'law' and 'society', as shown by the changing relationship between the form, content, and functions of law in particular societies in particular periods. The paper then discusses claims made by Tay and Kamenka concerning an alleged crisis in legal ideology as a result of movement towards what they described as a more 'bureaucratic administrative' use of law superimposed and in tension with its classical liberal 'gesselschaft' approach. After identifying their failure to show that a crisis in conceptions of law necessarily corresponds to a crisis in society I brought in the views of Habermas who argued that there was in fact such a social legitimation crisis. The discussion of key issues of the 1970s – the abandonment of liberal individualism, the move in tort law from fault to risk,

---

34 Some textbook writers have interpreted my argument here as an appeal for the sociology of norms to replace the sociology of law. Although this would be too radical, it is true that as a result of the network society characteristic of globalisation we are now seeing ever more processes of 'normalization' which do call for such a subject, see e.g. David Nelken (2006), 'Signalling Conformity: Changing Norms in Japan and China', in *Michigan Journal of International Law*, **27**, pp. 933–72.

from contract back to status, from individual to collective property ownership and so on – makes interesting reading now, a generation later, when there has been a sharp return to these older values as part of neo-liberal ideology, the weakening of the welfare state and the globalization of the economy.

Chapter 4, called 'Legislation and its constraints', the final chapter in this section, develops some ideas first tried out in my book about landlords and the law[35] and concerns legislative attempts in the 1960s and 1970s to change the behaviour of landlords and tenants. The point of this paper was to get away from the questions begged by talking about the 'impact' and effectiveness of legislation which had been the focus of work of the previous generation of socio-legal scholarship. The aim was rather to show that limited change was only to be expected once one took into account both the external and internal relationship between law and society.[36] The chapter offered a reformulation of the legal practices of legislation and judicial decision-making in relation to the ideas of social action and social structure as theorized by Steven Lukes and Anthony Giddens. It also discussed the homology between legal and social action, and explained why legal outcomes often exhibit 'coherence without conspiracy'.

The second part of this book is concerned with attempts to change the mainstream paradigm in the sociology of law. Chapter 5 dealt with what have come to be called 'correspondence theories' of the relationship between law and society whether, this is conceived as involving functionalist, structuralist, interactionist or hermeneutic linkages.[37] It offered an extended review of a book by Stuart Henry that showed that different types of labour regulation did not *correspond*, as he had expected, with the different types of social organization being regulated. I showed that Henry's work was at the cusp of paradigm change but that he was unable to show us what might replace the correspondence approach. I then discussed various theoretical arguments which did claim to be able to do this and which had in common an emphasis on the need to see not only how law affects 'society' but how 'society' is reproduced within law.

Chapter 6 is a chapter that came out of a workshop organised by Gunther Teubner at the European University Institute in Florence in 1985.[38] Going to this

---

35   David Nelken (1983), *The Limits of the Legal Process*, Academic Press.

36   In a way this anticipated the constitutive approach without going so far as to identify law with society.

37   The paper was given as the George Lurcey lecture at Amherst at the invitation of an emerging group of critical interpretative scholars, soon to become the dominant voices in the US law and Society association.

38   I had met Teubner some years before at a law and society conference where we had quickly agreed that too much attention to what Luhmann had called 'the sociology

meeting changed my life. This is not because I became a fully paid up believer in the autopoiesis theory that the workshop was intended to spread – although I do continue to find the approach both helpful and problematic. The reasons are more personal. I had asked – at a late stage – to join the participants in this workshop as it seemed a perfect excuse to return to Italy to meet up again with a fetching young Italian judge who eventually became my wife (and the reason for my permanent move to live in Italy in 1989). As this was a closed workshop however it was necessary to produce a paper in advance. Reading the already circulated essays by Luhmann and others was a daunting experience. The one I thought I best understood was the contribution by Richard Lempert, a leading American scholar in the field. But what I thought I grasped was that he had not properly examined all the differences between the Anglo-American idea of legal autonomy and Luhmann's theory of autopoiesis. Lempert was a friend – indeed he had been the person who had told me of the conference. I was not easy about criticizing his essay. But I was in something of a dilemma as between friendship and love.

My essay acknowledges the originality of Lempert's contribution to the theory of law's relative autonomy. This is seen, for example, where he says that, 'in the ideal case', legal autonomy and personal autonomy coincide, but adds that this is not his personal ideal. But I also sought to show why identifying autopoiesis with relative autonomy underestimated the novelty of Luhmann's theory. As with Pound's interpretation of Ehrlich, the 'misunderstanding' here was no doubt influenced by differences in legal culture between Germany and the USA as well as perhaps by different political leanings. Luhmann sees law as the great de-politicizer, taking over what politics cannot solve, and values it in that role. Lempert, on the other hand, values the idea of relative autonomy because it offers the chance to save law from total determination by politics (and from the US Critical Legal Scholars' charge that law is unavoidably political).

Chapter 7, an examination of the difficulties of putting criminal law 'in context', also makes reference to autopoiesis theory. The only chapter in this collection that focuses explicitly on an area of substantive law, it started with a paradox. Why (up till then) had no textbook in the law in context series been produced on the subject of criminal law despite this being the area where most social scientific studies of law had been carried out? The chapter accounts for this by pointing to the strong alliance between criminal law teaching and moral philosophy. It then discusses the three common strategies for contextualizing this or any legal subject matter. These are distinguished as adding information, drawing attention to the external social forces and conflict

---

of courts and lawyers' – meant that too little thought was given to furnishing a social understanding of law itself.

that shape the operations of law, and revealing the context inside the law. This last approach, pioneered by the Critical Scholars movement, also involved developing 'deviant' doctrine. The chapter then goes on to discuss what I called the 'irrelation' between law and contextualizing discourses, arguing that law's specificity is to be found not in the way it resists external influences but in the way it incorporates and responds to them.[39]

The next three chapters (8, 9 and 10) all deal with the theoretical significance of clashes between law and science.[40] Each developed out of a lengthy working paper called 'The Truth about Law's Truth' written at the European University Institute where I had gone to be a Jean Monnet fellow in 1987–1988. They all focused on identifying the sort of 'truth about law' being sought by the 'law and' movement as compared to 'law's truth' as it carries out its own operations. Seen from the perspective of, for example, economics, psychology or sociology, legal ways of doing things often rest on flawed assumptions or otherwise get things 'wrong'. The findings of these other disciplines are certainly relevant to legal practice – not least when it comes to matters of institutional design. But we can still ask: must the lessons of 'law and' research always be accepted? Each disciplinary approach to law, whether sociology, economics, psychology, political science, and so on, tends to create law 'in its image'. And the criticisms of legal practice they offer often carry different – and even competing – implications. What should we do if disciplines disagree (as they do) amongst themselves – and within themselves? Should law open up ever more to other disciplines? If not where should this process stop? How far should we be trying to find out and safeguard what is peculiar about law's way of doing things, not least its own forms of truth finding?

These essays used as an illustration of these issues the use of expert evidence at court – one of the most controversial areas in which law has to engage practically with different forms of knowledge. But they also emphasized that this is only one of many such contexts. I distinguished three approaches to understanding possible clashes between law and science: trial pathology, the competing institutions argument and the theory of incompatible discourses. I suggested that these different approaches are addressed to different participants: the judge, the legislator and the observer of social systems. In examining encounters between law and other disciplines it was important to learn how to distinguish real from only apparent disagreement, to decide what is a 'legal'

---

39 This formulation was quoted approvingly by Teubner (1989) in his influential paper 'How the Law Thinks: Towards a Constructivist Epistemology of Law', *Law and Society Review*, **23**, pp. 727–57. Law and Society Association.

40 'The Truth about Law's Truth' (1990), European University Institute Law, department Working Paper, Florence, Italy; reprinted in Alberto Febbrajo and David Nelken (eds) (1993), *European Yearbook of Sociology of Law*, Giuffrè: pp. 87–163.

question, that is, one appropriate for legal rather than other forms of process, and to find ways to introduce a constructive dialogue in which both law and more 'scientific' approaches were given their say.

The last section of the book then stands back from this specific problem of expert evidence so as to focus more generally on the question of limits to understanding. What is involved in going beyond the mainstream strategy for contextualizing law? What happens to the sociological search for legal meaning after the 'linguistic turn'? What follows if we see society as a text to be interpreted? Can we still draw a line between text and context? Can contextualizing approaches still be used if law does not belong to the context in which it is currently found? The question of how law relates to other types of knowledge can also be turned reflexively on the sociology of law itself. What, if anything, gives social theorizing about law a privileged status as compared for instance to understanding law with the conceptual resources of literary theory or theology? How far is social theorizing itself part of its context? Evidencing the coherence of this collection of essays, the last two chapters update and re-examine issues discussed in the chapters that introduce this volume.

Chapter 11 [41] discusses the implications of the so called 'linguistic turn' for social theorizing as reflected in the differences between 'law and literature' studies and more mainstream empirical sociology of law. It considers the claim that it is necessary to transcend distinctions between action and communication, and to learn to appreciate how law creates and participates in conversations. In questioning whether sociology of law can get at 'legal meaning' it also adumbrates criticisms of Roger Cotterrell's approach to the sociology of law. These comments (to which he replied) are then further developed in Chapter 12, 'Blinding insights? The Limits of a Reflexive Sociology of Law'. The exchanges in these chapters achieved a certain notoriety[42] and the issues raised range over a variety of topics including whether sociology of law as a sub-discipline of sociology can learn anything from considering the challenges faced by social theorizing about religion, art, knowledge and science.

Chapter 12 – which builds on the arguments of the earlier essays included in this collection – begins by contrasting two opposing approaches to sociology of law. The first accepts the need to make sociology relevant. The other sees its task as setting out to reveal what law is unable or unwilling to see and reconceptualizes legal phenomena, using its own conceptual armoury, in

---

41   Taken from David Nelken (ed.) (1986), *Law as Communication*, Dartmouth.

42   See e.g. Michael D.A. Freeman (2001), *Lloyd's Introduction to Jurisprudence*, 7th edn, Sweet and Maxwell; Reza Banakar (2000) 'Reflections on the Methodological Issues of the Sociology of Law', *Journal of Law and Society*, **27**, pp. 273–95 and, the unjustly neglected, Reza Benakar (2003), *Merging Law and Sociology: Beyond the Dichotomies in Socio-legal Research*, Galda and Wilch.

terms of social order, social control, regulation, governmentality and so on. Following this path social theorizing about law is less likely to compromise its own disciplinary progress or lose the possibility of external political critique. But what are its implications for legal practices? As we have noted, it is an open question how far law is capable of internalising information and concepts from other disciplines. As Teubner puts it, it may only manage to create hybrids that bear little resemblance to the discipline from which they are borrowed. More than this, the introduction of different styles of reasoning could have ill effects for legal practice by misunderstanding and thus threatening the integrity of legal processes or the values they embody.

Turning to Cotterrell, I pointed out that he had given different answers over time to these sorts of questions. He first treated law as a mere 'discipline-effect' and saw sociology, by contrast, as a special sort of discipline, particularly privileged in it ability to transcend its own limits (its self-questioning paradoxically constituting its strength). His views later changed, however. In responding to my paper about the difficulties social theorizing has in grasping legal meaning he now argued that social theorizing about law need have no disciplinary allegiance – except to broaden law's own understanding of the social world. Law and sociology are similar in that they both aim for knowledge that is social, systematic and empirical – law just needs its knowledge-base broadened. In my reply to this move I argued that it is not so easy to be 'undisciplined'. Whereas Cotterrell argued that the adoption of sociological insights was the most 'practical' of approaches for participants in legal processes, I suggested that there are important differences between using external disciplines to open up issues as opposed to trying to apply them so as to achieve legal closure.

The next two chapters – 13 and 14 – offer other illustrations of the limits faced by social theorizing when seeking to place law in its context. Here the problem is less about communication across legal and scientific cultures and more about what happens to legal concepts when they move across different national and cultural contexts. A key issue in comparative law in what is now the second (or, some say, the third) round of 'law and development', is what makes for successful legal change in, for example, Asia or Latin America. More generally, there is interest in studying how Europeanization and globalization are making new configurations of legal, economic and political spheres. Despite the overlap in the theoretical issues raised by each of these processes,[43] the literatures in these intellectual disciplines rarely refer to each

---

43 Leading some comparative writers to say that 'law is losing its context'. See David A.Westbrook (2006), 'Theorizing the Diffusion of Law in an Age of Globalization: Conceptual Difficulties, Unstable Imaginations and the Effort to Think Gracefully Nonetheless', *Harvard International Law Journal*, **47**, pp. 489–506.

other. The essays included here are amongst those I have written recently as part of my attempt to introduce more dialogue between the sociology of law and comparative law.

Do processes of legal transplant prove, as some legal historians argue, that any 'fit' between law and context is unlikely and unnecessary? Interestingly, Twining, Atiyah, Wilson, MacAuslan and the others who founded the law in context approach faced many of these same issues when trying to teach English common law in colonial contexts where the facts of daily life were so different from those at home. But they drew the opposite conclusions. In these chapters I look for the middle ground between those who claim legal transplants are impossible and others who claim that they are only too easy. While some authors worry whether such transfers can work, others are concerned that they may succeed only too well. And some seem to manage to hold both views simultaneously; claiming that legal transplants are impossible but also that they threaten the distinctiveness of different legal cultures. Chapter 14 'Comparatists and Transferability' examines the current debate on this point. Continuing the same theme, Chapter 15 considers what is meant by speaking of 'success' when writing about cross-national legal transfers. Who gets to define success?

Chapter 14 was written in response to an invitation to celebrate the 20th anniversary of the Canadian journal *Windsor Yearbook of Access to Justice*. This gave me the opportunity to revisit some of the questions I had discussed in the first issue of that journal (see Chapter 1 in this volume) showing the continuities between debates about introducing legal change domestically and cross-culturally. Chapter 15, the final essay in this collection, on the other hand, returns to some of the questions discussed in the paper about Pound and Ehrlich that is included here as Chapter 2. It asks about the relationship between social theorizing about law and the context within which it is produced.[44] What is the relevance of context for understanding the work of the classical founders of the sociology of law? And what implications does this have for deciding how this discipline should progress? As against what I had argued in my earlier paper, I now suggest that Pound's (re)interpretation of Ehrlich may have something to be said for it. This is because we need to acknowledge the need to distinguish the goal of seeking to get *a writer's ideas right* from that of trying to decide whether the ideas themselves *were right*. The relationship between the scholarly activities of contextualization, de-contextualization and re-contextualization is in fact quite complex.

---

44 This paper was written as part of a larger re-examination of Ehrlich's contribution to social theory of law; see my chapter in Marc Hertogh (2008), *Re-considering Eugen Ehrlich*, Hart.

As its main illustration of these points this chapter, called 'An e-mail from Global Bukowina', offers a commentary on a well-known essay by Gunther Teubner called 'Global Bukowina'. As its title suggests, Teubner set out to apply Ehrlich's insights to the changed world in which we live today by showing the relevance of his ideas for understanding the global spread of non-state law. Teubner's explicitly makes 'free' use of Ehrlich's writings so as to show that his ideas are more relevant now than they were in the past. Is this acceptable? If our goal is advancing the discipline, reading Ehrlich in the light of a major sociological theorist of the range and sophistication of Niklas Luhmann, as Teubner does, should not be rejected *tout court*, even if this interpretation does require some straining of Ehrlich's prose. Certainly it produces an unstable compromise between the aims of contextualization and de-contextualization, or between getting Ehrlich right and claiming that he is right. But, arguably, this is inevitable if traditions are to be kept alive and point beyond themselves. Whatever our conclusions about this, the discussions of Pound, Ehrlich, Teubner and Luhmann in this essay show how this sort of examination of 'books about books' can provide us with a valuable entrée into understanding some of the most significant current international legal developments.

[1]
The 'Gap Problem' in the Sociology of Law: A Theoretical Review

Mr. Nelken describes how the 'gap problem' was originally formulated and why it came to be displaced under the brunt of theoretical criticisms. He argues that such attacks were exaggerated and that the 'gap problem' could serve as the starting point of investigation provided that claims about law were themselves treated as a source of data. Mr. Nelken describes how similar concerns remain part of the hidden agendas of supposedly more theoretical enquiries and that this is now admitted. He then suggests how the 'gap problem' could be reformulated so that it could take its place as an element of some of the most lively contemporary theoretical approaches to law, both Marxist and. non-Marxist. More generally, the author's theoretical review has important implications for the conventional division of labour between 'socio-legal studies' and the 'sociology of law'.

Le problème de l'écart dans la sociologie du droit: un compte rendu théorique

M. Nelken décrit de quelle façon le "problème de l'écart" ("gap problem") fut formulé à l'origine et la raison pour laquelle il fut délogé sous le poids de critiques théoriques. Il affirme que de tels assauts étaient exaggérés et que le "problème de l'écart" pourrait servir de point de départ à l'enquête pourvu que les affirmations au sujet du droit soient elle-mêmes considérées comme une source de données. M. Nelken démontre que de semblables préoccupations font partie du programme caché d'enquêtes supposément plus théoriques et que cela est maintenant avoué. Il suggère ensuite comment le "problème de l'écart" pourrait être reformulé afin d'être reconnu comme un élément des plus vigoureuses méthodes théoriques contemporaines d'aborder le droit, aussi bien marxiste que non-marxiste. En termes généraux, le compte rendu théorique de l'auteur a d'importantes implications pour le partage des tâches entre les "études socio-juridiques" et la "sociologie du droit".

1. Introduction: Socio-legal Studies and Sociology of Law

According to the conventional wisdom, a prominent aspect of the present organisation of the sociology of law is the intellectual and sometimes also institutional division of labour between those who draw on sociology to improve their understanding of the workings of law and those who are

---

*Lecturer, Department of Jurisprudence, University of Edinburgh.

interested in law for the light it may throw on the nature of their society. These two pursuits are often described as socio-legal studies and sociology of law, and although the dividing line is drawn somewhat differently in Britain, Europe and America, in one form or another the two camps are fairly recognizable.[1]

Thus, on the one hand, there are those who investigate issues such as 'access to justice', 'legal effectiveness' or 'plea-bargaining', often with a view to finding some remedy to the 'problems' which, more or less explicitly, provide the parameters of such research topics. On the other hand, there are those who see law as an example or aspect of such sociological concepts as 'social solidarity', 'social control', 'social order' or 'capitalist discipline' whose theoretical and empirical properties they wish to document. Many of those in the first camp are quite content to restrict their interest in the finer points of sociological theory arguing that "sociologists should be on tap but not on top".[2] Conversely, sociologists of law insist that their discipline cannot be developed starting

---

[1] For Gr. Brit. see C. Campbell, "Legal Thought and Juristic Values" (1974), 1 *Brit. J. Law and Society* 13, C. Campbell and Paul Wiles, "The Study of Law in Society in Britain" (1976), 10 *Law and Society Rev.* 547, and C. Grace and P. Wilkinson, *Legal Phenomena and Social Inquiry* (London: Collier Macmillan, 1978); for the U.S.A. see Donald Black, "The Boundaries of Legal Sociology" (1972), 81 *Yale Law J.* 1086, Richard Abel, "Law Books and Books About Law" (1973), 26 *Stanford L. Rev.* 175, and Marc Galanter, "Notes on the Future of Social Research in Law", unpublished paper quoted in Lawrence Friedman and Stewart Macauley, eds., *Law and the Behavioural Sciences*, 2nd ed., (Indianapolis: Bobbs Merril, 1977). (The distinction seems less significant in Europe. Apart from the usual political and theoretical divides, what is most striking is the number of sociologists of law in both Western and Eastern European countries who explicitly adopt some type of social engineering perspective).

In the above writings the concerns of those who pursue socio-legal studies are seen as emerging from their interest in pre-defined problems with the functioning of law, and as arising from the fact that they are legally trained or work within the "lawyer's paradigm" which is replete with mistaken assumptions. But, as I argue in the text, it is not always clear whether their critics are (a) trying to explain which topics socio-legal scholars are likely to investigate *or* (b) trying to show why it is unsafe to rely on their findings. In Lawrence Friedman and Stewart Mcauley, eds., *id.*, 9-11, socio-legal type studies are characterized as "instrumentalist", and it is shrewdly commented that it is wrong to assume that such studies are necessarily theoretically deficient.

[2] I. Willock, "Getting on with Sociologists" (1974), 1 *Brit. J. Law and Society* 3.

Often these writers are dismissive of what they see as abstract theoreticism. B. Roshier and H. Teff in their book *Law and Society in England* (London: Tavistock, 1980) at 17, for example, defend their explicit socio-legal orientation with the assertion that neglect of "real world demands . . . makes analysis sterile or worse still resembles an attempt at spurious scientific objectivity" (sic).

from questions such as "how to make law more effective" or "how to make its benefits more accessible". They identify their task as the development of well-grounded social theory, leaving socio-legal studies to be characterized as some sort of applied science.[3]

However, superimposed on this description of the two concerns in terms of a necessary division of labour is another definition which declares socio-legal studies to be an inferior form of sociology of law. Much of the recent history of sociology of law has involved a series of theoretical attacks on the concerns of those associated with socio-legal studies. Indeed, the impression is sometimes given that the subject will only reach theoretical maturity when it has erased such concerns from its agenda.[4]

Similar worries about the narrowing or distorting effects of pre-definitions of problems on the development of a subject are encountered wherever a discipline or sub-discipline carries clear policy implications. In the sociology of the family, for example, complaint has been made of the tendency to ask 'why divorces occur' rather than to address the allegedly prior question of 'why people get married'.[5] Again, students of the sociology of organizations have argued that it is necessary to resist the tendency to ask why an organization is not fulfilling its goals until the prior issue of how members of organizations actually formulate their goals is better understood.[6] A particular fear of sociologists of law is that their sub-discipline will suffer the fate of criminology — the subject with which it has such close historical and topical connections. Sociologists of deviance struggled to get beyond a concern with 'correctional' issues such as how to reduce crime or deviance, or why people commit crimes so as to enquire instead into the question why certain behaviours come to be designated as criminal or deviant, and what this tells us about the society in question.[7] Similarly, sociologists of law are warned to avoid the mistakes made within criminology if they want to establish their subject on a sure footing.[8]

Thus there are two somewhat inconsistent pictures of the line between sociology of law and socio-legal studies; one of a

---

[3] See Roshier and Teff, id., 15. "The trend is likely to be a continuing divergence between its theoretical and practical branches: the theoretical consisting mainly of re-analyses of old sociological approaches to law, and the practical continuing with its problem-sorting approach. . . ."

[4] Grace and Wilkinson, supra note 1; and Richard Abel, "Redirecting Social Studies of Law" (1980), 14 Law and Society Rev. 805.

[5] M. Anderson, ed., The Sociology of the Family (London: Penguin, 1979).

[6] D. Silverman, The Sociology of Organizations (London: Heinemann Educational Books, 1970).

[7] S. Cohen, "Criminology and the Sociology of Deviance" in P. Rock and M. McIntosh, eds., Deviance and Social Control (London: Tavistock, 1974).

[8] Campbell and Wiles, supra note 2.

division of labour and one of a contrast between a more and a less acceptable approach to sociology. On the whole the second picture tends to blot out the first — at least in the eyes of sociologists of law! The notion of an 'applied' sociology existing in isolation from theoretical problems and developments is a difficult one to defend. The same is true of any claim that socio-legal studies is merely concerned with describing the law-in-action, if the theoretical difficulties of deciding how to describe and what to count as a 'fact' are taken seriously. Moreover, in practice, sociologists of law do not confine their attentions to the elaboration of 'theory' but engage in empirical investigations of the law in action, some of them in direct competition with those organized under the flag of socio-legal studies.

What then is so wrong with socio-legal studies and so right with sociology of law? Does the adoption of socio-legal concerns necessarily spell the kiss of death in organizing a sociological investigation? In this essay I shall not examine fully the objections that have been made to particular socio-legal concerns and approaches.[9] My interest here is mainly in using one example to suggest that concerns cannot be viewed as inherently a matter of either socio-legal studies or sociology of law and therefore that the distinction between them is of limited help in deciding whether and how they should be investigated.

But even a brief consideration of the objections levelled at socio-legal studies indicates that their inadequacies are more often assumed than demonstrated. It is rarely made clear whether objection is being made to the way socio-legal studies constitute the topics they investigate or the approach they use to study them. The very real difference between asking the wrong questions and merely tackling different and perhaps less ambitious questions is also obscured. It follows that it is at least possible that some socio-legal concerns may be of theoretical significance or may gain such significance when incorporated as an aspect or stage of theoretical investigation.

The resistance to this idea is based on the belief that concerns which emanate from a 'reformist', 'instrumental' and 'legalist' starting point should be seen as an 'ideological paradigm' to be struggled against, rather than as a set of substantive topics or approaches to be judged on their merits.[10] But it is wrong to confuse the question why a certain topic comes to be investigated with the question of whether or not it is worth investigating. Similarly it is mistaken to assume that only those topics are significant which are oriented to large macro-social

---

[9] See David Nelken, "Is There a Crisis in Law and Legal Ideology?", *Brit. J. Law and Society* (forthcoming, 1981).

[10] Richard Abel, "Redirecting Social Studies of Law" (1980), 14 *Law and Society Rev.* 805.

issues of social change. Significance depends on theoretical criteria and therefore criticisms of socio-legal concerns, if they are not simply pitting one theoretical position against another, must show why such concerns are necessarily theoretically barren. This is not so easy to demonstrate and, I would argue, cannot be demonstrated as a general proposition but only by examining particular pieces of work.

Much of the existing controversy between representatives of the different camps appears only to apply to some of the protagonists on the opposing side or else to fail to found a convincing theoretical basis for the distinction. One of the best known debates sets a behaviourist, who excludes the study of meaning from his conception of sociology, against a normative theorist who presupposes that law must be defined in terms of the achievement of legality.[11] But most sociologists of law are as unlikely to accept Black's version of positivism as they are to be comfortable with Nonet's modern natural law approach. Most of those pursuing socio-legal studies and sociology of law, unlike Black, do make reference to the meanings of the social action under investigation to those involved. They would probably also admit that 'values' entered at some stage into the choice and execution of their research and would reject Black's insistence on value-freedom as much as Nonet's argument that sociology and the promotion of one's values are inseparable.

It is sometimes implied that the weakness of socio-legal studies lies in its commitment to practical, policy-making objectives. But the purpose behind an investigation is not itself a guide to its theoretical adequacy or inadequacy, quite apart from the fact that some theoretical positions such as Marxism involve a specific commitment to 'praxis' and that sociologists of law often argue that it is only by taking their road that really workable practical solutions are to be found. A sustained argument has recently been made that what distinguishes socio-legal studies is its tolerance of eclectic theory and methodology.[12] But this rests on the doubtful premise that it is improper for a sociological investigation to have recourse to more than one theoretical 'perspective'.[13] Moreover, taken as a body of work both socio-legal studies and sociology of law will continue to bear the marks of the various competing sociological traditions and approaches.

The strongest argument levelled at socio-legal studies is its

---

[11] See Donald Black, *supra* note 1 and *The Behaviour of Law* (London: Academic Press, 1976); Philippe Nonet, "For Jurisprudential Sociology" (1976), 10 *Law & Society Rev.* 525. As a member of the "Berkeley School" of sociology of law Nonet would not describe his concerns and approach as mere "socio-legal studies" but as the right way at doing sociology of law. But his is a rare example of aggressive counter-attack by those whose work is committed to enhancing the achievement of legal ideals.

[12] Grace and Wilkinson, *supra* note 1; cf. Campbell and Wiles, *supra* note 2.

[13] See Nelkin, *supra* note 9 for an extended discussion of this point.

tendency to 'take' rather than 'make' the problems it investigates. It is true that taking problems ready-made can set up mistaken or misleading topics of enquiry. Most of the influential theoretical attacks on socio-legal objects of enquiry have exploited this weakness, asking for example, of studies of access to justice, 'who says that there is an 'unmet legal need'?' and in research into the implementation of legislation, 'what questions are begged by investigating why legislation 'failed'?' Frequently a topic comes to be a focus for socio-legal interests less because of inherent changes in the matter of concern than because of the growth of social concern about the particular 'problem'. Attention directed at the object of concern rather than at the reasons for concern may be misdirected.[14]

At the level of organizing empirical investigations the danger of 'taking' problems is that of bringing into the research setting a set of concerns which are not salient to those under investigation and, conversely, failing to discover what they do consider to be important.[15] It is true that such a procedure can be defended where the goal of investigation is strictly evaluative rather than descriptive but, in practice, the two goals are difficult to separate especially where the point of the exercise is to make policy recommendations. It is a fair criticism of many investigations into the law-in-action that they do not avoid this danger although, again, such work is by no means confined to or identical with that associated with socio-legal studies. But it has a corollary which is less often noted. For if it should be the case that the sort of concerns which are commonly pursued by those doing socio-legal studies *are* important to the social actors under consideration then this must be allowed for in the investigation. And it often will be the case that the ideals held out by law and the claims made by and for particular laws and legal institutions will be important to those being investigated.[16]

---

[14] Z.K. Bankowski and David Nelken, "Discretion as a Social Problem" in M. Adler and S. Asquith, eds., *Discretion and Welfare* (London: Heinemann, 1981).

The concerns of sociology of law are also not unaffected by changes in the social and political environment, but at least it is more likely to be reflexive about its changing concerns; see, e.g., David Nelken, "Capitalism and the Rule of Law: A Review Article" (1980), 8 *Int. J. of the Sociology of Law* 193.

[15] See Grace and Wilkinson, *supra* note 1.

[16] D. McBarnett, "False Dichotomies in Criminal Justice Research" in J. Baldwin and A. Bottomley, eds., *Criminal Justice: Selected Readings* (London: Martin Robertson, 1978), would reject this argument by insisting that talk of 'gaps' between the ideals of law and what actually occurs is misconceived because the ideals are not even built into the paper rules.

At the extreme this may only be to the extent that they are conscious of the possibility that others may call them to 'account' for failure to live up to these ideals. But in other cases it may enter into the 'internal' view by which legal officials orient their behaviour.[17] What I am proposing therefore is that many of the 'problems' associated with socio-legal studies can be reformulated for sociological purposes by asking (a) why the topic matters theoretically and (b) if, how and why it matters to those social actors whose behaviour is to be explained.[18]

2. The Gap Problem

Probably the most useful way of demonstrating these points is not by abstract argument but by displaying the intellectual history of a particular concern. I have chosen to discuss the problem of 'discrepancies' or 'disjunctions' between promises or claims held out for law and its actual effects, a concern which is often described as the 'gap problem'.[19] As will be seen, this concern has been treated by many writers as a typical example of a research problem which has been pre-defined by practical policy considerations and therefore as *the* exemplar of all that is wrong with socio-legal type concerns.

The purpose of the following review is therefore twofold. In the first place to work towards a reformulation of the 'gap problem' as a topic in the sociology of law and, secondly, by showing the possibility of such a reformulation of what is one of the most criticized of socio-legal topics, to call into question

---

Thus, in discussing the legal process, she argues that "due process *is* crime control". This seems to me an overstated argument and there is much sociological work on the legal process, as elsewhere, which shows how and why officials construct the impression that legal rules are being complied with as a gloss to their actual performance.

[17] H.L.. Hart, *The Concept of Law* (Oxford: Oxford U. Press, 1961).

[18] This point is hardly an original one and has recently again been well made by Roberto Unger, *Law in Modern Society: Toward A Criticism of Social Theory* (New York: Free Press, 1976). Unfortunately, Unger's work is a bad precedent to follow because he is content to make unverified (and sometimes unverifiable) assertions about the claims and promises that law is supposed to hold out to the citizenry, the expectations that the populations of different historical societies are supposed to have entertained and the consequent 'gap' between what law claims to achieve and actually can and does achieve. For further discussion of this point see David Nelken, "Is There a Crisis . . .", *supra* note 9.

[19] The 'gap problem' is both a topic and an approach. The process of reformulation which is undertaken here is designed to show that it is both a topic worthy of investigation and an approach useful as an aspect of a larger sociological investigation.

the present distinction which is drawn between sociology of law and socio-legal studies.[20]

In the review I shall describe the changing place of the 'gap problem' with special reference to the study of legislation.[21] The 'problem' will be located in terms of changing theoretical developments over the past two decades starting from those approaches in which the problem occupied pride of place, to those in which it played the role of serving as a symptom and pointer to wider issues. I begin by discussing the part played by the 'gap problem' in studies of the 'impact' of legislative enactments and judicial and administrative decisions and then comment on the criticisms to which these studies were subjected. I next consider how the 'gap problem' entered as an underlying concern and approach into work associated with the 'labelling' and 'conflict' perspectives in both the sociology of law and the sociology of deviance. After discussing the criticisms to which these frameworks were subjected I then provide a brief overview of some of the main contemporary trends within the sociology of law and deviance and defend one such contemporary approach to the study of law as a framework within which the 'gap problem' can be incorporated. My account of these changing developments will be roughly chronological in an attempt to follow the stages of theoretical debate. It can be argued that these stages mark the progress of sociology of law as its concerns widened to include ever broader issues of social structure and social change, but many of these ways of handling the 'gap problem' still have their adherents, who differ on fundamental questions of sociological theory and method and it is no part of my argument to elide such differences. What I do want to show, however, is that the 'gap problem' can be seen to have a continuing, if sometimes unacknowledged, significance is most of these developments and that such a concern cannot be seen as an irredeemably 'practical' and unsociological topic or approach.

---

[20] Insofar as this demonstration is successful, it may offer an example of how the division of labour that presently exists in the sociology of law can be made mutually beneficial (as any division of labour should be!). What commonly happens now may be characterized as follows. Practitioners of socio-legal studies find a promising new area for concern, for example 'legal effectiveness', 'unmet legal needs' or 'dispute processing'. Not long afterwards the 'theorists' move in, to argue, with some success, that these topics incorporate too many question-begging presuppositions. This critique all too easily becomes an end in itself until the process repeats itself, instead of being directed to working out the way in which such topics may be incorporated into sociological investigations.

[21] My definition of the 'gap problem' is necessarily somewhat restricted because no review of this sort could hope to deal with all the work concerned in some way with 'gaps' in the sense of whether or not legal rules form the basis of social conduct.

3. Early Studies of Legal Impact

The 'gap problem' was central to the revival of interest in sociology of law in America and Europe in the 1960's because so much of this early work took the 'impact' of law as its starting point.[22] Studies of the differences between the 'law in the books' and the 'law in action' provided the sort of incontrovertible evidence useful to pioneers of a new subject of the fact that the effects of normative legal or administrative guidelines to behaviour could not be understood without reference to the way in which they were refracted by the social environment. This problematic was present in a wide variety of studies, not only in work on the impact of legislation. Its influence may also be traced in such various research areas as those concerned with the 'penetration' of legal systems in developing countries; the degree of social change achieved by Supreme Court decisions such as those concerning race relations, bible-reading in schools and police arrest procedures; and the numerous studies of the divergence of the actions taken by legal and administrative officials from the norms that were supposed to govern their behaviour.[23] This style of research produces useful pay-offs for policy makers and others interested in law as a form of social engineering or social control; it also possesses the not inconsiderable attraction of allowing research to mimic the excitement of muck-raking, exposé journalism. But it has since come under heavy attack, much of it deserved, notably by American writers reflecting on the progress the subject had made by the early 1970's.

Perhaps the strongest line of criticisms was the accusation that this approach built into its problematic unexamined and

---

[22] Although this review concentrates on developments over the last two decades it is important to appreciate that neither the distinction between "the law in the books" and "the law in action" nor the accompanying concern to change one in the light of the other are original to these writers. Similar formulations and concerns were crucial in earlier attempts to provide a sociology of law such as that of Eugen Ehrlich, *Fundamental Principles of the Sociology of Law,* trans. Walter Moll (Cambridge, Massachusetts: Harvard Press, 1936) in Europe and the work of American Legal Realists, about which are Wilfred E. Rumble, *American Legal Realism* (Cambridge, Massachusetts: Harvard Press, 1968) and Alan Hunt, *The Sociological Movement in Law* (London: Macmillan, 1978). Moreover, the work of Thurman Arnold, *Symbols of Government,* 2d ed. (New York: Harbinger, 1962) and *The Folklore of Capitalism,* 2d ed. (New Haven: Yale University Press, 1971) represents an important precedent for a less practically-oriented attempt to explore the significance of the frequent gulf between the promise and achievement of law.

[23] See, e.g., the readers edited by Lawrence Friedman and Stewart Macaulay, *Law and the Behavioural Sciences,* 1st ed. (Indianapolis: Bobbs Merrill, 1969); Richard D. Schwartz and Jerome H. Skolnick, eds., *Society and Legal Order* (London: Basic Books, 1970); Joel B. Grossman and Mary H. Grossman, eds., *Law and Social Change in Modern American* (Pacific Palisades, California: Goodyear, 1971).

frequently implausible assumptions concerning the way in which norms might be expected to affect conduct. From a point of view based on sociological theory and evidence such a hypothesis of inevitable compliance was a straw-man — however important it might be from a normative, moral or practical point of view to show the lack of a perfect correspondence between norms and behaviour. From another angle some writers pointed out that it was no more than a cultural presupposition to suppose that law's essential role and justification lay in its capacity to direct social change. They argued that this was not so much a theoretical position concerning the nature of law but rather an unreflective parroting of contemporary cultural and ideological legitimations of the value of law.[24]

The brunt of the argument against gap studies was that, as a direct consequence of these unimpressive theoretical starting-points, much research in this mode tended towards the sociological commonplace. The exposure of discrepancies between the formal mandates of law and actual practice in courtrooms, police cars, or administrative agencies often amounted to little more than the rediscovery of the existence of informal organisation alongside formal organisation, or belated recognition of the fact that 'law-jobs' were, after all, also jobs, and therefore subject to the same kinds of pressures which could be found in other work contexts. One more specific criticism of the effect of this problematic on studies of the impact of legislation is particularly relevant here. Many early studies of the impact of law, in demonstrating the disparity between the object of legislation and its actual effect, assumed that it was a simple matter to identify the object or purpose of the legislation in question. But there was no foolproof way of extracting one authoritative object or purpose of a statute, which was almost always the compromise product of the various members of the legislature. The researcher was therefore often led (or willingly chose) to substitute his own moral view as to what the law was supposed to achieve. This made him part of the struggle for the passage and implementation of law rather than in any sense an independent observer.[25]

On the other hand, some of the criticisms levelled at this first stage of interest in the 'gap problem' went too far. Many of the studies attacked did not in fact limit themselves to the demolition of shaky hypotheses but went on to provide interesting and sometimes systematic descriptions of the various ways in which law was re-defined in its practical

---

[24] See Richard Abel, "Law Books and Books about Law" (1973), 26 *Stanford L. Rev.* 175; Black, *supra* note 1; Galanter, *supra* note 1; and Friedman and Macaulay, *supra* note 1, 21-27.

[25] See esp., Black, *supra* note 1.

operation. Nor is it obvious that moral assessments either can or should be entirely excluded from the investigation of legal outcomes, as some of the more extreme positivist critics urged. Indeed, an important 'school' of sociologists of law stands for the opposite viewpoint, that law itself can only be defined in terms of the values it is designed to serve.[26] More to the point in terms of the present argument is the fact that the difficulties which are alleged to vitiate studies of the impact of legislation are not insuperable. There is nothing invalid about a focus on the discrepancy between legislative promise and performance provided that the set of statements of the proclaimed objects of the legislation and the various accounts of its effects are treated as data worthy of investigation in their own right. The relationship that such claims may or may not bear to the facts revealed by independent investigation can then be regarded as a fertile source of research problems. Taken in this way the evidence of disparity between claims and performance can prove a useful starting point for research into the questions:

i. how and why these various claims and descriptions were made and what made them credible;

ii. why they diverged from what actually could and did happen; and

iii. how far, in what ways, and for what reasons, those discrepancies were concealed by those who implemented the legislation and/or made claims about its impact.

However, successful investigation of these problems does then require some larger theoretical framework in which they may be addressed and to which their study can contribute. It is these frameworks and their bearing on the 'gap problem' which I shall now discuss.

4. Labelling and Conflict Perspectives in the Sociology of Law

The second approach to the 'gap problem' which can be distinguished is the way it was handled in the labelling and conflict studies which were popular in the sociology of law and deviance in the 1960's and early 1970's. Those studies carried out under the influence of the labelling perspective were often intrigued by the frequent discrepancy between deviant labels and deviant behaviour; conflict studies placed considerable emphasis on the divergence between legislative promise and performance. There were, of course, differences of interest in the two bodies of research, but, despite this, there was much in

---

[26] See P. Selznick, "The Sociology of Law" in R. Merton, L. Broom, and L.S. Cottrell, eds., *Sociology Today* (New York: Basic Books, 1959); Schwartz and Skolnick, *supra* note 23; Philippe Nonet, "For Jurisprudential Sociology" (1976), 10 *Law & Society Rev.* 525.

common in the way each perspective explained the source and the significance of the divergencies they identified.

Both perspectives tended to view society as an unstable, temporary order in which various groups and individuals tried to impose their wills on their adversaries. In the competition for whose interests and definitions should prevail, victory went to the side with the greatest resources. Allegiance to some version of this framework of explanation was a particularly important common denominator for the various adherents of conflict theory, who were otherwise divided in their views concerning the number and character of the parties who were in significant contention for the control of society.[27] Many of those who used the labelling perspective shared a similar, if largely undeveloped, political sociology, though their particular focus was on the process by which officials and professionals dealt with their clients.[28] On the other hand, there was also a rather different minority approach which concentrated on the integrative functions of deviance.[29]

Explanations of the 'gap problem' fitted snugly within this common framework of explanation. The disparity between the claims made for a law and its outcome could be represented as a straightforward demonstration of the weakness of the law when faced with the resistance of powerful groups.[30] Similarly, the success of officials, professionals and the media in imposing stigmatising labels on deviants was seen to depend on and reflect their strength in relation to those they label.

There are three features of the way these perspectives discuss

---

[27] Amongst the better known examples of the conflict perspective in the sociology of law see Austin T. Turk, "Conflict and Criminality" (1966), 31 *Amer. Sociological Rev.* 338; Turk, *Criminality and Legal Order* (Chicago: Rand McNally, 1969); R. Quinney, *The Social Reality of Crime* (Boston: Little Brown, 1970); William Chambliss and Milton Mankoff, eds., *Whose Law, What Order: A Conflict Approach to Criminology* (New York: Wiley, 1976).

[28] For examples of this approach see H. Becker, *Outsiders* (New York: Free Press, 1963) and H. Becker, ed., *The Other Side: Perspectives on Deviance* (New York: Free Press, 1964); Edwin Lemert, *Social Pathology* (New York: McGraw Hill, 1951) and Edwin Lemert, *Human Deviance, Social Problems and Social Control* (Englewood Cliffs, N.J.: Prentice Hall, 1967); E. Schur, *Labelling Deviant Behaviour* (New York: Harper and Row, 1971); E. Rubington and M. Weinberg, *Deviance: The Interactionist Perspective* (London: Macmillan, 1st ed./1968, 2nd ed./1975).

[29] This is best represented by the work of Kai Erikson, "Notes on the Sociology of Deviance" in Becker, ed., *The Other Side: Perspectives on Deviance* (New York: Free Press, 1964); *Wayward Puritans* (London: John Wiley, 1966).

[30] For representative studies of the resistance to legal regulation by influential groups see, e.g., E. Sutherland, *White Collar Crime* (New York: Holt, Reinhart and Winston, 1961); Neil Gunningham, *Pollution, Social Interest and the Law* (London: Martin Robertson, 1974); F. Pearce, *Crimes of the Powerful* (London: Pluto Press, 1976).

the labelling of deviance and the sociology of law which have been found problematic in recent attempts to relocate these phenomena in terms of classical sociological concerns with social order and social structure. These are the narrow conceptions of power and social conflict which they employ; their tendency to reduce law, and other cultural phenomena, to the status of instruments which can be manipulated at will, and their failure to provide any overall perspective on how and why societies change.

The first of these issues arises from the fact that most labelling and conflict approaches concentrated on the social interaction of groups and individuals. The concept of power which they used tended to be that of the successful assertion of one's will over the opposition of another, which is what Lukes refers to as a behavioural, one-dimensional view of power.[31] It is possible, in principle, even within this framework, to broaden the concern with the way power is exercised so as to go beyond an exclusive focus on overt decision-making and conflict. These perspectives can, for example, take into account more subtle matters such as the indirect exertion of power over the contents of the agenda for decision-making and an emphasis on conflict in society could be extended to include many of the concerns of current theorising about law in society, provided that the requirement of evidence of overt conflict is pushed further and further away.[32]

In practice, however, the pursuit of these concerns within the framework of the conflict and labelling perspectives was not satisfactory. Conflict studies provided little discussion of the conditions which confine the scope and terms of conflict in society, or of the significance of the shared understandings which enabled the parties to social conflicts to know what it is they are fighting for and about. More generally, an interactionist methodology has an unfortunate influence on the analysis of social structure in relation to social conflict.[33] The theory of the state present in conflict theory often appeared over-simple and unconvincing. The state was defined institutionally and then presented as a passive tool in the hands of the most powerful social grouping.[34] When it was endowed

---

[31] S. Lukes, *Power: A Radical View* (London: Macmillan, 1973).

[32] For illustrations of this extension of interest within conflict theory see the discussion of Austin T. Turk, "Law as a Weapon in Social Conflict" (1976), 23 *Social Problems* 276 and J.J. McManus, "The Emergence of Legislation" (1978), 5 *Brit. J. Law and Society* 185.

[33] See Paul Rock, "Phenomenalism and Essentialism in Deviancy Theory" (1973), 7 *Sociology* 17; B. Meltzer, J. Petras and L. Reynolds, *Symbolic Interactionism: Genesis, Varieties and Criticisms* (London: Routledge, Keagan & Paul, 1975); K. Plummer, "Misunderstanding Labelling Perspectives" in David Downes and Paul Rock, eds., *Deviant Interpretations* (London: Martin Robertson, 1979), 85.

[34] E.g. William Chambliss and Robert Seidman, *Law, Order and Power* (Reading, Massachusetts: Addison Wesley, 1971).

with a life of its own it was seen as just another social group pursuing its particular interests.[35]

The second weakness of studies using these perspectives was their crude approach to the significance of the ideas and traditions embodied in law and deviant labels. It might almost be said that the hallmark of the conflict approach was its instrumentalist conception of law. Not only was the content (and form) of law seen as an epiphenomenon of the balance of power in society, but law itself was assumed to be no different in its essential characteristics from other sources of power such as money or political connections. The following programmatic statement by Chambliss and Seidman of their understanding of criminal law was not unrepresentative of this position:

> . . . The laws that define deviancy or illegality therefore, are the result of political activity. Deviancy is not a moral question, it is a political question. No act, nor any set of acts, can be defined as inherently "beyond the pale" of "community tolerance". Rather, there are in effect an infinite number and variety of acts occurring in any society which may or may not be defined and treated as criminal — which acts are so designated depends on the interests of the persons with sufficient political power and influence to manage to have their views prevail. Once it has been established that certain acts are to be designated as deviant, then how the laws are implemented will likewise reflect the political power of the various affected groups.[36]

Recent attempts to provide a more sophisticated treatment of law within this limiting framework have failed to advance far towards any new conception. Thus Turk was still content to *define* law as "a set of resources for which people contend and with which they are better able to promote their own ideas and interests against others."[37] He distinguished five kinds of resource control which are "represented in the cultural and social structural reality of law". These are (1) the control of direct physical violence (war or police power); (2) the control of production, allocation, and/or use of material resources (economic power); (3) the control of decision-making processes (political power); (4) the control of definitions of and access to knowledge, beliefs and values (ideological power); and (5) the control of human attention and living time (diversionary power). Despite the apparent latitude of this approach, the emphasis is still on the variety of ways in which groups make use of law in order to achieve their goals. The question which is never addressed is why law can serve as such a valuable resource for these purposes; why, indeed, it can come to be perceived as authoritative even by those who consistently lose out in the competitive struggle.

[35] Austin T. Turk, *Criminality and Legal Order* (Chicago: Rand McNally, 1969).

[36] Chambliss and Seidman, *supra* note 34, 67.

[37] A.T. Turk, *supra* note 32, 279-280.

Much the same applies to the otherwise interesting discussion by Jim McManus of the emergence and non-emergence of legislation.[38] Once again, his theoretical discussion of the role of law, as well as the associated empirical study of the regulation of credit provision, concentrates on the utility of both statute and common law to the pursuit of interests by powerful groups. Despite some reference to the fact that these groups ultimately derived their power from their place in society there is no close examination of the implications of this for the sources and limits of the power of social groups; there is also no real attempt to understand how institutions, ideas and traditions can serve as a source, a means and a restraint on power.

Within labelling theory, the corresponding discussion of the role of conceptions and ideas often suffered from a similar instrumentalism. Officials tended to be viewed as the bearers of ideas, including deviant labels, which usually originate in their professional stocks of knowledge or else are constructed subjectively to serve their purposes. The relationship of these ideas to the distribution of power in society was not followed up because of the astructural bias of the study of meaning within symbolic interactionism.[39] There was occasionally some recognition of the possibility that the ideas mobilized by officials and deviants alike were derived from a common stock of common-sense conceptions but this insight was not developed into an enquiry into the forces which shaped and sustained such conceptions.

These difficulties in conceiving law and conceptions of deviance as anything more than instruments of power, was connected with the artificial juxtaposition of so-called consensus and conflict approaches to society in studies of deviance, law and social problems in the 1960's. A common pattern here was for a writer to pose an over-simplified theory of willing acceptance of law by all members of society and then reject this in favour of a hard-headed recognition of the existence of conflict in society. In practice this meant that a mangled version of Durkheimian sociology was attacked and an approach ultimately derived from Weberian sociology put in its place. Consensus then became a dirty word and even Weber's notion of legitimate 'authority' became suspect as a description of the acceptance of law.[40]

---

[38] J.J. McManus, *supra* note 32.

[39] See H. Dreitzel, *Recent Sociology No. 2* (London: Macmillan, 1970); Paul Rock, *Deviant Behaviour* (London: Hutchinson, 1973); Meltzer, Petras, Reynolds, *supra* note 33.

[40] The problem here arose partly because of Max Weber's over-rigid distinction between force and legitimate authority. See M. Rheinstein, *Max Weber on Law and Economy in Society* (New York: Simon and Schuster, 1954); Hunt, *supra* note 22, 112-118 and 130-132. But cf. R. Bendix, *Max Weber: An Intellectual Portrait* (London: Methuen, 1973), 481-482.

50   *Windsor Yearbook of Access to Justice*   *1981*

The third drawback of work using these perspectives was the manner in which they handled the topic of social change. This follows in part from the other characteristics of the framework of explanation which I have been describing. When social groups and the powers they wield are the beginning and end of analysis it becomes difficult to come to grips with forces which make a once-powerful group decline in influence. For example, the argument that it is only possible to criminalise those outside the 'moral centre' of society, and that criminalisation therefore reflects shifts in the social status of those engaging in the behaviour being regulated has a superficial attractiveness.[41] But were this argument pressed to its limits it would raise the problem of how and why the moral centre of a society should ever change. Even those labelling and conflict studies which did focus directly on the problem of change demonstrated the restricted range of issues which could be examined using their framework of explanation. Thus Paulus conducted a study into the factors which explained the emergence and growth of legislation concerned with the regulation of food and drug manufacture. Typically, however, most stress was placed on the way in which this process depended on the willingness of powerful groups to accept that their own interests lay in accepting such regulation: "[t]hose to be controlled often changed their perceptions and instead of opposing control, in turn called for further and more stringent control, generally supporting the activities of the law enforcers as long as the personal and social costs of such law-enforcing activity can be borne easily and without too great stigmitization."[43]

My criticism is not so much of this argument as such, but of the way this approach allows the problems concerning the relevant broader changes in economic and political structures and ideas to be too easily avoided. Even the best of these studies, when examining the process by which legislative outcomes are achieved and transformed, necessarily placed all their stress on the activities of interest and status groups engaged in competitive struggle. Thus, apparent divergence between legislative objectives and actual consequences (the 'gap problem') is sometimes explained by saying that the group pressing for legislation was resigned to a symbolic rather than instrumental achievement. Alternatively, in more careful statements of this approach, the argument is put that the actual outcome was the result of an unfolding process which involved

---

[41] Troy S. Duster, *The Legislation of Morality: Law, Drugs and Moral Judgment* (N.Y.: Free Press, 1970); P. Bean, *The Social Control of Drugs* (London: Martin Robertson, 1974).

[42] I. Paulas, *The Search for Pure Food* (London: Martin Robertson, 1974).

[43] *Id.*, 48-49.

both symbolic and instrumental dimensions.[44] But too little attention was given to explaining how the ideas mobilized by these social groups were related to wider social and economic changes.

5. Recent Theoretical Developments in the Sociology of Law and Deviance

There is an obvious danger of imposing a superficial uniformity on the disparate trends that make up recent theorizing about law and society. But one central characteristic does appear to be a move away from a concentration on the conflicting purposes of social groups towards a renewed concern with the sources of shared understanding and ideas and how this 'common-sense' is maintained. Moreover the particular focus of interest in these topics is their relation to the larger structures of society.

The retreat from over-simple versions of the conflict perspective became evident on many fronts at once. On the one hand, Paul Rock criticised labelling theorists for their unreasonable assumption that officials and deviants inhabited completely separate moral worlds, and argued instead that they often shared a large number of common conceptions without which they could hardly sustain their mutual interaction and communication.[45] From a different theoretical position, Sumner was making the same point in his critique of conflict-type Marxist explanation of crime, arguing that ". . . the question is raised: how does a consensus, a shared social stock of meanings come into existence in what they agree is a class-divided society?''[46] The point is an important one in the context of developments in this field of study. But it must be admitted that the logical and empirical dependence of social conflict on the existence of some consensus, and the fact that a consensus on goals could itself fuel conflict had been noted long before in mainstream sociological theorizing. Cohen, for example, discusses the question at some length.[47] It is, of course, precisely the argument of Merton's explanation of crime.[48] Moreover, what was still required at this stage was the development of a theoretical conception which transcended the

[44] J. Gusfield, *Symbolic Crusade* (Urbana, Illinois: U. of Illinois Press, 1963); W.G. Carson, "Instrumental and Symbolic Aspects of Factory Legislation" in Roger Hood, ed., *Crime, Criminology and Public Policy* (London: Heinemann, 1974).

[45] Paul Rock, "Conceptions of the Moral Order" (1974), 14 *Brit. J. Criminol.* 139.

[46] C. Sumner, "Marxism and Deviancy Theory" in P. Wiles, ed., *The Sociology of Crime and Delinquency in Britain: Vol. 2. The New Criminologies* (Oxford: Martin Robertson, 1976).

[47] P. Cohen, *Modern Social Theory* (London: Heinemann, 1968).

[48] R. Merton, *Social Theory and Social Structure* (New York: Free Press, 1968).

artificially opposed concepts of conflict and consensus, and which linked this conception to the part played by social groups or classes in society and to an overall perspective of social structure and change.

Although I shall be concentrating on the recent progress of this development in the different form it has taken in Marxist and non-Marxist writing, it is important to relate it to some of the other major trends in contemporary sociological studies of law and deviance. All these trends represent vital movements in theory; they must be distinguished from the approach of some writers who still continue to characterize as 'conflict theory' almost everything that has been written in the last twenty years in the sociology of law and deviance.[49]

One of the most pronounced of these other major trends is the attempt to produce a Marxist theory of the form and content of law which returns to the work of writers such as Pashukanis so as to advance beyond the instrumentalism of conflict theory.[50] A relevant feature of this work is the attempt to formulate a viable theory of ideology. Another relatively self-contained trend is the continued pursuit of a critical social theory of law based on an overtly normative definition of legality and its characteristics. This was originally identified

---

[49] For a bad example see R. Reasons and C. Rich, eds., *Sociology of Law: The Conflict Perspective* (London: Butterworths, 1978).

[50] The recent growth of Anglo-American interest in analyses of the form of bourgeois in law may be traced in M. Cain, "The Main Themes of Marx and Engels' Sociology of Law" (1974), 1 *Brit. J. Law and Society* 136; I. Taylor, P. Walton, J. Young, *The New Criminology* (London: Routledge, Keagan & Paul, 1973) and *Critical Criminology* (London: Routledge, Keagan & Paul, 1975); I. Balbus, "Commodity Form and Legal Form" (1977), 11 *Law and Society Rev.* 571; C.J. Arthur, ed., *Law and Marxism by E.B. Pashukanis* (London: Ink Links, 1978); John Holloway and Sol Picciotto, eds., *State and Capital: A Marxist Debate* (Austin, Texas: Univ. of Texas Press, 1978); R. Kinsey, "Marxism and the Law" (1978), 5 *Brit. J. Law and Society* 202; M. Cain and A. Hunt, *Marx and Engels on Law* (London: Academic, 1979); C. Sumner, *Reading Ideologies* (London: Academic Press, 1979); B. Fine, et al., eds., *Capitalism and the Rule of Law* (London: Hutchinson, 1979). Cf. David Nelken, "Capitalism and the Rule of Law: A Review Article" (1980), 8 *Int. J. of the Sociology of Law* 193. E.P. Thompson's remarks on the significance of the "rule of law" at the end of his study of the "Black Acts", have stimulated considerable interest in the ideological significance of law but his approach is better considered with regard to the development of Gramsci's notion of hegemony. See E.P. Thompson, *Whigs and Hunters* (Harmondsworth: Penguin, 1975) and A. Gramsci, *Prison Notebooks*, ed. and trans. Q. Hoare and G. Howell-Smith (London: Lawrence & Wishart, 1971).

with a number of sociologists of Berkeley but it has since made at least one important recruit elsewhere.[51]

A third aspect of contemporary theorizing is the defence and counter-attack by adherents of versions of labelling and conflict theory. Thus, Friedman and Macaulay, in the second edition of their influential Reader, argue that the criticisms of their version of conflict theory made by recent radical and Marxist approaches to law do not in fact shake their position because they can easily be absorbed into it.[52] Similarly, the collection of papers edited by Downes and Rock, as a response to recent radical and Marxist theorizing in the sociology of deviance, includes two articulate defences of labelling theory.[53] Rock[54] takes further his earlier claims that the labelling perspective rests on an authentic alternative conception of what social theory can and cannot achieve.[55] Plummer, on the other hand, argues that the problems concerning the labelling of deviance which are the common denominator of studies in this perspective can and should also be addressed by those interested in developing and understanding what he terms 'the master institutions of society'.[56] The important point here is that the imposition of labels, whether they are accurate or not, can be shown to benefit groups and institutions other than those immediately engaged in pressing for or implementing them. However, although Plummer is right to argue that there is room for such an extension of interest starting from the questions addressed within the labelling perspective, he is much less convincing when he claims that this can be done by applying those conceptions of power and understandings of social structure which serve in the analysis of face-to-face interaction.

It is useful to pause at this point to note that the 'gap problem' has again come to the fore in many of these recent writings, albeit in a slightly different form from the way in which it figured earlier. It is hardly surprising that the critical normative school of sociology of law, as well as some other writers responding to 'radical' attacks on the achievements of 'liberal legality', have renewed their interest in the 'gap problem' and have called for the study of how law can better

---

[51] See Selznick, *supra* note 26; Schwartz and Skolnick, *supra* note 23; Phillippe Nonet, "For Jurisprudential Sociology" (1976), 10 *Law & Society Rev.* 525 and cf. now D.M. Trubek, "Complexity and Contradiction in the Legal Order: Balbus and the Challenge of the Social Theory about Law" (1977), 11 *Law and Society Rev.* 529.

[52] Friedman and Macaulay, *supra* note 1.

[53] David Downes and Paul Rock, eds., *Deviant Interpretations* (London: Martin Robertson, 1979).

[54] Paul Rock, "Conceptions of the Moral Order" (1974), 14 *Brit. J. Criminol.* 139.

[55] See also, Grace and Wilkinson, *supra* note 1.

[56] Plummer, *supra* note 33.

deliver the ideals it is supposed to represent.[57] For, as a result of the moral expectations they impose on law, these writers are constantly brought up against its failures as measured by these expectations and are forced to examine how this 'gap' can be overcome.

It is more significant perhaps that 'radical' sociologists of law and deviance are now prepared to concede that both the major theoretical approaches in their field have hitherto, as Jack Young puts it, started from a concern with "the gap between the ideals of law and their actual practice".[58] For those writers whom Young describes as 'Left Idealists' such a gap is an "unbridgeable chasm . . . the central strategy as far as law is concerned is to debunk it. That is, to expose the unequal reality underneath the rhetoric of equality and to cast doubt on the legitimacy of the system". On the other hand for 'Reformist' sociologists "likewise it is the gap between bourgeois reality and ideals which can be used to prise open capitalism, but this is part of a piecemeal process of reconstructing the social order."

Even Richard Abel, whose attacks on the early version of the gap approach were so trenchant, now appears ready to admit that it is necessary for sociologists to tackle the 'gap problem' as an empirical problem. He argues that the questions raised by the frequent evidence of the failure of legal reforms are whether and by whom this 'gap' is perceived, with what effects, and how far the legitimacy of the state and law necessarily rests on persistent actions of concealment.[59] The issue remains however how best to organize such investigations in relation to broader developments in social theory and law.[60]

---

[57] See, e.g., Trubek, *supra* note 51.

[58] Jack Young, "Left Idealism, Reformism and Beyond. From New Criminology to Marxism" in Fine et al, *Capitalism and the Rule of Law* (London: Hutchinson, 1979), 11.

[59] See R. Abel, "From the Editor" (1978), 12 *Law and Society Rev.* 199.

[60] This paper was written before the appearance of B. Roshier and H. Teff's *Law and Society in England* (London: Tavistock, 1980) but their attempt to revive the gap approach cannot be counted a success. They begin their book by arguing (at 15-17) that disjunctions between the 'law in the Books' and the 'law in action' can serve as a 'unifying' framework for research in the sociology of law despite the criticisms that have been levelled at it. Unfortunately their all too brief consideration of this approach suggests that they adopted it as a convenient way of organizing their book rather than as the result of a radical reformulation of why 'gaps' and 'disjunctions' are of theoretical significance. This is confirmed by the authors unconcerned acceptance of the early version of the 'gap problem' which, as has been seen, came under deserved attack in the early 1970s. Thus, they assume that the concern with disjunctions must mean that "the reality of law is measured against some ideal, usually taken to be implicit in the formal 'book' content of the law, or in the constitutional proceedings

For those interested in the 'gap problem' as one aspect of the social significance of the impact of particular pieces of legislation and of specific episodes of labelling, the most promising recent theoretical developments are those which have tried to go beyond the crude juxtaposition of consensus and conflict. It is significant that these developments have been contributed to both by explicitly Marxist writers as well as those concerned with the ambit of sociological theory more generally. Thus, on the one hand, Marxist writers have tackled this issue as part of their recent re-examination of how law helps to maintain the 'hegemony' of the ruling class(es) in capitalist societies.[61] On the other hand, some leading British sociological

---

available for formulating and changing laws" (at 15), and then admit that this means that "the researcher is usually, implicitly at least, introducing his own version of these ideals as a measuring rod". They then go on to claim that "arguments about the existence of disjunction between the reality of law and its ideal forms reflect varying conceptions of the nature of power in society", although it is not clear why this helps their case. Their main defence of their version of the gap approach comes to rest on the assertion that it represents a special kind of interest in the law. Their interest in the "disjuncture between intent and reality" and "the reality of law in action" can be justified by their commitment to understanding law "in the real world" and by the fact that they see themselves as concerned with 'socio-legal problems' rather than sociology of law. But if these two enterprises cannot really be distinguished, as I argue in this paper and elsewhere ("Sociology of Law v. Socio-Legal Studies: The False Divide", a paper presented at the Conference on Critical Legal Scholarship, University of Kent, April, 1981), this escape-clause will not suffice. Instead, the concern with disjunctures must be defended in its own right and, if necessary, such a concern must be modified and reformulated in the light of theoretical criticisms.

[61] See E. Currie, "Sociology of Law: The Unasked Questions" (1973), 81 *Yale Law J.* 134; Sumner, *supra* note 46 and *supra* note 50; Alan Hunt, "Perspectives in the Sociology of Law" in Carlen, ed., *Sociology of Law* (Sociological Review Monographs: Keele U. Press, 1976); "Law, State and Class Struggle", [1976] *Marxism Today* 178; and *The Sociological Movement in Law* (London: Macmillan, 1978); M. Cain, "Optimism, Law and the State: A Plea for the Possibility of Politics" in B.M. Blegvad, C.M. Campbell, C.J. Schuyt, eds., *European Yearbook of Law and Society* (The Hague: Martinus Nijhoff, 1977); S. Hall, "Culture, the Media and the Ideologicl Effect" in Curran et al., *Mass Communications and Society* (London: Edward Arnold, 1977); S. Hall, C. Critcher, T. Jefferson, J. Clarke, B. Roberts, *Policing the Crisis: Mugging, the State, and Law and Order* (London: Macmillan, 1978). See also R. Miliband, "The Capitalist State: Reply to Nicos Poulantzas" in R. Blackburn, ed., *Ideology in the Social Sciences* (London: Penguin, 1972), *The State in Capitalist Society* (London: Quartet Books, 1973), *Marxism and Politics* (Oxford: Oxford U. Press, 1977); and R. Williams, *Marxism and Literature* (Oxford: Oxford U. Press, 1977).

theorists have also tackled what is substantially the same issue in their concern to understand the interrelation of power and meaning in the reproduction of the social structure of contemporary societies.[62]

The notion of hegemony was originally put forward in the 1920s by the Italian Marxist Antonio Gramsci as part of his re-working of Marxist theory of the role of the political, social and cultural superstructures in the maintenance of bourgeois rule in late capitalist societies.[63] Gramsci wanted to explain what he saw as "the 'spontaneous' consent given by the masses of the population to the general direction imposed on social life by the dominant fundamental group."[64] He claimed that this consent was won and retained through the exercise of hegemony, by which he meant the success of the bourgeois class in projecting its own particular way of seeing the world, human and social relationships so that this becomes accepted in general as part of 'commonsense' and an aspect of the natural order of things.[65] As a method of maintaining political dominance, the exercise of hegemony always relies ultimately on more coercive methods of imposing order; it comes particularly to the fore during certain periods of late capitalist society. The concept of hegemony has since been made use of in a number of theoretical and empirical investigations by Marxist writers.[66]

However Gramsci's use of the concept of hegemony as well as that of those who have adopted it since, suffers from a number of ambiguities.[67] There is therefore some danger that the term may come to be used merely as a shiny new label for the well-worn theoretical tools of the labelling and conflict perspectives.

To avoid this happening there are at least three areas of conceptual and empirical difficulty which need to be given

---

[62] See esp. the work of S. Lukes, *Power: A Radical View* (London: Macmillan, 1973); "Political Ritual and Social Integration" (1975), 9 *Sociology* 289; and *Essays in Social Theory* (London: Macmillan, 1977). See also A. Giddens, *New Rules of Sociological Method* (London: Hutchinson, 1976).

[63] A. Gramsci, *Prison Notebooks,* ed. and trans. Q. Hoare and G. Howell-Smith (London: Lawrence and Wishart, 1971). See esp. 12, 57, 155, 157, 160-161, 165-168, 170, 177-181, 184-185, 195, 210, 235, 242-243, 246-247, 250, 259, 377.

[64] *Id.,* 12.

[65] Carl Boggs, *Gramsci's Marxism* (London: Pluto Press, 1976), 35 ff. and cf J. Merrington, "Theory and Practice in Gramsci's Marxism", [1968] *The Social Register* 145.

[66] See note 50.

[67] See P. Anderson, "The Antimonies of Antonio Gramsci", [1976] *New Left Rev.* 100.

further consideration.[68] Firstly, what is meant by talking of hegemony? It is, for example, sometimes used to describe a state of affairs and at other times used to indicate a characteristic of leadership or dominance, which applies to a social group or to a set of ideas. In view of the derivation of the word, it is best to use it in such a way that one or other of these latter referents is implied. But the fact that hegemony can be ascribed to either of these latter referents raises the further problem how far the two sorts of hegemony can be considered separately. Can particular social groups be said to possess hegemony in the form, for example, of military or economic dominance which then enables them to dictate the content of dominant ideas? Or is it preferable to say that a social group has hegemony only because it uses and complies with dominant ideas or conceptions (or because its structural power is constituted by them)? There are grounds for using the term in both these ways, indeed it is the essence of Gramsci's use of the notion of ethico-political hegemony that they are fused together. But how does this work in practice?

Secondly, what is meant by saying that hegemony rests on the 'spontaneous consent' of subordinate groups? By what means are these groups induced to accept the legitimacy of ruling groups and/or their ideas and practices, and in what sense do they consent? Do they voluntarily embrace them, are they rendered incapable of formulating alternatives or do they co-operate in a spirit of 'teeth-gritting' harmony? The issues raised by an attempt to examine these alternative possibilities include the difficult problem of whether a method exists through which to discover what the members of a subordinate group 'really' believe and want.

Thirdly, is hegemony the name of a result or a process? If it is the latter, how and why does the hegemony of a particular group or set of ideas ever change? More specifically, how do ruling groups succeed in maintaining their hegemony despite the process of change in dominant conception (and vice versa). How are the ideas and practices which lie outside the range of the dominant set either incorporated or neutralized? These questions raise the vexed problem of the nature and explanation of social change.

Underlying these three issues is the question of whether to adopt a 'voluntarist' or structuralist conception of hegemony. Does the use of the notion of hegemony imply that ruling

---

[68] My comments here are concerned with the applicability of Gramsci's notion within the sociology of law and are not intended as an exegesis of what Gramsci himself intended. As it happens, the applications of Gramsci's ideas which I reviewed all departed to a large extent from his original conceptions of the relationship of hegemony to his other guiding concepts such as 'civil society' and 'organic intellectuals'.

groups and their agents maintain the dominance of the ideas that favour them through a series of deliberate actions (whether or not this is their aim)? Or, alternatively, should hegemony, and the activity of these agents rather be viewed as an 'effect' of the structural location of social classes and their practice in terms of the social relations of production?[69]

The first type of approach can be difficult at times to distinguish from the labelling and conflict modes of explanation and it is subject to the same objection, namely that it gives an exaggerated account of the capacity of agents to manipulate their social and cultural environment.[70] On the other hand, the drawback of the opposite approach is that it places so much stress on structural influences and limits that it becomes difficult to see in what way these are made secure and reproduced through the activity of agents.

The continuing vitality of the controversy over these two approaches in Marxist theorizing is evident in the recent argument and polemic of E.P. Thompson.[71] According to Thompson, hegemony is disclosed "in certain fixities of concept: of property and the rights of money: of innate human nature: of political 'realism': of academic objectivity (itself concealing such concepts): of dominative modes of communication, education, and government: of utilitarian criteria of economic and social decision: of negative freedoms, various active institutional mediation . . . [and] delicate institutional selectivities, reticencies and resistances."[72] The essence of his argument is the necessity to examine this process historically and empirically as an active process which consists, on the one hand, of active direction and control and, on the other, of resistance and struggle. He therefore attacks the structuralist approach, best represented by the work ·of

---

[69] The opening contributions to this important debate within Marxism are to be found in R. Milliband "The Capitalist State: Reply to Nicos Poulantzas" in R. Blackburn, ed., *Ideology in the Social Sciences* (London: Penguin, 1972), and Nicos Poulantzas, "The Problem of the Capitalist State" in R. Blackburn, ed., *id.*

[70] This is seen in the following formulation by Miliband, an exponent of the first conception of hegemony. "Hegemony is not simply something which happens, as a mere superstructural economic and social predominance. It is, in very large part, the result of a permanent and pervasive *effort,* conducted through a multitude of agencies, and *deliberately intended to create . . .* a higher order of solidarity." R. Miliband, *The State in Capitalist Society* (London: Quartet Books, 1973) 163, emphasis added. But see now R. Milliband, *Marxism and Politics* (Oxford: Oxford U. Press, 1977).

[71] E.P. Thompson, *The Poverty of Theory and Other Essays* (London: Merlin Press, 1978).

[72] *Id.,* 183.

Althusser[73] which, he claims, assumes that the state has only to 'hail' passive individuals to recruit them instantly to whatever imaginary relationship it requires.[74] Yet Thompson himself is well aware that this historical process takes place within limiting and facilitative economic, political and cultural structures, which he has explored in his work.[75] What has yet to be demonstrated is the way in which it may be possible to draw on both the voluntaristic and structural approaches to the way hegemony is maintained.

A remarkably similar set of issues has been the focus of attention for some leading British sociologists who have not been so concerned to develop their ideas according to explicit Marxist presuppositions (although one can detect the ghost of Gramsci past). Within recent British sociological theorizing the renewed interest in the sources and dimensions of power arose largely from a dissatisfaction with the major forms of pluralist political analyses of the 1960s. This is particularly true of the work of Stephen Lukes who stressed the need for sociologists to appreciate the way in which structures could serve as a source of power.[76] There are also close parallels to the ideas surrounding the notion of hegemony in Giddens' call for the study of 'structuration', the conditions which govern the continuity and dissolution of structures or types of structures.[77] Giddens' argument that "[t]he reproduction (of structure) is not a mechanical outcome but an active constructing process accomplished by, and consisting in, the doings of active subjects . . ." points to what may be seen as distinctive of the Gramscian type of Marxist approach to social structure. His emphasis on the constraining influence of structures illustrates the other side of that approach. Thus he asserts that "[w]hat passes for social reality in immediate relation to the distribution of power, not only on the most mundane levels of everyday interaction, but also on the level of global cultures and ideologies, whose influence may be felt in everyday social life itself."[78]

These authors have also been forced to deal with the crucial question, which I noted with regard to hegemony, of how far to base explanations on the activity of agents and how far to rest explanation on the effects of structures. Lukes, for example, has argued that the part played by agents and structures must

---

[73] L. Althusser, "Ideology and Ideological State Apparatuses" in *Lenin and Philosophy and Other Essays* (London: New Left Books, 1971).

[74] *Id.,* 366.

[75] E.P. Thompson, *The Making of the English Working Class* (Harmondsworth: Penguin, 1963); *Whigs and Hunters* (Harmondsworth: Penguin, 1975).

[76] S. Lukes, *Power: A Radical View* (London: Macmillan, 1973).

[77] A. Giddens, *supra* note 62, 122 ff.

[78] *Id.,* 113.

be carefully analysed both as a conceptual problem and as an empirical question in any sociological investigation and has offered a useful conceptualization of the internal and external 'constraints' which exert influence over an agent's behaviour.[79]

Both these lines of theoretical development can be used to provide a serviceable framework for examining the part played by law, and legislation in particular, in the reproduction of social order.[80] Moreover, such an investigation may include a concern over the ways in which politicians, officials and others come to make certain claims on behalf of law, the factors which effect their achievement and the extent to which such a 'gap' is perceived by others in the society.

Conclusion

A number of findings emerge from this theoretical review of the 'gap problem' in the sociology of law and legislation. I described how the 'gap problem' was originally formulated and why it came to be displaced under the brunt of theoretical criticisms. But I argued that such attacks were exaggerated and that the 'gap problem' could serve as the starting point of investigation provided that claims about law were themselves treated as a source of data. I described how similar concerns remained part of the hidden agendas of supposedly more theoretical enquiries and how this was now admitted. I then put forward some suggestions to show how the 'gap problem' could be reformulated so that it could take its place as an aspect of some of the most lively contemporary theoretical approaches to law, both Marxist and non-Marxist.

This review also has implications for my argument that topics of concern cannot be categorized as belonging either to 'socio-legal' studies or to the 'sociology of law'. Like the 'gap problem', many other concerns can be reformulated so they can be seen to possess theoretical significance. It will often be true that errors are more likely until some conscious effort at reformulation is undertaken.[81] But all that may be said about one or other example of sociological research is that it is misconceived or well-founded according to specified theoretical and methodological criteria. To allocate work to one or other of the two categories, as such, neither adds nor takes away from this task of assessment. On the contrary, amongst other

---

[79] S. Lukes, *Essays in Social Theory* (London: Macmillan, 1977).

[80] For examples of the kinds of studies of legislation framed with these concerns in mind see William Chambliss, "On Lawmaking" (1979), 6 *Brit. J. Law and Society* 149; P. O'Malley, "Structure and Negotiation in Legislative Process" (1980), 7 *Brit. J. Law and Society* 22; David Nelken, *Landlords, Law and Crime* (London: Academic Press, 1981).

[81] Richard Abel, "Redirecting Social Studies of Law" (1980), 14 *Law and Society Rev.* 805.

dangers, it has the effect of automatically belittling the theoretical adequacy of work associated with 'socio-legal studies' and of giving an undeserved 'cachet' to work in sociology of law merely because of its claims to be advancing the theoretical development of sociology. As far as the 'gap problem' is concerned there are still many studies which fall into the errors associated with over-simple assumptions concerning the goals of law in general or particular instances of legislation, but these 'mistakes' are made even by those who disavow any socio-legal policy-making ambitions.[82] And if they are mistakes, they are such whoever makes them, however they come to be made and whatever flag they fly under.

---

[82] Examples of the early basic errors in the formulation of the 'gap problem' in recent Marxist studies of legislation are discussed in David Nelken, "Capitalism and the Rule of Law: A Review Article" (1980), 8 *Int. J. of the Sociology of Law* 193, 196-197 (regarding legislation against sexual discrimination) and David Nelken, *Landlords, Law and Crime* (London: Academic Press, 1981), c. 1 (regarding housing legislation).

[2]
Law in Action or Living Law? Back to the Beginning in Sociology of Law[1]

Sociology of law often seems to be marked by a form of intellectual apartheid. Whilst social theorists refine their conceptual frameworks, those with more practical concerns robustly set out to investigate the 'law in action'. Mixing of the two approaches is thought likely to impede their necessary separate development. One recent survey of the field concluded that:

'The trend is likely to be a continuing divergence between its theoretical and practical branches: the theoretical consisting mainly of re-analyses of old sociological approaches to law, and the practical continuing with its problem-solving approach without confronting the theoretical problems implicit in what it accepts as problems and solutions'.[2]

This conclusion is somewhat overdrawn and rather unjust to theorists and problem-solvers alike. Yet the germ of truth it contains stems from the fact that many of those researching in the sociology of law (including the authors of the recent survey) take the view that a focus on the 'law in action' represents a sufficient starting point for empirical studies. The concern with the 'law in action' thus serves to isolate research from much of the apparently grander social theory. In this article I shall discuss the historical origins of this focus on the 'law in action' which has its roots in the work of Roscoe Pound, and contrast it with the idea of the 'living law' put forward by Eugene Ehrlich, with which it is often confused. By re-examining the beginnings of sociology of law I also hope to throw some light on alternative starting points for theory and research in this subject.

I. Comparing the views of Pound and Ehrlich

Pound (1870–1964) and Ehrlich (1862–1922) were near contemporaries. Ehrlich was a professor of law at Czernowitz in the province of Bukowina on the edge of the Austrio-Hapsburg empire at the time at which Pound was beginning his long and distinguished career in American law schools, which culminated in his Deanship at Harvard. Pound's seminal article 'Law in Books and Law in Action'

1. This paper was first presented as 'Pound and Ehrlich on the Living Law' at the IVR Conference on Legal and Social Philosophy, Helsinki, 22 September 1983 and as 'Is there life in Ehrlich's concept of the Living Law?' at a Seminar at the Sheffield Centre for Criminology and Socio-legal Studies, 3 February 1984. I am grateful to the responsive audiences on both occasions for their helpful comments.
2. B. Roshier and H. Teff, *Law and Society in England and Wales* (1980) p 13.

158   Legal Studies

was published in 1910; Ehrlich introduced the notion of 'living law' in his rambling but perceptive text on the *Principles of the Sociology of Law* issued in 1913[3]. Ehrlich is the more neglected of the two authors, partly because Pound had the advantage of longevity, but also because he it was who introduced the translation of Ehrlich's book to English-speaking audiences. Pounds' concerns have become today's orthodoxies. Few today question the need for law to adapt itself to meet changing social needs or question the value of Law Commissions set up to keep the effectiveness of legal rules under review. But Ehrlich left behind no similar inheritance. His book was suppressed by the Nazi's after its second edition and most of his European interpreters concentrated on his later arguments for judicial creativity but rejected what they saw as his conservative approach to legislative intervention, which was so strong a feature of his textbook.[4]

Pound and Ehrlich: The False Equation
Some modern commentators take the view that Pound faithfully captured the essence of Ehrlich's concerns and ideas.[5] Zeigert, for example, in a wide ranging recent discussion of Ehrlich's work, argues that:

'Pound spread the idea of a possible "sociological jurisprudence" and Ehrlich's book *could only prove* that he thought along *exactly* the same lines.'[6]

But whereas I shall argue that this sounds ironic in terms of the way Pound transformed Ehrlich's message, Zeigert is quite serious. For him:

'Ehrlich sketches the way for Pound's social engineering . . . Ehrlich's ideological background and optimistic spirit as regards the auspices of modern legal science are *exactly* those conveyed in Pound's writings.'[7]

Both writers, claims Zeigert, were committed to a search for the 'social causality' behind law and the need to use science to provide the answers to questions of legal engineering. They differed only in the

---

3. Roscoe Pound, 'Law in Books and Law in Action' 44 Amer Law Rev, 1910, p 12. E. Ehrlich, *Principles of the Sociology of Law* (trans W Moll) (Harvard U P 1936) (first published 1913). Ehrlich coined the term 'Sociology of Law'.
4. See, for example, the early critical views of Sinzheimer, the famous German Labour lawyer and mentor of Otto Kahn Freund, discussed in M. Rehbinder, *Die Begründ ung der Rechtsoziologie durch Eugen Ehrlich* (1967). Similar criticisms can be found in Wolfgang Friedman's *Legal Theory*, (1949), pp. 187-188
5. See especially K. Zeigert, 'The Sociology behind Eugene Ehrlich's Sociology of Law', Int J Soc of Law 7, 1979, p 225. Illustrations of the many discussions which confuse Pound's and Ehrlich's distinctions are J. O'Day, 'Ehrlich's living law Revisited – Further Vindication for a Prophet Without Honour', Case Western Law Rev, 18, 1966, p 210; J. Harris, *Law and Legal Science* (1979), p 27 and W. Chambliss and R. Seidman, *Law, Order and Power*, (2nd edn, 1983), p 68. The better view is found in D. Schiff, 'Socio-legal Theory': Social Structure and Law', 1976, MLR p 287 at 303–308, but I have found no satisfactory comprehensive survey of Ehrlich's ideas in English.
6. Zeigert, *op cit*, p 231, my emphasis.
7. Zeigert, *op cit*, p 233, my emphasis.

reception their work received. America offered fertile territory for Pound's approach because of its high regard for science and technology and its pragmatic concern with the resolution of social problems. Ehrlich's ideas fell on barren soil in the over-centralised régimes of Continental Europe with their codified legal systems. The alleged similarity in the programmes of the two writers leads Zeigert to the conclusion that Pound and Ehrlich shared the same conceptual tools:

'The famous distinction of 'law in books' versus 'law in action' is very much Ehrlich's pair of opposites '*rechssatz*' (legal proposition) versus '*rechtsleben*' (legal life).'[8]

In fact, Pound's programme and the conceptual tools designed to further it were very different indeed from those of Ehrlich. Pound *used* Ehrlich's ideas, as he used so many others, to help make that eclectic amalgam of diverse theories which is unique only in the range of positions it synthesises. His discussion of Ehrlich in his *Jurisprudence* made his reservations quite clear. Although he hailed Ehrlich's text as 'one of the outstanding books of this generation', he argued that:

'[He] had only the beginnings of a technique of ascertaining patterns of popular action and getting at the relation of these customs to the '*law in books*' and the judicial and administrative process in *action*.'[9]

It is important to note here now Pound carefully distinguishes Ehrlich's concerns from *both* of his own concepts. This difference itself was based on a deeper contrast between what Pound called 'the European tradition of sociology of law' to which Ehrlich belonged, and the American 'sociological jurisprudence' school which Pound represented. In Pounds view:

'The sociological juristic thinking of Europe has developed what might be called a phobia of the State and of Sovereignty. But this has entered little into Anglo-American thinking.'[10]

Pound admitted without embarrassment that the Europeans criticised the Americans for their:

'. . .preoccupations with problems of the legal order and the judicial and administrative process.'

But he stood firm on his view that the focus of attention should be:

'. . .the legal order of a politically organised society rather than the order implicit in all groups, associations and social relations'.[11]

Unfortunately for later interpreters of Ehrlich's work, however, in his introduction to the Harvard translation of Ehrlich's text in 1936,

---

8. Zeigert, *ibid.*
9. R. Pound, *Jurisprudence*, Vol 1 (1959), p 335.
10. R. Pound, 'Introduction' to S. P. Simpson and J. Stone (eds), *Cases and Readings on Law and Society* (1948), Vol 1, p xiv.
11. *Ibid.* In fact, Pound's ideas were also derived from a different European tradition, in particular the work of Ihering.

160   Legal Studies

Pound failed to emphasise these points of contrast. Instead, he went some way to giving the impression that his concerns were interchangeable with those of Ehrlich. Thus we are told that the value of obtaining knowledge of the 'living law' is that it provides a way of measuring the 'functional validity of legal requirements'.[12] Such knowledge can then be used to criticise the law by showing, as Pound puts it, that 'it is not a part of life, it is a norm for decision, not a norm for life and practice'.[13] It is this *amalgamation* of Pound's and Ehrlich's ideas which has most influenced later writers.

The Distinctions between Pound's and Ehrlich's Ideas
In order to appreciate the extent of the differences between Pound's and Ehrlich's concepts and the alternative routes which they chart for the sociology of law, it is essential to examine the background to their ideas. I shall look in turn at their approach to the definition and purpose of law and their conceptions of norms and society and then re-examine the way in which their distinctions fit into the larger framework of their views.

For Pound there is only one criterion of valid law. This is equated with the rules laid down by the authorities in a politically constituted society. But not all of such rules count as law:

'What makes a precept law is that it obtains as a rule of conduct and of decision and what makes a legal right is that the precept which stands behind it obtains in action. This means that its psychological efficiency is guaranteed, that is that the authority which has prescribed it is so backed by social-psychological power as to be in a position to give effect to the precept, as a motive for action, in spite of counter-acting individual motives.'[14]

Pound thus recommends an imperative theory of law coupled with a Realist stress on effective prediction of legal outcomes. That this is a philosophically weak solution to the problem of defining law is well seen in Pound's own comment that:

'Judge-made and statutory *law* fail continually because they have no social and psychological guarantee.'[15]

Here Pound himself calls ineffective rules law. In a sense, Pound's preoccupation with 'law in books' and 'law in action' can be seen as an attempt to resolve the tension inherent in his definition. Later writers who have attempted to use his distinction in their research have also found it difficult to decide whether what legal officials do in practice counts as law even if there are good grounds for saying it is at variance with the legal rules.[16]

---

12. R. Pound, 'Introduction' to E. Ehrlich, *Sociology of Law, op cit*, pp xxxiii-xxxiv.
13. *Ibid.*
14. R. Pound, quoting the German theorist Jellinek. *Jurisprudence*, Vol 3 (1959), p 361.
15. *Ibid*, p 362 (my emphasis).
16. McBarnet reviews research employing this distinction in the study of the criminal process and herself reaches the paradoxical conclusion that, far from serving as constraints on official action, the rules of due process are *for* crime control. See McBarnet, *Conviction*, 1981.

Ehrlich, on the other hand, distinguishes two (and more) kinds of law. In particular, norms for decision were the rules and propositions found in the civil codes, in judicial decisions and in statutory enactments. These were the 'norms which would be enforced by the courts in case the parties resort to litigation'. For some purposes Ehrlich breaks down this category further into legislative and judge-made law. By contrast to norms for decision, 'living law' is defined as:

'the law that dominates life itself, even though it has not been printed in legal propositions. The source of our knowledge of this law is, first, the modern legal document. Secondly, direct observation of life, of commerce, of customs and usages, and of all associations not only of those that the law has recognised but also of those that it has overlooked or passed by, indeed of those that it has disapproved.'[17]

As soon as Ehrlich formulated this definition of law, he was immediately attacked by Kelsen on the grounds that he confused normative and descriptive analysis. Whilst the sociologist might want to distinguish several types of law, legal theory was necessarily monist. Ehrlich gave as an example of the living law of Bukowina the fact that the wages of children placed in service were pocketed by their parents, even though this was contrary to the provisions of the Austrian Civil Code. Ehrlich said it was an example of the reigning 'living law' in Bukowina:

'If we were to ask why children put up with such behaviour, we would be told that resistance would be unheard of.'[18]

Kelsen could make no sense of this. Surely Ehrlich appreciated that this left the true legal situation unaffected:

'Will Herr Professor Ehrlich reply, you are legally obliged to put up with the fact that your parents dispose of your income without your consent? I don't doubt that Ehrlich would help the child obtain his rights – even in Bukowina.'[19]

In Kelsen's view and that of most 20th century analytic philosophers, Ehrlich's 'living law' is misdescribed as law. But this criticism may rest on a misconception concerning the purpose of Ehrlich's definition.

Both Pound and Ehrlich were less concerned with analytic solutions to the problem of defining law than with the uses to which their definitions could be put. Pound's scientific background and sympathy with Pragmatism led him to view law in terms of its purpose. Law was seen as an instrument which could be used to solve social problems. The influence of the German legal theorist Rudolf Ihering and the early American sociologists Ross, Small and Ward, led Pound to conceive law as a method of 'social control'.[20] Industrial growth and the

17. E. Ehrlich, 1936, *op cit*, p. 493.
18. E. Ehrlich quoted in Rehbinder, 1967, *op cit*, p 104.
19. H. Kelsen, writing in 1915, quoted in Rehbinder, 1967, *op cit*, p 104.
20. See G. Geis, 'Sociology and Sociological Jurisprudence: Admixture of Lore and Law' 52 Kentucky L J, 1964, p 267.

162   Legal Studies

increasing size of cities had led to rapid social change and social disorganisation; the decline of controls based on primary groups and religious traditions had left a vacuum which had to be filled by law. Law served as a tool of social engineering in the sense that it could help to prevent and resolve social conflicts with the least waste and inefficiency. With these purposes in mind, it was essential to define law in terms of its effectiveness.

Ehrlich's vision was rather different. Law in the sense of 'norms for decision' did have a part to play in engineering solutions to social conflicts. Thus Ehrlich discusses the problem of assigning relative weights to the competing interests of farmers and crop growers in Africa as well as considering examples nearer home, such as freedom of contract and restraint of trade, the rights of workers to protection from dismissal and the general problem of welfare rights.[21] It was important, in his view, for the lawmaker to decide which claim was nearer to the path of evolutionary progress. But all this is seen as belonging to the emergency task of law rather than the slowly unfolding, more fundamental, social order produced by living law. Whereas emergency law was essential to reconcile ruptured social relationships, it was quite wrong to assume that norms appropriate for that task were also those that should be applied or self-imposed in circumstances where relationships were 'at peace'. Hence law was to be seen more as an *outcome* of social processes and social change rather than as a *tool* of intervention. It was one aspect of social and economic life, organically connected with and created by common patterns of life, work and relationships in groups and other collectivities. Behind the 'living law' stood the ever active relations of interaction, domination, possession and agreement and the changing requirements of collective production and consumption. These in turn gave rise to the legal relations of ownership, property rights, inheritance, contracts and corporate and family life. Overall Ehrlich insisted on the importance of social forces and developments as the major influence on 'living law' as compared to mere legislative and judicial enactments.[22]

Much of this difference of emphasis can be explained by each writer's constrasting view of norms. For Pound and many of those who follow him, norms are seen mainly as claims and counters put forward and bargained over by competing groups. Legislatures and judges produce norms for the satisfaction of as many of the demands of the citizens as possible, much as producers try to satisfy the needs of consumers. There is something of this view in Ehrlich's approach to 'norms for decision'. But his appreciation of the genesis and maintenance of the norms of 'living law' offers a far more subtle and

---

21. E. Ehrlich, 1936, *op cit*, esp pp 203-205.
22. This has something in common with the views of his Austrian contemporary, Karl Renner, in *The Institutions of Private Law and their Social Functions*, ed Kahn Freund (1949). But Renner's legal positivism led him to confine the title law to what Ehrlich called the 'norms of decision' whilst his Marxist framework made him focus on the *economic* forces that shaped the slowly unfolding life of social associations. As a result, he neglected the point that such associations generated their own form of normative life – the 'living law'.

Law in action or living law?   163

penetrating insight into norms than anything produced by Pound. For Pound norms are instrumentally useful to groups or individuals or they are nothing. But in Ehrlich's work we find discussions of the connection between norms, social action and social structure in the best sociological tradition. That norms are instrumentally useful does not mean that they are *chosen* to meet such needs. Norms are seen by Ehrlich to express common patterns of behaviour and feeling, to unify groups and bolster identity. They have to be understood at the level of meaning rather than merely in terms of their usefulness.

But Ehrlich's fascination with norms poses a problem for him which Pound can avoid. That is the difficulty of distinguishing the norms of 'living law' from other norms. Pound says that legal norms are those backed by the State, therefore, other norms do not count as law. Law is a distinctive form of 'social control' which can be easily distinguished in its source from other influences on social behaviour such as the family or public opinion. But Ehrlich is in difficulty because 'living law' is identified by its norms yet cannot be taken to include all social norms without over-extending the notion of law too much. His solution is that, despite the scientific difficulties in distinguishing legal norms, it is possible to distinguish them 'practically' on the basis of people's attitudes:

'Compare the feeling of revolt that follows a violation of law with the indignation at a violation of the law of morality, with the feeling of disgust occasioned by an indecency, with the disapproval of faithlessness, the ridiculousness of an offence against etiquette and lastly with the critical feeling of superiority with which a votary of fashion looks down upon those who have not attained the heights which he has scaled.'[23]

But this not altogether happy solution to the problem has been much criticised.[24] It is denied that our reactions do fall into such neat gradations, and it is not thought obvious that law necessarily regulates matters of particular social concern. Yet some of these criticisms miss the point because they use examples of regulatory law to demonstrate public apathy to legal matters whilst Ehrlich is concerned with 'living law' and not such 'norms for decision'. In any event, in practice Ehrlich avoided the necessity for psychological introspection by choosing as his sub-set of legal norms those which have a parallel form and content to the norms found in Roman and Western legal systems such as those associated with contract, property and inheritance rules. This offered a practicable, if still questionable, basis for isolating the norms specific to 'living law'.

There are related differences in each author's view of society. For Pound society was composed of overlapping groups competing for

23. E. Ehrlich, 1936, *op cit*, pp 164-165.
24. See, for example, N. Timasheff, *An Introduction to the Sociology of Law* (1939), p 26; and J. W. Harris, 'Olivecrona on Law and Language – the Search for Legal Culture' in *Tidsskrift for Rettsvitenskup* (1979), p 625 at pp 638–640.

scarce resources. Despite his rejection of unbridled individualism as a political or legal ethos, he remained a methodological individualist in his approach to social life. His philosophical anthropology, developed as it was in conscious opposition to Puritanism as well as to classical Liberalism, still retained strong elements of the positions he opposed. Groups were seen as collections of individuals united by the pursuit of common interests. Their members required social control 'to supplement the exercise of willpower' so as to enable them to restrain their desires and harmonise the aggressive and co-operative sides of human nature. Similarly, groups required the mediation of law to prevent destructive conflict. Only then could individual and group energy be used for the common good.

Ehrlich, on the other hand, did not share either Pound's methodological individualism or his residual belief in the view of man and society inherent in classical liberalism. His attention was focussed on the life of groups, institutions and associations. Individual behaviour for him was channelled by the norms of group life, social relationships and social and economic development:

'Organisation is the rule which assigns each individual his position and his function.[25]

Only exceptional individuals were seen as possessing the capacity to create or change group norms. If Pound erred on the side of seeing norms as too manipulable by individuals, Ehrlich's tendency was the opposite, to see men as moulded by norms.

The social circumstances in which each writer put forward his views were also importantly different. Pound wanted to see a more interventionist role for creative law-making by Congress and the Supreme Court because he faced an American Federal legal system where pluralistic and competing cultures and interests were all too evident. By contrast, Ehrlich, living in an outlying region of a ramshackle Empire and observing in the province of Bukowina a harmonious mix of distinct cultural groupings each with their own form of life, saw centralised law-making from Vienna as a crude intrusion into a set of working normative orders. Yet Ehrlich's views should not be thought suited only to circumstances such as Bukowina, as is commonly asserted, because his point was not so much the need to respect the *cultural* pluralism of Bukowina, even though that sometimes helped to illustrate his argument, but instead the importance of the *normative* pluralism inherent in different working normative orders. The general point that emerged from his consideration of Bukowina was the claim that *lawmakers never confront a normative vacuum*. This claim remains valid today in other social circumstances than those of Ehrlich, even if his more particular views about the limited scope for state activity now seem outdated.

The Point of Pound's and Ehrlich's Distinctions
Against this background it becomes easier to contrast both the

25. Ehrlich, 1936, *op cit,* p 85.

meaning and point of Pound's and Ehrlich's distinctions. Pound's concepts 'law in books' and 'law in action' both refer essentially to the activities of lawmakers and law enforcers.[26] They apply only with difficulty to action by citizens. That is why the distinction has been so commonly used to address dubious police practices of arrest and interrogation as compared with the rules supposedly governing such practices – an issue debated from Pound to the present day. But the distinction is more awkward when it is applied to actions by citizens such as the way contracts are made and used as compared to text-book expectations. Although this too has been examined as an example of 'law in books' versus 'law in action' by Pound himself and by those who have followed him, it is harder to see the point of this exercise. It is not clear why citizens should be expected to use the rules of contract as they are laid down. It is hard to tell when they diverge from the possible purpose to which contract can legitimately be put, and it is not clear why it even matters. In fact, the value of the distinction even for studying the work of legal officials also becomes suspect once it is recognised that many of their responsibilities are also cast in terms of legal powers rather than duties. This creates the same problems of deciding whether activities by officials count as an exercise or an abuse of their powers.[27]

Ehrlich's distinction, on the other hand, is clearly bifurcated. 'Norms for decision' refer exclusively to action by legislators, judges, jurists and other legal officials. But 'living law' refers mainly to the norms recognised as obligatory by citizens in their capacity as members of associations. It can be seen now why the two distinctions do not map on to each other. 'Law in books' refers solely to rules and norms. It is only in this way that it can be distinguished from the 'law in action'. But 'norms for decision', which are said to be its equivalent, include in Ehrlich's usage not only norms and rules but also the actual patterns of decision by legislative and judicial bodies. Conversely, 'living law' does not correspond to what Pound meant by the 'law in action' because it refers essentially to obligatory *norms* rather than action. Indeed, from the point of view of the members of a group, 'living law' represents their 'law in books' as compared to what actually happens in practice when the norms are breached, avoided or transformed. Ehrlich's concept of 'norms for decision' therefore encompasses most of what Pound was getting at in his discussions of 'law in books' *and* 'law in action'. But Ehrlich's notion of 'living law' has no parallel in Pound's distinction. Its nearest relative is the idea of informal norms within formal organisations. 'Law in action' and 'living law' tend to be assimilated when the actions of legal officials in organisations are said to be attributable to the 'living law' of the organisation. But in other respects the idea of informal norms excludes the formal norms of the

---

26. Pound's extensive discussion of jury equity only confirms this point because the members of the jury are seen as 'licensed' to shape the 'law in action' in a way which is not normally open to the ordinary citizens.
27. See McBarnet, *op cit*, footnote 16.

organisation which Ehrlich *would* include as part of 'living law' and includes the activities that go on in the organisation beyond the point at which Ehrlich would consider them to represent the norms of 'living law'.

The different point of each set of distinctions can be understood in terms of each writer's practical concerns. It is essential to refer to both writers' concerns because it is all too tempting to argue that Pound's ideas were shaped by his interest in reform whereas Ehrlich's conceptual classification was intended purely as a theoretical contribution. However, such contrasts between sociological jurisprudence on the one hand and sociology of law on the other are usually misleading because discussions of law and society have both a theoretical and policy-oriented component, however implicit either of these may be.[28] Ehrlich's work must therefore also be understood in terms of his policy concerns even though these are different from those of Pound.

Pound was preoccupied with the need to harmonise the 'law in books' and the 'law in action'. Since both of these referred to the same subject matter under the same conditions, they could not both be right and appropriate; one or other must be changed. Pound is quite aware that as a matter of fact divergent 'law in books' and 'law in action' can co-exist in the world and that there may be reasons for this. But he cannot accept that there are any *good* reasons for the perpetuation of such discrepancies. They represent at best 'legal fictions' which conceal for the time being the fact that law is out of touch with the needs of society or with public opinion. Valuable as such fictions are to facilitate gradual change, they are also a warning signal. The policy response must be to change the law so as to meet the changing needs of society or else risk the law's effectiveness and good name. As long as discrepancies persist, says Pound, they distort legal procedures, encourage deception, cast doubt on the state of the law and prevent the emergence of the least wasteful, most efficient, solution to social problems. Pound had little sympathy for the view that law can serve to educate 'public opinion' precisely by being out of touch with it, nor did he recognise the importance of symbolic law where the existence of 'law in books' is itself of intrinsic value to some social groups whatever the actual effects of the law in practice.[29]

The simplest policy solution to the problem of divergence was:

'. . .to make the law in books such that the law in action . . . can conform to it.'[30]

Pound saw this as a solution for example to the need for collusive evasion of the contemporary over-strict divorce laws. This was also the remedy

---

28. See D. Nelken, 'The Gap Problem in the Sociology of Law: A Theoretical Review' in *Windsor Yearbook of Access to Justice* (1981), pp 35–63 and 'Sociology of Law vs Socio-legal Studies: A False Divide', unpublished paper delivered to the Conference on Critical Legal Scholarship, University of Kent, April 1981.

29. See, for example, V. Aubert, 'Some Social Functions of Legislation', *Acta Sociologica* (1961), 10, pp 99-110; J. Gusfield, *Symbolic Crusade*, 1963; W. G. Carson, 'Instrumental and Symbolic Aspects of Factory Legislation' in R. Hood, ed, *Crime Criminology and Public Policy* pp 107–138.

30. R. Pound, 1910, *op cit*.

Law in action or living law? 167

for the over-complicated exceptions developed by judges to escape the harsh impact of the common-employment rule on employees' chances of obtaining compensation for injuries sustained from their colleagues. But incorporating the 'law in action' into the 'law in books' was less easy to advocate in other cases. Pound, like later writers, was equivocal about this with regard to police methods of bending the rules even though he worried about the police view that this was forced on them by the difficulty of achieving convictions. As this suggests, it is always possible to beg the question whether the 'law in action' *should* dictate the 'law in books' and why. At most it can provide one defeasible argument in favour of a particular change but there may be independent reasons for and against such a change. That Pound appeared to give so much weight to the 'law in action' seems to be the result of two considerations. Firstly, 'action' as compared to mere 'paper rules' or moral argument had a special ontological significance for him. It was part of the world of reality to which law-making must submit:

'Men will do what they are bent on doing, law and tradition to the contrary notwithstanding.'[31]

Simply to reassert existing 'law in book' requirements therefore would not change the effects of social developments.

'In a conflict between the 'law in books' and the national will, there can be but one result, let us not be legal monks.'[32]

The second argument for favouring 'law in action' as the model for new law was that it was likely to reflect some felt need or function on the part of those who had resorted to it, needs which the lawmaker ignored at his peril. But even Pound conceded that neither of these arguments could be decisive in any particular case and for this reason he tended to delegate the decision as to whether 'law in books' or 'law in action' should prevail to the discretion of an activist judiciary.

For Ehrlich, on the other hand, divergence was not the policy issue. 'Norms for decision' and 'living law' were not necessarily in competition because they applied under different conditions. The need for 'norms for decision' arises only in cases of dispute and conflict, whereas 'living law' prevails under normal circumstances. For example, Ehrlich argued that the normative régime of male ownership of peasant family property in Bukowina was acceptable under normal conditions, even though the Austrian civil code's rules about joint ownership of property were the norms more appropriate to follow if the parties should seek to break-up their relationship. What Ehrlich was worried about, then, was the dangerous consequences of intrusive law making. He reclassified the law that came from Vienna as mere 'norms for decision' so as to restrict it to its proper scope and function.

31. *Ibid.*
32. *Ibid.*

168 Legal Studies

The Overlap Between Pound's and Ehrlich's views

Having shown some of the crucial differences between Pound's and Ehrlich's ideas, it is now possible to complete the picture by discussing the simiarities, both apparent and genuine, where they do exist. This helps to explain how Ehrlich's ideas came to be misinterpreted and also ensures that my efforts to save Ehrlich from Pound's use of him does not lead to any opposite distortion.

Both writers employ the same metaphor of 'living' and 'dead' law. Pound was concerned throughout his career to contrast the 'law in action' with 'mere paper rules', and Ehrlich shared the same sense of the contrast between law as a collection of prescriptions and law as it was lived. For him, the law of the civil codes was often the clearest embodiment of dead law and the life of the law was to be found not merely in the way legal officials adapted this law or citizens avoided it, but in the definite normative patterns of group life. In Ehrlich's view:

'To attempt to imprison the law of a time or of a people within the sections of a code is about as reasonable as to attempt to confine a stream within a pond. The water put in the pond is no longer a living stream, but a stagnant pond.'[33]

There are even closer parallels to Pound's distinction elsewhere in Ehrlich's work. Thus, in one of his later articles, Ehrlich comments that:

'The old principle of personality was thus living on in fact while having – on paper only – long been substituted by the principle of territoriality.[34]

On the other hand, both authors also use metaphors in ways which do not fit with each other's work. Thus, Ehrlich argues that:

'The law of possession . . . is the true law of the economic order and is most closely related to the living law of economics.'[35]

This notion of 'living law' clearly has nothing in common with Pound's idea of the effective 'law in action'.

Pound and Ehrlich also had something in common in the views to which they were opposed. Both rejected the values of economic individualism which were present in contemporary legal theory. Both were critical of the conceptual jurisprudence of their time and also of the historical jurisprudence which was the other leading approach. If their disavowal of conceptual jurisprudence, however, was sometimes over-simple for modern tastes, their relationship to historical jurisprudence was more complex and interesting. Pound disliked the

---

33. E. Ehrlich, 1936, *op cit*, p. 488.
34. Quoted by K. Zeigert, 1979, *op cit*, p 229 from M. Rehbinder (ed), *Eugen Ehrlich: Recht und Leben,* 1967, p 43. But even here there is a characteristic difference between Ehrlich and Pound. Ehrlich is emphasising the way in which paper rules fail to change long-standing patterns of normative behaviour whereas Pound placed more stress on the extent to which social action transforms the significance of paper rules.
35. E. Ehrlich, 1936, *op cit*, p 98.

arguments of historical jurists because they described and advocated a role for law as a guarantor of individual liberties, which he saw as time-bound. Their views prevented the use of law to meet collective needs and solve social problems and also stood in the way of enlarging judicial discretion so as to meet the substantive needs of particular cases. Yet he himself made use of the historical viewpoint in drawing on the work of Kohler so as to establish the 'jural postulates' for given historical periods. Ehrlich, for his part, provided the definitive refutation of the historical theory of the *volksgeist* and called for a shift of attention from the historical archaeology of law to the dynamic sources of law in daily life. But his stress on the 'living law' of diverse social and cultural groups as opposed to the static formalist emphasis on autonomous legal traditions owes much to the theories of the historical school.

Pound and Ehrlich were particularly close in their views of the importance of judicial decision-making. Both were convinced that judges needed to be relieved of the belief that their role was a narrow one. Pound insisted that judges had a responsibility to adapt and apply the law to changing circumstances. Ehrlich polemicised for 'free law finding', by which he meant the attempt to base judicial decisions on the appropriate criteria which emerged from a situation under consideration rather than from legal propositions. Both writers were therefore interested in methods of discovering the nature of the situations with which law dealt. But whereas Pound was concerned with the unmet social needs which were made evident by these social circumstances, Ehrlich was more concerned with the existing normative orders which it would be perilous to disregard.

II. Is there life in Ehrlich's concept of the 'Living Law'?

Having recovered the sense of Ehrlich's notion of the 'living law', the question now arises whether it was worth saving, especially in the light of the enormous political, social and economic changes such as the growth of state intervention and legislative activity which might seem to render his assumptions out of date. I shall offer a necessarily brief outline of why Ehrlich's work can be seen as a still relevant contribution to research, theory and policy-making in the sociology of law.

Ehrlich's ideas provide a better starting point for empirical research than a focus on the 'law in action', because the idea of 'living law' is less isolated from sociological theory. The 'law in action' perspective will always recommend itself to those interested in aspects of the interaction between legal officials and others which involve the conscious use and manipulation of rules. But it proves unhelpful when relied on for any broader purposes because of the intrinsic limitations of Pound's concerns which have already been noted. Not surprisingly, work employing the 'law in action' focus has been the repeated target for attacks which allege it to be over-preoccupied with discrepancies between legal rules and legal practice and a failure to examine the

170 Legal Studies

actual sources of social action in the rush to criticise departures from rules.[36]

Even as a classificatory device, Pound's distinction seems to bring together the most diverse and unrelated topics. Pound himself included such unlikely bedfellows as jury equity in court verdicts, third degree methods of interrogation by the police, modification of the strict rule of common employment in industrial injuries law and judges' reluctance to admit the extent of discretion they allegedly possessed.[37] The recent effort by Roshier and Teff to present socio-legal studies in terms of Pound's distinction once again ranges over such well-worn examples as police behaviour at variance with the judges' rules, the extent to which the use of contract law reflects contract law text books, whether divorce law meets the needs of the parties, and more surprisingly perhaps, the existence of an unmet need for legal services.[38] They make no distinction between discrepancies between *stereotypes* of legal behaviour and the actuality, or between *ideals* about how law ought to operate and how it actually does operate. The only thing such classifications provide insight into is the remarkably consistent policy concerns of legal reformers from Pound to the present day.

The differences between investigations couched in terms of a study of the 'law in action' and those concerned to explore the 'living law' may not always be substantial. But they can be important even at the margin. A good example is provided by Macaulay's classic study of non-contractual relations between businessmen, work which has justly been paid the compliment of international replication.[39] Macaulay's investigation was conceived very much in the Pound tradition of studies of legal effectiveness, even if its findings transcended this starting point. The question was whether contract law as taught in the universities was actually used or not, and how it might be changed so as to make it more useful to businessmen. Macaulay revealed that businessmen made only limited use of contract law in planning their transactions, and were reluctant to rely on their contractual remedies. Business relationships were governed more by the need to maintain a good reputation in the market place, and stand behind a good product, than by the rules of contract law. These findings were very similar to those Ehrlich had emphasised when illustrating the existence of living law amongst businessmen. For example, be noted:

'There are large mercantile houses, which as a matter of principle, do

---

36. See, for example, D. Black, 'The Boundaries of Legal Sociology', 81 Yale L J, 1972, p 1086; R. Abel, 'Law Books and Books about Law', 26 Stanford L Rev, 1973, p 175; D. Nelken, 'The Gap Problem', *op cit* at footnote 28; and C. Grace and P. Wilkinson, *Legal Phenomena and Social Inquiry*, 1978. M. McConville and J. Baldwin's latest study of the criminal process, *Courts, Prosecutions and Conviction*, 1981 is an intriguing illustration of research which has reached the limits of usefulness of the 'law in action' approach but which has yet to find an alternative focus of enquiry.
37. R. Pound, 1910, *op cit.*
38. B. Roshier and H. Teff, *op cit*, n 2.
39. S. Macaulay, 'Non-contractual relations in Business: A preliminary study', Amer Soc Rev, 28, 1963, p 55.

Law in action or living law?   171

not bring suit on a matter arising in their commercial relations, and as a rule do not permit themselves to be sued but satisfy even an unfounded claim in full. They meet refusal of payment and frivolous demands by severing commercial relations.'[40]

It is arguable that Macaulay's investigation would have been even more fruitful if it has started from this type of fascination with explaining the working norms of business life rather than the problem of how far contract 'law in the books' misrepresents what actually occurs. In addition to showing how the exigencies of business life affect contract law, research using Ehrlich's ideas would seek to account for the origin and maintenance of the specific norms of business life including the neglected point which Ehrlich makes about the relevance of honour and business self-respect to the organisation of transactions.

But the theoretical stimulus of Ehrlich's ideas goes well beyond the suggestion of 'living law' as a topic for empirical investigation. Ehrlich's arguments have become an essential starting point for those writers (often anthropologists) concerned to emphasise the 'legal pluralism' of modern Western societies.[41] One of the most fertile ideas to come from this school is the suggestion that particular social settings should be conceived as 'semi-autonomous social fields' which are the site of overlapping and competing normative obligations which arise from the internal activities of the association as well as from external influences.[42] The connection between this and Ehrlich's ideas about the living law is clear, although where later writers have improved on him is their greater sensitivity to the interpenetration of state and 'living law' norms.[43] In any event, even the basic implications of legal pluralism have hardly begun to be properly absorbed into the sociology of law.

The policy relevance of Ehrlich's ideas relates to the contemporary re-examination of the limits of legal intervention. Voices on both the political right and left warn that modern Western societies are suffering from excessive state intervention. This is seen either as arising from an over inflation of citizens' claims and expectations or else as a development by the state of ever-more subtle methods of 'discipline' by which to penetrate everyday life.[44] None of the proposed alternatives to

40. E. Ehrlich, 1936, *op cit*, pp 64–65.
41. The best recent survey, unfortunately as yet unpublished, is J. Griffiths, 'What is Legal Pluralism?', a paper presented at the Law and Society Association meeting, Amherst, USA, June 1981. See also the acute overview in Peter Fitzpatrick, 'Law, Plurality and Underdevelopment' in D. Sugarman (ed), *Legality Ideology and the State*, 1983, p 159; Stuart Henry, *Private Justice: Towards integrated theorizing in the Sociology of Law*, 1983, Ch 2. All these writers pay their respects to Ehrlich but are rather too quick to accept the over-critical account of Ehrlich's ideas in Gurvitch, *Sociology of Law* (1947), pp 116–122.
42. S. F. Moore, *Law as Process*, 1978, Ch 3.
43. See Stuart Henry, *op cit.*
44. See, for example, I. Jenkins, *Social Order and the Limits of Law* (1980), and Stan Cohen, 'The Punitive City', 3 Int J for the Sociology of Law, 3, 1979, p 339; cf D. Nelken, 'Is there a Crisis in Law and Legal Ideology?' Journal of Law and Society, 9, 1982, p 177.

state regulation, such as the 'spontaneous order' of the market, or 'community justice', or even participatory democracy in the creation of state norms, carry much persuasive power. Ehrlich's idea of working normative orders could at least provide a basis for proceeding beyond the present, often inconsistent, ad hoc justifications for deciding on legal intervention in particular cases.[45] Many sociologists of law have demonstrated that the unpredictable outcomes of legislative or judicial interventions largely result from the fact that the law is deflected or neutralised by pre-existing patterns of 'living law'.[46] This has led some to urge a new role for law by which it should reflexively monitor the agreements reached by parties rather than attempt to transform their social relationships.[47] Again, the relevance of Ehrlich's work hardly needs stating.

A useful illustration of the application of Pound's and Ehrlich's different ideas on legal intervention is the contemporary debate whether to give legal recognition to co-habitees on the same basis as those who are married. In many jurisdictions the legislatures and courts have gone a long way to equating their legal status as also that of legitimate and illegitimate children. In Pound's terms this would be seen as bringing the law up to date so as to meet changing social needs and also deal with the 'social problem' of deserted co-habitees and disadvantaged children. It is perhaps no accident that the Law Commissions, whose establishment Pound advocated, have often been in the forefront of recommending such changes. But a number of writers have argued that these developments are misjudged. Some have merely wished to retain the traditional preferred status of marriage and the social values it is supposed to uphold. But others, of more interest for present purposes, have argued that people should retain the freedom to make agreements which will not be incorporated into 'state' or 'official' family law.[48] They argue that family law is itself repressive and in need of reform and that people are entitled to autonomy in their relationships on a basis of contract rather than have a particular legal status conferred upon them. The case against the assimilation of co-habitation to marriage is made to rest on liberal premisses of the right to privacy and the existence of areas of life beyond the law's business. But these classical liberal ideas seem rather unpersuasive in a society in which state interference can be found in every area of social life and where the boundaries of private and public are increasingly hard to draw. Resort to Ehrlich's ideas, on the other hand, could provide a different basis for their arguments. Ehrlich's advocacy of normative pluralism could be seen to complement Mill's liberal ideal that truth

45. A good current example of such ad hoc decisions over intervention is the rejection of the Kahn-Freund view that the law is best kept out of industrial relations and union affairs, at the same time that the 'self-regulation' of the stock exchange is endorsed.
46. See, for example, D. Nelken, *The Limits of the Legal Process: A Study of Landlords, Law and Crime*, 1983.
47. G. Tuebner, 'Substantive and Reflexive Elements in Modern Law', Law and Society Review, 17 (1983), p 239.
48. M. Freeman and C. Lyon, *Cohabitation without Marriage*, (1983).

best emerges from competition. It would therefore justify non-intervention on the ground that people should be allowed to experiment with new normative patterns of family relationships in the interest of everyone.

Even with so much in their favour, it must be admitted that Ehrlich's ideas do need further elaboration and modification at many points both from a theoretical and policy-oriented point of view. One crucial problem concerns Ehrlich's distinction between the norms of the 'living law' and other norms. Ehrlich models the former on the 'norms for decision' of Western legal systems. But this is a historically contingent matter and does not justify Ehrlich's assumption that this is an analytical distinction. But no analytical basis for such a distinction has yet been discovered. What, if anything, do the norms which help structure the normative life of families, organisations and business activity actually have in common?[49] How far do these organisations and associations reproduce within themselves Ehrlich's two type of law, having *both* 'norms for decision' and 'living law'? Can groups and associations be defined apart from the norms that constitute them? How do the norms of 'living law' arise?[50] What are the relationships of opposition, incorporation and symbiosis between state 'norms for decision' and the 'living law' of groups? How do the norms of some groups affect the norms held dear in other associations?

The answers to these questions depend on the development of a sociology of norms rather than a sociology of law. But whilst this might be a more realisable objective, it does have the implication of swallowing up the sociology of law in general sociology. This involves arguing that sociology of law can make its best contribution by identifying issues which are problems in general sociology and which are highlighted by the study of law.[51]

There are also difficulties in developing clear policy implications from Ehrlich's ideas. The most drastic problem is deciding what is meant by a 'working normative order'. Is there any empirical yardstick by which to judge whether an order is working? Who is to make the decision? To rely on whether the participants of an association call for outside intervention would be circular if the question is whether to allow such intervention. In any case, there is nothing to stop the members of a group from invoking the norms for decision even where this will sow the seeds of a conflict which was not already present. Members of associations will tend to choose between the 'norms for

---

49. Cf P. H. Partridge, 'Ehrlich's Sociology of Law' in G. Sawyer (ed), *Studies in the Sociology of Law* (1961), p 1.

50. The deeper question here is the ontological status of social norms. Are they collectively generated 'social facts' which constrain individuals, as Durkheim and Ehrlich presuppose, or 'reasons for action', as Pound or Raz claim, or 'moral commitments' as Dworkin's critique of Hart's social rule theory of law would have us believe?

51. See the attempt to examine the isomorphism between social action and legislative action in D. Nelken, 'Legislation and its Constraints: A Case Study of the 1965 Rent Act' in C. Whelan and A. Podgorecki (eds), *Social Systems and Legal Systems* (forthcoming).

174 Legal Studies

decision' and the norms of 'living law' in terms of which best serves their interests, thereby making it impossible to maintain the integrity of Ehrlich's two schemes of law.[52] Ehrlich's ideas also seem very conservative in their rejection of social and legislative interventions. Ehrlich certainly does not favour Conservative doctrines of facilitating 'the spontaneous order of the market place' but he does appear to justify leaving working orders alone even when they are themselves based on the dominance of some individuals or groups by others. One answer to this is that a lot depends on how a working normative order is to be identified. On Habermas's view, for example, this is a question best left to the members of the association themselves. But for them to be able to conduct such debates on a relatively equal footing it is a prior condition that existing patterns of dominance be reduced.[53] And this may require social or legal intervention. This is undeniably an extension of Ehrlich's ideas because it accepts the necessity of interfering in relationships ostensibly at peace. But the promise of developing Ehrlich's work in this direction is that it makes it possible to find a mode of allowing law to intervene in social life which is different from Pound's legacy of social engineering.[54]

52. I am grateful to Joseph Raz for suggesting this point. See also M. Galanter, 'How the Haves come out Ahead: Speculations on the Limits of Legal Change', 9, Law and Society Review (1974), p 95.

53. See, for example, J. Habermas, 'Systematically Distorted Communication' in P. Connerton (ed), *Critical Sociology* (1976), p 348.

54. Ehrlich's ideas can be used to develop what may be called an ecological approach to legal intervention which concerns itself with the *mode* rather than the *merits* of intervention. A sound ecological approach to law would see intervention as a continuing process with various forms of feedback, rather than as an 'event' with an 'impact'. It would see the focus of intervention as a 'social field' rather than as the actions of an individual or group or a 'social problem', would start by mapping the existing normative patterns at work in the field and would attempt to achieve change through communication, learning and adaptation rather than the adjustment of rewards and punishment. Finally, it would recognise that the intervener and his mode of intervention are themselves part of the social field in question and subject to reciprocal change. This mode of intervention (especially when coupled with the requirement of 'non-distorted communication') could represent a genuine alternative to present forms of intervention such as those based on social engineering, disciplinary surveillance or professional parcelling out of 'problems'. See G. Bateson, *Steps towards an Ecology of the Mind* (1973) and D. Nelken, 'The Ecology of Norms', unpublished paper presented to the Centre for Human Ecology, Edinburgh, 25 January 1984.

[3]
Is there a Crisis in Law and Legal Ideology?

The task of a macro-social theory of law is two-fold: firstly to examine the nature of the connection between "law" and "society" and, secondly, to establish the specific, changing, relationship between the form, content and functions of law in particular societies at particular periods. Both these endeavours are interrelated in such a way that examination of one problem entails and contributes to the study of the other topic. My concern here is with a number of recent changes in law in western industrial societies which are alleged to constitute a crisis in law and which are said to be related to a crisis in society.[1] In order to evaluate such claims three issues need to be addressed: (i) What concept of crisis is being employed? (ii) What is the nature of the alleged crisis in law and in society and what is the supposed relationship between them? (iii) What distinguishes a crisis from a change or transformation?

I shall base my discussion on two important recent arguments concerning the way law and society are changing although some of my analysis could be applied to other recent contributions to the debate.[2] The first argument I shall consider here is that put forward by Alice Ehr-Soon Tay and Eugene Kamenka, a lawyer and a philosopher; the other is by the sociologist and philosopher Jurgen Habermas. There is much that is common in the portrayal by each of these writers of the implications of the growth of state intervention into and management of increasing areas of social and economic life, and this agreement is the more remarkable because Tay and Kamenka explicitly reject a Marxist approach to these matters whereas Habermas claims to be a Marxist theorist. Tay and Kamenka are rather better at providing an account of the alleged crisis in law than they are at explaining how this is related to changes in society: it is for this reason that it becomes important to look at ideas such as those of Habermas concerning the contemporary crisis in society. In examining both these arguments I shall be particularly concerned with the adequacy with which they deal with the three issues mentioned previously. I shall also illustrate how their theoretical defects are not merely a matter of academic significance but help to explain why their accounts failed to allow for a number of recent changes in law in directions contrary to those predicted.

On the other hand, if there is something to criticize in these arguments, there is also much of interest, not least because they can be used to provide a background against which to develop alternative interpretations of these developments in the law. For example, I shall conclude by suggesting that, far from being in crisis, legal institutions and concepts help to prevent the emergence of a social crisis by playing an important role in preventing wider recognition of significant social changes which might otherwise be perceived as threatening.

Is there a Crisis in the Form of Law?

Tay and Kamenka's account of the supposed crisis was set out in 1975 in an influential essay entitled, quite explicitly, "Beyond Bourgeois Individualism: The Contemporary Crisis in Law and Legal Ideology".[3] The argument rests on evidence of a number of historical changes in the character and functioning of various areas of private law and the extensive growth of public and administrative law. Throughout private law they detect a move from a concern merely with the protection of individual rights towards an increasing appreciation of law as an instrument for the realization of approved collective purposes. In the area of Tort Law, for example, this century has seen an erosion of the assumption that liability for negligence must be based on proven fault; instead no-fault schemes as an alternative to Tort Law together with changes in the operation of the law itself appear to be leading towards the notion that victims of accidents should receive compensation, either from those whose activities create risk and who can insure against this or else from the state itself. A similar trend is evident in the area of family law, with the move here away from divorce based on fault to a utilitarian concern with irretrievable breakdown of the marriage and the interests of children. In the law of contract both the Courts and the legislature increasingly infringe on the concept of the contract as a bargain between two parties deemed to be equal before the law. Instead efforts are made to prevent gross examples of unfair or unconscionable contracts consequent on real inequalities of bargaining power. In property law, owners have had their property rights steadily restricted in the name of the social good and quasi-property rights have been created in welfare benefits, security of tenure and employment. In criminal law, the principle of retribution in terms of fault and responsibility has long been joined to the strategic goal of deterrence and both are allegedly yielding to the rehabilitative ideal with its assumption that the criminal is a victim of society who needs to be helped or treated. The move towards law as an instrument of policy to achieve collective goals is obviously even more apparent in the area of public and administrative law, in matters such as the regulation of the economy, industrial law, conciliation and arbitration, rent and price control, the control of resources and the protection of the environment.

All this signifies, according to Tay and Kamenka, a crisis in the individualistic view embodied in the framework of legal conceptions and goals which was so well attuned to the needs of the individual home or property owner rather than to the needs of less privileged members of society, or collective purposes. There is a tendency to play down individual rights, especially property rights, since all such rights are ultimately subservient to public policy. These changes undermine the autonomy of legal institutions and legal traditions and the separation of law, politics and morality because legal argument becomes inseparable from political and moral argument; they also throw into doubt the separation of power doctrine and the notion that there are limits on what matters can be considered justiciable.

Much of their evidence seems sound as far as it goes, although there is clearly a careful choice of supporting illustrations and there is also some indication that these allegedly irreversible trends have come to a stop and may even be going into reverse in certain areas of law. A more cautious sociological interpretation might also want to distinguish amongst the changes in the various areas of law they cite according to some sociologically-based distinctions as to the role of different laws such as, for example, Durkheim's contrast between the different part played by criminal and civil law in the maintenance of social solidarity.

However, the major problems with their approach result from their failure to theorize why these changes in law constitute a crisis and their superficial reference to the concomitant changes in society to which the changes in laws are said to be related. They nowhere explain what conception of crisis they are employing but they do imply a number of accounts of the crisis nature of these changes, none of them particularly persuasive. Thus, at times, they seem to suggest that the crisis lies in the attitudes and conditions of work of lawyers in relation to the structure of the institutions they service. Lawyers try to cope with these changes, they argue, by separating courts from tribunals, law from regulation, and justice from administration. But this is doomed to failure and the institutional separateness of the legal system cannot ultimately survive. This argument is not developed at length but it must be said that there is little evidence that lawyers or legal institutions are facing such a crisis of identity. Nor indeed does it appear that lawyers' willingness to hive off certain areas as not strictly requiring the full panoply of legalism has been anything but successful, and they retain the option of de-colonizing or re-colonizing such areas, a point to which I shall return later.

Tay and Kamenka's insistence on the crisis seems to derive mainly from their perception of the incompatibility between the existing framework of legal conceptions and the new tasks law is being asked to assume. For them, these changes in law are not merely changes of content, they constitute nothing less than a change in the *form* of law. There is a crisis because the new role of law must cause it to explode its existing framework. To demonstrate this point they offer a typology of three forms of law which are present in varying degrees in all societies. The first, *gemeinschaft* law, expresses the will and traditions of an organic community. A person is seen as a member of a community and is dealt with in terms of his status and other fixed relationships rather than as an isolated individual. Law in feudal societies provides one illustration of this form of law. The second,

gesellschaft law, is the form of law built up through the growth of individualism, the market economy and the associated political revolutions.
Men are treated as equal political and legal citizens each capable of bearing
both rights and duties, and most of their actual social status and particular
history is legally irrelevant. The law serves to adjudicate between disputing
parties or to facilitate their transactions. Where the state or public interest
is involved it is treated as if it was just another private interest. The third
form of law is *bureaucratic-administrative* law. This treats human beings
not as members of an organic community or as bearers of private interests
but as the functionaries or carriers of continuing social activities and
concerns. Law is here an instrument for the regulation and management of
activity and its rules are oriented to what is best for the national or
collective interest rather than acting as a resource for the use or
adjudication of rights. The growth of this form of law leads to a crisis
because its implicit ideological position on the role of law in society cannot
be reconciled with that of *gesellschaft* law.

   However, even in these terms, their explanation of the crisis fails to
persuade, and not merely because they fail to locate this critical clash of
ideas in any existing institutional or political arena. There seems at first
sight to be a plain methodological mistake here. Of course, "ideal types",
such as their distinctive types of law, appear to be irreconcilable for they
are precisely designed with that aim in mind. A contradiction in concepts,
especially a methodologically required contradiction, does not equal a
contradiction in reality. What is required is surely a close examination of
the diverse elements in the social formation being studied to see whether
conditions are appropriate either for their mutual co-existence, or for a
slow transition, or for revolutionary change. Only in this way too can battle
be joined with the Weberian view that these trends are no more than one
swing of the ever-oscillating pendulum between a bias towards either
formal or substantive justice.[4] I will return to this topic later in my
argument.

   There is also room for further enquiry as to whether even in theory
gesellschaft and *bureaucratic-administrative* law are in truth mutually
incompatible forms of law. After all, Fuller stigmatized the positivist
definition and philosophy of law, so closely associated with the development of *gesellschaft* law, as one which reflected and lent itself to a "managerial directive" approach to the regulation of human affairs.[5] Historically such a role of law is clearly apparent in the work of theorists and
social reformers such as Bentham or Beccaria whose concern was with the
use of law as an instrument of utilitarian philosophy designed to maximize
the sum of human happiness. Certainly it is not unimportant that their
views coincided in the main with a period of relatively limited state intervention but the possibility of legislative intervention in their approach to
law was often quite explicit.[6] Although their goal was only social in the
sense of the sum of individual happiness, most, if not all, of the legislative

interventions to which Tay and Kamenka refer can be interpreted as having the same goal. The same applies to the operation of the courts and the reasoning of the judiciary. Whilst it is true that Courts and judges do not usually take part in the day to day administration or regulation of an area of social activity it is just as untrue to argue that they can or do exclude matters of public or collective purpose from their deliberations or that they ever desired to do so. Dworkin's insistence in *Taking Rights Seriously* that judges must only act as adjudicators between parties in dispute so as to confirm which party is in the right appears very much a prescriptive rather than a descriptive account of what judges do.[7] This becomes even clearer when set against the historical record of shifts from "formal" to "grand" styles of reasoning as judges alternate in making their advertence to public policy considerations either more or less explicit. In practice, no hard and fast line can be drawn between adjudication and policy-making; judges do take into account the various larger "consequences" of the different decisions open to them, a process well described in MacCormick's recent study of *Legal Reasoning and Legal Theory*.[8] That there is nothing essentially new about this can already be seen in Durkheim's investigations of the role of contract — that exemplar of *gesellschaft* law. He noted that the way in which judges read in "objective" interpretations of the intentions of parties to a contract and the notion of contracts contrary to public policy both demonstrated that contract was more than a bargain between individuals.[9] Finally, whilst it is true that there has been a quantitative increase in the extent to which the law places limits on individuals' purposes as well as in the extent of administrative and regulatory law it is not clear why this should constitute a contemporary crisis; since these trends have been gathering strength at least since the emergence of European welfare states it is not self-evident that they cannot continue as before. If, as will be illustrated later, there is already some apparent reversal of these trends this begs the question what are the underlying social changes to which such movements in law correspond.

Tay and Kamenka's discussion of such changes is disappointingly superficial. They note the increase in human interdependence consequent on changes in technology, increases in the scale of economic production and enterprise, the ramifications of "property" and the increased role of the state, but they do not specify how this is linked to particular legal changes. Above all, perhaps, their ready acceptance that such social changes in no way reflect or presage a crisis in society weakens their claim that corresponding changes in law do represent a crisis.

Is there a Crisis of Legitimation?
It is with reference to these points concerning what constitutes a crisis and the nature of the crisis in society that I wish to make selective reference to the arguments of Jurgen Habermas in *Legitimation Crisis*, a work published at about the same time as the paper by Tay and Kamenka.[10]

Habermas's concept of crisis is a considerable improvement on what is offered by Tay and Kamenka. He distinguishes the objective and subjective dimensions of a crisis. On his view of society as a functioning social system, the objective dimension of a crisis stems from problems of system integration which occur where the steering mechanisms of the society are overloaded or pursue incompatible ends. The subjective dimension exists where such breakdowns communicate themselves to the consciousness of individual members of society; this happens when the problems of system integration lead to a weakening of the socialization processes by which motivation and a sense of shared meaning and conditions is built up — thus engendering a crisis in social integration. A virtue of Habermas's presentation is the care he takes to explain both that he is talking all the time of potential crises and to note the factors that work against their materialization; I shall take this cue later in this paper when I shall make use of it to turn Habermas's argument on its head. But Habermas's generally satisfactory definition of crises does seem to have one weakness. According to him, a crisis necessarily involves both objective and subjective elements, one without the other being insufficient; the same assumption, incidentally, is present in Gramsci's analysis of the conditions under which a new hegemony can emerge. Yet, hypothetically at least, it is possible to envisage a crisis built out of disturbances in processes of social integration which did not necessarily correspond to genuine or equally serious problems of system integration. For Habermas, however, this possibility does not need to be considered because welfare-capitalist societies have no lack of real problems of system integration.

These problems are not simply what Marxists have always seen as the economic "contradiction" and crisis tendencies inherent in capitalism. For Habermas, like other members of the Frankfurt school, takes the view that the intervention of the modern state has allowed these tendencies to be overcome or at least has displaced them into the political arena. The actual and perceived responsibilities of the state now extend to the generation of prosperity, the fair distribution of the social product and even the fixing of appropriate wage levels — thereby replacing the market mechanism which used to be the self-legitimating locus of these functions. But the modern state faces a number of obstacles in the course of meeting its dual objectives of, on the one hand, facilitating successful economic performance within the requirements of a largely capitalist mode of production and, on the other hand, sustaining its own legitimacy. Habermas is more willing than colleagues of his such as Offe and Altwalter to allow that the requisite administrative tight-rope can be successfully negotiated. But the ultimate stumbling block in his view arises from the necessity to refer more and more crucial management decisions to administrative and technical élites which requires the general public to take these decisions on trust. Will people be content to play such a passive role with regard to decisions that crucially affect their lives? Will they content themselves with the pursuit of consumer goods and the increments of status bought by conformity at work? Habermas thinks not, insisting that the legitimacy of any order requires that those in positions of authority provide reasons for their actions which justify their decisions in terms of some widely accepted criteria and which in turn provide people with reasons for obedience. Unlike Luhmann, his chief protagonist in this as in many other important current European debates, he does not accept that legitimacy can be achieved by mere compliance with legally prescribed procedural requirements. Indeed, Habermas elsewhere takes issue explicitly with what he takes to be Weber's position on this point, arguing that the legal-rational mode of dominance can never be its own circular legitimation. It must itself be justified by the wider claims to authority in which it is embedded. Habermas believes that the need to avoid giving reasons is likely to lead to a deficit in social motivation and in people's reasons for obedience and will threaten the stock of shared meanings amongst the population at large — hence there arises what he calls a legitimation crisis, which will be particularly evident as the process of socialisation of young people becomes ever longer under conditions of decreasing levels of employment.

There are, of course, a number of difficulties associated with Habermas's whole theoretical project of which his argument in *Legitimation Crisis* forms only a part. For present purposes it is particularly important to examine why he assumes that no new form of legitimation can be developed to justify the present operation of welfare capitalism. Habermas is surely right to claim that there can be no "administrative creation of meaning", that legitimating values and meanings are still-born as soon as they are seen as artifices or deliberate social constructions. Those who govern must perforce make use, in their ideological retailing of meaning, of terms which are already traditional currency. Habermas may also be correct in his assertion that neither technology, science nor art possess the capacity to serve as new legitimating devices, although with regard to the former he perhaps underestimates the extent to which a concern for the most effective means to an otherwise "obvious" goal such as economic prosperity can become an end in itself. What is more problematic is his assumption that because the market no longer plays the primary role in structuring economic relationships or allocating resources the various meanings and values associated with commodity-exchange such as the notion of fair-exchange, responsibility and the like have therefore also lost their potency as legitimating notions and sources of motivation. Habermas himself argues that the rise of an economic and political order based on the market relied heavily on pre-existing cultural traditions such as those associated with the acceptance of family or other hierarchical relationships. Even if these traditions have now finally been eroded, which is far from obvious, the logic of Habermas's own argument dictates that values arising from the market order are still likely to be powerful cultural elements, whatever technological changes may have occurred or be impending.

Law and the Management of Social Change
This brings me back to the starting point of this paper. Legal institutions
and legal conceptions are one of the major repositories and living sources
of such *gesellschaft* traditions. It is therefore possible that they play an
important role in preventing the disappearance of the sense of common
meaning and motivation on which Habermas lays emphasis. Yet *Legitimation Crisis* contains no discussion of this possible role of law.[11] Similarly, if this argument is correct Tay and Kamenka may have organised a
premature wake for *gesellschaft* law. Indeed were this not so, it would be
hard to credit what they hoped to achieve in their more recent, explicit, call
for a return to such values. Nor is this simply a matter of a "lag" between
economic and cultural change. Habermas's own projections for the ideal
community of the future are based on Kohlberg's notion of the ethically
autonomous individual but this notion bears much more than a trace of the
gesellschaft values of the individual bearing responsibility for his own
actions and malfeasances. Tay and Kamenka, for their part, admit that
there is much in common between the forms of *gesellschaft* and
bureaucratic-administrative law and, as I have argued previously, there is
in fact even more in common than they concede.

What is needed therefore is a more sensitive appraisal of the complex
relationship between law and society in general and at this transitional
period. On the one hand, it is necessary to avoid the prevailing error of
thinking that law is no more than an "instrument" responsive to the
purposes of powerful groups or the dominant authorities; law is also a
repository of meaning and tradition and this indeed is part of the explanation for its potentiality as an instrument and resource. On the other
hand, the current revival, under the influence of Marxism, of a conception
of law and society as two ways of conceiving a social formation leads to the
opposite error of identifying law so closely with the form of the society that
it becomes difficult to examine the special role performed by legal institutions and conceptions as a repository of traditional and cultural meanings.
Neither of these mistaken viewpoints offer the opportunity of a satisfactory
assessment of current changes in law because they both lead to the very
conclusion which has been criticized in this paper, that as we move to an
increasingly "managed" society law must necessarily follow suit and be
shaped accordingly.

In other respects the under-estimation of the role of law as a repository
of meanings and values seems to derive from certain features of the work
of some of the leading theorists in the sociology of law. Durkheim, for
example, stipulated that in modern society it was only really criminal law
and that to a residual degree, which served to provide a sense of shared
meanings and values. Complex societies were united by the consciousness
of interdependence and mutual reliance, not by agreed principles and
sentiments which had necessarily grown too various and diverse to serve
this function. When Parsons turned this argument of Durkheim's on its

head and conceptualized society as being built up out of social action oriented to common expectations and values, he allocated only a minor role to law which was seen as external and superficial as compared to informal norms and role expectations. Even Bredemeier's application of Parson's approach made light of law's contribution to meaning and motivation — what Parsons calls pattern-maintenance — and emphasised instead law's contribution to system integration through its role of dispute-processing.[12] Weber also underestimated this aspect of law, despite his concern with legitimate domination through formal rational law, because he kept referring to the public or democratic consciousness as one which was basically out of sympathy with *gesellschaft* values and procedures.[13] Yet whilst it is correct that decisions on *gesellschaft* principles can give rise to criticism based on considerations of substantive justice and the equity of the particular case, it is also true that decisions made on such substantive grounds can often give rise to public disquiet on the *gesellschaft* grounds of their unfairness, or disproportionality in relation to other allegedly "like" cases.

To show that these points are not merely matters of theoretical interest I want finally to illustrate my argument and its implications by reference to some area of recent legal change and controversy. I shall try to show how law can avoid being caught up and shaped in the image of social developments and changing social relations and suggest that it may play a special role even when it does become involved in such developements. The implications of this argument are perhaps particularly relevant for those "radical" law teachers and activists who have responded to the upsurge in conservative politics and philosophy and the corresponding cutback in welfarist interventions by stealing the liberal-reformist's clothes and rediscovering the value of law. If my argument is correct they may find that they have chosen to fight for progressive legal changes at a time which is particularly unsympathetic to the use of law as a tool of social engineering.

To avoid misunderstanding, some preliminary points should be made regarding what the following examples are designed to prove. Firstly, I am not claiming that law has the capacity to halt the developments portrayed by both Tay and Kamenka and by Habermas in which crucial political decisions concerning the economy, employment, energy, defence etc. are turned into technical matters of social engineering devised by administrative and scientific elites. On the contrary, my point is that such developments can more easily continue because, within certain spheres of social life, *gesellschaft* traditions continue to provide a sense of meaning and motivation and legal institutions and conceptions provide one of the main sources of such a living tradition. Secondly, the analysis of recent changes in the law is complicated by the fact that they largely coincide with, and are even an outcome of, the trend in many Western countries towards the election of Conservative governments dedicated to a reduction in state intervention in the economy and society. In principle, it would be possible to distinguish cases where resistance to the onward trend of *bureaucratic-administrative* law is to be attributed to the reluctance of such governments to become involved in greater expenditure, from cases which are more to do with rejection of this trend on other grounds. This could be on the basis of conservative ideology as a new version of *gesellschaft* values, or the activities of interest groups such as lawyers or others, or the result of a more or less mobilized "public opinion". It could be argued that we are witnessing a phase of over-determined withdrawal from interventionist forms of law. Governments attempt to pull back from their interventionist role because of the conspicuousness of their failures in resolving problems such as inflation, unemployment etc.; if less is expected of them there is less risk to their legitimacy. Concomitant with this, as a justification of it and an outcome of it, legal traditions stressing individualism, self-help and responsibility are preferred to those concerned with successful regulation of activity. However, important as these points are, they do not affect my main line of argument and will not be pursued further here.

In studying legal change in relation to social change at the present time, attention must be given to the way in which law resists, fights back and incorporates social developments. The first example of resistance comes, appropriately enough, from the area of Tort, the very area of law used as the best illustration of the relentless march of the *bureaucratic-administrative* form of law. The transformation of this area of law into an arena for risk allocation and insurance has come to an apparent full stop, at least for the present. The all-embracing New Zealand scheme of state compensation was flatly rejected in Australia shortly after it was introduced in New Zealand. The fifteen American states which introduced no-fault insurance schemes to deal with the car accident cases previously processed by their Tort systems are not likely to be joined by many more. In England the relatively modest recommendations of the Pearson Commission to remove some cases dealt with by the Tort system stand little chance of being implemented. Yet nothing has outwardly happened to weaken the arguments in favour of such schemes and it still remains true that up to half the money produced by a Tort system goes to pay lawyers and run the system itself rather than to compensate accident victims.

Part of the explanation for this hiatus must obviously be sought in the relative power of the interest groups most active or potentially concerned in such changes in the law. But, in the view of some of those with long experience of trying to bring about such changes in Tort systems, this is not all there is to it. There does seem to be some growing resistance by some people to the assumption that law has no other role to play than one to be evaluated in terms of costs and benefits; opposition focussed, predictably enough, around the argument that it is not "right" for "the law" to be seen to be compensating those clearly at fault such as drunken drivers.

If there is some evidence of resistance to further movement along the lines of what were alleged to be almost inevitable trends in the law, there are also indications that *gesellschaft* procedures and conceptions are even coming back into favour in some areas where it would seem they had been definitely expelled. This can be seen in at least two areas of law and politico-legal controversy. In the area of criminal justice, arguably the area with the closest relation to cultural traditions and meanings, we are witnessing a sharp move away from the justificatory principles of the rehabilitative ideal if not always from the "treatment" practices associated with it. In many Scandinavian countries, in the United States and elsewhere the system of juvenile justice has come under attack precisely on the grounds of its abandonment of the *gesellschaft* litany of rights and duties, responsibility, consistency and proportionality. Not unconnected with these changes, there is also a wider debate in Britain, the United States and elsewhere over the so-called problem of discretion which makes an issue of the lack of rule-governed accountability in the decision-making of officials, experts and others. I have argued elsewhere that the terms of this debate are far too narrow and that there are other alternatives to those represented by either a *gesellschaft* or a bureaucratic mode of taking and justifying decision-making.[14] There is no doubt also that concern over discretion is sometimes used, as in recent Conservative welfare legislation in Britain, to rationalize cutbacks in the extent of assistance offered. The point here is simply to document once again the power of *gesellschaft* traditions and illustrate some of the contexts in which they are drawn on.

On an overall view, however, the most significant contribution of law lies in the way it can so easily be adapted, where necessary, to bless administrative purposes with legitimacy. There need not be any incompatibility between these two institutional practices, for the reasons stated earlier with regard to whether the *gesellschaft* and *bureaucratic-administrative* forms of law were really essentially different and irreconcilable. Pursuing administrative objectives through statutory means can impose some slight costs in terms of flexibility of manoeuvre, in terms of easier oversight by the courts, in terms of *intra vires* requirements etc. but the price is usually found acceptable by governments, especially as the resulting instrument is then presentable as not only "legal" but also "democratic". The resulting "laws" may or may not have much in common with the traditions of *gesellschaft* law but they share in the reflected glory of the principles of that tradition.[15]

In sum, my argument is this. A proper appreciation of the role of law in modern capitalist societies must be based on appreciation and further investigation of the various institutional and ideological practices which are represented by law. Care must be taken to allow for a lack of congruence between social relations and legal traditions, in particular for the likelihood that the traditions of *gesellschaft* law still play an important cultural role and do so all the more because men's social relations in production and elsewhere may be now less based on simple exchange relations than previously. Behind this argument and, if it be accepted, as a corollary to it, is the claim that there is no real crisis in law and legal ideology as such and that the conditions for such a crisis have not been correctly identified by the authors whose work I have discussed.

NOTES AND REFERENCES

[1] This is the text of a paper presented at the joint meeting of the Law and Society Association and International Sociological Association held at Madison, Wisconsin in June, 1980. Its theme should be distinguished from related but somewhat different problems, such as the claim that there exists a crisis in respect for legal authority and official hierarchies (e.g. E. Rostow (ed.), *Is Law Dead?* (1971); R. O. Wolff (ed.), *The Rule of Law* (1971)), or that centralized legal institutions are declining in favour of informal and local methods of dispute-processing (R. Abel, "Delegalization: A Critical Review of its Ideology, Manifestations, and Social Consequences" in *Alternative Rechtsformen und Alternative zum Recht* (1979; ed. E. Blankenburg *et al*, 27–47), and M. Galanter, "Legality and its Discontents: A Preliminary Assessment of Current Theories of Legalization and Delegalization", *Ibid.*, pp. 11–26).

[2] For example, the analysis of the crisis in law in R. M. Unger, *Law in Modern Society* (1976) especially 192–213.

[3] E. Kamenka *et al*, *Law and Society: The Crisis in Legal Ideals* (1978).

[4] Kamenka and Tay are well aware of this point about their ideal types which they explicitly derive from Weber's "ideal-types" and Tonnies' "normal-types", both of which are heuristic theoretical constructs. Moreover, they freely concede that these types of law are mixed in reality and may even be mutually supportive, see A. E.-S. Tay and E. Kamenka, "Beyond the French Revolution: Communist Socialism and the Concept of Law" (1971) XXI *University of Toronto Law Journal* 109–140, and E. Kamenka and A. E.-S. Tay, "'Transforming' the Law, 'Steering' Society" in *Law and Social Control* (1980; ed. E. Kamenka and A. E.-S. Tay 105 ff). Why did they come to posit the existence of a "crisis" in their 1975 paper and why they maintained this view, with variations, in their other more recent discussions? See, for example, A. E.-S. Tay, "Law, the Citizen and the State" in *Law and Society: the Crisis in Legal Ideals* (1978; ed. E. Kamenka *et al*. 1); *Ibid.*, p. 48; E. Kamenka, "What is Justice" in *Justice* (1979; ed. E. Kamenka and A. E.-S. Tay 1); A. E.-S. Tay, "The Sense of Justice in the Common Law", *Ibid.* pp. 79–96; Kamenka and Tay, 1980, *op. cit.*. The answer seems to lie mainly in their changing appraisal of the merits of these types of law and of the growing threat to *Gesellschaft* law. The "crisis" arises from what they see as the need to counter the developments leading to *Gesellschaft* society. Thus in 1965 Kamenka is broadly sympathetic to *Gemeinschaft* aspirations and highly critical of what he sees as the "widespread tendency . . . to accept as hallowed presuppositions the concepts characteristic of *Gesellschaft*", see E. Kamenka, "*Gemeinschaft* and *Gesellschaft*" (1965) 17 *Political Science* 3. From 1971 onwards there is a re-appraisal of *Gemeinschaft* (in the light of contemporary student protests?) on the basis that claims made in its name can only be met by increasing the role of the state as provider. This would inevitably hasten the growth of a collectivist bureaucratic-administrative order in which a man is no more than "a cog in a wheel" or a "case in the eyes of a social worker", see Tay, "The Sense of Justice . . ." *op. cit.*. To resist this development it is essential to re-assert the virtues of *Gesellschaft* law with its tried and tested, modest but careful, procedures for truth-finding and dispute-processing. By this point their biographical reappraisal has moved full circle so that Tay now insists that *Gesellschaft* law alone has "a bias towards freedom and equality and against arbitrary coercion" (*Ibid.*, p. 26).

[5] L. Fuller, *The Morality of Law* (1969).

[6] The fact that Tay and Kamenka develop their argument by combining the approaches of Tonnies, Weber and Pashukanis means that they run the risk of taking over some of the weaknesses of the component theories and missing some of their strengths. Paradoxically, in view of their concern about the rise of collectivism on the model of "communist" societies, their exaggerated distinction between *Gesellschaft* and bureaucratic law is a result of their uncritical acceptance of the arguments of the Marxist theoretician, Evgeni Pashukanis, who rejected the view that law was a form of domination so as to demonstrate the contrast between bourgeois "law" and technical administration, see E. Pashukanis, *Law and Marxism* (1978). By contrast Tonnies' view of the contrast between *Gemeinschaft* and *Gesellschaft* led him to see *Gesellschaft* as the simultaneous rise of both (arbitrary) individual freedom and (arbitrary) governmental power, see F. Tonnies, *Community and Association* (1955), 109, 333.

[7] R. Dworkin, *Taking Rights Seriously* (1977).

[8] D. N. MacCormick, *Legal Reasoning and Legal Theory* (1978).

[9] E. Durkheim, *The Division of Labour in Society* (1964) 206–219.

[10] J. Habermas, *Legitimation Crisis* (1975).

[11] See now H. Rottleheuthner, "The Contribution of the Critical Theory of the Frankfurt School to the Sociology of Law" in *Approaches to the Sociology of Law* (1981; ed. A. Podgorecki and C. Whelan). For a similar conclusion see also J. Habermas, *Communication and the Evolution of Society* (1979) especially 178–205.

[12] H. Bredemeier, "Law as an Integrative Mechanism", *Sociology of Law* (1969; ed. V. Aubert).

[13] M. Rheinstein (ed.) *M. Weber: On Law in Economy and Society* (1954) especially chapter 11.

[14] Z. K. Bankowski and D. Nelken, "Discretion as a Social Problem" in *Discretion and Welfare* (1981; ed. S. Asquith and M. Adler), 247–269.

[15] These propositions are well illustrated by the extensive use of the language of rights in recent Conservative legislation in Britain, see P. Taylor-Gooby, "The New Right and Social Policy" (1981) 1 *Critical Social Policy* 18–31.

[4]
Legislation and its Constraints: A Case Study of the 1965 British Rent Act

Discussions of the relationship between social systems and legal systems face not only the difficulty of separately identifying each system, but the problem that the connection between 'law' and 'society' is an <u>internal</u> one. For the sociologist, the legal system is an <u>aspect</u> of a social system. Theoretical conceptualization of what is meant by the social system must include a place for the features and contributions of the legal system; the same goes for the terms 'law' and 'society'. Obviously, theoretical models are one thing and social reality another (at least on one view of ontology), and there may be value sometimes in distinguishing legal systems and social systems so as to consider how one affects the other. But the value of such models is likely to be much greater if they offer some specification of the internal as well as the external relationships between law and society and succeed in showing how law is one part of the processes which make up social life.

One of the most fruitful ways of achieving this goal is to explore the relationship between law and society as aspects of the process of 'structuration' by which the actions of members of society reproduce, but also alter, the structural configurations and cultural understandings which constitute their society (Giddens, 1976). This approach is particularly useful for a study of legislation, which is the feature of the law and society relationship upon which this chapter concentrates. A recurrent issue in the study of legislation concerns the extent to which legislation is capable of changing society. How much does it reflect the existing distribution of power and respectability and how far is it capable of transcending and changing them? In this chapter I shall be developing a framework with which

to examine how legislation incorporates existing
features of society which shape and limit its
'effects' which arise as it confronts obstacles in
the course of the implementation. In particular, I
shall be developing the argument that there is an
isomorphism between the way in which legislation is
part of society but yet is capable of changing it
and the way in which all social action is at the
same time part of social structure but also that
which upholds and changes it.

The process of making and enforcing legislation
is certainly no everyday incident in the life of
society. At least some of its stages are particularly public, institutionalized and often dramatic
events. Legislation may even amount to a self-
conscious experiment in planned but contained social
change. Yet there are nonetheless parallels between
the way in which social actors make and remake
society and the legislative process. Moreover,
legislation is always part of the everyday social
activity of some social actors and arises from and
returns to the everyday social activity of the rest
of society. The claim being made here is that we
can advance the study of legislation by attending
more closely to what we mean when we talk about
social actors being able to effect a change in their
society.

A stimulating recent discussion of the conceptual linkage between human agency and social structure is that provided by Steven Lukes (Lukes, 1977,
ch. 1). He points out that the boundary line
between what we choose to call the agent and what we
choose to call social structure is inevitably an
arbitrary one which depends on how strictly social
structure is seen to define the potential area of
choice open to agents. The parallel here is that it
is not so much that an agency 'affects' social
structures or that law 'affects' society; both the
agent and the law are dynamic elements of the
continuing process that is society. It is the
theorist who decided where the line is to be drawn
between these concepts so as to examine the internal
and external relationship between them. What are
described as the constraints of social structure
over an agent or limits which social structure
exerts over the effects of legislation is just a way
of talking about these conceptual boundary lines.
However, whilst Lukes' analysis offers a valuable
starting point for a study of legislation, it cannot
be carried over wholesale. In examining the relationship between agency and structure Lukes chooses

to identify internal constraints with the limits on
the abilities of agents to achieve particular outcomes and to equate external constraints with limits
on the opportunities available to them. In applying
these ideas to the study of legislation I have
preferred to consider internal constraints as the
self-imposed or unconscious limits on the ambitions
of those advocating, framing and implementing legislation. External constraints, on the other hand, I
choose to define as those obstacles which confront
the making or implementing of these ambitions and
projects. In developing the analysis I also distinguish the relevant constraints that apply to the
groups involved in making legislation as compared to
those engaged in implementing legislation and I also
emphasize the importance of distinguishing different
levels of analysis of these constraints. This bring
out the importance of the fact that social actors
belong to political or legal hierarchies. There is,
of course, much more to be said concerning the
appropriateness and the detailed working out of this
theoretical framework but these general points will
suffice for present purposes.

Rather than developing the conceptual points
further in an abstract way, I want instead to provide an illustrative case study which will demonstrate these basic points. For this purpose I shall
draw freely on a recent empirical study of the
making and implementation of rent legislation in
Britain (Nelken, 1983). My discussion of the
effects of this legislation may sound all too similar to the typical studies of 'legal effectiveness'
which were the bread and butter of sociology of law
studies in the 1960s, and therefore some points of
clarification are in order. The point of this case
study is <u>not</u> to demonstrate the 'impact' or 'effect'
of the legislation; indeed, the point of the
argument is to show why this way of approaching
legislation must be reformulated. Nor is my concern
with the 'gap' between the promises of legislators
and the actual performance of legislation. Claims
about intended outcomes and reports of effectiveness
are all data worthy of investigation and understanding but no relationship between them can be assumed.
Often we are in the realm of persuasive argument as
different interpreters fight for the soul of legislation (see Nelken, 1981). It is obviously wrong to
say that there are never clearcut discrepancies in
the results of legislation compared with the purposes of some of those who framed it. But it is
just as foolish to presuppose that legislative

72

results are always wayward. Insofar as the question
of intention and outcome will yield to description
rather than evaluation, it will be found that consideration of the internal and external constraints
on the social actors. involved in making, implementing and resisting legislation will prove an
illuminating approach.

It also has to be conceded that no single case
study could hope to demonstrate by itself the
utility of a new framework for studying the relationship between law and society. There is no sense
in which this study can be said to be representative
of all kinds of legislative activity and still less
of all kinds of law. But I have deliberately tried
to keep the points which I want to derive from this
case study at a high level of generality concerned
with methodological rather than substantive issues.
In addition, there are at least some features of the
1965 Rent Act which make it particularly apt for
illustrating the internal and external constraints
on legislation. For this was legislation passed in
a context free of the more obvious constraints. The
Labour Government returned in 1964 had a remarkably
free hand to do something about London's housing
crisis which had been one of the important issues of
the election. 'Interest groups representing landlords did not and could not play a major part in
shaping the legislation. Even the Civil Service,
having the wreck of the 1957 Rent Act on their
hands, were willing to allow a coterie of expert
advisers an unusually free hand to employ novel
ideas and the legislation had the backing of one of
the most thorough social research reports yet
commissioned. Thus, whatever constraints we may
call in explanation of the outcome of this law are
likely to be exaggerated in other cases of legislation. On the other hand, rent legislation is a
particularly interesting illustration of the constraints on interference with property·rights in a
mixed economy where housing is seen partly as a
matter of public need and partly a matter of market
provision.

SOME EFFECTS OF THE 1965 RENT ACT

Legislation to control rent and to provide security
of tenure in privately-rented property goes back in
Britain as far as 1915. Typically, however, such
measures were treated as a series of temporary
expedients and were subject to violent swings of the

political pendulum, as in the Conservatives' attempt in 1957 to reintroduce free market criteria into the privately-rented sector. The 1965 Rent Act, however, represented a major restructuring of what was left of this declining sector of housing by introducing the concept of rent regulation and 'fair rents' in place of rigid rent control and by extending security of tenure to all tenants of unfurnished accommodation. Despite some significant later changes such as the extension of security to furnished tenants and the relaxation of security for resident landlords in Labour's 1974 Rent Act, and the introduction of various exemptions from rent regulation and security in the Conservatives' 1980 Housing Act, the provisions introduced in 1965 have remained fundamental to housing law in the private sector (Partington, 1980; Farrand and Arden, 1981). The blanket removal of rent regulation is no longer a live political issue. The law against harassment - the crime of threatening to evict or actually evicting a tenant from his accommodation - has become a permanent feature of the law governing rented accommodation, the only public criticism being of its alleged lack of sufficient severity or effectiveness. To this extent, then, the legislation has altered existing features of social structure and culture.

On the other hand, the changes introduced by the legislation are not all they were said to be. At the time of its passage through Parliament the 1965 Rent Act was hailed as 'a tenants' Magna Carta' and 'one of the most courageous and valuable Bills ever placed before Parliament'. Yet this new form of rent regulation seems to have been at least of as much benefit to landlords as to tenants. Landlords were the main ones who took advantage of the new schemes for fixing fair rents and some landlords actually made enormous profits out of rented accommodation after the Act, using methods which were not dissimilar to those adopted by Rachman, the property speculator whose activities helped stimulate the passing of the law. One property magnate made such a fortune out of residential property after the 1965 Act that even when the property bubble burst, he set a record for bankruptcy at £142,978,430. The landlords prosecuted and convicted of harassing their tenants, by contrast, tended to be small resident landlords caught up in personal disputes with their tenants in situations very different from those in which Rachman had been involved. As many as 70% of landlords prosecuted for harassment were resident in the same house as their tenants and a similar percentage were from immigrant backgrounds.

As Table 4.1 shows, rent legislation had relatively little effect on the practices characteristic of business landlords (which were affected far more by changes in the property market). The most severe sanctions were directed at practices which were characteristic of amateur and often immigrant small landlords.

Table 4.1   The legal response to malpractices of different types of landlord

Types of Malpractice	Type of Landlord	Types of Response
CRIMINAL OFFENCES		
Harassment and Illegal Eviction	Mainly resident foreign-born landlords	Regular prosecution of illegal eviction but difficulties in proving harassment
Overcharging in furnished tenancies	Business and non-business landlords	Rarely prosecuted, repayment of over charge usually required
NOT CRIMINAL OFFENCES		
Overcharging in unfurnished tenancies	Systematically by business-oriented landlords	Tenants allowed to recover up to two years overpayment
Avoidance and evasion of security of tenure and rent regulation	All types: systematically by business-oriented landlords	Some effort by Rent Officers, Housing Advice Workers and Law Centres to defeat weak schemes
Winkling (financial inducements to tempt tenants to vacate)	Business-oriented landlords and developers	No official action
Abuse of Improvement	Systematically by business-oriented	Some local authorities

Table 4.1 (cont'd)

Malpractice	Type of Landlord	Types of Response
Grants (where property is not improved for the bene- fit of exist- ing tenants)	landlords and developers	claimed discretion to refuse grants in these circum- stances
Gentrifica- tion (buying working-class tenanted hou- sing for con- version for up- market owner- occupation).	Systematically by business-oriented landlords and developers	Limited efforts by some local authorities to safeguard or develop Housing Action areas for existing tenants
Legal Rach- manism (Var- ious tech- niques used to raise rent levels; thereby increase the mortgage value of blocks of residential property)	Large business- oriented landlords	Occasional resistance by Rent Officers or Rent Assessment Committees, otherwise left to Tenants' Associations

The purpose of discussing the limited effects of the 1965 Rent Act is not to show that it 'failed'. That would be to offer an evaluation which would rightly be challenged by those who would stress other features of how much the law did achieve, or would place a higher value on what I admitted it did achieve. Some commentators would even argue that it 'failed' because it went too far in restricting landlords' powers rather than, as I have been implying, because it had relatively little effect on the legitimacy of property rights. The point of showing that the 1965 Rent Act had only limited effects is only intended to show which are the features of social structure which remained relatively unchanged. This is a different under- taking from assessing the effectiveness of legis- lation. Firstly because however successful a piece of legislation, there will always be some features of social structure that remain unchanged. Secondly

because some of the matters which best show the
constraints on legislation are those which never
formed part of the purpose of the legislator in the
first place and therefore represent the deepest
constraints of all. Even so, in order to ensure
that relevant features of social structure are being
discussed, it is important not to pluck imaginary
legislative outcomes out of the air or to believe
the rhetorical promises of politicians when they
make legislation, which may sometimes be the same
thing. The practices listed in Table 4.1 meet the
criterion of relevance because they are all matters
which, at some point in the '60s and '70s, gave rise
to minor scandals concerning the legitimacy of the
exercise of property rights by landlords and specu-
lators. Insofar as these practices remain immune
from official control, they testify to the continuing and, in fact, now reinforced constraints over
interference with property rights in contemporary
British society. I turn now to a more specific
discussion of the constraints which influenced the
making and implementation of the 1965 Rent Act.

EXTERNAL CONSTRAINTS

Landlord and tenant interest groups had remarkably
little direct influence on the content of the 1965
Rent Act (Banting, 1979; Nelken, 1983). Some return
to rent and scarcity regulation was recognized as
inevitable by landlords after the furore following
the Rachman scandal, and was even welcomed as
restoring some stability to the market. But providing that conditions were not made too uneconomic,
landlords did not expect to influence the details of
the legislation. This is not to say that they did
not have an important indirect influence in conditioning what the lawmakers saw as realistic. This
indirect influence is highlighted by the 1974 Rent
Act, where the legislators mistakenly allowed
themselves to be persuaded that it was safe to
ignore this constraint because the landlords
affected by the new extension of security of tenure
would be unable or unwilling to move out of the
private sector. The importance of interest groups
and pressure groups in shaping legislation varies
greatly from case to case but there are a number of
features that stand out from this study which may be
of more general application. The first is to note
that in the political process of framing legislation
it is the legitimacy of particular practices that is

77

at issue rather than the size or type of landlord
who engages in the practice. Not surprisingly,
there was a strong correlation between the respectability of given practices and the type of landlord
involved. Large business landlords were more likely
to employ practices that were allowed as compared to
amateur resident landlords. But legislators also
recognized the legitimate interests of groups such
as seaside landladies or parsons living in tied
cottages, who were economically insignificant. A
second and not unrelated point is that the capacity
of a group to dispose of large economic resources
does not of itself represent an external constraint
on the lawmaking process, even if such resources
constitute a formidable obstacle to the implementation of the law. Private landlords are a good
illustration of this point because of the gulf
between the economic power of some of them and their
lack of political respectability in a situation
where neither Labour nor Conservative parties considered private renting the ideal form of housing
tenure.

If the economic resources of different landlords were less important than might be expected in
the passage of the law, they were certainly crucial
in effecting its implementation. Both Rent Officers
in fixing rents and Harassment Officers responding
to complaints of harassment tended to be reactive
rather than proactive. They waited to be mobilized
by complainants and it was typically the tenants of
non-business landlords who came to them for assistance. Business landlords, by contrast, developed a
number of devices by which they were able to turn
the scheme of rent regulation to their advantage so
as to increase the rental and mortgage value of
their property and preserve the immunity of practices by which they made considerable profits
(Nelken, 1983, ch. 2). When such landlords did find
themselves at odds with the law, they were likely to
co-operate; on the other hand, small landlords, with
more at stake in any particular case, were less
willing to co-operate and this increased the likelihood that they would be subject to legal sanctions.
Whereas harassment was an insignificant feature of
normal business practices by large landlords, small
landlords did resort to harassment as part of their
methods of self-help to remove unwanted tenants.
But from their point of view this was one aspect of
the informal norms that governed the letting of
accommodation in housing stress areas (norms to
which tenants gave considerable assent). To insist

as the law did that tenants could only be removed by
the use of a Court order was at odds with the
willingness of small landlords to take tenants into
their accommodation without checking their bona
fides, relying on the fact they would ask them to
leave if things did not work out. In these, and of
course in many other ways, the results of the Rent
Act were influenced by the external constraints
arising from differences in economic power and
respectability.

INTERNAL CONSTRAINTS

Some explanations of the effects of legislation
reject the emphasis on external constraints in order
to re-examine the internal constraints which condition the purposes of the legislator. Alleged
shortfall in achievement often turns out to be
precisely what would be expected on closer analysis
of the reasons and purposes for particular legislative intervention. Although such an analysis has
the danger of assigning prescience to who make
legislation, it offers an important corrective to
focussing solely on external constraints. This is
demonstrated by recent investigations of what
Richard Crossman, then Housing Minister, really
meant to achieve by the 1965 Rent Act. Investigations based on both his published and unpublished
diaries demonstrate that Crossman and his advisers
were far more concerned to introduce a stable system
of rent regulation than to fleece business landlords
and that they indeed clearly recognized that rent
would rise under their new system (Banting, 1979).
Part of Crossman's difficulty in steering the Rent
Bill through Parliament was the need to simulate a
rather greater radicalism than the Bill possessed in
order to placate the left-wingers of his Party.
This is the true explanation of his strange confes-
sion in Committee that he had a prejudice against
landlords.
        Consideration of the aims and purposes of
Crossman and his advisers merges almost impercep-
tibly into discussion of their assumptions. These
were particularly important here because the Civil
Servants were unusually receptive to the ideas of
outsiders. Both Crossman and his advisers wanted to
provide a scheme of rent regulation which could
'take rent out of politics'. They assumed that the
application of successful technique and the introduction of a neutral third party could achieve this.

They assumed, too, that some incentive was needed to keep landlords in the rent property market, but that excessive profits could and should be removed. In addition, they shared an ideology of 'fairness' which Crossman referred to as his 'public school' sentiments, which dictated that landlords deserved to be treated fairly as well as tenants and which predisposed them to prefer 'fair rents' to 'controlled rents'. Finally, insofar as they gave any attention to the question of which forms of landlord behaviour should be made criminal, making harassment a crime evidenced their assumption that displacing tenants by the use of petty violence was to be treated in a different manner from the exercise of more subtle financial methods (such as those listed in Table 4.1), which indirectly achieved similar goals.

Somewhat different internal constraints affected the implementation of the legislation. Rent Officers and Local Authority solicitors and Harassment Officers all had their own aims and assumptions. Solicitors' attitudes to the problem of harassment, for example, related mainly to their role of assessing legal sufficiency and their sensitivity to, whether it was the policy of their local authority to encourage prosecution. Harassment Officers, on the other hand, worked within the day-to-day constraints of obtaining co-operation from landlords. Back in the office, their main concern was working out whether the harassment complaint should be pursued and whether the case they dealt with involved a sufficient degree of desert (including moral desert) to justify recommending prosecution of the landlord (Nelken, 1983, ch. 4).

LEGAL CONSTRAINTS

The constraints on legislation imposed by the form of modern law and the nature of legal institutions can be considered to be both internal and external. Some of these, such as the need for any one law to conform to the form and to some extent the content of the rest of the legal system, is a matter which is internal to the legal process; but the effect of legal institutions on restricting what politicians and enforcement agents are able to achieve may properly be considered an external constraint. The influence of legal constraints is a particularly intriguing topic because those who framed the 1965

Act made some effort to avoid or nullify them. One reason for the creation of the new Rent Officer service and the Rent Assessment Committees was to avoid the existing legal system. Together with Rent Tribunals they testified to the belief that there would be easier access and better justice for tenants in administrative settings rather than having to use Courts with their associated costs, complicated procedures and property-minded lawyers. Even the crime of harassment was created partly as a means of bypassing the existing civil legal remedies. It was thought to be cynical to ask the type of tenants who were subject to harassment to rely on civil remedies so as to take the landlord to court for breach of their right to 'quiet enjoyment of their occupation'.

Studying the effects of the legislation, however, shows that this attempt to bypass legal constraints was less successful than anticipated. Quasi-administrative methods of regulation in practice also depended on which complainants were likely to invoke them. These tended to be the poor tenants of poor landlords, who had few other resources when disputes arose (including a reluctance or inability to use lawyers). Thus Rent Officers and Harassment Officers found themselves dealing mainly with poor landlords. In any case, decisions of Rent Officers could be appealed to Rent Assessment Committees which were slightly more sympathetic to landlords and their decisions in turn were under the jurisdiction of the Courts; business landlords were able to take advantage of all of this. They were also able to use the well-documented advantages of 'repeat players' to challenge decisions by Rent Officers and others when it best suited them (Galanter, 1974). Quite often, when cases reached the Courts, judges displayed a preference for common law property rights as compared with the philosophy implicit in the statutory framework of the Rent Acts. This was often the case with their responses to practices by landlords which were on the borderline of avoidance and evasion of the Rent Acts. Interestingly, some judges even attempted to incorporate into the law the recognition of external constraints which they assumed the legislator must have meant to respect. For example, considering whether to give leave to appeal against a decision in favour of a landlord after the 1974 Rent Act, some Court of Appeal judges took into account what they saw as the danger of discouraging landlords from continuing to let their accommodation

(Griffith, 1979). In Scotland some judges tried to guide Rent Assessment Committees to an interpretation of their functions in deciding on fair rents, which would take into account the importance of ensuring a fair return for landlords on their investment (Robson, 1981).

Even the law against harassment failed to offer tenants the protection they required. It was of little help to tenants to know that their landlord would be prosecuted for harassment if this left them without accommodation. What they needed, therefore, was an effective <u>civil</u> remedy to prevent their landlord from harassing them or to reinstate them. This was in practice only available in those areas where free legal advice centres were set up and where there was good liaison with the Local Authority. It should be added, however, that some of the legal obstacles which commentators have seen as limiting the effectiveness of rent legislation may have been misinterpreted. For example, magistrates are wrongly thought to impose low fines in cases of harassment because they sympathise with the landlords as men of property. In fact, rightly or wrongly, magistrates are influenced more by their conception of the situation of harassment as having much in common with domestic disputes. Those cases involving clear financial motives, especially involving business landlords, tend to be dealt with severely (Nelken, 1983, ch. 6).

TYPES AND LEVELS OF ANALYSIS

Even the most summary outline of the constraints on rent legislation reveals the necessity for different types and levels of analysis. Legislation involves a series of complexes of social action over time and these can be distinguished by function, for example law-making and law enforcement. Those involved in these legislative processes occupy different roles in legal and administrative hierarchies and are subject to different constraints. Moreover, the constraints which affect these stages are not independent and may incorporate or at least affect each other.

One interesting question that arises is the nature of the reciprocal relationship between constraints. A recent excellent study of the regulation of safety on the North Sea oil rigs argued that the crucial factor leading to neglect of safety standards as compared with those demanded in factories is the emphasis on the speed required to maximize North Sea oil revenue. The stress on speed, which hampered the enforcement activities of the regulatory agency, was in turn traced back to the constraints on oil companies who had to repay the heavy costs of their initial investment and the pressure on the British Government to improve the balance of payments. This latter concern was linked to the dominance of the Treasury in Government policy-making and the weak position of Britain in the international economy (Carson, 1981). Here the influences seem relatively one-way. But in a study of rent legislation it would also be possible to show a more reciprocal chain of influence. Clearly the choices made by Rent Officers and Harassment Officers are influenced to some extent by the constraints on the supply of houses at a national and local level. But action taken in the course of implementing the legislation also constrains what the law can achieve and, through the effects and feedback reports which are communicated to law and policy-makers, they then influence further development of the legislation. Thus the question of whether to 'tighten up' on the prosecution of harassment may be affected by the accounts provided by Harassment Officers of the type of cases with which they dealt. It should be added, however, that those in closest contact with the results of legislation often occupy a low status in the 'hierarchy of credibility' in policy-making.

DISCUSSION

A number of theoretical points follow from this survey of some of the constraints relevant to rent legislation. Firstly, it is clear from the case study that the distinction between what I have called external and internal constraints is necessarily an arbitrary one. Many of the factors dealt with under one heading could equally have been dealt with under the other without any loss of plausibility. Just as in Lukes' terms 'abilities' can be assimilated to 'opportunities' in the study of human agency so there is no strict dividing line between analysis of aims and achievement in the study of legislative outcomes. The distinction between internal and external constraints, like the distinction between types and levels of analysis, serves only as a heuristic tool to ensure coverage of relevant factors and to help focus attention on which factors are being examined and which features of the environment are being held constant. There are therefore no factors which are intrinsically external or internal constraints. Wider recognition of this point could help avoid fruitless discussions of whether the results of particular legislative interventions owed more to external obstacles or original purposes. The answer will often be, it depends where you choose to draw the line.

Secondly, it may have been noticed that at least some of the factors which I have described as constraints represent projections by social actors of what they take to be external constraints on their behaviour. The makers of the 1965 Rent Act, unlike those who framed the 1974 Rent Act, took the view that some incentives had to be left for landlords otherwise they would move out of the rented sector. It may have been that in this case they were correct. But the possibility remains that such projections could be made in error, but nonetheless have a real effect on legislation in so far as law-makers and enforcers act on what they believe to be true rather than what actually would occur. Projections of likely outcomes can lead to action or inaction. Thus, in 1963 at the height of the Rachman scandal over exploitation of tenants by property landlords, there were some who urged that no methods of regulation could help to improve conditions. Sir Keith Joseph, then Housing Minister, for example, argued that the 'sweating of property' was an inevitable concomitant of market pressures on scarce resources. The Estates Gazette commented at the time that trying to control rents went against human nature and would be bound to fail like the Prohibition experiment in America! The significance of these sorts of beliefs is perhaps neglected by those who study the effects of legislation because they focus too much on situations where the legislators' plans are frustrated by real obstacles in the world which they had not anticipated.

Thirdly, study of legislative processes as complexes of social action requires a work of synthesis as well as analysis. The relationship between external and internal constraints must be posed and we have already seen the need to move between the constraints relevant to different types and levels of analysis. Internal and external constraints may clash, they may be unrelated, they may even reinforce each other. For example, the internal constraints which influenced Crossman and his advisers to 'play fair' with landlords were in

turn reinforced by more external constraints built
into legal institutions and the philosophies of
those who manned them which dictated that the property rights of landlords would be given sympathetic
treatment. This example of over-determination of
constraints is perhaps hardly surprising given that
most of Crossman's advisers, whatever their political sympathies, were also lawyers. But it does show
in addition the overlap between political and legal
culture and the way in which both share certain
'hegemonic' common sense assumptions about what is
right and fair.

At this point it may be as well to sum up the
arguments of this chapter. I suggested at the outset that a useful framework for studying the legislative process would be to see it as a set of social
actions framed by internal and external constraints.
Rather than talking in terms of the 'impact' or
'effect' of law on society, legislation was to be
understood as one aspect of the way in which society
is maintained and changed. I then illustrated the
application of this framework with reference to a
case study of rent legislation. But while I may
have pointed the way to reformulating questions
concerning the relationship between law and society,
it would be disingenuous to suggest that this
framework itself resolves all the relevant issues
that now arise. The parallels and the differences
between social action and legislative interventions
need to be further studied. The meaning of 'constraints' and the way in which constraints shape
social and legislative action need much more careful
specification. Pursuing this approach to the
legislative process and its constraints requires
engagement with enduring questions of agency and
structure and the relationship between them. But
that, I suggest, is its strength.

REFERENCES

Banting, K. (1979) Poverty, Politics and Policy:
    Britain in the 1960s, London, Macmillan
Carson, W.G. (1981) The Other Price of Britain's
    Oil, London, Martin Robertson
Farrand, J. & Arden, A. (1981) Rent Acts and
    Regulations (2nd edn.), London, Sweet & Maxwell
Galanter, M (1974) 'Why the "Haves" Come Out Ahead',
    9 Law and Society Review 95
Giddens, A. (1976) New Rules of Sociological Method,
    London, Hutchinson
Griffith, J. (1979) 'Playing the Game on Fair

Rents', New Society, 13 December, p. 600.
Lukes, S. (1977) Essays on Social Theory, London,
    Macmillan
Nelken, D. (1981) 'The Gap Problem in the Sociology
    of Law: a Theoretical Review' in Windsor
    Yearbook of Access to Justice, pp. 35-61
            (1983) The Limits of the Legal Process: a
    Study of Landlords, Law and Crime, London,
    Academic Press
Partington, M. (1980) Landlord and Tenant (2nd
    edn.), London, Weidenfeld & Nicolson
Robson, P. (1981) 'Sabotaging the Rent Acts' in P.
    Robson & P. Watchman (eds.) Justice, Lord
    Denning and the Constitution, London, Gower

[5]
Beyond the Study of
'Law and Society'?

STUART HENRY, *Private Justice: Towards Integrated Theorizing in the Sociology of Law.* Boston: Routledge & Kegan Paul, 1983. Pp. ix + 245. Paper $13.95.

TIMOTHY O'HAGAN, *The End of Law?* Oxford: Basil Blackwell, 1984. Pp. vi + 183. Cloth $29.95; paper $12.95.

1. Changing Paradigms in the Sociology of Law

There can be little doubt that "law and society" studies are at a crossroads. When an editor of the *Law and Society Review* gives it as his opinion that "social studies of law have reached a crucial point in their development. The original paradigm is exhausted,"[1] and the president of the Law and Society Association writes a justification of the most fundamental assumptions of his field,[2] we may be sure that we are witnessing what appears to be a struggle over paradigms in the sociology of law.

But even on the assumption that this sort of language is appropriate for explaining changes in this outlying region of the social sciences,[3] it is still not at

David Nelken is Lecturer in Law at University College, London. B.A. 1972, Dip. Crim. 1973, Ph.D. 1981, Cambridge University. In 1985 he received an American Sociological Association Distinguished Scholar Award.

1. Richard Abel, Redirecting Social Studies of Law, 14 Law & Soc'y Rev. 805, 826 (1980). In this piece Abel explains the 'paralysis' of the field as a result of the fact that "sociolegal studies have borrowed most of their research questions from the object of study—the legal system . . . and [from] legal scholars" (at 826). For a similar analysis of the field in Britain see Colin Campbell & Paul Wiles, The Study of Law and Society in Britain, 10 Law & Soc'y Rev. 547 (1976). I have argued against this view that taking "practical" topics for investigation *can* lead to theoretically interesting problems and that, conversely, more "theoretical" starting points are themselves permeated by specific cultural assumptions and normative concerns. See David Nelken, The Gap Problem in the Sociology of Law: A Theoretical Review, 1 Windsor Yearb. Access Justice 35 (1981). What is significant about current debates is that this latter point has increasingly become the crux of the argument. In an earlier prescient article, Law Books and Books About Law, 26 Stan. L. Rev. 175 (1978), Abel contributed a masterly discussion of this issue.

2. Stewart Macaulay, Law and the Behavioural Sciences: Is There Any There There? 6 Law & Pol'y 149 (1984).

3. Thomas Kuhn, The Structure of Scientific Revolutions (Chicago: University of Chicago Press, 1970). Although disagreements between social scientists provided Kuhn with the stimulus to discover similar problems in the progress of natural science, the notion of paradigms was designed to explain why

324   AMERICAN BAR FOUNDATION RESEARCH JOURNAL   1986:323

all easy to make out the shape of things to come. What appears to be happening is something like this: There is increasing rejection of a starting point that juxtaposes the terms "law" and "society"—however these are concretized —and then investigates the way they "influence" or "affect" each other. At the same time, at a more fundamental level the field is becoming more self-conscious about what it means to say that law in some way 'fits' or 'corresponds' to the society or social context in which it is found. This "domain assumption'"[4] of scholars of law and society is now itself being called into question. Whereas the previous generation of scholars battled to show the structural and interactionist sources of legal behavior, which alone could explain the continued discovery and rediscovery of "gaps" between legal rules and social action,[5] their successors disdain the prize for which they fought.[6]

There is an obvious risk of oversimplification in drawing too clear a distinction between the older and newer paradigms.[7] Adherents of the older approach are likely to complain that what is portrayed is a travesty of their position, whilst the diverse criticisms and alternatives to their work may be united merely by lying outside the mainstream rather than by what they have in common.[8] But in the current ferment of intellectual activity a few broad contrasts may be detected. These concern, first, the questions thought worth asking about "law and society"; second, the way the relationship between "law and society" is conceptualized; and finally, what is meant by "law" and "society." I shall try to show how these problems are connected.

Although mainstream studies of law and society used a framework within which it was possible to ask "how society affected law" as well as "how law affected society," there is little doubt that the stress was on the latter.[9] The reason for this was the strong practical interest in helping law achieve

---

practitioners of the "hard" sciences were *less* dogged by controversies over fundamentals than social scientists.

4. See Alvin Gouldner, The Coming Crisis of Western Sociology 52–54 (London: Heinemann, 1971; N.Y.: Basic Books, 1970).

5. Nelken, *supra* note 1.

6. See for example John Griffiths, Is Law Important? 54 N.Y.U. L. Rev. 339 (1979); Robert Gordon, Critical Legal Histories, 36 Stan. L. Rev. 57 (1984); Franz von Benda-Beckmann, Why Law Does Not Behave, *in* H. Finkler, ed., Papers of the Symposium on Folklore and Legal Pluralism 232, 11th ICAES, Ottawa, Canada, 1984.

7. Leading writers such as Richard Abel, Marc Galanter, Stewart Macaulay, or Dave Trubek were at the forefront of the old paradigm and are active in current attempts to revise it. But in some of their recent work there may be detected a defensiveness about the achievements of earlier law and society studies as correct only for the period at which they were written, which can sound like a lament for a failing paradigm. See, e.g., Marc Galanter, Vision and Revision: A Comment on Yngvesson, 1985 Wis. L. Rev. 647. However, the notion of legal pluralism has always been central to Marc Galanter's work, no doubt because of his concurrent research interest in Asian legal systems. See, e.g., Marc Galanter, Justice in Many Rooms: Courts, Private Ordering, and Indigenous Law, 19 J. Legal Pluralism 1 (1981).

8. For further discussion see David Nelken, Changing Paradigms in the Sociology of Law, European University Institute Conference on Autopoiesis in Law and Society, Dec. 1985 (forthcoming in the Conference Materials, ed. Gunther Teubner) and his What Next in the Sociology of Law? George Lurcey Lecture, Amherst, Mass., Mar. 28, 1986.

9. In the influential casebook, Lawrence Friedman & Stewart Macaulay, eds., Law and the Behavioral Sciences (2d ed. Indianapolis: Bobbs-Merrill, 1977), chapter 3, entitled On the Impact of Law on Society, is followed by chapter 4's On the Impact of Society on Law.

desired measures for social change.[10] The new approach, by contrast, is more interested in social constraints on law, possibly because of the mounting evidence of the limits on legal intervention.[11] But it is more than a matter of changed practical concerns. Whether it is plausible to ask about law's "effects" on society may be debatable, but it is certainly unproductive to talk about society's "effect" or "impact" on law, because the idea of "society" necessarily includes law.

This new focus has led to a move away from conceiving the relationship between "law" and "society" as an *external* one towards investigating instead the way "society" is produced *within* "law." Instead of demanding that law be placed in its social context, interest has grown in the context which is assumed and reproduced by law as a bearer of traditions[12] or of ideological constructions[13] or forms of discourse.[14] In consequence, the line between law and society becomes difficult to detect. Law comes to be seen as "imbricated"[15] within social practices or relationships or even as "constituting"[16] social reality, in a way that poses problems for the previous style of research. And although mainstream scholars try to "domesticate" some of these challenges by arguing that they call for empirical investigation of law's ideological "effects" on society,[17] proponents of the newer approach continue to appear uninterested in reformulating its concerns in a way that would promote compatability between the older and newer paradigms. An especially important stimulus to the collapse of the "law" and "society" distinction was the debate within Marxist theory that concluded (though not without dissent) that since law belonged to both the "base" and the "superstructure" such a distinction had little to offer the social study of law.[18] This was generalized to the broader field of sociology of law

---

10. According to Macaulay, *supra* note 2.

11. There are numerous studies addressing or confronted by this problem. See, e.g., David Nelken The Limits of the Legal Process: A Study of Landlords, Law and Crime (New York: Academic Press, 1983), and *id.,* Legislation and Its Constraints: A Case Study of the 1965 British Rent Act, *in* Adam Podgorecki, Christopher J. Whelan, & Dinesh Khosla, eds., Legal Systems and Social Systems, (London & Dover, N.H.: Croom Helm, 1985).

12. See Martin Krygier, Traditions and Their Types, paper presented to the Australian Political Studies Association Conference, Aug. 1984.

13. This is a somewhat inadequate summary of the approach to law taken by critical legal scholars. Although there is as yet no good introduction to the underlying assumptions of these writers, some insights may be gained from David Kairys's The Politics of Law: A Progressive Critique (New York: Pantheon Books, 1982), and the 1984 *Stanford Law Review* special issue (vol. 32, nos. 1-2) on critical legal scholarship.

14. See Peter Goodrich, Rhetoric as Jurisprudence, 4 Oxford J. Legal Stud. 88 (1984).

15. Edward P. Thompson, Whigs and Hunters (Harmondsworth, Eng.: Penguin, 1975; N.Y.: Pantheon Books, 1975), "'law was deeply imbricated within the very basis of productive relations which would have been inoperable without this law'" (at 261), and cf. E. P. Thompson, The Poverty of Theory 288 (London: Merlin, 1978; N.Y.: Monthly Review Press, 1978).

16. See, for an extreme view of this CLS conception of law, Peter Gabel, Reification in Legal Reasoning, *in* 3 Research in Law and Sociology 25 (Greenwich, Conn.: JAI Press, 1980).

17. See especially David Trubek, Where the Action Is: Critical Legal Studies and Empiricism, 36 Stan. L. Rev. 575 (1984).

18. Raymond Williams, Marxism and Literature (Oxford: Oxford University Press, 1977); G. A. Cohen, Karl Marx's Theory of History (Oxford: Oxford University Press, 1978; Princeton, N.J.: Princeton University Press, 1978); Richard Kinsey, Marxism and the Law, 5 Brit. J. Law & Soc'y 202

so as to bolster resistance to any attempt to locate law on only one side of any postulated dichotomy between law and society, structure and action, idea and practice, etc.[19] What is less clear, however, is whether this disillusion with research into the "effects" of law represents a downgrading in the significance of law or presupposes an even more ambitious conception of law, for example as the key ideological form which encapsulates a society's self-understanding.[20]

All this is linked to recent theoretical developments in what is understood by "law" and "society." In place of the mainstream notion of law as a system of commands or resources, rules or norms, law is now seen increasingly as a framework of interpretation,[21] a specialized discourse,[22] or a source of (exclusionary) reasons for actions.[23] Such changes in the definition of law have implications for the way law is connected to society and how such a relationship is to be investigated. Of particular interest for the books to be discussed here has been the revival of interest in "legal pluralism." Mainstream writers were, of course, well aware of the multiple normative systems that coexist with the official legal system, but the critics concentrate less on the way the formal and informal interact with each other and more on the sense in which they *constitute* a total (yet pluralist) normative order even in contemporary Western societies.[24]

Why should any of this internecine academic debate be of wider interest? Certainly, it is interesting and instructive to see how new ideas emerge from intellectual struggle, and I shall be particularly concerned in this review with the problems that arise when an attempt is made to use evidence to discredit a style of inquiry whilst remaining within its own framework of as-

---

(1978); Hugh Collins, Marxism and Law (Oxford: Clarendon Press, 1982; N.Y.: Oxford University Press, 1982); and Steven Lukes, Can the Base Be Distinguished from the Superstructure? *in* D. Miller & L. Siedontop, eds., The Nature of Political Theory (Oxford: Oxford University Press, 1983).

19. See the articles by Robert Gordon and Franz von Benda-Beckmann, both cited *supra* note 6.

20. Thus, while a critical legal scholar such as Robert Gordon insists on the "indeterminacy" of law, he goes on to add that "the critical claim of interdeterminacy is simply that none of these regularities are *necessary* consequences of the adoption of a given system of rules." Gordon, *supra* note 6, at 124. Whilst expressing some uncertainty whether law is in fact influential, by diffusing legal consciousness through society (at 121) he soon makes up his mind that the forms which go into the "constitution of legal relations are manufactured, reproduced and modified for special purposes by everyone, at every level all the time." *Id.* at 123. Similar ambivalence within the critical camp may be detected in the debate between Kennedy and Gabel that introduces the *Stanford Law Review* special issue, *supra* note 13 (see Peter Gabel & Duncan Kennedy, Roll Over Beethoven, at 1). On the other hand, writers such as John Griffiths, *supra* note 6, whose disillusion with law's effects stems more directly from a review of empirical sociological findings, also create ambiguity by affirming *both* that law's effects are unimportant or undemonstrable *and* that law nonetheless plays a vital role as a "collective good" which allows society's members to cooperate without the fear of "free-riders."

21. Ronald Dworkin, Law as Interpretation, 60 Tex. L. Rev. 527 (1982).

22. See, e.g., Bernard S. Jackson, Semiotics and Legal Theory (London & Boston: Routledge & Kegan Paul, 1985).

23. Joseph Raz, Practical Reason and Norms (London: Hutchinson, 1975).

24. See Marc Galanter, Justice in Many Rooms, *supra* note 7; John Griffiths, What Is Legal Pluralism? paper presented at the meeting of the Law and Society Association, Amherst, Mass., June 1981; and the important papers by P. Fitzpatrick: Law, Plurality and Underdevelopment, *in* D. Sugarman, ed., Legality, Ideology and the State (London: Academic Press, 1983); Marxism and Legal Pluralism, 1 Australian J.L. & Soc'y 45 (1983); and Law and Societies, 22 Osgoode Hall L.J. 115 (1984).

sumptions. But there are also important practical and political implications, even if these are not always intended by the protagonists. For different images of law and society necessarily condition the strategies recommended for producing social change and the extent to which regulation of social activity is thought desirable or possible. This is particularly relevant in the current period of political and economic retrenchment. But the issue is also a timeless one. The question of *whether* and *how* law fits a given society is closely bound up with proposals for deciding how law *should* fit society. The recurrent concern generated by discovering gaps between the law in books and the law in action represent one of the less interesting examples of this linkage.[25] More fascinating are the attempts by sociologists of law to ground what has been called "a science of morality" on the facts of social order.[26] Whilst a little learning concerning the social roots of legal order can lead to a loss of legitimacy and respect for law, serious engagement with the problem, on the other hand, promotes secular attempts to found the sacredness of law on its harmony with the needs of the times.[27] But such practical concerns, whether modest or ambitious, would appear to presuppose that there is a determinate and determinable relationship between law and society. How far the newer approach can retain the same concerns whilst attacking the previous presuppositions remains to be seen.

2. Two Studies of Pluralism in Modern Society

Many if by no means all of these issues are raised by two valuable recent contributions to the sociology of law: Stuart Henry's *Private Justice* and Timothy O'Hagan's *The End of Law?* These books are an interesting contrast in themselves, showing the range of literatures and approaches being drawn on in current work. Henry's book (with which I will be mainly concerned) is primarily a report of an empirical investigation into methods of workplace discipline in a variety of organizational settings. O'Hagan, on the other hand, tries to justify the need for law in modern society from a largely left-wing point of view, and draws his arguments from writings on

25. See David Nelken, Law in Action or Living Law? Back to the Beginning in the Sociology of Law, 4 Legal Stud. 157 (1984).

26. Emile Durkheim, The Division of Labor in Society, trans. George Simpson (New York: Free Press, 1964). "The same method must be followed in ethics. A moral fact is normal for a determined social type when it is observed in the average of that species; it is pathological in antithetical circumstances. That is what makes the moral character of the particular rules vary; they depend upon the nature of social types." *Id.* at 432.

For an illustration of the way Durkheim employed this idea in political controversy, see Steven Lukes, Durkheim's Individualism and the Intellectuals, 17 Pol. Stud. 19 (1969).

27. Jurgen Habermas, Theory and Practice, trans. John Viertel (Boston: Beacon Press, 1973; London, HEB, 1974); Roberto Unger, Knowledge and Politics (New York, Free Press, 1975), and Law in Modern Society (New York: Free Press, 1976); and Alasdair McIntyre, After Virtue: A Study in Moral Theory (London: Duckworth, 1981; Notre Dame, Ind.: University of Notre Dame, 1981, 2d ed. 1984). On this view the sociology of law becomes almost a form of secular natural law, in pursuit of the "immanent rationality" which connects law and social life (to use Gordon's phrase in his paper prepared for the European University Institute Conference on Autopoiesis in Law and Society, R. Gordon, Questions of a Fascinated Skeptic, 7.)

328   AMERICAN BAR FOUNDATION RESEARCH JOURNAL   1986:323

social theory, jurisprudence, and civil liberties.[28] Nonetheless, these writers do have much in common. Both are attacking what they regard as an unsound orthodoxy.[29] For Henry this is the fundamental methodological assumption of much of the literature in the sociology and anthropology of law—that law corresponds to its social milieu. For O'Hagan this is the Marxist or libertarian rejection of the need for law in favor of either communal or market autonomy. Both writers share roughly similar political aspirations; they seek the basis for a viable communitarian form of association within the all-embracing influence of the interventionist state. It is also interesting that in advancing their arguments, both writers criticize those approaches that claim a necessary correspondence of legal structures with social structures. Henry does this by showing the multiplicity of forms of legal and social order involved in the maintenance of workplace discipline in modern society. O'Hagan builds his case against Marxist theorists, who claim that law in capitalist society must necessarily represent and serve capitalism, by demonstrating law's potential for doing more than these theorists allow.

But these books are also significantly different in style and content and therefore reach in some ways rather different conclusions. Whereas Henry's work is contemporary and descriptive, O'Hagan's is historical and prescriptive. In one way it could be said that where O'Hagan ends, Henry begins—by setting out to explore the empirical interactions between the sort of partially autonomous social orders whose viability O'Hagan wishes to protect. On the other hand, through his exegesis of Hegel, Marx, and Tönnies, O'Hagan provides us with a larger theoretical framework for understanding the necessary continuation of pluralistic orders in modern society and provides the jurisprudential justification for this that Henry's work lacks. The authors also use characteristically different methods to arrive at their conclusions concerning the impossibility of isolating a communalistic or any other self-contained social order within modern society. O'Hagan claims that it is impossible to achieve a socialist *gemeinschaft* in modern society because problems such as the growth of information technology mean that privacy can never be safeguarded from interventionist governments nor protected without their help. Henry, by contrast, shows the implausibility of creating an encysted arena of solidarity by revealing the unavoidable mutual interpenetration of social and organizational settings.

In many respects the approaches of these books may be thought of as broadly complementary; they provide us with both normative arguments

---

28. O'Hagan's title is rhetorical. His aim is to show why even within a broadly Marxist perspective law must be seen as essential.

29. It is probably no accident that both writers are slightly maverick in the research interests which bring them to this field. This is especially true of Henry, who comes to the sociology of law having previously investigated informal organization in the context of the "black economy," amateur crime, and self-help organizations. O'Hagan too is unusual in bringing together ideas from social theory and jurisprudence in a re-examination of Marxist ideas about law.

and empirical evidence about the relationship between legal and social orders. But their different methods, as will be seen, lead them to different conclusions about the scope for successful legal intervention. Henry mounts a sustained attack on ideal-typical theorizing as opposed to theoretically informed descriptions of empirical detail. He rejects such theorizing even as a heuristic device, because it obscures what should be highlighted: the facts of interdependence between social orders rather than the extent to which they diverge from some a priori model. On the other hand, O'Hagan is happy to employ typologies of law and society throughout his argument, perhaps because he is more interested in persuading us that there must be an overlap between the characteristic forms of social organization in different historical periods which can be demonstrated even with the use of ideal types. The part played by the rediscovery of pluralism in each book is correspondingly different. Henry wants to convince us of the need to adopt modes of theorizing that are fully alive to the existence of pluralistic orders and able to offer an integrated theoretical approach to such mutually constitutive areas of social life. For him, pluralism is a *fact* that raises problems for existing *theory*. O'Hagan, however, is more interested in showing how pluralism raises problems for the legal regulation of social order. For his purposes it is *law*, not *theory*, that is needed to (re)integrate plural orders. It can do this only by embracing a logic of intervention not reducible to that of any local constitutive orders. Because of these contrasts in their methodologies, the problems raised by Henry's book have to do mostly with its empirical attack on mainstream work in the sociology of law, whereas O'Hagan's work opens up interesting political issues that will become significant if the renewed emphasis on pluralism is to have practical implications. I shall deal with each of these topics in turn.

3. The Attack on Correspondence Theory

Henry's *Private Justice* is an ambitious attempt to interweave theoretical inquiry and empirical investigation into a combined attack on mainstream work in the sociology of law. After two theoretical chapters that consider past theories of legal pluralism, he goes on to describe five contrasting examples of workplace discipline ranging from the type he calls "punitive authoritarian" discipline, which is found most commonly in small firms with weak unions, to "celebrative-collective discipline," which characterizes small-scale cooperative type organizations. He provides comprehensive accounts of the contexts, rules, and procedures, as well as attitudes toward crime, deviance, justice, and sanctions characteristic of each type of discipline. But all this has a definite theoretical purpose, as is evident from the book's subtitle—*Towards Integrated Theorizing in the Sociology of Law.* As this suggests, Henry's real interest lies not in the varieties of workplace discipline or even labor law in general but in developing an adequate approach to theorizing in the sociology of law. Yet although his empirical material is carefully harnessed to this purpose, there is much to learn from

330   AMERICAN BAR FOUNDATION RESEARCH JOURNAL   1986:323

the book about each of the organizational settings he investigated, and there is no sense of his empirical data being preselected so as to fit the procrustean bed of theorizing.

But there is more in this than meets the eye. For if Henry had provided too "tidy" an account of his findings it would have been against the point of his exercise. His theoretical argument concerning the mutual interpenetration of different plural orders *requires* him to display the full *untidy* complexity of each network of discipline. In this way he hopes to persuade us of the inadequacy of more schematic theoretical approaches. Henry uses his empirical material to show us how he was forced to move beyond the original hypotheses that had guided him in framing his investigation. As will be seen, however, Henry's argument moves uneasily between the claim that his findings provided no support for existing approaches in the sociology of law and the far stronger assertion that his data offers the basis of the new approach he calls "integrated theorizing." It is, therefore, perhaps most useful to understand Henry's book as situated in the transition between older and newer paradigms in the sociology of law since this vacillation is exactly what would be expected during a period of paradigm change.[30] It explains why his argument is couched in terms of the concerns and methods of the preceding paradigm whilst it reaches out to a new framework of assumptions.

Seen in this light the most interesting issue raised by Henry's book is how far the findings which he claims cannot be explained by the previous paradigm really do force a choice between old and new ways of theorizing in the sociology of law. The transitional quality of Henry's work (which is written almost as if he were trying to persuade himself to move from one position to the next) is evident throughout the book. The title—*Private Justice*—correctly describes his interest in relatively localized forms of workplace discipline. But the whole point of his argument is that there cannot in fact be any such thing as private justice. His conclusion is that even the most localized relationships are shaped by the social controls emanating from the state and the official legal system. Thus it would appear that Henry is at first committed to explaining what he eventually explains away. But in other respects Henry is surely right to keep the term, which at least requires explanation at the level of ideological constructions (and which is more useful than competing concepts such as "informal" or "lay justice"). For an important weakness of the argument of early legal pluralists was to neglect the problem of how the centralized system succeeds in so shaping competing normative orders that these orders come to be responded to or treated as merely private.[31]

30. The stimulus for this way of reading Henry's book was provided by Steven Lukes's discussion of Mathew A. Crenson, The Unpolitics of Air Pollution: A Study of Non-Decision Making in the Cities (Baltimore: John Hopkins University Press, 1971), as a study operating on the margin between what he calls the two-dimensional and three-dimensional conceptions of power. See Steven Lukes, Power: A Radical View 31 (London & N.Y.: Macmillan, 1974).

31. For an excellent attempt to overcome this drawback of legal pluralist work, from within the Marxist tradition, see Boaventura de Sousa Santos, On Modes of Production of Law and Social Power,

The same ambivalence can be detected throughout Henry's attack on what he treats as "the correspondence thesis" in the sociology of law. He rejects outright the idea that there is necessarily a match between types of law and types of society or social organization. But the extent of his rejection of this idea is hardly clear. For though his findings lead him to deny the evidence of correspondence between hypothesized forms of workplace discipline and the social context in which they are found, this does not show that it is necessary to reject the very idea of correspondence itself. Henry's emphasis on the importance of plural legal orders can therefore be seen either as representing an alternative to established ways of studying the relationship between law and society or as merely a sophistication of these. At the outset of his book Henry asserts: "Arguably the most important contribution made by sociologists and anthropologists to theorising about law is to identify the structural conditions that appear to give rise to particular kinds of law" (at 1). But by the end of the book he argues that his findings have led him to reappraise this approach drastically. His "major conclusion and indeed the most overriding of the study" is to reject the assumption he took from the "considerable literature in the sociology and anthropology of law" (at 220) that suggested particular social structures have corresponding types of law. Contrary to his expectations, different types of organizational structures at work did *not* have their own corresponding systems of discipline. Instead, his case studies show that each organizational structure accommodated aspects of the whole range of theoretically identifiable forms of private justice. Thus, organizations that had established formal disciplinary procedures also relied on informal methods of discipline whilst, at the other extreme, cooperative groups drew regularly on the official legal system whenever they felt necessary.

Rarely has a null hypothesis been presented with such enthusiasm! But does Henry's finding that forms of workplace discipline fail to correspond entirely to organizational structures really demand the wholesale reappraisal of theoretical perspectives, which he claims it does? Henry is, I think, right in identifying the correspondence thesis as lying at the heart or near the heart of much work in the sociology of law.[32] But serious doubts may be raised about the meaning, point, and scope of his use of empirical findings in challenging this thesis and about the way in which these findings are used to support his theoretical critique.

Above all, perhaps, it is unclear what Henry means by the correspondence thesis. This is because he does not tell us which version he takes

---

13 Int'l J. Soc. L. 299 (1985). For a historical attack on this problem, see Harry Arthurs, Without the Law: Administrative Justice and Legal Pluralism in 19th Century England (Toronto: University of Toronto Press, 1985), and see also his Understanding Labour Law: the Debate over "Industrial Pluralism" *in* Current Legal Problems 83 (London: Stevens, 1985).

32. This may be evidenced from both the title and content of textbooks in the field, such as Robert L. Kidder's Connecting Law and Society (Englewood Cliffs, N.J.: Prentice-Hall, 1983). It is hard so see how Marxist theorizing can avoid this focus either, whatever the problems it raises. See E. P. Thompson's discussion of the correspondence thesis in Marxist theory in his The Poverty of Theory, *supra* note 15, at 349-52.

332   AMERICAN BAR FOUNDATION RESEARCH JOURNAL   1986:323

himself to be disproving. His reference to the "considerable literature" could, and perhaps is intended to, encompass the very different theoretical positions of Marx, Durkheim, and Weber. Coming to more contemporary studies, it is uncertain whether Henry's quarrel is with structural, functional, interactionist, or hermeneutic ways of understanding the correspondence between legal and social structures.[33] He appears to be arguing mainly with attempts to make structural connections between law and social organization, but his rhetoric would also deny the possibility of the interactionist linkages between interest groups and the mobilization of law that his findings themselves display.[34]

The point of Henry's argument is also in some doubt. Because he does not identify which theorists he is addressing, we do not know whether he is more concerned with those (like Durkheim[35] or Sorokin[36]) who tried to show a link between the "law in books" and social structure, or with those more interested in proving correspondence at the level of the "law in action" (such as Lawrence Friedman).[37] Because his hypotheses about the shape of discipline in the workplace were based on a priori expectations of correspondence and, moreover, were particularly concerned with macrosocial linkages, much of his evidence has the familiar ring of the discovery that law in action is at variance with law in the books. But since his expressed interest is in the degree of correspondence in practice between organizational structures and patterns of social control, rather than in legal rules as such, he does appear to be committed to proving that it is law in action that does not operate as would be expected. One of the dangers of Henry's proposed "integrated theorising" is that it may conflate the three separate problems of explaining law in books, law in action, and the relationship between them.

Other ambiguities of Henry's project are still more serious. Different theorists have tried to show correspondence between social structures and either the rules, procedures, or functions of law; sometimes they have tried to show why these may vary independently.[38] But it is not clear which of these projects Henry is trying to undermine. Henry tells us he is interested in the different forms of "social control" in each organizational setting, then he describes how each expected (or ideal-typical?) mode of control is in fact penetrated by alien forms of reasoning and external sources of disci-

---

33. The mainstream approach, according to both its critics (see Gordon, *supra* note 6) and its sympathizers (see Robert Summers, Instrumentalism and American Legal Theory (Ithaca, N.Y.: Cornell University Press, 1982)), incorporates an amalgam of functionalist and instrumental approaches to correspondence.

34. Henry neglects this point, perhaps because these are linkages between powerful groups and disciplinary decision making rather than between organizational types and types of social control.

35. See Durkheim, *supra* note 26, and Durkheim and the Law, ed. Steven Lukes & Andrew Scull (Oxford: Martin Robertson, 1983).

36. Pitirim A. Sorokin, 11 Social and Cultural Dynamics ch. 15 (New York: American Books, 1937).

37. Lawrence Friedman, The Legal System: A Social Science Perspective (New York: Russell Sage Foundation, 1973).

38. See especially Karl Renner's discussion of the form and function of law in the Institutions of Private Law and Their Social Function (London: Routledge & Kegan Paul, 1976).

pline. The metaphor of penetration is used to describe such disparate matters as reference to external forums for adjudication, drawing on due process considerations in internal decision making, and the fact that those involved in such decision making have prior experience of official courts or
tribunals outside the organization. Added together, his examples certainly
show that workplace discipline relies on a variety of legal forms and
forums. But it might be possible to make more sense of each pattern of discipline if attention were restricted to one feature of social control at a time.
Why should Henry assume that all evidence of reference to external forms
of control disproves the correspondence thesis? Is it reasonable to expect
each setting to have its own distinctive and self-contained type of dispute
processing and discipline or only that each should have a distinctive way of
drawing on the modes of control available? Many apparent examples of
noncorrespondence can be dealt with relatively easily. For example, someone sympathetic to the mainstream approach could reinterpret much of
Henry's evidence as support for the well-established argument that informal and formal types of social control vary inversely.[39]

Leaving these conceptual problems aside, Henry also does not make it
easy to determine the scope of his attack. He never indicates in what proportion of cases the hypothesized correspondence between types of organization and types of discipline breaks down. In fact his methodology does
not even enable him to do this because he has sampled the *accounts* given by
participants concerning the range of different methods of discipline they
have witnessed, rather than independently assessing the occasions of their
use. All but proponents of the most extreme versions of the correspondence
thesis would be willing to concede some divergence in practice; there is after
all a difference between correspondence and perfect correspondence. And
in all his settings, with the exception of the cooperative organizations he
studied, workplace discipline did mainly take the form he predicted. The
exception of the cooperatives (with which, it is true, Henry is particularly
concerned) may only represent Henry's idealized expectations about communal self-sufficiency within cooperatives rather than any reasonable hypothesis that could be attributed to correspondence theory. But even if we
accept Henry's claims for the purpose of argument, what has he proven?
His case study is drawn from a very specific area of social life and his particular examples can make no claim to be representative, even of workplace
discipline.[40] There may be something about labor law more generally that
can explain the peculiar mix of forms of social control Henry has discovered. Possibly there is also something special about labor law in Britain

39. See, e.g., Richard Schwartz, Social Factors in the Development of Legal Control: A Case Study
of Two Israeli Settlements, 63 Yale L.J. 471 (1954); Donald Black, The Behavior of Law (New York:
Academic Press, 1976). This argument has of course incurred considerable criticism but its relevance to
Henry's findings should have led him to give it some consideration. It would also have served to highlight the problem of drawing the boundaries of correspondence theory.
   Does a claim of determined and determinable *non*correspondence count as within or without the
theory?
40. See Peter Fitzpatrick's review of Henry's *Private Justice,* 13 Int'l J. Soc. L. 212 (1985).

that makes it incompatible with any version of the correspondence thesis. After all, it is particularly true of this sphere of law in Britain that it uses various forms of direct and indirect state intervention in a context of supposed nonintervention.[41]

It would be quite possible, therefore, to see Henry's findings, at best, as merely exceptions to the ambit of correspondence theory. The fact that Henry does not take this route suggests that he relies more on his theoretical critique of correspondence theory than on his particular empirical findings. His findings are offered as illustrations of a wider argument against any approach that fails to incorporate an appreciation of the interaction between the parts and the whole in understanding social life: "dichotomous theorising results in the conception of a range of forms of private justice, each of which is seen as the product of a certain kind of organisational structure and each as operating at a different level of formality. . . . such theorising not only misunderstands the nature of factory law, but is actually part of the process whereby it is constituted as a reality" (at 71). The search for correspondence is not merely wrong, but outdated! "What has occurred . . . is no less than a Kuhnian style paradigm revolution whereby theorising whose analysis proceeds in any one dimension alone will be ignored rather than debated, discredited rather than discussed" (at 66). But what exactly is Henry offering us in his alternative "integrated theorising" approach? And how does his argument relate to the characteristic differences between the older and newer paradigms in the social study of law that I outlined at the start? Henry's critique draws support from all three contrasts between the older and newer paradigms. This leads him to reject the task of searching for a determinate relationship between law and society on the basis that there are, instead, numerous "semi-autonomous" social fields, each conditioned both by their internal influences and those emanating from fields external to them.[42] The trouble here is that this approach can easily turn out to be a restatement of the problem rather than a theoretical advance. Henry hardly improves matters by applying the notion of semi-autonomous fields to such conceptually incommensurable objects as "the state," "the firm," "the economy," and "individual workers." He does not explain whether each of these possesses autonomy in the sense of actual freedom of action or only in the sense that each may be analytically distinguished from other theoretical objects. As a result, the numerous forms of interdependencies that, according to Henry, escape the purview of correspondence theory, may represent no more than conceptual choices by the theorist when to separate or synthesize these conceptions of the different "agents" and "structures" under investigation.[43] In a sense Henry would be the first to admit this. He claims that many of his categories represent *choices* by the

---

41. Bob Hepple et al., The Making of Labour Law in Europe: A Comparative Study of Nine Countries up to 1945 (Netherlands: Kluwer, 1986).
42. Sally Falk Moore, Law as Process ch. 2 (London & Boston: Routledge & Kegan Paul, 1978).
43. See the acute discussion in Steven Lukes, Essays in Social Theory ch. 1 (London: Macmillan, 1977).

agents to view the world in particular ways rather than structural constraints over their actions. He argues that the alleged structural influences that form such an important plank of correspondence theory represent no more than the imposition by theorists and agents alike of structure upon reality.[44] But because he tells us so little about whether these structures can *in this way* exert real influence over the choices and opportunities open to agents,[45] it is hard to see why this forces him to break with correspondence theorizing.

To sum up: Henry's argument is that it is a fundamental mistake to distinguish types of law and social control and attempt to match them to differentiated organizational and social forms, and he offers his own empirical study as confirmation of this. But, although his work is presented as a test of the older approach rather than as an illustration of his new position, it wavers uncertainly between the two. The chapters of the book are actually divided up on the basis of the *expected* differences between workplace discipline in each organizational setting, and charts are provided detailing the characteristic features (or mix of features) of workplace discipline in each of these settings as if these represent descriptive *aide-memoires* rather than discredited hypotheses. At various points, Henry even talks as if he were still committed to the correspondence thesis. Thus he explains: "the same kinds of problems arise with those companies and organisations whose structure leads to them adopting a more overtly participative approach" (at 131). Henry's attempt to stand simultaneously inside and outside correspondence theory leads to an an uncertain combination of theoretical critique and empirical evidence. What remains is a provocative and often fascinating account of the diversity of forms of workplace discipline among and within different organizational settings.

4. Pluralism and Politics

I have concentrated so far on the theoretical issues raised by Henry's attempt to revive pluralist thinking in the sociology of law. But there are also some important practical and political issues to be considered. If it is true, as some critical legal scholars have argued, that "law" and "society" is a peculiarly liberal distinction, bound up with the separation of "the state" from "civil society,"[46] the concern to dismantle such a distinction is itself a

---

44. There are times when Henry's "integrated theorising" seems to conflate rather than overcome the problems deriving from analytical dichotomies between macro and micro theorizing, official and local normative orders, and structural or action (including ethnomethodological) explanations. More fruitful work on these issues has been done in anthropological studies such as John Camaroff & Simon Roberts, Rules and Processes (Chicago: University of Chicago Press, 1981); cf. Robert M. Hayden, Rules, Processes, and Interpretations, 1984 A.B.F. Res. J. 469.

45. As argued by Unger in Law in Modern Society, *supra* note 27.

46. See, e.g., Gordon, *supra* note 6, at 124: "The whole point of the critics' critique is that the 'economy' isn't something separable from the 'law' which reacts on law and is in turn reacted upon by it. The idea of their separation is a hallucinatory effect of the liberal reification of 'state' and 'market' (or public and private) into separate entities." But for arguments that this distinction is no illusion, see Niklas Luhmann, The Differentiation of Society (New York: Columbia University Press, 1982), or from a different perspective. B. de Sousa Santos, *supra* note 31.

significant political choice. Henry and O'Hagan see these issues differently. Whereas Henry uses evidence of pluralism as part of his attempt to strengthen the prospects for a more communalistic order, O'Hagan sees pluralism, as always within orthodox liberalism with its concern for the protection of diversity, as the very justification for liberal rather than collectivist forms of regulation.

Henry's practical interest lies in discovering what capitalist, and ostensibly more socialist, forms of organization actually involve in practice. Much of the apparently serendipitous path taken by his research can be explained by this interest, for if capitalist organizations had corresponding forms of social control and the same were true of socialist or communal ways of living, it might be possible to chart a way forward for his preferred form of life. In fact, as we know, he discovered that these forms of life could not be disassembled in this way. However, this is not the end of the story. Henry's political concerns are set out at greater length in a recent paper using the same empirical research into workplace discipline.[47] In this he takes issue with the claim of Richard Abel and others that moves toward informal justice necessarily end up supporting the master institutions of capitalist society.[48] Henry argues instead that the growth of communal forms of organization necessarily shapes capitalist institutions as well as being molded by them. He then discusses this in relation to the way the cooperative organizations he studied reinforced and helped constitute official law as well as being partially independent of it.

The points of comparison and contrast between the ways in which Henry and O'Hagan use evidence of pluralism is instructive in showing the different political implications that may be drawn from such evidence. Both Henry and O'Hagan are skeptical about the possibility of autonomous forms of life within capitalist society. For Henry such autonomy is just not possible, for O'Hagan it is not even desirable.[49] Both object to the alternative option of collectivism as a means of achieving viable communality and see pluralism as giving the lie to any plan for total transformation of society. As Henry's concluding lines show, he regards his findings as proving that the achievement of valued social change requires "revelation rather than revolution" (at 222). At the same time both writers deny that total transformation of the official legal order is actually necessary for the assertion of counterhegemonic values as represented by more communal forms of order.

But the points of divergence are again equally if not more significant. O'Hagan takes the existence of plural orders as providing the mandate for the limited but essential oversight characteristic of a *Rechtstaat*. In particular he sees the need for centralized law to correct the potential abuse of indi-

47. Stuart Henry, Community Justice, Capitalist Society and Human Agency: The Dialectics of Collective Law in the Cooperative, 19 Law & Soc'y Rev. 303 (1985).
48. Richard Abel, ed., The Politics of Informal Justice (2 vols. New York: Academic Press, 1982).
49. It is a pity that neither author refers to the insightful study by Philip Abrams and Andrew Mc Culloch, Communes, Sociology and Society (Cambridge, Eng. & N.Y.: Cambridge University Press, 1976), which bears directly on this point.

vidual rights within localized orders as well as to check the abuse of governmental power itself (but he offers little insight into how law can serve both
aims simultaneously). Henry is much less sanguine about the capacity of
centralized intervention to transform activity within localized social arenas
in predictable ways. His detailed descriptions of patterns of workplace discipline show the unexpected effects and feedback consequences of intervention, the likelihood of either avoidance or co-option by more powerful parties, and the difficulty of preventing procedures designed for one purpose
being used to achieve very different aims. O'Hagan is so intent on persuading us that there is no logical contradiction between the capacity for centralized intervention and the viability of pluralist orders that he fails to take
seriously Henry's point that the *interdependence* between central and local
orders also means that intervention often produces unpredictable results.
On the other hand, O'Hagan may be satisfied with a more modest conception of what local autonomy requires. For Henry any sort of constraint or
"penetration" by external influences is taken to represent a reduction in autonomy. But for O'Hagan autonomy is necessarily conditional on some specific constraints. In a particularly interesting reexamination of Tönnies'
ideas concerning *Gemeinschaft* and *Gesellschaft*, O'Hagan discusses the
possibility of "Gesellschaft unions" in capitalist societies and addresses the
question of how law can encourage and protect them.[50] Such unions fall
short of the self-governing communal organizations for which Henry
sought, but O'Hagan is more concerned with the classical liberal problem of
how to protect individuals' rights within groups, and their rights to form
groups, rather than Henry's attempt to defend the independence of plural
legal orders as such. In the end, therefore, political and theoretical concerns
shape each other. Henry starts from a pluralist conception of law and examines the social conditions of its reproduction; this focus is both cause and
consequence of his attempt to develop an integrated theory of legal and
social action. O'Hagan, on the other hand, works with a unitary idea of law
but sees pluralism as something that an appropriate form of law can help
maintain and reproduce.

Conclusions

Because both these books raise such significant issues it would be easy to
pay them the doubtful compliment of faint praise. Instead, their achievement should be taken as showing how much remains to be done in working
through both the theoretical and political implications of the rediscovery of
pluralism. At a theoretical level scholars in the mainstream will take some
convincing that Henry's findings could not be both discovered and reconciled with their own approaches. They might object that Henry's stress on
the constitutive character of plural orders can be easily translated into the

---

50. At 86–98. Whilst Tönnies can be used to support a variety of viewpoints it cannot be denied that
his major argument was that the simultaneous rise of the centralized state and individual rights would
depend on and accompany a decline in the power of intermediate groups and associations. See Ferdi-
nand Tönnies, Community and Association 109, 333 (London: Routledge & Paul, 1955).

more familiar language of mutual influences and interdependencies. This misapprehension, for I think it is one, is made possible by Henry's attempt to try and discredit the mainstream paradigm whilst accepting so many of its working assumptions. Other criticisms that may be levelled at Henry do at least make it more obvious that a choice does have to be made between the older and newer paradigms. For Henry's recommended theoretical approach requires the abandonment of the careful, piecemeal, but always testable mainstream methods for investigating the mutual effects of law and society in favor of a more holistic understanding that does not easily lend itself to the establishment of determinate relationships. Even on his chosen territory of legal pluralism, Henry, like other pluralists, may be criticized for failing to explain the special significance of centralized official law as more than merely *primus inter pares* amongst competing normative orders. Perhaps as a consequence of these difficulties in seeing what is distinctive about Henry's theoretical contribution, some of his practical conclusions would appear self-evident to others working in this field. It is hard to disagree with his claim that "any attempt to change society through merely changing formal laws must fail because formal law is only one part of an interrelated set of semi-autonomous constituent parts" (at 222).

Much the same applies to O'Hagan's vision of the *Rechtstaat*. Whilst it is important to show the theoretical and political "space" within Marxist jurisprudence for liberal values it remains a problem to show how liberalism can escape the logic of market or welfare capitalism with which it is so bound up. Nonetheless, putting the works of Henry and O'Hagan together may help to discover and support new forms of order that can incorporate liberal and communitarian values. For the key to this may lie in better appreciation of how local orders are both shaped by and help constitute the total normative order. This is a useful corrective to other recent work in the sociology of law that has tended towards a too radical separation between law and society. Thus it has been argued that law can only regulate social life by regulating itself.[51] Alternatively, it is claimed that law appears to regulate social life only by virtue of self-imposed constraints over our creative imagination.[52] The great merit of Henry and O'Hagan's arguments is to provide a stimulating way of moving beyond the paradigm concerned with law's "effects" on society without abandoning the enterprise of investigating how law enters into the production and reproduction of society. But the characteristics of any revised version of the sociology of law enterprise and the nature of its ambitions still remain far from settled.[53]

---

51. See the forthcoming papers of the European University Institute Conference on Autopoiesis in Law and Society, Dec. 1985, especially those by Luhmann.

52. Gabel, *supra* note 16.

53. See *supra* note 8.

[6]
Changing Paradigms in the Sociology of Law

> "System theories are not concerned with encouraging right action but rather with the meaning-based systems-building connections among actions."
> (Luhmann, 1982: 107)

> "Use of the concept of autonomy is motivated by [the] answer to the question of why the ability to set the terms for legal discussion matters." (Lempert, supra: 175)

My aim in this paper is to place the theory of autopoiesis within the larger theoretical corpus the work of Niklas Luhmann in order to consider its potential contribution to a paradigm change in the sociology of law. This means that, unlike some other contributors, I shall not be attempting to develop or work with the theory as such; nor, on the other hand, do I try to refute it. I shall also have little to say about the controversial implications of the theory of autopoiesis for legal regulation or the design of new strategies for legal intervention, even though my initial interest in this work was certainly kindled by such issues (Nelken 1983; 1985). This is partly because this subject has already been well covered by other contributors, including an explicit discussion of the theory of autopoiesis as compared to the findings of Anglo-American studies on the implementation of law (Clune, 1987). But it also can suggest that reconsideration of Luhmann's larger theoretical approach may reveal other routes for observing and initiating contact between law and other sub-systems than are allowed for by those who draw policy conclusions from autopoietic theory alone.

My interest lies instead in the theoretical problem of formulating the relationship between "law" and "society". My paper has most in common therefore with those contributors who have sought to pose questions for the theory of autopoiesis from perspectives informed by one or other position within Anglo-American sociology of law (e.g., Gordon 1985; Lempert, supra; Trubek, 1985). In particular I shall be following the lead given by Richard Lempert in the careful paper in which he compares and contrasts the theory of autopoiesis with what he takes to be the relevant features of a mainstream Anglo-American approach to the sociology of law (Lempert, supra). However, there are a number of significant differences between Lempert's assumptions and aims and those of this paper. My goal is to investigate and to clarify what is at stake in the theoretical disagreements between Lempert and Luhmann.

Lempert devotes most of his effort to examining autopoiesis as a vision or version of *legal autonomy*, although he does at points (somewhat inconsistently) concede that these two concepts may not have been intended to serve the same theoretical purpose. He concludes that the view of legal autonomy assumed or implied in the theory of autopoiesis (insofar as there is one) is less tenable than that of the Anglo-American perspective he advances.[1] By contrast, I shall focus on the differences between the concepts so as to show why they are *not* to be equated and how they reflect different theoretical assumptions and practical concerns (as suggested by my introductory quotations). I shall develop my argument by drawing on Luhmann's writings on the theory of social systems in addition to the work he presented at the Autopoiesis Conference (to which Lempert's considerations were confined). On this basis I shall consider the feasibility of *reconciling* the notions of autonomy and autopoiesis *within Luhmann's theory*. Finally, I shall come to the main purpose of this paper which is to argue that the disagreement between Lempert and Luhmann rests on and can contribute to paradigm change in the sociology of law. With slight exaggeration, it may be said that while Lempert comes to praise the Anglo-American framework for studying "law and society", I come to bury it.[2] Because of the difficulties of the subject my argument will necessarily be somewhat complex and tentative. In brief it runs as follows.

I shall claim that autopoiesis is to be seen as a further development of what Lempert understands by legal autonomy. But though Luhmann's theory of autopoiesis therefore presupposes a considerable degree of autonomy, it does *not*, as Lempert suggests, assume that it can or must be absolute. But more than this, I shall argue that the current approach to understanding legal autonomy within the Anglo-American mainstream paradigm recommended by Lempert is itself theoretically unsatisfactory

---

[1] A number of other contributors have been persuaded by Lempert's arguments or else sympathized with his criticisms (see, for example, Dupuy, supra; Gordon, 1985; Trubek, 1985).

[2] In fairness it should be said that Lempert did not intend to deal with the wider issues raised here. But my argument, as will be seen, reflects the fact that his version of empirical sociology of law makes it too easy to sidestep these issues.

and needs to be replaced by the sort of framework used by Luhmann in his general sociology of law. It can be seen, therefore, that though I agree with Lempert that a comparison of autonomy and autopoiesis raises important questions, and I offer this paper partly as a response to his invitation to provide a more persuasive account of Luhmann's position than he can make, it is unlikely that he would approve of my argument. Whether or not I have correctly entered into Luhmann's thought must necessarily be a matter of some doubt, though I think the reconciliation worked out here is of interest in its own right.

I. The Differences between Autonomy and Autopoiesis

An understandable and predictable reaction to Luhmann's theory of auto-poiesis from those working within Anglo-American empirical sociology of law is to question the credibility of any theory which appears to suggest that law is in some way hermetically sealed off from other aspects of society. Despite some equivocation[3], criticism of this implication of Luhmann's proposal seems to be the main purpose of Lempert's sustained comparison of autonomy and autopoiesis. Nor is this a parochial or tangential problem. It is worth attending to this debate because a close examination of these conflicting approaches to legal autonomy does offer insight into some of the fundamental difficulties of the current framework of sociology of law and the need to reconceptualize theoretical strategies in understanding law in post-industrial societies. Without claiming either Lempert or Luhmann as ideal representatives of the Anglo-American or European traditions, it is possible to see Lempert as champion of the influential Anglo-American pragmatic empirical approach with Luhmann, on the other hand, working to develop and up-date classical European social theory.

Lempert offers a number of telling observations and critical comments on the approach to autonomy he takes to be implied by Luhmann's theory, which he finds to be *a priori*, ambiguous, untestable and unnecessarily complicated. In particular he questions the idea that law's autopoiesis is secured through its "normative closure". This, he argues, is either empirically untrue or amounts to the trivial claim that only the law can change the law. Lempert argues that "norms must come from somewhere", and

---

[3] Lempert has added a number of "clarifications" to his original paper. In footnote 19, for example, he comments that "ultimately I suggest that ... autopoiesis and autonomy are not to be equated", and later, at p. 177, he argues that "autopoietic systems should not be seen as a species of autonomy in the Anglo-American sense of the term". But these riders and qualifications sit awkwardly with the rest of the paper which is devoted to examining the approach to autonomy implicit in the theory of autopoiesis.

194   David Nelken

there are many examples of law incorporating or being changed by extra-legal norms and values such as the doctrine of "good faith", jury decision-making or legal capitulation to collective deviance. If the theory is saved by enlarging what is meant by "cognitive openness" to incorporate such matters, there seems no bite to the idea of normative closure. Likewise, if all that is meant is that legal ratification of extra-legal influences is always required, this would mean that legal endorsement of naked political manipulation of the courts would be sufficient to include it within law's autopoiesis. Whereas Lempert is prepared to concede that Luhmann's theory has some application to judicial adjudication, he claims that it breaks down entirely in relation to legislation which he characterizes as standing "at the intersection of the legal and political spheres". The Anglo-American approach to autonomy, which sees it as a matter of *degree*, is recommended as a better starting point for empirical research, although Lempert insists that he is more concerned to expose the weaknesses of autopoiesis theory than to advocate the virtues of his rival conception. He concludes that "Treating the idea of autopoiesis not as a metaphor but as a theory, it appears to be either an erroneous, an inadequate, or an unnecessarily complicated approach to understanding what we mean by legal autonomy" (Lempert, supra: 188).

How are these criticisms to be answered? The way forward begins from Lempert's admission that the ideas of autonomy and autopoiesis may not be equivalent and may have different theoretical purposes. There is justice in Lempert's argument that there needs to be more clarification of the implied relationship between these concepts, especially as discussions of autopoiesis often use the term autonomy quite loosely in association with or as a substitute for that of autopoiesis. But the best means of identifying the differences between these two is to locate them in the context of the wider theoretical and practical concerns which give them their point. This strategy will show that most of the questions which Lempert levels at autopoietic theory cannot and need not be answered in his terms. They are dealt with (if not always perhaps in ways with which Lempert would be happy) elsewhere in Luhmann's social systems theory. However, this will not of itself solve the whole problem. For, as Lempert claims, many of the empirical points he adduces are so patent that the question cannot be, "does Luhmann know of them", but rather, "what does he make of them", and how can they be reconciled with his claims about autopoiesis. If it is true, as we will see, that Luhmann is willing to talk about *degrees* of autonomy and that he does discuss the mutual interchange between legal and other sub-systems of society, it still needs to be explained how this is consistent with his own ideas about autopoietic systems. It is this issue which Lempert's probing places firmly on the theoretical agenda.

What are the main differences between autonomy and autopoiesis? One way to compare and contrast autonomy and autopoiesis is to see how they are defined. According to Lempert, autonomy is "the degree to which the legal system looks to itself rather than to the standards of some external social, political or ethical system for guidance in making and applying law" (Lempert, supra: 159). Autopoiesis, on the other hand, means that the legal system produces and delimits the operative unity of its elements (i. e., legally relevant events and decisions) through the operation of its elements and in this way lends unity to the system. (Luhmann, 1985e: 281 − 82). These different definitions go a long way to indicating the gulf between the two conceptions. But this is not sufficient to sort out all the theoretical difficulties here. Autonomy and autopoiesis are both used in a variety of senses which are only weakly captured by these definitions; moreover, they are each used to deal with a diversity of problems which cannot be deduced from the way they are defined. Moreover, the need of further exegesis of the unfamiliar notion of autopoiesis suggests that the compatibility of these ideas depends on the relationship between the different theoretical languages in which they are being communicated rather than on any surface similarities or dissimilarities.

In an effort to introduce greater clarity, Tables 1 and 2 set out some of the different senses and theoretical projects in which the ideas of autonomy and autopoiesis are used (many of which are found in the Autopoiesis Conference papers themselves). The contrasts which I have drawn in Table 1 relate to the theoretical frameworks and characteristic meanings of each term. The focus of Table 2 is on the presumed sources of each phenomenon, and the associated policy concerns and the methods of investigation used to study them. Naturally, what is presented here is no more than a schematic outline of the way in which autonomy and auto-poiesis figure as building blocks in their various respective theoretical projects, and my emphasis is on the differences between them rather than on the question of overlap (to which I shall return later).

One obvious conclusion which emerges from this exercise is that each of these terms conveys a number of not necessarily coherent meanings (some of which may be assigned more to the core with others as the penumbra as suggested in Table 1). These variant meanings sometimes reflect different points and not only different ways of putting the point. They therefore include a number of possible inconsistencies which are of theoretical interest in their own right. For example, the Anglo-American approach to autonomy embraces *inter alia* the idea that law has short-run organizational and temporal independence, that it is *functionally* required to be independent of power holders (and in this sense, its "independence" is exactly what secures its usefulness to them), that its independence is founded on *resistance* to outside influence and control and that, conversely,

196   David Nelken

Table 1. *Autonomy and Autopoiesis: Theoretical Frameworks and Characteristic Meanings*

	Legal Autonomy	Legal Autopoiesis
1. *Theoretical Framework*	a) Input-output paradigm of system-environment relations between actions (including messages)	a) Closure paradigm of recursive production of elements (and boundaries) through distinctive forms of communication of meaning and expectations
	b) The sub-system is open insofar as not closed	b) The sub-system is open because closed
	c) Autonomy lies in extent of independence from external factors	c) Autopoiesis means operating a particular selective mechanism for responding to the environment
	d) Autonomy is a matter of degree, ranging from autarchy to total dependence	d) Autopoiesis is an all or nothing category
	e) Therefore, more independence means less dependence	e) Therefore, it involves simultaneous increased independence of, and increased dependence, on the environment
	f) Legal autonomy is something special	f) All sub-systems are auto-poietic, in their own ways
2. *Characteristic Meanings* *core*	a) Independence as freedom from outside control	a) Independence as *self-* dependence
	b) Non-correspondence to other social factors	b) Reflexivity (circularity)
	c) Not reproducing external power or value differences	c) Unity
	d) Neutrality	d) Identity
	e) Responsive to plurality of interests therefore not only responsive to some interests	e) Self-observation/awareness of own autonomy
	f) Cause and justification of legitimacy	f) Operating according to its own code
	g) Short-run independencies in time (e. g., bureaucratic independence or historical lags)	g) Positivity
penumbra	h) "relative autonomy" (in Marxist theories)	h) Legal point of view
	i) Systems actions not predictable from outside	i) Performance of unique functions of sub-system
	j) Systems actions not predictable from inside	j) Maintenance of functional differentiation

Table 2. *Autonomy and Autopoiesis: Their Sources, Associated Policy Concerns and Methods of Investigation*

	Legal Autonomy	Legal Autopoiesis
1. Sources	a) Derives from *Institutional* (e. g., organizational), *Occupational* (e. g., legal profession) and *procedural* (e. g., specialized rules and principles and intellectual methods) *spezialization*	a) Derives from *Functional Differentiation* of legal sub-system operating according to its own code
	b) Derives also from functional requirement of *legitimacy* needs of powerholders/the "state"	b) Autopoiesis is a *fact* about law as a distinctive "ontological epistemology"
2. Associated Policy Concerns	a) Ideal of separation of powers/rule of law	a) Problems and prospects for maintaining increasing evolutionary complexity and avoiding de-differentation
	b) Threats to separate identity of law	b) Problems in legal modelling and regulation of other social spheres
	c) Limits of law's ability to transcend political and economic interests	c) Internal limits on law's conditional programs
3. Methods of Investigation	Analysis of variance between legal and extra-legal factors and law's independent effects	Study of theoretical and empirical implications (including tendencies and tensions) as suggested by the theory. Theory must also be autopoietic.

such independence is best facilitated by law being *responsive* to *all* comers and so not merely to some.

Lempert's own version of the Anglo-American approach is not without its peculiar difficulties. For example he does not appear to integrate his conception of legal autonomy as the result of institutional, occupational and procedural specialization (legal formalism) with the theoretically distinctive attempt to derive autonomy from the functional requirements of legitimacy. His further, somewhat idiosyncratic, claim that legal autonomy depends on status and normative neutrality and on equal legal competence is also problematic. In essence, for law to be autonomous it must be able to resist the penetration of the social, political and ethical systems that surround it. But in addition, "the autonomy of the legal system ... also depends on the degree to which all actors can invoke the law effectively" (Lempert, supra:

175, 166). Thus, it would seem, the state of the environment (the extent to which social equality already exists) conditions the autonomy of law even without needing to penetrate it. Lempert goes on to argue that perfect legal autonomy could only be achieved in an already equal society but he insists that the theoretical idea of perfect legal autonomy does make sense even if it is empirically impossible; "in the ideal case legal autonomy and personal autonomy coincide. Freedom is at a maximum" (Lempert, supra: 168). In practice the idea of legal autonomy is a reality insofar as the effects of legal specialization and the pluralist competition of interest groups do create a "meaningful level" of independence for law. As a rider he adds that his preference would not in any case be for the "ideal-type" situation of complete but equal individualism but would include a built-in element of communality. But is all this a coherent vision? Lempert seems to be motivated by the understandable desire to reconcile the *Gesellschaft* conception of legal autonomy as neutrality, with an understandable refusal to see law as autonomous when it merely reproduces external differentials in power and values. But is this anything more than a heroic but ultimately doomed effort to straddle formalist and substantive notions of legal autonomy? It is not even clear that perfect autonomy in the substantive sense is in fact theoretically conceivable. What would the coincidence of legal autonomy and personal autonomy actually be like? Would there be a need for a perfectly autonomous legal system in an already equal society? Lempert notes in passing that where law reflects everyone's values it could be said that the separation between law and external values has collapsed; why is the same not true where law reflects everybody's interests?

    If there is some ambiguity and uncertainty about the meaning of legal autonomy, this also applies to the idea of legal autopoiesis. The nature and implications of autopoiesis are certainly given different interpretations by Luhmann, Teubner, Deggau and others. To take only one illustration from the work of Luhmann (but one which will turn out to be crucial in considering the relationship between autonomy and autopoiesis), why is there a connection between what Luhmann sees as the specific *tasks* of law in a functionally differentiated society and the *elements* whose reproduction constitutes and reconstitutes its autopoiesis? The question of functional differentiation surely *is* a matter of degree whatever may be true of autopoiesis. The safest assumption therefore is that such notions as reflexivity or self-observation tell us nothing about the *substantive nature* of such reflexivity. This could consist of something *other* than the requirements of "normative closure" and "cognitive openness" which Luhmann takes from his own systems theory. In fact Luhmann concedes that the notion of autopoiesis is, strictly speaking, applicable to any sociological theory provided that it is in some (unspecified) way "compatible" with it. It will be seen, however, that it is far from easy to disentangle *his* understanding of autopoiesis from his wider theory.

However, we are not yet ready to pursue these questions further. Whatever the *internal* inconsistencies within the notions of autonomy and autopoiesis the main object of Tables 1 and 2 is to demonstrate *the gulf between them*. And although Lempert provides us with a searching examination of the differences between autonomy and autopoiesis, he never succeeds in finding the source of these differences.

II. Wider Theories and Contrasting Concerns

At the outset it is important to appreciate that what autonomy and autopoiesis have in common is that they both refer to *self-determination*. But each concept deals with different aspects of what this entails. The idea of autonomy focuses on self-direction as an alternative to direction by others. It presumes that independence is a *relational* category signifying *non-dependence* on others. For example, one of the dictionary definitions of autonomy, drawn from the political context, is *"limited self-government"*. What is to be noticed here is that this is the definition of autonomy itself — not of *partial* or *relative* autonomy. This approach to self-determination therefore fails to ask another question — or rather it assumes it away so that it becomes impossible to ask. This is what is *further* required in being *"true to oneself"* beyond being free of outside interference (and what is involved in the self-monitoring which sustains this process).

If we are interested in studying legal autonomy we might well be satisfied with a framework which allows investigation of the relationship between legal and extra-legal factors and produces findings concerning their variation.[4] In terms of the historical development of sociology of law the study of autonomy represents exactly the converse of the search for the extent to which law "corresponds" to other social phenomena, whether geographic, political, economic or whatever (see Nelken, 1986).

The theory of autopoiesis, on the other hand, concentrates on understanding law's correspondence to *itself*. Hitherto, as Luhmann concedes, this was a question thought appropriate to legal rather than social theory. And indeed part of the difficulty in appraising autopoiesis is deciding whether it does make any sense to search for the nature of law's "identity" or "unity" from a sociological point of view. Autopoiesis theory (like all theory) does beg the question. On the other hand, whereas the theory of autonomy does seem to pre-empt any further inquiry into the nature of law's self-determination (independence *is* non-dependence) the converse is not the case. Those characteristics which make for law's reflexivity —

---

[4] There are some unexpected difficulties even in following through this project, for which, see Griffiths (1979).

assuming they exist — do not necessarily explain its freedom from outside control. The question of the degree of such control can still be posed, even though, as Lempert successfully demonstrates, it is certainly not easy to reconcile the idea of determination by outside factors with reflexive self-determination. (We will see later that though it is difficult, it is *not* impossible.) In any case, the appropriate framework for examining auto-poiesis is as different as might be expected from that which can be used in investigating autonomy. It is matter of developing the paradoxical logic of reflexivity, on the basis of stipulated characterizations of law's elements and specificity, looking, on the model of the approach used by Talcott Parsons, for emergent tendencies and contradictory tensions.

The reason for the different routes which these enquiries take derives from the theoretical traditions from which they arise. Lempert associates his approach with the reaction against "crude Marxist" attempts to reduce law to an economically determined phenomenon. In positive terms, his description of legal autonomy is said to be related to Weber's attempt to delineate the causes and conditions of "legal rationality". But it is instructive that Weber's interest was in the broader processes of the rationalization of Western life rather than simply the degree of law's autonomy: law took the form it did partly as a result, and aspect, of wider processes of social change. Again this suggests that autonomy presupposes dependence on other social processes. On the other hand, Luhmann's theorizing draws on Durkheim's theory of functional differentiation as well as on Weber but revises their arguments in the light of recent intellectual developments in the areas of systems theory, cybernetics, philosophy of science — and now the theory of autopoiesis. Since Luhmann criticizes the classical sociologists on which Lempert bases himself (Luhmann claiming that they have misconceived the nature of functional differentiation in late industrial societies), it is no surprise that their sociologies of law are different.

These differences come to a head in their contrasting approaches to examining the relationship between system and environment in modern conditions. Lempert is satisfied to demarcate law from extra-legal factors in terms of law's activities and communications which are located in designated organizations and occupations. These are seen as performing a variety of functions, including the significant task of lending legitimacy to the political system, but we are not given any theoretical argument concerning the necessary boundaries set by these functions. This would appear to be a matter of empirical mapping of the actual interactions between law and the environment. Lempert's approach to "relative autonomy" is thus not to be identified with Marxist efforts to explain the origins of the autonomy of law and "the state" (as in the "state derivation" debates discussed in Holloway and Picciotto, 1978 and Jessop, 1982).

Luhmann also works with an institutional and functionalist definition of law. Yet there are significant divergences from Lempert's starting point.

His definition of law includes all actions oriented to law, not merely those of organizations and legal occupations. Although he defines law in terms of its stabilizing of congruent expectations, his approach to the functions of law also includes a host of tasks which it performs for other sub-systems. These include not merely the allegedly "unique" function of resolving disputes which Lempert sees emphasized in Luhmann's autopoiesis papers. In addition there are the jobs of handling politically contentious problems, preventing too close an interdependence between social sub-systems, and acting as an "externalities" device to "remind" other sub-systems such as politics and administration of the existence of an external environment (Luhmann, 1982; 1985 e; Poggi, 1985).

In Luhmann's view a focus on legal institutions alone would not provide a good method of appreciating the full extent of law's functions or those of its functional equivalents. The real break initiated by Luhmann already in his *Rechtssoziologie* (1972) was his rejection of what he called "the sociology of courts and lawyers" and its replacement by an enquiry into the "unity of law". And Luhmann argues that even now "the sociology of law is interested only in connections between legal and extra-legal variables and although it may talk of the unity of the legal system, it never clearly perceives this unity" (Luhmann, supra: 13). In pursuit of his new project Luhmann adopted developing ideas in systems theory and has now incorporated the theory of autopoiesis. The result of this "break" however means that it is uncertain what significance, if any, Luhmann still attaches to the approach and findings of the "sociology of courts and lawyers" which Lempert may be said to represent. Has his theory superseded them or are they answers to a different question? We will see that although this is the crucial issue at stake between Lempert and Luhmann, it has not yet been satisfactorily addressed.

The choice to focus on different aspects of law's self-determination may be taken to reflect different concerns and "problematics". These derive from different practical and political debates which, at least in part, may even have shaped the development of each theoretical project. But it would be wrong to *reduce* the ideas of these authors to practical concerns (seeing autopoiesis, for example, as a rationalization of legal deregulation and autonomy as concerned with establishing the degree of law's independence as a force for social change and reform). Apart from anything else, the introductory quotations at the beginning of this article make it clear that each author has a different view of the point and potential of sociological theorizing. They have different theories of the relationship between the process of understanding and the problem of "encouraging right action". Nor need we assume that each author has drawn the correct practical conclusions from his theory (some of the implications concerning law's internal limitations which Luhmann derives from autopoiesis seem particularly suspect). Yet some light can be thrown on the disagreement between

Lempert and Luhmann by investigating the inner connection between each author's contrasting "concerns". Luhmann's main concern seems to be to understand and preserve law's contribution to evolving functional differentiation. He wants to know how it can provide legitimacy to the political sub-system, how it can maintain its own legitimacy even while being subject to constant revision; how, above all, it can help sustain the contingent and fragile mixture of complexity and simplifying techniques characteristic of modernity. His analysis of the conditions of such differentiation means that the contributions of law are identified in *post-instrumentalist* terms. Lempert's interests lie in the instrumental capacities of law whereas Luhmann's ideas, if not a straightforward reaction to claims of a regulatory crisis, are clearly relevant to these debates.

Each author's discussion of law in relation to other sub-systems of society reflects their concerns. For example, while both are clearly interested in the way that law and politics affect each other, Lempert is engaged by problems of how political influence can endanger law's autonomy, whereas Luhmann is worried by what happens to law when it usurps the function of politics. Lempert considers that law can best maintain its own legitimacy and that of power-holders by showing its independence from political *input*. He argues that its legitimacy is put in question if it is not "responsive" and merely reproduces rather than attempts to change external interests and values. On the other hand, for Luhmann, law's "responsiveness" lies in the way its processes are differentiated from other social sub-systems and "interrupt" their interdependency. The threats to its legitimacy have more to do with law's functions rather than with its "inputs". (This may explain why he does not deal with Lempert's question concerning legislation as an obvious example of political "input" into law.) In his view, the attempt to use law to compensate for power differentials in society, as Lempert advocates, would re-politicize it and risk its legitimacy which would then be tied to the success of its interventions. For Luhmann the function of law is to absorb and de-politicize those problems which the political process does not or cannot resolve, by using conditional programs whose consequences will not affect law's validity as such.

It can be seen therefore that Luhmann takes for granted (rather than denies) the "threats" to autonomy discussed by Lempert and even the more fundamental attacks on the very possibility of legal autonomy characteristically levelled by the American Critical Legal Scholars movement. Law is *exactly* a method of de-politicizing social problems as these critics allege. There is no possibility of emancipating the content and overall goals of legal intervention from the requirements of politics. "Positive law is an unavoidably politically chosen 'state' law. Its destiny is bound up with that of the political system in society" (Luhmann, 1985 e: 187). But nor is it a statement of the obvious, as Lempert thinks, to argue that the law reproduces itself even when (or exactly when) doing the work of politics and yet not working *as* politics (cf. Luhmann 1982: 168). For Luhmann, law is the great concealer, hiding the fact of violence at the basis of social order, handling irreconcilable political and moral choices in a world without either consensus or absolutes, teaching people not to learn from their disappointed expectations and to respect law even while recognizing its contingency (Luhmann, 1985 a; 1985 b; 1985 c; 1985 d; supra; 1987). But all this can be achieved, according to Luhmann, only if law rests on and reproduces its way of seeing the world in terms of legality and illegality and suppresses all possibility of querying the foundation of this distinction (which in itself can be either legal, illegal or neither!).

III. The Relationship between Autonomy and Autopoiesis

We have seen so far that Luhmann's approach to the problem of legal autonomy is significantly different from that assumed by Lempert. What is more, autopoiesis theory does not represent the key to Luhmann's approach to this problem, which can only be appreciated by reviewing the larger corpus of his work. If this does not quite answer Lempert's criticism of autopoiesis as a theory of autonomy it has at least shown why this theory was not designed to answer the questions Lempert raises. But we must now move on to ask how the concepts of autonomy and autopoiesis relate to each other. My aim here is *not* to find a way of reconciling the approaches of Lempert and Luhmann. There is no reason to think an amalgamation of their views to be either possible or desirable, despite Lempert's suggestion that something like this theory of autonomy needs to be inserted into autopoiesis theory. What does need to be explained is how Luhmann himself deals with problems concerning autonomy, including points raised by Lempert, in the course of developing *his own theory*. What is the relationship he envisages between these two ideas? Put differently, how far has the adoption of autopoiesis theory led Luhmann to reject previous parts of his work? An answer to this question may also enable us to see how far others who have embraced the idea of autopoiesis have remained consistent with Luhmann's larger scheme.

There is little doubt that Luhmann's earlier work in the sociology of law did not deny the importance of some of the questions about legal autonomy which interest Lempert. In reviewing what he describes as classical sociology of law, Luhmann commented:

> It is exactly the *relative autonomy* and the inherent laws of legal terminology, the question regarding *the degree* to which legislation can direct it, its functional specificity, its receptivity to social effects, its power when in the hands of certain groups ... all these would be interesting problematics of sociology (Luhman, 1985 e: 18—19, my emphasis).

204   David Nelken

But he felt that contemporary empirical sociology of law (circa 1972) had
not made much progress with these questions. Instead of formulating his
problems in these terms, however, he chose to develop a theory of the
positivity of modern law and the strengths and limits of its functioning in
relation to other sub-systems. It is for this problem that Luhmann later
recruited the theory of autopoiesis. This marked a new and important stage
in his theory, and in some respects it does appear to alter or replace earlier
discussions in his *Rechtssoziologie*. This is especially true of the way law is
said to "see" and affect its environment. For example, Luhmann would
now probably want to reformulate the use made of Podgorecki's three-
step hypothesis of how legal messages permeate the social environment,
so as to substitute the idea of autopoietic reproduction of meaning. Some of
the theoretical language used to expound system-environment relationships
would also no doubt now be changed, such as the following passage:

> The system becomes more sensitive to the environment … the system *sees itself*
> confronted with an excess of possible causes of change between which it must choose.
> In other words, the system has to see environmental complexity as relevant and cope
> with improved selection techniques if it wants to circumvent crises. This consideration
> makes us suspect a connection between structural variability and complexity in the
> relations between system and environment (Luhmann, 1985 e: 186).

There also appear to be some inconsistencies between Luhmann's account
of the hierarchalization of norm-structures in his earlier work and the
emphasis on circularity within autopoietic theory.

On the other hand there are good reasons to think that Luhmann is still
committed to most, if not all, of his previous systems theory. This includes
his approach to functional differentiation as the characteristic of modern
society and the particular part law plays in the facilitation and reduction
of complexity. Most important, for present purposes, there is also no sign
of any rejection of the claims put forward in the chapters on positivity in
the *Rechtssoziologie* or the lecture entitled "The Autonomy of Law" delivered
in 1976 (see Luhmann, 1982).

In a new conclusion in the recently translated second edition of his
Rechtssoziologie, Luhmann offers an important but tantalizingly brief account
of the relevance of autopoiesis theory to his sociology of law. Here he
presupposes that we are dealing with a legal system which has "relative
autonomy" or "high autonomy" (Luhmann, 1985 e: 281, 286). These ideas
of degree are similar to what Lempert describes as "meaningful independence", but they differ by stressing *positivity* as much as insulation from
outside control. However the important point is that this *degree* of self-
determination and autonomy constitutes the background and basis of
autopoiesis rather than serving as an equivalent concept. The idea of
autopoiesis has other functions in Luhmann's systems theory. For it is put
forward as a sociological answer to the problem of how law can see itself
as a "unity". His description of the way autopoiesis works to reproduce

the unity of the system is explained from the perspective of the legal system, without denying the possibility of describing relationships between law and other sub-systems in other terms than this. Autopoiesis theory is best seen therefore as a development, culmination and perhaps also a justification of Luhmann's systems-theory rather than as a deviation from it. This explains why and how Luhmann has altered the theory to fit in with his ideas, not only by applying it to social systems (which had been anticipated) but in reducing the significance of "the observer" and in other ways choosing between the now somewhat different formulations of the two founders of the biological basis of the theory.

Some of the alleged inconsistencies between Luhmann's earlier and later propositions about the relationship between law and its environment (including those quoted before) may therefore be resolved if they are taken as directed at different problems within his theory. Luhmann even provides various clues as to how such reconciliation should be sought, stressing for example, that,

> This closure does not, however, mean ... complete determination by itself. Rather, closure consists in the fact that all operations always reproduce the system (Luhmann, supra: 15 and footnote 11).

A reconstruction of the place of autopoiesis within Luhmann's systems theory would run as follows: Luhmann originally distinguished three forms of society/sub-system relations, in terms of the *functions* that the sub-system served, its *performance* conceived as an input-output relation and the sub-system's relation to itself as *reflection* and *internal differentiation* (Luhmann, 1982: 264 ff.; cf. Murphy, 1984: 610). The differences between these three types of relationship, or three ways of conceiving the relationship between law and other sub-systems, help to explain the differences between autonomy and autopoiesis because autopoiesis theory comes in only as a replacement or reformulation of the third kind of relationship. By contrast the considerations raised by Lempert can and should be dealt with in terms of what Luhmann calls *performance*. If Luhmann does not discuss these problems much it is because of his conscious effort to distance himself from empirical (often small-group) studies in the sociology of law. As Poggi puts it, Luhmann is primarily interested in law at the social rather than the organizational level (Poggi, 1985).

The results of this reconstruction of Luhmann's ideas are presented in Figure 1.

But have we now answered all Lempert's questions about the relationship between autonomy and autopoiesis? There still seems to be some uncertainty about the way one affects the other. This is partly because the idea of autopoiesis, along with that of autonomy, tends to be defined in a variety of ways. As shown earlier (in Tables 1 and 2) autopoiesis refers, *inter alia*, to the "identity", "unity", "reflexivity" and "self-observation" of

206   David Nelken

Figure 1. *Relationship between the Legal System and the Environment in Luhmann's Social Systems Theory.*

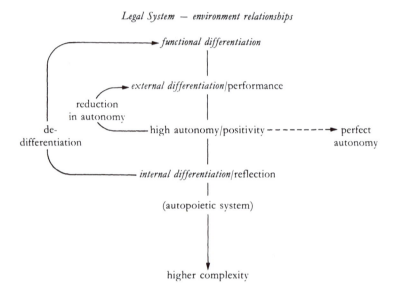

Legal System — environment relationships

functional differentiation

external differentiation/performance

reduction in autonomy

de-differentiation

high autonomy/positivity - - - - - - - -▶ perfect autonomy

internal differentiation/reflection

(autopoietic system)

higher complexity

law. In consequence formulations of the specific conceptual interrelationship of autonomy and autopoiesis are similarly various. We are told, in the Conference papers, that autopoiesis "explains the nature of law's autonomy" and that is a description of a state of affairs which arises "when law becomes aware of its own autonomy". Autopoiesis is seen, both as a historical "fact" *and* a different way of understanding and talking about law's reflexivity (thus constituting its status as an "ontological epistemology"). Autonomy, for its part, is also a distinctive phenomenon and a different way of talking about it. This accounts for the way autopoiesis can be described by Teubner as "a more radical and precise definition of law's autonomy" and also as a "functionally higher level of autonomy" reached through the logical/historical progression from "social autonomy" to "legal autonomy" to "legal autopoiesis" (Teubner, 1985 b). As Figure 1 indicates, autopoiesis therefore both presupposes a high degree of autonomy and represents a new phenomenon.

What difference does this new phenomenon produce? In responding to Lempert's paper at the Conference, Luhmann explained that autopoiesis dealt with the situation where there was a simultaneous growth of both dependence and independence of the legal sub-system in relation to its environment. Thus the more closed (independent) the reflexivity of law the more it served its various functions in its dependent connections to other sub-systems. Another example taken from Luhmann's papers is the claim that as an autopoietic system, law no longer serves the function of resolving or pre-deciding conflicts (as Lempert still takes him to be arguing), but instead *uses* the existence of disputes to reproduce its elements. This, according to Luhmann, helps explain and perhaps even justify empirical evidence of the extent to which adjudicative procedures sharpen and even exacerbate disputes rather than serve to mediate them. As this last example suggests, however, autopoietic theory tends to be used to provide novel interpretations of established findings about the legal system rather than to generate new methods of discovering its empirical connection with other sub-systems. It is this tendency which lies at the very basis of Lempert's critique of Luhmann's approach to theorizing. In order to evaluate this foundational issue it will be necessary to consider what is at stake in the challenge thrown down by Luhmann in urging us to abandon older-style empirical work on the "sociology of courts and lawyers".

IV. Towards a New Paradigm in the Sociology of Law

There can be little doubt that the Anglo-American approach to sociology of law which Lempert draws on in examining Luhmann's theory is itself going through a crisis. Such a conclusion does not seem unreasonable when a past editor of the *Law & Society Review* gives it as his opinion that "Social studies of law have reached a crucial point in their development. The original paradigm is exhausted" (Abel, 1980: 826), and the President of the Law & Society Association writes a justification of the most fundamental assumptions of empirical work in the field (Macaulay, 1984: 149). Although it is hard to summarize the various and sometimes conflicting critiques which have been levelled at the mainstream, many of these reflect increasing dissatisfaction with a search for ways in which law and society "affect" or "influence" each other and a redirection of energies towards internal connections between legal and social relations, and the way law is "imbricated" within social practices (See Nelken, 1985; 1986).

Although the work of Luhmann has not yet played much part in these intellectual cross-currents, it would seem valuable to look to him for further guidance on how to move beyond the study of "law and society" or even "law in society". As already noted, as early as 1972, Luhmann saw himself as rejecting and transcending what he called the "sociology of courts and lawyers" in order to further develop the sociology of law as such. The editors of the recent English translation of the *Rechtssoziologie* summarize this theoretical break in terms which reflect precisely on the disagreements between Lempert and Luhmann:

> The sociology of law is not, then, an examination of the influence of one set of factors on another but an inquiry into what is found to be a necessary inner connection between law and any kind of social life (King-Utz and Albrow, 1985: viii).

Nor does it seem an exaggeration to use that over-worked term "paradigm change" to indicate the shift in theoretical language and problem focus that adopting Luhmann's perspective would entail.

> One could more or less talk of a change in paradigm, which replaces the concept of environmental openness with the concept of self-reference, which then in turn makes it possible to combine the openness and closedness of a system. The insights gained thereby also give new lift to a sociological theory of legal systems (Luhmann, 1985: xii).

Other contributors at the Autopoiesis Conference also noted that Luhmann's work offers a way of replacing "misleading" or "unexpressive" ways of conceiving the law and society relationship (see Willke, 1987; Gordon, 1985: 2).

However, the possibility of misunderstanding Luhmann's approach is also considerable, especially if attention is confined too closely to his work on autopoietic theory. Roger Cotterell, for example, recently noted that:

> critical legal scholarship, reflecting wider intellectual concerns, has done much to undermine the idea that we can relate two discrete entities, 'law' and 'society'. Law is best thought of as an aspect of society, or part of the means by which social relations are constituted; not as some independent phenomenon which acts on (or is acted upon by) another phenomenon we can call 'society'. Analytically separating legal systems and social systems seems unpromising as an organising strategy. On the other hand, as Luhmann's and Teubner's influential work has suggested, if we do try to identify, for purposes of analysis, a distinctively legal realm of social life it may well be that we should start from the assumption that such a realm does *not* interact extensively with or impact upon other social spheres. Perhaps what is most significant about legal discourse and legal systems is their isolation; their *lack of relationships with other social systems* (Cotterrell, 1986: 495).

As the previous discussion of the relationship between autonomy and autopoiesis should have demonstrated, this may unwittingly over-emphasize Luhmann's closure paradigm to the neglect of his wider discussion of legal system and environment relations. But when this is taken into account, Luhmann's framework seems even more fertile as an inspiration to new enquiries in this field.

On the other hand, we may also anticipate considerable resistance to the adoption of Luhmann's ideas from those still adhering to the mainstream. Lempert speaks for many when he argues that elements of Luhmann's theory appear to be not susceptible to disproof and objects that the concept of autopoiesis itself does not seem designed for heuristic testing (and accompanying examination of variance) in the manner of positivist social science. Like Macaulay, in his recent review and defense of mainstream work, the impression is given that European theorizing (especially of the alleged Teutonic variety) builds "theory on the back of definition" and is more interested in theory construction for its own sake than in painstaking middle-range empirical discoveries (Macaulay, 1984). There is much that could be said about these different traditions of sociology and social theory (see Nelken, 1984). Certainly if Luhmann's work is taken as a whole it can be defended both as prefering to incorporate existing empirical findings in the sociology of law and as generating suggestions for new work. But what I would prefer to argue here is the need to avoid presenting the choice as the stark one between continuing empirical work in the mainstream paradigm or the wholesale adoption of Luhmann's theory — autopoiesis and all. In my view Luhmann's work should rather be used as a stimulus to change the *framework* within which sociology of law is pursued. The problem with Anglo-American theorizing (and investigating the degree of law's autonomy from social influences provides a perfect example of this) is that it is less a theory than *a place on a map*. The best that can be said about the mainstream framework is that it is apparently hospitable to a variety of different theoretical approaches and methodologies. It makes it possible for the connection or lack of connection between law and society to be examined in the light of functional, structural, interactionist, conflict or even some Marxist theories and methodologies. But the apparent openness of the framework is also misleading insofar as it conceals the fact that it necessarily occupies a distinctive theoretical space.

Figure 2 provides an intellectual map of the place of mainstream "law and society" work in relation to some illustrative alternative approaches. It shows that this work operates best at the intersection of two axes which demarcate the possible conceptual linkages between the ideas of "law", "society" and "sociology". The first deals with the relationship between law and society (conceived ontologically), the second axis that between sociology and law (conceived as epistemologies). Firstly, then, for mainstream empirical sociology of law to make sense it is forced to presuppose that "law" and "society" can be conceptualized as sufficiently similar phenomena for their relationship to be worth investigating. This is as opposed to the alternative possibilities that, on the one hand, law is too distinct from society or, on the other hand, too inextricably interdependent for it to be possible to pursue such enquiries. Secondly, the mainstream project is forced to presuppose that law can be a theoretical object for sociology — thus excluding at the one extreme those sociological theories which do not focus on "law" as one of their organizing concepts, and — at the other extreme — those approaches which view law as a rival competing discourse. It is of particular import here to contrast the mainstream approach (represented by Lempert) and the quite different perspective (with which Luhmann and Teubner are associated) which resists characterizing law as a mere passive *object* of the sociological gaze and treats it rather as a *subject* reproducing its own conceptions of itself (and of society).

The assumptions which lie behind the mainstream framework may not be indefensible; the point is rather that they are not in fact defended. And

210   David Nelken

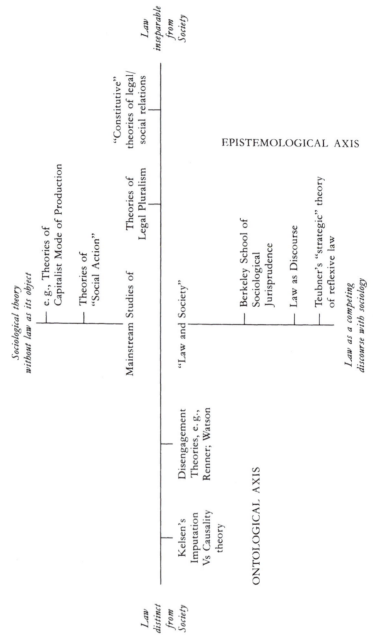

Figure 2. *Intellectual Map of Mainstream Law and Society Studies and some Alternatives*

that they are not uncontroversial is easily seen by considering some of the illustrative alternative positions which I have added to each of the axes which presently frame enquiry in this field. At the very least, mainstream work must justify the positions it takes. But the great merit of Luhmann's work in sociology of law is actually to collapse these axes into each other by showing how the extremes do in fact meet up (it is noteworthy, for example, that Kelsen can be seen as making both ontological and epistemological claims about the distinctiveness of law). What is more, Luhmann's approach is a positive one. It is not intended, as is so often the case, to demonstrate the impossibility of doing sociology of law but rather to create a theoretically justifiable *starting-point* for this field. If law, society and sociology are to be analytically distinguished for the purposes of developing sociology of law (and it is hard to see how this can be avoided) Luhmann offers us a model of how to justify this in theoretical terms rather than merely adopting pragmatic positions along the relevant axes. We can learn from the way he poses his theoretical questions even if we cannot always accept his answers. What Luhmann does is what all theorists in this field should do: he starts from the problem of how, where and why law, society and sociology actually become distinguished from each other. For Luhmann the differentiation of law and society is represented as the historical (evolutionary) outcome of the emergence of functionally differentiated societies. The "positivity" of law and its reproduction as an autopoietic system is then seen as a further historical stage of this evolution (although the theory is certainly presently unclear as to when this final stage was reached and how it is to be identified). It is this same attention to starting points which underlies Luhmann's (and Teubner's) attempts to offer a sociological explanation of law's reproduction in relation to the way one autopoietic system may understand another.

The merit of Luhmann's framework can be assessed by examining it in relation to the recent critique of mainstream sociology of law coming from some members of the Critical Legal Studies Conference in the United States (see e. g., Gordon, 1984). It can be seen that Luhmann's approach provides a sociologically articulate anticipation of their attempt to deny the very possibility of the sociology of law. They focus on legal institutions and doctrine in an effort to show that law and politics cannot be distinguished. Luhmann's theory, however, includes an account of how and why these sub-systems have different functions, and stresses exactly the "de-politicizing" function of law. The Critical scholars reject the mainstream approach to investigating the relationship between "law" and "society" with the argument that law is in fact *constitutive* of society (see Figure 2). But Luhmann argues that this is going too far for, as Willke helpfully explains, this is to misunderstand functionally differentiated societies. Although law is indeed everywhere, it becomes both *more* and *less* relevant than in segmented or hierarchically organized societies. Though entering into all social action it

212   David Nelken

does so as only one (separable) aspect of it. It follows that it is in truth possible to examine the relationship between law and other features of society (Willke, 1987). Interestingly enough Gordon himself does admit that Luhmann's work marks an advance on existing approaches in sociology of law. In his view, "Autopoiesis provides a more elaborate metaphor for the law-society relationship than the unexpressive, neo-Marxist notion of relative autonomy" (Gordon, 1985: 2).[5] This is because in his opinion the latter idea is only a negative rather than a positive explanation of the nature of legal autonomy. By contrast to this, Lempert explained that this theory could be seen as a reaction *against* earlier Marxist theories of the economic determination of law (so that for him "relative autonomy" is used as a poor synonym for "partial autonomy"). In these terms, his Anglo-American perspective could therefore be seen as a *doubly* negative theory by comparison with Luhmann's starting point.

Having argued for the value of Luhmann's framework and questions, why not go all the way and also accept his answers? Perhaps, as some contributors undoubtedly assume, the really interesting and important problems only arise in applying the theory and drawing out its practical and political implications. I cannot follow this route because I have too many reservations about Luhmann's claims concerning the actual relationships between law and society and sociology, both where these derive from his general systems theory as well as from autopoiesis theory more narrowly. And it is precisely the practical implications which he (and others) derive from some of these hypothesized relationships which make me want to pause and re-examine their theoretical force.

Let us consider first Luhmann's approach to the relationship between "law" and "society". It is hard to deny that this suffers from all the defects of the neo-Parsonian functionalist and evolutionary scheme in which it is embedded. Like Parsons, Luhmann is consciously engaged in a process of re-writing and synthesizing Durkheim's ideas about functional interdependence in modern society with Weber's theorems on social action, rationality and legitimacy. But Luhmann also introduces characteristically original elements into Parsonian theory. Just as systems theory was used to reformulate Weber's approach to the way organizations control themselves and their environment, so autopoiesis theory is invoked to revise the notion of internal functional differentiation derived from Durkheim. Luhmann also breaks with Parsons' argument that law provides normative integration

---

[5] For a sophisticated recent attempt to use the idea of "relative autonomy" to provide a new starting point for sociology of law, see De Sousa Santos (1985). Although Marxist in conception, it has some similarity to Luhmann's approach perhaps because being influenced by Althusser it shares a common derivation from Parsons. But De Sousa Santos is explicitly concerned to integrate legal pluralism into this theory, which Luhmann in his *Rechtssoziologie* was disposed to dismiss.

for the social system (see Bredemeier, 1962), challenging the idea that such integration is necessary or possible. But his more complex (and not always clear) explanation of how the legal sub-system maintains congruent expectations in a society without a center is still recognizably Parsonian.

The difficulties of this functionalist mode of explanation are familiar enough, and Luhmann tries to deal with some of them. He insists that it is always possible to find "functional equivalents", and indeed argues that sociological "enlightenment" lies in the discovery of functional equivalents. He even applies this insight to the debate over de-legalization and the increasing resort to lay forums and mediation, arguing that this does not necessarily indicate any reduction in the function of law itself even though the forums themselves may be changing. At other times, however, Luhmann's arguments about the way law must function do seem to assume that legal *institutions* themselves must keep to their functions without allowing for the possibility that these could and would be achieved regardless (see especially Luhmann, 1985 d). Nor is it obvious that the functions Luhmann attributes to the legal sub-system must actually *be* achieved. According to his theory it would often be sufficient if the impression was successfully given that they *were* being achieved. This applies especially to his arguments about the need for law to handle certain contentious problems on behalf of politics. Luhmann fails to take his own arguments to the conclusion that law needs only to *conceal* its "political" resolution of political choices, not actually behave non-politically.

These weaknesses of functional explanation matter because Luhmann draws important practical and political conclusions from his analysis of law's functions, warning of the dangers of functional de-differentiation if law should come to resemble politics in its concern for attaining predictable consequences. Such apparently prescriptive theorizing may or may not be justifiable.[6] But it is regrettable that his view of law's functions does lead him to dismiss the manifest evidence of law's efforts to achieve such "result-oriented" outcomes. As Lempert rightly notes, Luhmann's approach is hard to square with legislative initiatives. But even adjudicative decisions are shaped by "policy" considerations or "goal-reasoning" and debates over the justifications of specific types of decision-making such as sentencing do not make sense if it is *assumed* that they cannot be concerned with outcomes. Luhmann makes two points in reply. He argues that the "validity" of these decisions is not called into question by their predictive inadequacy and that the level of consequentialist reasoning employed by the courts is often primitive. But this cannot dislodge the need to explain why courts make attempts at such reasoning (which may improve under the influence of external influences such as the "law and economics"

---

[6] See the attempt to defend Weber from accusations of similar charges in Brubaker (1984).

214   David Nelken

movement). Luhmann's criticisms of law's departure from its functions echo arguments that are sometimes heard in American or German jurisprudence and constitutional law theorizing. But it might be more *sociologically* profitable to show how and why legal institutions succeed in fusing such apparently incompatible functions as adjudication and regulation. It is not always easy to follow why Luhmann sees some tendencies as irreconcilable and at other times embraces them as evidence of the paradoxal requirements of modernity. For Luhmann "the critique of law is the critique of social differentiations", but this seems to owe more to his preference for delegated decision-making, conditional programs and the rest, than to any inherent requirements of modern development. And even he admits that his propositions would not apply to a centrally organized (socialist) state.

There are also difficulties about understanding (let alone accepting) Luhmann's revisions of the way we should view the relationship between "law" and "sociology." As the previous discussion of consequentialist reasoning might have suggested, another way of thinking about law and consequential reasoning is in terms of the various overlapping and contrasting *discourses* which interact with law and on which law relies (see e. g., Fitzpatrick, 1984; Garland, 1985; Nelken, 1987). But Luhmann's approach is quite different from that of Foucault even if it is just as sensitive in its own way to the reflexivity of knowledge and the contingent status of "truth" and "justice" (see Murphy, 1984). Autopoiesis theory carries implications for the very form and focus of theorizing (see e. g., Heller, infra and Hutter, 1987). Yet the standpoint from which Luhmann's sociology of law is written is still not clear. Luhmann insists that the social theory of law has an essential part to play in explaining *to law* the nature of its autopoiesis and its limits (see Luhmann, 1985, conclusion to second edition). But if "law" cannot work these matters out for itself, how is it able to understand when the explanation comes from outside? There are also other difficulties of interpretation. Luhmann claims that the nature of law's autopoiesis lies in its distinctive normative elements (which allow it to remain "cognitively open"). But it is at least as arguable that the boundaries of law's understanding are set by its idiosyncratic way of knowing and categorizing the social world (cf. Nelken, 1987). Thus law is *not* cognitively open. The distinction "legal/illegal", upon which Luhmann lays such stress, hardly serves to capture the full range of law's normative vocabulary of rights, duties, permissions, obligations and so on. Moreover, as Teubner has shown, it offers little insight into law as a proto-social science interested in understanding and regulating and not only evaluating the social world (Teubner, 1985 a).

It is possible that some of these difficulties reflect the cultural divide between common law and civilian legal traditions and practices. But even if that is true it limits the wider applicability of Luhmann's approach. A more generous assessment of Luhmann's contribution would be that these problems arise because of the effort to provide a sociological understanding of law's self-understanding. In any event it is proper to end on a positive note. For it would certainly count as sufficient evidence of paradigm change if theoretical debates in the sociology of law were now to be conducted within Luhmann's framework and around Luhmann's questions even if his own formulations and answers were to be subjected to criticism and revision.

This is a considerably extended version of the paper of the same title presented at the Colloquium on Autopoiesis in Law and Society held at the European University Institute, Firenze, December 12–15, 1985. It attempts to take into account the revisions which Richard Lempert incorporated into his paper, partly as a result of the questions raised in mine (Nelken, infra), and I am grateful to him for allowing me to see the revised version of his paper in preparing my own.

Bibliography

ABEL, RICHARD (1980) "Re-directing Social Studies of Law", 14 *Law & Society Review* 805.

BREDEMEIER, HARRY C. (1962) "Law as an Integrative Mechanism" in W. M. Evan (ed.), *Law and Sociology*. New York: Free Press.

BRUBAKER, ROGER S. (1984) *The Limits of Rationality*. London: Allen and Unwin.

CLUNE, WILLIAM H. (1987) "Implementation as Autopoietic Interaction of Autopoietic Organizations" in G. Teubner (ed), *State, Law, Economy as Autopoietic Systems*. Berlin: de Gruyter (forthcoming).

COTTERRELL, ROGER (1986) Review of A. Podgorecki, C. Whelan and D. Khosla (eds.), *Legal Systems and Social Systems in Public Law* 495.

DE SOUSA SANTOS, BOAVENTURA (1985) "On Modes of Production of Law and Social Power", 13 *International Journal of the Sociology of Law* 299.

DUPUY, JEAN-P. (1987) "On the Supposed Closure of Normative Systems", in G. Teubner (ed.), *State, Law, Economy as Autopoietic Systems*. Berlin: de Gruyter.

FITZPATRICK, PETER (1984) "Law and Societies", 22 *Osgoode Hall Law Journal* 115.

GARLAND, DAVID (1985) *Punishment and Welfare*. London: Gower.

GORDON, ROBERT (1984) "Critical Legal Histories", 36 *Stanford Law Review* 57.

— (1985) "Autopoiesis — Questions of a Fascinated Skeptic". Paper proposed for the Conference on Autopoiesis in Law and Society, European University Institute, Firenze (December 12–15).

GRIFFITHS, JOHN (1979) "Is Law Important?" 54 *New York Law Review* 339.

HELLER, TOM (1987) "Accounting for Law", in G. Teubner (ed.), *State, Law, Economy as Autopoietic Systems*. Berlin: de Gruyter (forthcoming).

HOLLOWAY, JOHN and SOL PICCIOTTO (1978) *State and Capital: A German Debate*. London: Edward Arnold.

HUTTER, MICHAEL (1987) "How the Economy Talks the Law into Co-Evolution: An Exercise in Autopoietic Theory", in G. Teubner (ed.), *State, Law, Economy as Autopoietic Systems*. Berlin: de Gruyter (forthcoming).

JESSOP, BOB (1982) *The Capitalist State,* Oxford: Martin Robertson.

KING-UTZ, ELIZABETH and MARTIN ALBROW (trans.) (1985) Introduction to N. Luhmann, *A Sociological Theory of Law*. London: Routledge & Kegan Paul.

216   David Nelken

LUHMANN, NIKLAS (1982) *The Differentiation of Society*. New York: Columbia University Press.
— (1985 a) "The Autopoiesis of Social Systems". Paper presented at the Conference on Autopoiesis in Law and Society, European University Institute, Firenze (December 12—15).
— (1985 b) "Meaning". Paper presented at the Conference on Autopoiesis in Law and Society, European University Institute, Firenze (December 12—15).
— (1985 c) "The Self-Reproduction of the Law and its Limits" in G. Teubner (ed.), *Dilemmas of Law in the Welfare State*. Berlin: de Gruyter.
— (1985 d) "The Sociological Observation of the Theory and Practice of Law". Paper presented at the Conference on Autopoiesis in Law and Society, European University Institute, Firenze (December 12—15).
— (1985 e) *A Sociological Theory of Law* (German original, 1972). London: Routledge & Kegan Paul.
— (1987) "The Coding of the Legal System" in G. Teubner (ed.), *State, Law, Economy as Autopoietic Systems*. Berlin: de Gruyter (forthcoming).
MACAULAY, STEWART (1984) "Law and the Behavioral Sciences: Is There Any There?" 6 *Law and Policy* 149.
MURPHY, TIM (1984) "Modern Times: Niklas Luhmann on Law, Politics and Social Theory", 47 *Modern Law Review* 603.
NELKEN, DAVID (1983) *The Limits of the Legal Process: A Study of Landlords, Law, and Crime*. London: Academic Press.
— (1984) "Law in Action or Living Law? Back to the Beginning in Sociology of Law", 4 *Legal Studies* 152.
— (1985) "Legislation and its Constraints: A Case Study of the 1965 British Rent Act", in A. Podgorecki, C. Whelan and D. Khosla (eds.), *Legal Systems and Social Systems*. London: Croom Helm.
— (1987) "Criminal Law and Criminal Justice: Some Notes on their Irrelation" in I. Dennis (ed.), *Criminal Law and Justice*. London: Sweet and Maxwell.
— (1986) "Review Essay: Beyond the Study of Law and Society?" *Amer. Bar Foundation Research Journal*, Spring 328—338.
POGGI, GIANFRANCO (1985) "Niklas Luhmann on the Welfare State and its Law", European University Institute Working Paper 85/157.
TEUBNER, GUNTHER (1985 a) "After Legal Instrumentalism? Strategic Models of Regulatory Law" in G. Teubner (ed.), *Dilemmas of Law in the Welfare State*. Berlin: de Gruyter.
— (1985 b) "The Hypercycle in Law: Self-description, Self-constitution and Autopoiesis of the Legal System". Paper presented at the Conference on Autopoiesis in Law and Society, European University Institute, Firenze (December 12—15).
TRUBEK, DAVID (1985) "Normative Openness and Closedness in American Civil Procedure". Paper prepared for the Conference on Autopoiesis in Law and Society, European University Institute, Firenze (December 12—15).
WILLKE, HELMUT (1987) "Societal Guidance through Law" in G. Teubner (ed.), *State, Law, Economy as Autopoietic Systems*. Berlin: de Gruyter (forthcoming).

[7]
Criminal Law
and Criminal Justice:
Some Notes on their Irrelation

There is something odd about the teaching of criminal law in Britain. The standard textbooks on the subject make little or no use of the information and arguments to be found in studies of criminal justice and criminology.[1] Yet, paradoxically, there are incomparably more studies available here than on subjects such as Tort, Company and Administrative Law in which valuable "law in context" works have been produced.[2] Nor is the answer to be found in textbooks on criminal justice or the criminal process, which rarely contain informed discussions of the substantive criminal law[3] and may not mention it at all.[4]

The subjects of Criminal Law and Criminal Justice (in which I include the study of crime and the criminal process)[5] obviously presuppose each other. Criminal law scholars do appreciate that they may be overly "court-centred" in their interests and so sometimes seek to extend the principles of their subject to the governance of the pre-trial and post-conviction stages of the criminal process.[6] Criminologists and criminal justice scholars, for their part, usually acknowledge that criminal law defines what counts as criminal behaviour. But when they come to examine the use and effects of the law in the criminal process they may be led to argue that the value of different provisions of the criminal law can only be estimated in the light of the way they are likely to be used.[7] But there is little systematic discussion of what is involved in the different approaches adopted by each group of scholars. In particular it is hard to find explicit consideration of the discontinuities or incongruities—what I call the irrelation—between what each takes as their task. How far can these different subjects be brought into a fruitful dialogue? Does it make sense, for example, to pursue "coherence" as an object of the criminal law whilst admitting that the realm of criminal justice is one of unavoidably uncoordinated activities? Are criminal law and criminal justice scholars concerned with the same subject matter? Is the difference perhaps to do with "insider" and "outsider" perspectives, and, if so, are these reconcilable? My tentative answers to these questions will be discussed under the loose headings of "texts," "contexts" and

140   *Criminal Law and Justice*

"differences." I shall first review some relevant characteristics of standard works in criminal law, then consider some existing strategies for contextualising its subject matter; finally I shall return to the problem of the obstacles which stand between the study of legal doctrine and the effort to contextualise it.

Texts

The most usual explanation for the gulf between criminal law and criminal justice has to do with pragmatic factors. Criminal law is asked to play a special role in the law school curriculum—typically as a first year course introducing students to the techniques of legal analysis. The standard textbooks double as respected guides for practitioners—their main aim to help provide coherent and accurate directions to juries rather than engage in wider debates. Above all, the sheer bulk of material on crime and the criminal process now available reflects and encourages academic specialisation: perhaps this is the solution to the apparent paradox that criminal law is so little contextualised with more opportunities to be so than other subjects. But none of these pragmatic arguments are unanswerable. Criminal law as a first year course could surely be integrated with studies of the criminal "law in action", which now get taught under the heading of English legal institutions or English legal system. Practitioners could arguably learn more about the practicalities that face them from sound studies of the criminal process than from books about the "elevated doctrine" of the appeal courts. The lack of a law-in-context book in this area may in any event only be happenstance; there are already relevant contextual studies of sentencing[8] and evidence[9] and there is now, with Clarkson and Keating's new text, at least a partial attempt to contextualise the substantive law.[10] In any case, the really interesting question is not whether "criminal law" and "criminal justice" can be squeezed into one textbook, or even one course, but rather how, if at all, they are to be related to each other.

Criminal law and legal philosophy. The reason why so little attention has been given to this problem is not that criminal law scholars have confined themselves to the exposition of the criminal law but the way in which they have sought to further its development. They have chosen to make an alliance with *philosophy* rather than, for example, with the *social sciences*, as may be seen from the lead given by such central figures as Herbert Hart and Glanville Williams (himself previously a Professor of Jurisprudence). It is not hard to see the attractions of philosophy to criminal law scholars.[11] Ordinary language philosophy, in particular, has much to offer in the work of conceptual clarification and reformulation of judicial utterance and statutory expression. The crucial importance of justifying punishment means that criminal law scholars are heirs to a long tradition of moral and political philosophising. Moreover, philosophy and law tend to share similarities of style and approach which set them apart from much of the social science used in the study of the criminal process. Both concentrate on constructing persuasive arguments within normative frameworks, both are often dismissive of empirical fieldwork, they each succeed (too easily) in speaking the language of the "unhistorical present", in the name of "everyman".

The affair between criminal law and philosophy is still vital. The most recent textbook to appear, for all its adventurousness, is explicitly dedicated to "subject(ing) the law to the beginnings of a philosophical analysis."[12] Likewise, Richard Tur in a recent important paper, argued that criminal law was the ideal medium for teaching jurisprudence.[13] Is there anything wrong with this? Conceptual clarification and normative critique are essential parts of the study of criminal law and, for that matter, criminal justice and criminology. Nor does an alliance with philosophy necessarily produce complacency about the social effects or justifications of the criminal law.[14] But it *has* produced or reinforced a number of blind-spots in the study of criminal justice in relation to criminal law which can easily be illustrated from current writing.

First, too exclusive a reliance on philosophical critique has led to concentration on some subjects at the expense of other potentially more important ones. Commonly discussion revolves around the justification of punishment, or the problems of sentencing, but is less likely to examine the significance of "conveyor-belt" guilty pleas[15] or the practicalities of law-enforcement.[16] This may reflect the lack of a sustained literature on the *philosophy* of enforcement or of negotiation (the work of Lon Fuller constitutes an important exception here).[17] The development of adequate administrative law concepts to govern decisions in the criminal process[18] can hardly be achieved without more careful consideration of the approaches and findings of empirical studies of these topics.[19]

Other examples have to do with the particular commitments built into philosophical work. So-called "strict liability" offences are typically attacked as problematic exceptions to the requirements of criminal responsibility. There is a reluctance to examine them as widespread, prototypical illustrations of the regulatory processes of the welfare state which are enforced by means of specialised "compliance" (not punishment) strategies.[20] Perhaps the most striking evidence of the perverse results of a philosophical

142   *Criminal Law and Justice*

approach to criminal law may be seen in Clarkson and Keating's decision to entirely exclude the substantive law of theft from their recent student text. They justify this on the basis that cases on the Theft Act reveal only the familiar problems of judicial interpretation (or misinterpretation) of statutes, and are not apt for discussing the underlying principles of criminal liability. But this means that students are not asked to think about offences of dishonesty even though these constitute up to 70 per cent of reported serious crimes[21] and play such an invaluable instrumental and ideological part in the defence of private property.

A second drawback of the philosophical approach relates to policy-making. Those who offer philosophical analyses of doctrinal puzzles in the criminal law may be willing to admit that they can only clarify but not resolve any remaining policy choices.[22] They may even concede that there is a danger that seeking for unifying principles can obscure the competing pulls of law and administration which can best be reconciled only through practical politics and public discussion.[23] But this proper caution can have the unfortunate side-effect of presenting an exaggerated and artificial contrast between those matters which are seen as susceptible to reasoned analysis and those which are deemed to be irredeemably political. This can easily slight the value of those other disciplines and approaches which can inform rational policymaking even after the resources of legal and philosophical analyses are exhausted. Too often evidence gained from studies of the "working logics" of the agencies of the criminal justice system is ignored. Law and philosophy both have a strain towards a "top-down" approach which tries to *impose* consistency and coherence rather than discover the endogenous rationalities of those involved in criminal justice.

Thirdly, and most relevant to the present discussion, the "natural affinity" between legal and philosophical approaches can give the impression that the rationalisation and development of the criminal law *is itself an exercise in philosophy*—and that it falls to be evaluated by the same criteria. Yet philosophers who examine the assumptions of the criminal law quickly point out that it does not appear to adopt the philosophically most respectable position (or even any one consistent position) in its definitions of responsibility, voluntariness, intention, fault and the like.[24] Nor is there any good reason to suppose that the law must necessarily be more concerned with philosophical respectability than with the acceptability of its conceptions in terms of any other disciplines or approaches to human behaviour.[25] Although writers on criminal law have accepted that whether determinism is true or not may be treated as irrelevant from a legal point of view,[26] they have not offered an account of the conditions under which it may nevertheless be appropriate to criticise the law for holding on to discredited or implausible philosophical viewpoints. What is perhaps more important is that it may not be in the capacity of an exclusively philosophical approach to produce an account of the extent to which law can escape its aegis. In sum, arguments in and about the criminal law *may* adopt the assumptions, methods or conclusions of (particular) philosophical approaches or they may reject them. But once it is seen that neither philosophical articulacy nor correctness are essential features of the criminal law it becomes more possible to examine what other approaches connected with the study of criminal justice may have to offer.

Demands for Contextualization. It is in fact increasingly being recognised by teachers of criminal law that "lack of reference to criminal process matters leaves very important and highly relevant questions unanswered."[27] And there have been a number of attempts to forge links between criminal law and criminal justice. As early as 1963 Alan Milner responded to the publication of Elliott and Wood's case-book by stigmatizing the teaching of the subject as a course in "intermittent moral prurience."[28] He suggested instead that "the core of the teaching and learning of the law relating to criminal problems must be the understanding of how these problems arise and the operations of the various social techniques for dealing with them."[29] The syllabus he proposed along these lines discussed the court-centred rules of criminal law as part of a system whose ambit ran from enforcement to disposal. It covered the value-structure of the community in relation to crime, statistics on the distribution of crime, different stages in the regulation of crime, difficulties in designing effective sanctions, the meaning of criminal responsibility and ended with an outline of sentencing and penological aspects of the criminal process.

Clearly there is too much here for any manageable course nowadays. But apart from the sheer volume of material that has accumulated since these ideas were put forward (and the redistribution of some of these topics to different courses) there are other ways in which both Milner's critique and his alternative approach have dated. The teaching of criminal law has gained in philosophical depth but has lost in breadth of subject-matter. Conversely, the recommendation to treat criminal law as a method of "social engineering" designed to deal with a particular social problem now seems naive and even suspect. It ignores or distorts the many other symbolic and ideological features and functions of the criminal law.

144   *Criminal Law and Justice*

If the 1960's saw the conception (but still-birth) of a "social problems" approach to the teaching of criminal law in Britain, the 1970's was a period of slightly greater success in examining the part played by the criminal law as an *influence* over decision-making in what was described as "the criminal justice system" or, "the criminal process." This approach did not produce textbooks here as it did in the United States,[30] but did lead commentators such as David Thomas to call for a "functional approach" to the design of the criminal law. This meant that discussions of types and levels of criminal liability should be related to the stage and levels of the criminal justice process. The substantive law should be seen as affecting where discretion was best used in handling the offence in question.[31] As will be seen, this approach could be used to build a bridge to enquiries in the field of criminal justice but as yet the intellectual two way traffic has not really begun to flow.

Instead, some criminal law teachers of the 1980's have aspirations to a more wide-ranging critique. Amongst the most trenchant recent criticisms of contemporary criminal law scholarship are those made by Celia Wells. In commenting on the Report of the Criminal Law Reform Committee on sexual offences she criticised the Committee's approach to law reform as being both "too narrow" (because it avoided empirical investigation) and "too broad" (by engaging in sweeping policy judgments in the guise of uncontroversial reform proposals).[32] Likewise in attacking the Law Commission's approach to the revision of the criminal law, including the codification project undertaken on its behalf by representatives of the SPTL, she questioned its reluctance to examine the factual assumptions and value preferences underlying the criminal law. In addition she cast doubt on the meaningfulness of reshaping the criminal law without a more informed understanding of the way it operated in practice.[33]

Most of her arguments are well-aimed but they are directed at a variety of different targets. In order to get a clearer idea of current perspectives on relating criminal law and criminal justice it may be useful to try and distinguish more carefully amongst her points. This will show that not all of her criticisms have the same implications for the way in which those topics should be realigned and that some of her points may even in some ways be mutually contradictory. Her criticisms include evidence of the empirical sloppiness of much law reform effort, such as mistaken assumptions about public beliefs about the definition of rape which are then used to justify proposals designed to protect these (non-existent) expectations. On the other hand, at a more basic level, she objects to the presupposition of moral consensus in British society. This means

Criminal Law and Criminal Justice 145

that proposals for reform are limited to those which reproduce existing inequalities and rules out, for example, extending the definition of criminal violence to include companies knowingly marketing dangerous products or ignoring safety hazards in their goods. She does not, however, make it clear whether her suggestions reflect a newly emergent consensus or whether the search for consensus is itself futile. This ambiguity is still more pronounced in her demand for more awareness of the arguments of (some) jurisprudents concerning the limits of language in predetermining decision-making and the need to appreciate that definitions of criminal liability can only take on their full meaning in the context in which they are used. Again the question where such reflections lead is left open. Are her criticisms to be taken as additive or in the alternative? For example, what, if anything, can better use of empirical evidence do to resolve her other more basic criticisms? In order to answer these questions it may be helpful to discuss in more detail the differences in the approaches to contextualising the study of criminal law which she draws on in her critique.

Contexts

Any approach to contextualising criminal law must adopt some criterion of relevance to select its topics[34] and disciplinary orientations.[35] I shall consider here only some of the sociological studies of crime and the criminal process which may be roughly described under the heading of criminal justice. It is also true that these studies themselves require to be placed in a wider context[36] whereas I shall be focusing more on their application to the narrow topic of criminal law. My sole purpose here is to provide illustrative examples of the differences between three strategies for contextualising criminal law. The first is introducing more information into the study of criminal law and the others are the more consciously theoretical exercises of either placing the criminal law in context or revealing the context implicit in the law itself.[37]

Useful Information. The introduction of more "facts" and findings into textbook discussions of criminal offences and their processing would seem to pose few conceptual difficulties. It could certainly be useful for textbooks to categorise and sub-categorise offences according to their characteristic "fact situations", and the typical motives and circumstances surrounding them (as the American Realists argued many years ago). An illustration may be found in the report of a recent Home Office Research Study which stated:

146   *Criminal Law and Justice*

"Offences of personal violence are more readily understood when categorised in a way which focusses on the circumstances surrounding them: for example violent crimes associated with alcohol or drugs; racially motivated violence, domestic violence, armed robbery, street robbery (mugging). Looking at offences in this way makes it easier to concentrate on measures to combat them."[38]

This strategy may throw up interesting contrasts between legal and criminological categories which would not be obvious from the unrepresentative sample of cases adjudicated in the higher courts. For example, given the law's preoccupation with distinguishing levels of criminal responsibility it is instructive to learn that the peak age for criminality is fifteen for men and fourteen for women.[39] In considering how to draw the boundaries between murder and manslaughter it may be useful to bear in mind that those at greatest risk of murder are babies under one year old who are the victims of non-accidental injuries.[40] Going further it maybe possible to show that the criminal law operates with distinctions between offences such as drug-pushing and drug-using[41] or stealing and receiving[42] which may be positively misleading when it comes to dealing with actual cases.[43] In the same way greater awareness of (changing) patterns of prosecution, sentencing and punishment, like the information provided by criminal statistics and typologies, may have much to contribute to the justification and reform of offence categories such as offences against the person.[44] Clarkson and Keating do make some definite moves in these directions in their textbook. But the result is somewhat patchy, and not only because of the narrow range of offences they discuss. Their approach to culpability—which they say should be based on a combination of "harm" and "blame"—leads them to recommend that more information about motive and circumstances of offences should be considered at the trial rather than the sentencing stage.[45] But they do not offer any criminologically informed scheme of offence categories or resolve the problems of relating this to legal doctrine. They equivocate, for example, over whether the law could conceive provocation in terms of the degree of "victim precipitation," as in some criminologists' classifications, or whether the defence should rather be seen as a matter of compassion towards the offender.[46] It is only in connection with rape that they offer anything like a full discussion in a section entitled "sociological context" in which they examine the "level of rape in society" and "societal attitudes towards rape."[47] Nothing like as systematic an approach is provided in relation to any other

Criminal Law and Criminal Justice   147

offences, although it is hard to say why rape should be so singled out,[48] and it is interesting to note that there is no similar discussion (or even any mention) of "wife-battering" although it raises many similar issues of under-enforcement and criminal definition. Significantly, this may be because it does not correspond to any single criminal offence.

Whatever the weaknesses of current textbooks the advantages for law reform of obtaining more information about crime and the criminal process can hardly be in doubt—as was recognized by the Royal Commission on Criminal Procedure. But there are some pitfalls in attempting to integrate findings about crime and criminal justice without an appreciation of the theoretical frameworks and methods with which such "facts" are generated. Criminal statistics—even with the availability of the *British Crime Survey* and various Victimisation surveys—are notoriously difficult to interpret. Nor is the problem merely technical—as sociological theories and investigations of the definition and redefinition of criminal labels amply document.[49] Above all, when "facts" are detached from the perspectives which produce them the opportunity is lost to see that what is at stake is law's way of approaching problems and not merely its factual assumptions.

Theoretical Approaches to Contextualisation. Two competing strategies designed to encourage a more explicit confrontation between a doctrinal perspective and alternative approaches may be characterised as "placing the *law in context*" and "revealing the *context in law*" (they are not of course confined to criminal law).[50] The first approach draws attention to the social forces and conflict that shape the operation of law, the second tries to illuminate (or de-construct) the source and significance of legal categories and rules. The two approaches may overlap (as in studying the making of law) and could perhaps complement each other. But the former approach has tended to dominate investigations of the criminal process over the last 20 years, whilst the latter represents a recent, but increasingly influential unorthodox form of criminal law scholarship. There are a number of interesting differences between these two strategies for contextualising criminal law. Law in context writers might be said to examine the operation of law so as to show how "context determines meaning." The more recent approach, on the other hand, looks for the context which shapes the production of legal texts. The law in context strategy is particularly likely to use empirical methods to investigate the "law in action" but often leaves unquestioned the values and much of the aspirations of the substantive law. The alternative approach, by contrast, is mainly distinguished by its rejection of these values

148   *Criminal Law and Justice*

and aspirations, and its reinterpretation of doctrinal categories as
unsuccessful attempts to resolve underlying social dilemmas.
Those who place the law in context therefore tend to stress the
contradictions between aspiration and achievement. They
threaten the coherence of the criminal law by suggesting that it
needs to take into account an increasing (and unpredictable)
number of factors if it is to make sense. The message of those who
reveal the context in law, on the other hand, is that contradictions
are necessarily inherent in the law itself. Coherence is not a
question of the scope of the law's viewpoint but reflects an ultimately arbitrary decision to foreclose alternative options. For
example, whereas "law in context" scholars would stress the *limits*
of what can be achieved by the current codification proposals, the
exponents of critical legal studies would offer an appropriate form
of *de-codification.*

The "law in context" approach also challenges criminal law
scholarship by questioning the importance and efficacy it attaches
to law. By comparison, those who uncover the context within law
take law at least as seriously as doctrinal scholars—and perhaps
too seriously, albeit for different reasons. In this respect at least
"law in context" studies adopt an outsider's standpoint on the role
of criminal law within the criminal process, whereas those who
examine the context in law may be said to share the insiders' perspective (even if they do not restrict themselves to the forms of
reasoning which are conventionally accepted).[51]

Criminal Law in Context. A short survey of some of the main
findings of "law in context" studies will indicate their implications
for the study of criminal law.

First, they point out how rarely legal doctrine is invoked in the
practical adjudications of criminal cases, 97 per cent of which are
tried by magistrates' courts and most of which turn on facts rather
than law. Innovations in doctrine have little effect on the sorry
parade of criminals through the lower courts which are deputed to
do the "dirty work" of disposing of allegedly "trivial" cases.[52]
Even in the higher courts, cases more often end in guilty pleas
rather than contested trials and there is an uncertain relationship
between doctrinal niceties and the reasons for negotiated pleas.[53]
The most far-reaching and influential decisions are those taken by
the "gatekeepers" to the criminal process: the police, other
enforcement agencies as well as victims and other complainants,
all of whom act on their imperfect knowledge of the law.

Secondly, doctrinal prescriptions may often be sidestepped or
ignored. Thus a recent training manual for newly appointed magistrates contains the following advice:

Criminal Law and Criminal Justice 149

"It is sometimes said on the defendant's behalf that he did not intend to inflict the particular injury which the victim suffered. This is always a weak point because any sane person who commits an act of violence must expect injury to result. The fact that it happens to be greater than anticipated provides no excuse whatsoever."[54]

At one blow these remarks appear to cut straight through the endless debate over intention in the criminal law. They may represent no more than an enthusiastic over-simplification of the conditions of liability for what have been characterised as half *mens rea* offences under the Offences Against the Person Act 1861. Straining credulity, they may perhaps indicate endorsement of the wide application of the *Caldwell* definition of recklessness (as advocated by Clarkson and Keating).[55] But it is most likely that they simply indicate the common blurring of the different questions of culpability and mitigation which puts in doubt much of the effort that goes into doctrinal clarification in the criminal law.

Thirdly, "law in context" work on agencies in the criminal process argues not so much for the *irrelevance* of legal doctrine as for the *malleability* of legal rules. Law must be seen as a resource (rather than a constraint), which is available for use by those who work for these agencies for the purpose of achieving their organisationally (or personally) defined goals.[56] It is rare for rules to be employed for their own sake.

Fourthly, it is true that changes in the substantive law may sometimes affect these processes and purposes by affecting the stock of available legal resources and bargaining chips.[57] But such changes may also be neutralised or re-formed in ways which can only be understood (but not always predicted) by close examination of localised networks of decision-making.[58] In consequence, desirable alteration of the substantive law may have undesirable effects elsewhere. As Andrew Sanders has argued, increased emphasis on "subjective" mens rea may translate in practice into intensified efforts by the police to extract confessions as the surest way of providing the necessary evidence.[59]

The upshot of much of this work has been to demonstrate the recurrent "gaps" between "law in books" and the "law in action," and the relevance of this for standard textbook discussions can be drastic. It is now many years since Carson showed how strict liability rules governing factory safety were enforced in such a way that the only offenders prosecuted were those who deliberately ignored repeated warnings and advice as to their breach of the rules (in addition to those prosecuted after incidents of serious

150   *Criminal Law and Justice*

injury and death).[60] The same pattern has been shown to exist in
the enforcement of laws dealing with other regulatory offences
involving business and industry.[61] Offenders against these criminal
provisions therefore benefit from the reduced stigma attaching to
what are seen as merely "regulatory" or "quasi-crimes" whilst in
actuality they often may possess more than the usual requirements
of intentional mens rea.[62] Whilst not all strict liability offences are
enforced in this way, it is nonetheless strange to see textbooks continue to agonise over the justifications of strict liability without
building on this work.[63]

The importance of "law in context" studies for problems of
institutional design in the criminal law should not need to be
further demonstrated.[64] But this strategy is not without its weaknesses. The division of labour between the concerns and methods
of doctrinal scholarship and those who specialise in the description
of the criminal process (reproduced in the distinction between
"law in books" and "law in action") is too neat. It makes it too
easy for criminal law scholars to minimise the importance of these
contextual findings. They may treat them as unrepresentative or
idiosyncratic reports of particular institutional settings or local
practices. They may deny that there is anything problematic about
any given use of law,[65] or, even if some deviation is acknowledged,
may insist that it is the nature of normative standards that they be
distorted or broken without this detracting from their significance.
Some doctrinal scholars even give the impression that they see
themselves as providing a framework which is important in its own
right, as something which can appeal directly to citizens over the
heads, as it were, of the legal actors (not excluding the judges!)
who operate the criminal process in such a way as to confuse their
counsels.

Furthermore, the distinction between 'law in books" and "law
in action" is often (wrongly) equated with Packer's contrast
between the "due process" model for protecting criminal defendants' rights and the "crime control" imperative of those working to
process crime efficiently.[66] Properly understood it is not clear that
Packer was offering these as descriptions or that the clash between
these models can be overcome.[67] However, the most important
recent contribution to this debate has been that of Doreen McBarnet who has argued that the legal rules associated with "due process" protections do not need to be undermined or distorted in
order to expedite the "conveyor-belt" conviction of criminal
offenders characteristic of the lower courts.[68] Rather than focus on
the way law is undermined by being used to achieve organisational
goals we are urged to study the *form* and *content* of the law itself.

Criminal Law and Criminal Justice 151

In her view "Due Process" is *for* "Crime Control"[69] McBarnet's argument has in turn been criticised for ignoring the difference between those rules which offer illusory safeguards because they are unenforceable, those which could protect but are in fact unenforced, and those which, despite her polemic, do exercise some inhibitory influence over the enforcement of the law and the processing of offenders.[70] McBarnet's analysis may also have other flaws. Her description of the methods used by judges to narrow down the scope of defendants' protections may be partly understood as the result of case-law growing on the back of unworthy defence appeals rather than as some inevitable development.[71] McBarnet's view of "law" may still be too monolithic.[72] Judicial choices in extending or restricting protections may be better seen as a further example of the 'law in action" *undermining* the law in books rather than, as she assumes, representing the enunciation of the "law in books." Her contrast between the world of "rhetoric" (where procedural safeguards do exist) and the law itself—which fails to make such claims a reality—runs the risk of reproducing, at a higher level, the artificial distinction between "law in books" and the "law in action" which she is at such pains to reject. The view that "rhetoric" lies *outside* the law rests on an unexamined positivist separation between the rules of law and the broader principles which animate it and ignores the argument, (as Dworkin might put it),[73] that "rhetoric" serves as the source of principles which can generate or limit legal rule-making even though it does not and cannot function in the same way as rules. In a sense, McBarnet has not so much overturned previous work into the workings of law in the criminal process as extended it. She has demonstrated that the reason why criminal law so easily serves as a *resource* for police, prosecution *or judges* to achieve their aims is that it is so often *permissive* rather than duty-imposing. Yet, more than anyone else, she has directed students of criminal justice to look more carefully at the possibilities built into the formulation of the substantive law itself rather than merely the way it is used or abused.[74]

A number of other factors have contributed to this important shift in focus. Within criminology growing disappointment with the search for the causes of crime had led many writers to turn instead to the way particular forms of misconduct were singled out for "criminalisation."[75] The anti-positivist trend within critical criminology led some writers to argue that questions of "blame" and "guilt" should be put back on the agenda of their subject.[76] More recently, other radical writers within criminology have, for reasons of political strategy, complained of the emphasis given to the study of exotic forms of "deviance" or a preoccupation with "crimes of

152   *Criminal Law and Justice*

the powerful." They urge the importance to working-class neigh-
bourhoods (as well as to the middle class) of offences such as burglary, violence or vandalism which are the standard fare of
textbook discussions of criminal law.[77] From a different angle,
feminist writers have helped to widen the debate over sexual
offences such as the crimes of rape and indecent assault.[78] Changing attitudes to the justification of punishment such as a loss of
belief in rehabilitation (and even deterrence) and a return to "justice" conceived in formal, retributionist and denunciatory terms
also underlined the significance of legal doctrine in its own right.
Finally, renewed interest in law was encouraged by a number of
developments in the sociology of law which gave rise to increasing
doubts about the possibility of "reducing" legal doctrine to external social or economic structures.[79] This helped to fuel the rise of
the Critical Legal Studies movement in the United States of
America and Europe.[80] The result of these various factors is that
anyone producing a contextualising textbook on criminal law in
the 1980's is at least as likely to offer an approach geared to
revealing (and reshaping) the context-within-law as they are to
seek to incorporate findings concerning the operation of the "law
in action".[81] For this reason it is worth examining this approach
more carefully.

The Context in Law. This alternative strategy for contextualising
law has its forerunners in work such as Jerome Hall's classic study
of the historical emergence of the larceny laws in *Theft, Law and
Society*.[82] But the distinctive feature of the critical legal scholar's
approach is to seek to reveal political and moral *choices* which are
made to seem matters of *social necessity*. Unfortunately this movement has shown comparatively little interest so far in the criminal
law.[83] But some idea of its style may be gained from a short consideration of Kelman's paper "Substantive Interpretation in the
Criminal Law"[84] (which was drawn on by Celia Wells in her
critique of the Law Commission).[85] Kelman's arguments are concerned with the way "concrete situations are reduced to substantive legal controversies"[86] so as 'to avoid dealing with fundamental
political problems."[87] Consciously and unconsciously, solutions
for legal dilemmas are produced which tend to favour the power-
holders in society.[88] Kelman suggests that doctrinal analysis oscil-
lates, as required, between broad and narrow "time-frames"; dis-
jointed and unified accounts of the criminal act; and broad and
narrow views of intent and of the offender. He claims that the law
incorporates both voluntarist and determinist conceptions of
human conduct and vacillates between an insistence on rules or a
preference for standards. Law's claim to rationality can be under-

mined by revealing the arbitrariness of its selection of one choice or the other.

One example which can be used to follow the thread of his often complex argument concerns the distinction between ordinary and strict liability offences. Kelman claims that the conduct penalised by strict liability offences could be viewed as intentional if the time-frame was expanded to include preceding actions.[89] He argues that such a wider perspective is already used in dealing with omissions,[90] attempts[91] or abandonment of offences.[92] But the law avoids consistent use of a broad time-frame because this would allow in too much information about victim involvement or social pressures on the defendant, which could not be properly subjected to judicial scrutiny. It might also threaten criminal law's assumptions about responsibility by showing how particular incidents were "determined" by previous events. Focussing on the criminal incident is justified by the requirements of "legality," which discountenances vagueness in the ambit of the criminal law. But it has various other implications. For example, it artificially separates theft offences from the problems of justifying the wider property regimes in which they are embedded and it confines us to the stereotype of "the unremorseful and non-restitutionary thief."[93] Kelman's view of strict liability offences is remarkably similar to that reached by "law in context" studies, although arrived at by a different route.[94] In his view much of the concern over alleged departures from the usual standards of mens rea gives the misleading impression that *other* offences are only penalised where these have been deliberately broken. But in all cases this depends on how carefully antecedent events are examined.

Kelman's arguments about how the categories of culpability emerge—how the context gets into the law—are more tentative. For example, he suggests that excusing conditions such as duress are confined to the criminal incident rather than embracing the long-term grinding effects of social deprivation because power-holders can envisage themselves facing immediate psychological pressures but have not been exposed to the social pressures.[95] Other connections are structural rather than being related to the attitudes of the law-makers. Thus rules about the determination of consent are seen to parallel (and reinforce) definitions of consent in the market place.[96]

It is too early to assess the value of the approach represented by Kelman's article. It is certainly capable of being applied to English material, indeed his method of analysing the pull of competing conceptualisations could usefully be extended to the way law distributes choices between culpability and mitigation, matters of law

154   *Criminal Law and Justice*

and matters of fact and even to the debate over subjectivist and objectivist approaches to responsibility. But the strategy as presently developed still suffers from serious ambiguities about what it is purporting to reveal. As Kelman admits,[97] it is unclear whether we are being offered an interpretation of the reasons legal categories take the form they do, or, instead, an avowedly "external" account of the "structure" of legal doctrine which the commentator imposes on the legal materials. It is also uncertain whether this approach is committed to showing the superficiality of the apparent coherence which masks underlying incoherence or, alternatively, the coherent purposes which force legal doctrine to be incoherent. In fact both of these types of argument are developed but (ironically) we are not told how to decide *when* one or the other is appropriate. In consequence, it is easy to accuse Kelman of incorrect, or at least unsupported, attributions of the rationales for various of the legal doctrines he discusses.[98] For example, he assumes that the excuse of duress reflects the intrusion of a determinist perspective into the criminal law.[99] But others justify it on the basis of not setting law's standards too high.[1] Many commentators would freely concede that the law marshals competing rules and principles in resolving particular cases, but would stress the importance and possibility of rational persuasion for all that; others would insist on the viability of law as a method of policy determination.[2] At worst, they will refer law's incoherence to the case by case "flexibility" of the common law rather than to fundamental contradictions in society.

The difficulty of dislodging these more conciliatory accounts of legal doctrine is partly caused by the extent to which Kelman's work remains unhistorical. We are given little insight into the movements in ideas and social forces which lie behind the different and allegedly incongruous conceptions in the law.[3] Accordingly, claims concerning contradiction and incoherence often amount to little more than evidence of inconsistency rather than demonstrating the insoluble conflicts within the liberal world-view or capitalist social structure which Kelman wants to prove. Or, more specifically, it is hard to pick out *which* of the inconsistencies he describes can bear this weight of argument.

The reason for all this ambiguity appears to lie in the extent to which this approach to contextualisation purports to adopt the "insiders" perspective on the law. Much like other commentaries on legal doctrine it runs together the question of explaining legal doctrine with the rational reconstruction of arguments and justifications for particular legal provisions. The strengths and weaknesses of this approach are therefore the reverse of those of "law in context" studies. It is closer to doctrinal scholarship because it concentrates on substantive law, is sometimes willing to engage in normative argument and prescription, and is relatively unconcerned with empirical investigation. But these very similarities make it subject to many of the drawbacks of mainstream criminal law scholarship (in addition to those which are self-inflicted). The choice which faces this approach is whether to continue to try to demonstrate the incoherence of existing legal doctrine or whether to seek to develop what Unger calls "deviationist doctrine" and create a new groundwork of offence categories and conditions of culpability.[4] In either case, however, it is unlikely that it can dispense with the methods and insights of "law in context" studies[5] and it would be regrettable if new British textbooks in criminal law were to "leapfrog" over the extensive contributions made by the other approach. But, as the mutual inattention of these two approaches to contextualisation would seem to show, there remain considerable difficulties in the way of weaving together doctrinal commentary, whether seen from a mainstream or deviationist perspective, with description and explanation viewed more from an outsider's viewpoint. It is time to ask where these difficulties may lie.

Differences

Writers interested in contextual approaches to law have always appreciated that legal doctrine operated its own view of the world, the so-called "legal paradigm" of lawyers and legal scholars.[6] But they understood their task to be to demonstrate the *mistakes* or *inconsistencies* in the legal perspective. However, there are now signs of a renewed respect for law's ability to maintain and reproduce its way of categorising the social world and a new concern with how best to characterise this process. Roger Cotterrell, for example, argued recently that, "Legal discourse . . . protects itself from (perhaps is immune to) interference from external knowledge fields."[7]

There may be some dangers in this opposite tendency to see law as self-contained. Much depends on noticing that law's autonomy lies not in its freedom from being influenced by external causes and influences but in the way in which it incorporates and responds to them.[8] In any case we should not assume that law is a unitary discourse. Studies of different branches and levels of law and diverse arenas of social life are required before we can map the characteristics and variations of law's specificity. Yet it is surely

156   *Criminal Law and Justice*

correct to say that contextualising approaches must develop a fresh
understanding of what is *distinctive* about legal discourse—and the
way in which this is understood by textbook writers—if they are to
get any further with their own project. This is the route, I suggest,
which may allow us to understand, if not wholly to overcome, the
irrelation between criminal law and criminal justice.

   From Domain to Discourse. The distinction between Criminal
Law and Criminal Justice is often related to the apparently contrasting *domains* of court adjudication as compared to pre-trial
and post-conviction processes.[9] These are seen as arenas in which
the distinctive ideals and purposes of "due process" and "crime
control" compete. Investigating their relationship therefore
becomes a matter of seeing how these domains and purposes
actually intersect. We now know that it is an oversimplification to
identify the judicial role with the pursuit of "due process."[10] Less
well recognised, perhaps, is the danger in taking the world of
police and prosecutions to be one uniformly dedicated to "crime
control."[11] There are also those who collapse these distinctions
between the domains and purposes of the different actors in the
criminal process. They propose instead that we view criminal justice as a united search for "crime control"[12]; "bureaucratic justice"[13] or even "substantive equity."[14]

   Whatever the value of these debates, it is clear that this
approach does not help us answer the question how criminal law
(and those textbooks which try to rationalise it) succeed in paying
so little attention to external disciplines and findings.[15] When
writers such as Clarkson and Keating and others begin to confront
legal doctrine with evidence concerning the operations of the
criminal process they are placing a *new* type of problem on the
agenda. *Under what conditions (in both senses) is legal doctrine
open to learning about these or any other perspectives and findings
"external" to itself?* It will not do simply to juxtapose the claims of
medicine, psychology, sociology or even philosophy to the corresponding assumptions made by the law. We must also have a
theory (or rather a meta-theory) of what is distinctive about the
self-understanding and reproduction of law in relation to these
potentially competing approaches. We have to consider not only
the first-order problem of the way in which the activities and ideas
of police and lawyers impinge on those of judges (who may be
senior in the "hierarchy of credibility" and power but less close to
the realities of crime processing). We need to develop a method of
discussing second-order questions regarding the obstacles which so
often prevent the approaches and findings characteristic of the
study of criminal justice from being perceived as relevant to the

Criminal Law and Criminal Justice 157

development of legal doctrine.[16] A variety of theoretical perspectives and frameworks may be employed for this purpose.[17] I want to consider here, at a relatively concrete level, three features which can help to explain the distinctiveness of legal discourse as compared to that of the contextualising disciplines used in criminal justice scholarship. These are differences in the *functions* (or better *"functioning"*) of each type of discourse; differences in their sources of *authority* and differences in their claims to *legitimacy*. I will also show how these differences are interrelated. My purpose is not to attempt a comprehensive account of these issues but to illustrate what is entailed by moving from talking about the relationship between *domains* or *purposes* to discussing instead the confrontation between *discourses* or *rationalities*.

The Distinctiveness of Doctrine. Much of what is distinctive about criminal law discourse stems from its ostensible concern with the function of setting standards. Thus criminal law scholars, including those involved in the codification project or the authors of the standard textbooks, try to discover or establish a framework in which appropriate degrees of blame and punishment are attached to corresponding kinds of harmful rule-breaking.[18] This project may assume certain sociological or other suppositions about the causes and cures of criminality but as Kelsen would argue it is not itself geared to developing such knowledge. When criminal law is conceptualised by criminal justice scholars as an instrument of social control viewed in terms of its use in the criminal process, the distinctiveness of this endeavour is easily missed. This function largely explains the differences of emphasis and subject-matter between the way law is discussed in books on criminal doctrine and in criminal justice. The many pages devoted to the insanity defence in criminal law textbooks, for example, represent a conscious effort to sustain the normative framework of the law by patrolling the boundaries of criminal responsibility.[19] It is not justified by the number of practical difficulties within the criminal process which are raised or resolved by the existence of this defence. Likewise, it is not every day that prosecutors face the question of what to do with a drunk who wakes up and seizes control of a car hurtling downhill.[20] Its significance lies elsewhere, as a "hard case" (in Dworkin's sense)[21] which can be used to clarify the underlying principles of the law. Criminal justice scholars, for their part, may wonder why the case was prosecuted at all and may point out that much tactical decision-making over prosecution appears to have only a loose linkage with the need for norm-clarification. Contextualising approaches question whether there are "hard" and "easy" cases, whether the distinction, if it exists, is the

158 *Criminal Law and Justice*

same for the judge and other criminal justice actors, and whether those which are "hard" in the doctrinal sense are necessarily those which make it to trial.[22] But insofar as doctrinal scholarship concentrates on this unrepresentative and peculiar sample of contested criminal cases it does so because, as a matter of social as well as legal fact, these are the only ones which can be used to create and convey doctrinal messages.

A second function of legal doctrine which is assumed by criminal law textbooks is the need to provide a conceptual framework suitable for its specialised methods of adjudication.[23] This explains (and justifies?) the use of sometimes arbitrary but expeditious cut-off points between life and death,[24] the age of criminal responsibility,[25] sexual maturity,[26] and so on. It may also help to account for differences in "factual" and "legal causation"[27] and many of the features of the law's fact-finding processes where these diverge from those adopted by psychology or statistics.[28] Alternative disciplines may be admitted to offer expert *diagnoses* of particular problems but not to displace legal *definitions* by their own[29] (and law retains the right to distinguish diagnosis from definition).[30]

However, it is plain that legal discourse does not develop in a vacuum. Its reliance on certain methods of fact-finding may reflect their past popularity in other *fields* in a way that can no longer be justified.[31] Similarly, many of the distinctive doctrinal assumptions connected with this function relate to the special strengths and limitations of *judicial* scrutiny. Greater reference to criminal justice studies would raise serious questions about how far the same doctrinal presumptions do and should apply to the various forms of "judging" which effectively take place at other stages of the criminal process (under very different circumstances).[32] Moreover, criminal process considerations do already play some part in shaping legal doctrine. The familiar contrast between "due-process" and "crime control" may be re-cast as an *internal* difference in the principles justifying various doctrines. On the one hand, there are those principles and rules, mainly in the realm of procedure, which demand that legal guilt reach a higher level of proof than factual guilt. On the other hand, the criminal law is sometimes more willing to impose responsibility where other approaches might be less likely to do so. Thus "victims must be taken as they are found" (not as possessing average states of health),[33] drink or drugs may be disallowed as an excuse even where they actually influenced the individual's ability to make decisions,[34] other defences may be confined or extended in ways that make little sense from a behavioural point of view. For example, provocation is confined to murder, but duress is currently avail-

Criminal Law and Criminal Justice 159

able for all crimes except principal to murder.[35] To some extent then, legal doctrine incorporates a concern for "crime control" as part of its distinctive tasks of creating and adjudicating its own normative standards. This allows law to treat similar behavioural situations differently and makes it difficult for contexualising disciplines to substitute their own assumptions without risking law's achievement of its self-imposed tasks.

Criminal justice scholars may challenge or add to the textbook view of law's functions.[36] Contextualising approaches also appear to be on strong ground when they challenge law's claims to *regulate* behaviour rather than simply lay down standards to be followed by citizens or used in adjudication. The training of judges and magistrates does now include criminological evidence concerning, for example, the effects of different sentences. Yet it still remains important to see why this sort of information is unlikely to be generated *inside* the legal and fact-finding processes itself. This is something which contextualising approaches can help to explain. They can show how "facts" about crime and criminality are constructed and reconstructed in the criminal process so as to make them fit doctrinal categories and processing requirements.[37] They can reveal the structural limitations which govern how far normative decision-making can be made subject to evidence derived from other forms of understanding or prediction. Beyond a certain point judging and understanding may be incompatible.[38] If law pays too much attention to the *consequences* of its decisions this can threaten the *validity* of its normative order and the *autonomy* of its reproduction.[39] This last argument has been developed by a leading German scholar of criminal law into the view that punishment must be based on the voluntary breach of criminal law rather than on the harmful consequences of behaviour as such.[40]

Paradoxically, therefore, contextualising approaches can actually be used to show the extent of their own "irrelevance" to the reproduction of criminal law. Whilst this view can be taken too far it does provide a useful corrective to the haste with which some contextualisers have *assumed* their work to be relevant to doctrine. In fact what is really needed is a method for distinguishing which are the more, and which are the less, insulated features of legal reproduction and how these features are interrelated.[41]

A further difference between criminal law and contextualising disciplines lies in the sources of their claims to *authority*. Criminal law scholars generally see doctrine as growing through the search for coherence, supplemented by deliberate choice by legislatures and judges. *Who* or *what* is authorised to interpret doctrine or recommend change is crucial. Unlike other disciplines, change in

160   Criminal Law and Justice

law is not linked to the discovery of new truths or the resolution of
anomalies. The ideal virtues of criminal law—its certainty, uniformity, consistency and so forth would represent faults in contextualising approaches. For these it is disunity, uncertainty and
constant change which are a necessary part of their existence. The
subservience of law to changing developments in other disciplines
would be incompatible with the basis of its authority (including the
doctrine of judicial independence). What textbook writers mean
by "theory" is the best and most parsimonious account of the principles which would "generate" the criminal law, *not* what best
'explains" the criminal law in terms of its causes and functions.
Furthermore, the *point* of their theorising is to show as much
coherence as possible, not to unpick claims to coherence.[42]

There are other related problems which arise from the way criminal law seeks *legitimacy* as compared to that sought by contextualising approaches. A particularly interesting feature of this branch of
law is its attempt to derive legitimacy from its ability to incorporate
commonsense conceptions and judgments. This is said to reflect the
need for citizens to be able to guide their conduct in accordance with
the law, to allow law to reproduce popular distinctions between
kinds and levels of blame and to ensure that the law is intelligible to
juries when these are directed as to their duties. On the other hand,
contextualising approaches, such as medicine, sociology, psychology or statistics, typically pride themselves on their ability to
challenge or *undermine* commonsense conceptions and values.

However, many of the same questions arise here as in law's relations with competing disciplines. Is law capable of modelling lay
conceptions and introducing them into its processes? Or, as with
other elements of its self-identity perhaps, is this no more than a
rhetorical gloss (but important for all that)? There are certainly
criminal lawyers who question this feature of legal doctrine.
Richard Tur, for example, argues that:

> "the nature of excuses in crime . . . is, however, so particular-
> istic and so dependent upon the facts of the case that it strains
> credulity to imagine someone seeking in advance to bring his
> case under such categories."[43]

Kenny offers an even more biting comment on this self-
imposed task of criminal lawyers:

> "The elaborate efforts of lawyers and academics to sort
> offences into precise categories and to fit crimes to punish-
> ment on impeccable theoretical grounds may well strike a lay-
> man as resembling an attempt to make a town clock accurate
> to a millisecond in a community most of whom are too short-

Criminal Law and Criminal Justice 161

sighted to see the clockface, too deaf to hear the hours ring, and many of whom set no great store on punctuality in any case."[44]

But Kenny actually appears to blame the public for their lack of appreciation of lawyers' efforts at fine distinctions. And, like Tur himself, he continues to seek some match between criminal law conceptions and those of the public.[45]

Law's concern to match the public's viewpoint seems curiously ambivalent and selective. Little effort is made to establish what is the public's perception.[46] Whereas some elements of offences are left for juries to define, such as the meaning of "dishonesty" in theft,[47] other matters are predetermined to avoid their participation, such as what counts as provocation[48] (and the whole recourse to legal definition of what is reasonable behaviour). Law is expected simultaneously to reflect the public's perceptions and yet represent a standard to which they should aspire in their attitudes. And in any case public conceptions may themselves have previously been shaped by law.[49]

What all this suggests is that it does not matter too much if legal and public conceptions do sometimes differ. As with law's exchanges with other disciplines, what seems to be important if law is to reproduce itself as an independent discourse is not that it should originate all its own categories and ideas but that they should not be reducible to those of any other approach. Legal discourse retains the choice whether and when to homologate the views of other disciplines or those of the public. As long as there is *some* support this will be deemed sufficient even if the view relied upon is not the most favoured, or up to date one within the relevant discipline.[50]

The irrelation between criminal law and the approaches used in criminal justice and criminology derives, *on both sides*, from these differences in function, authority and legitimacy. For the distinctive features of criminal law which have been discussed so far are exactly what can threaten the integrity of contextualising approaches when they are pressed into its service. Policymakers who work within the categories of criminal law look for approaches and findings that can help it achieve its goals and secure its authority and legitimacy. But scholars in other disciplines who tackle problems defined in this way are unlikely to advance their own subjects.[51] Nor, it is claimed, will they even produce useful policy conclusions.[52] For this to be achieved they have to pose problems in terms of their *own* theoretical frameworks, even if this undermines the working assumptions of the law

162   *Criminal Law and Justice*

by changing law's definitions of the problem or the solution. Maintaining a "dialogue" between doctrinal and other approaches to criminal law is therefore fraught with intellectual and political difficulties.[53]

But, partly for this reason, law and other disciplines should not always be taken as trying to achieve each other's tasks. For example, those who examine criminal law from contextualising perspectives disagree radically amongst themselves both over whether criminal law *is* turning into a form of social policy regulation[54] and whether it *should* do so.[55] Whereas some criminologists would undoubtedly welcome closer involvement with the criminal law, others would resist such licensed technocracy. Conversely, the criminal law does not always seek collaboration with those perspectives which are apparently closest to its own style and viewpoint (it often treats them as redundant)[56] it looks rather for *contrasting* approaches to which it can delegate those problems which it cannot fit into its own framework. It may also be hypothesised that there will always be more resistance to marginal criticisms of law and its administration than to more radical critiques which can either be ignored or co-opted.[57]

All of this suggests (or should suggest) that the relation or irrelation between criminal law and contextualising disciplines is at least as much a matter of power as it is of intellectual competition. Or rather, as Foucault has shown, we must speak of struggles between different constellations of power/knowledge.[58] The struggle referred to here is not the one presented in some textbooks which ranges an inconsistent and sometimes incoherent judiciary against the combined efforts of Parliament and commentators.[59] Rather, it includes, on the one side, *all* those committed to maintaining and developing the juridical mode of discourse as against those writing within alternative discourses. In these terms, whilst Foucault may have been correct to emphasise the growing importance of surveillance and disciplinary techniques in place of law,[60] it is important not to exaggerate the decline of law. Nor should we neglect the influence legal discourse may have beyond the boundaries of its institutional domain.[61]

Some conclusions (and beginnings)

At this point we should perhaps return to the starting point of this paper. Are there any conclusions to be drawn from this discussion for the content of textbooks or courses in criminal law? Is the only choice that between either reflecting law's own self-understanding or adopting an "external" point of reference which must therefore fail to engage with law's internal discourse? Obviously the answer depends on the point of the exercise and its intended audience. Those writers who want to be "insiders" in the development of law, or to be accepted as "authorities," are rightly wary of drawing on other disciplines except where these are easily assimilated or "domesticated" by legal discourse. But the price of such a hermeneutic adoption of the legal point of view is to be unable to see the limits of its way of seeing the world. It means accepting its own systemic misunderstandings.

Too many problems are avoided or distorted in this way. It prevents appreciation of how law assumes, depends on and opposes competing and supplementary discourses—including those of "criminal justice" and "criminology."[62] It ignores the extent to which legal institutions and strategies embrace competing discourses such as law, social work and psychiatry whether in the work of courts or penal agencies or in creating the realm of "the social."[63] It obscures understanding of the past sources of legal categories and conceptions and the circumstances in which these change. And it hides the critical historical processes which encourage the rise and fall of legal discourse and which lie behind the particular mixture of discourses currently used in dealing with crime.[64] Fuller understanding of these matters is essential to understand, for example, what is a question of culpability or mitigation as well as the mutually constitutive definitions of mental illness and normality or adult and juvenile responsibility. It will also shed light on the blend of neo-classical and positivist views of human nature which Kelman and others claim to find reflected in the structure of excuses in the criminal law.[65]

This sort of contextualisation of the criminal law does not necessarily involve rejecting the boundaries between doctrinal and other disciplinary approaches to crime (that would be to participate in a struggle *against* legal doctrine). It means making clearer the way law *makes* its boundaries so that practitioners, teachers, students and law reformers may be in a better position to know what is happening when legal discourse and other approaches conflict or diverge.[66]

If these questions are outside the current agenda of textbooks it should not be thought that this is because these are *compelled* merely to reproduce law's self-understanding. In fact, just as theology has its own special autonomy within religious practice, so do legal commentators within legal practice.[67] Textbook writers help to create different branches of law and their underlying leading principles.[68] In criminal law, at present, the most authoritative writers are even advocating a vision of these principles so at vari-

164   *Criminal Law and Justice*

ance with that put forward by the judges that they have been accused of misrepresenting the law so as to sustain their subjectivist account of criminal liability.[69] Their vision, in turn, reflects their chosen interpretation of the wider political principles at the basis of law. Thus there must be serious doubts about how far textbooks in criminal law do feel themselves bound to offer a hermeneutic account of judicial reasoning.[70] This could provide the warrant for attempts to develop "deviationist" doctrine in criminal law on the basis of an alternative and perhaps more informed and updated social theory.[71]

My argument, then, is that the study of criminal law would benefit from more systematic consideration of what is known about crime and the criminal process, *provided* that this is related to a more explicit acknowledgment of the specificity of legal discourse. But this analysis, inevitably, leaves many questions unanswered. Are the characteristics of legal discourse I have been describing essential and unvariant? Are they part of the structure of its claims or its practice? More important, are they part of law's reflective understanding or can they only be constructed by outsiders?[72] Is there really such a contrast between legal discourse and contextualising disciplines? The answer certainly depends on which discipline we are discussing. We have seen that law and philosophy make good bedfellows and the same seems to be the case with law and economics. But the point is more fundamental. What if law should be seen as a distinctive form of *knowledge*, even of social knowledge, and not just a source of authoritative norms and principles?[73] Or, to put the argument the other way round, many have claimed that contextualising disciplines are very like law in their drive to order and control the social world.[74] Nor can they erase from their explanatory schemes a concern with blaming, accounting and attributing responsibility.[75] Even the authority and legitimacy claims of other disciplines may be compared to those of law if we are to accept Kuhn's description of how paradigm change depends on the authority of communities of scholars.[76] The thrust of much recent post-structuralist theorising in semiotics, rhetoric, deconstruction or discourse theory is to place law and other disciplines on an equal footing.[77] Thus both as theory and practice, there may be more in common between law and contextualising disciplines than I have allowed for in my discussion (and therefore less opportunity for co-operation as opposed to colonisation). The same uncertainties attach to the question of standpoints. Can there ever be an "outsider" perspective on law rather than just another standpoint connected with some other existing or possible "practical interest"? (And if the "interest" is emancipation might not law

Criminal Law and Criminal Justice 165

be as good a place to start as any?)[78] From what standpoint has this paper been written? These and other difficulties cannot be resolved here. But, fortunately, of this I am certain: understanding, unlike judging, need never and can never end.

NOTES

* I gratefully acknowledge the helpful comments of Matilde Betti, Ian Dennis, Nicola Lacey and Robert Reiner, none of whom is to be held responsible, in legal or other discourse, for the faults of this paper.

[1] It should be explained that this paper was provoked by returning to the criminal law after ten years of teaching criminology and criminal justice. The standard textbooks referred to are:
Smith and Hogan, *Criminal Law* (5th ed. 1983)
Glanville Williams *Textbook of Criminal Law* (2nd ed. 1983)
Elliott and Wood *Casebook on Criminal Law* (D. W. Elliott and Celia Wells (eds.) (1982).
A partial exception is the recent text by C. M. V. Clarkson and H. M. Keating *Criminal Law: Text and Materials* (1984) which is discussed later.

[2] Patrick Atiyah *Accidents, Compensation and the Law* (3rd ed. 1980)
Tom Hadden *Company Law and Capitalism* (2nd ed. 1977)
Carol Harlow and Richard Rawlings *Law and Administration* (1984)
The strategies used in these books could all have been applied to criminal law. *e.g.* treating tort law as one amongst many methods of compensating victims; comparing the legal categories of company law with the social characteristics of types of company: or examining administrative law as a restraining or shaping force on government action.

[3] For an illustration of the need for more careful analysis, see the attempt to extend the law of rape by drawing an analogy to the consent requirements in the law of theft, in Steven Box's *Power, Crime and Mystification* (1983) p. 125 ff.

[4] Keith Bottomley and Ken Pease *Crime and Punishment: Interpreting the Data* (1986) does not have an index entry for Criminal law.

[5] I am using Criminal Justice simply as a shorthand term for these areas of study. However, as will become clearer later in this paper, "criminal law" and "criminal justice" may either be seen as contrasting *domains* (*i.e.* the realm of substantive doctrine versus that of other decisions in the legal process) or as competing *discourses*—juridical versus contextualising approaches to crime and the criminal process.

[6] See the discussions in Martin Wasik "Towards Sentencing Guidelines in England"; Nicola Lacy "Discretion and Due Process at the Post-Conviction Stage"; Denis Galligan "Regulating Pre-Trial Decisions," in this volume.

[7] See Andrew Sanders "Some Dangers of Policy Oriented Research: the Case of Prosecutions," in this volume.

[8] Andrew Ashworth *Sentencing and Penal Policy* (1983).

[9] William L. Twining *Theories of Evidence: Bentham and Wigmore* (1985). See also Nigel Walker *Sentencing; Theory Law and Practice* (1985).

[10] *Op. cit.* see n. 1 above.

[11] Although less pronounced in other branches of law there has also been a

166   *Criminal Law and Justice*

recent plethora of books on the philosophy of contract law (which can perhaps be seen as the opposite of crime, raising the question of the basis and limits of voluntary obligation).

[12] Clarkson and Keating *op. cit.* n. 1 p.V.

[13] Richard Tur "Criminal Law and Legal Theory" in W. L. Twining *Legal Theory and Common Law* (1986) 195–215.

[14] *e.g.*, see Anthony Duff *Trials and Punishments* (1985) and Alan Norrie "Marxism and the Critique of Criminal Justice" (1982) 6 *Contemporary Crises* 59–73. This work is particularly important in showing the dependence of criminal *justice* on social justice, especially at a time when the retributive approach to punishment is once again fashionable. However law in context studies also raise problems for this justification of punishment, for example by showing the differential power available to different groups and individuals in the making and enforcement of law. Of course the boundaries between "philosophy" and sociology or social theory are neither strict nor uncontroversial.

[15] But see (1979) *13 Law and Society Review* (special issue on Plea Bargaining) pp. 509–583.

[16] The important exception here, Herbert Packer's *The Limits of the Criminal Sanction* (1969), is discussed in the next section of this paper.

[17] For a recent comprehensive overview see Robert Summers *Lon Fuller* (1982).

[18] Denis Galligan "Regulating Pre-Trial Decisions," in this volume.

[19] See *inter alia* Eugene Bardach and Robert Kagan *Going by the Book* (1982); Jerry Mashaw *Bureaucratic Justice* (1983); Jeffrey Jowell "Implementation and Enforcement of Law" in L. Lipson and S. Wheeler (eds.) *Law and the Social Sciences* (1987) Chap. 6.

[20] Keith Hawkins and John Thomas *Enforcing Regulation* (1984) and *cf.* Nicola Lacey "The Territory of the Criminal Law" (1985) 5 O.J.L.S. 453–462.

[21] Keith Bottomley and Ken Pease *op. cit.* n. 4 above p. 26 quoting the British Crime Survey (1982). Theft and related offences constitute a smaller percentage of those crimes *not* reported to the police because of the high reporting of burglary and car theft for insurance purposes.

[22] Kenneth Campbell "Offence and Defence," in this volume.

[23] Nicola Lacy "Discretion and Due Process at the Post-Conviction Stage," in this volume.

[24] Anthony Duff "Codifying Criminal Fault: Conceptual Problems and Presuppositions," in this volume.

[25] But see the works of Ronald Dworkin who does come close to casting judges in the role of philosophers.

[26] Glanville Williams *op. cit.* n. 1 above pp. 92–93.

[27] Nicola Lacey *op. cit.* n. 20 above at pp. 459–460.

[28] Alan Milner "On the University Teaching of Criminal Law" (1963) J.S.P.T.L. 192 at p. 197.

[29] *Ibid.* at p. 192. There is a noticeable and understandable similarity to the project Atiyah was executing for tort Law at about the same period.

[30] See especially Sanford Kadish and Monrad Paulsen *Criminal Law and its Processes* (2nd ed.) (1969).

[31] David Thomas "Form and Function in 'Criminal Law' " in P. Glazebrook *Reshaping the Criminal Law* (ed.) (1978) 21–37. *e.g.*, at p. 30 Thomas instructively dismisses the terms of the textbook debates over strict liability by arguing that it really amounts to a procedural issue of when it is acceptable to delegate power to prosecutors to define offences. Also influential were Keith Bottomley's *Decisions in the Penal Process* (1973) and the studies by John Baldwin and Michael McConville.

Criminal Law and Criminal Justice 167

[32] Celia Wells "Law Reform, Rape and Ideology" in (1985) 12 Journal of Law and Society, 63–77.

[33] Celia Wells "Restatement or Reform" [1986] Crim.L.R. 314–323; but see Ian Dennis "The Codification of English Criminal Law" (1986) 23 Coexistence 43–53 for a different view of how the codifiers saw their task.

[34] Perhaps the most urgent need for up-dating of *topics* in current textbooks is to give greater consideration to "private" and "informal" types of social control (*e.g.* within organisations or forms of self-regulation) and the growth of alternative methods of dealing with crime such as mediation. The value of the textbook view that criminal law is defined as a proceeding which is followed by punishment is put in some doubt when offences are handed over to community forums or others to mediate. Do they cease to be crimes? If not, why are they not subject to the criminal law? For an overview of some of these developments see David Nelken "Community Involvement in Crime Control" [1985] C.L.P. 239–269.

[35] Various problems other than those discussed in the text are raised by introducing approaches and insights from history, economics, psychology, medicine or statistics, for example.

[36] See Doreen McBarnet "False Dichotomies in Criminal Justice Research," in John Baldwin and Keith Bottomley eds. *Criminal Justice: Selected Readings* (1978). For some illustrative broader studies see *e.g.* Stuart Hall et al *Policing the Crisis* (1978); W. G. Carson *The Other Price of Britain's Oil* (1981) or David Nelken *The Limits of the Legal Process* (1983).

[37] William Twining has developed a series of important contributions to the problem of contextualisation and the task of "broadening legal education from within." See, for example, his "The Bad Man Revisited" (1973) 58 Cornell L.R. 275, "Some Scepticism about Some Scepticisms II" *11* (1984) N.J. of Law and Society 285 at pp. 296–300 and "Talk about Realism" (1985) 60 N.Y.U.L.R. 324–384 at pp. 372–380. But whilst I agree with his stress on the significance of distinguishing "standpoints" and "purposes" in viewing law it does not quite deal with the problems of choosing different strategies for contextualising law or the specificity of legal discourse itself.

[38] Summary of HORPU Report No. 89 (1986) by Roy Walmsley.

[39] Bottomley and Pease *op. cit.* n. 4 above at p. 14.

[40] See n. 38.

[41] Jock Young *The Drugtakers* (1973).

[42] See David Thomas *op. cit.* n. 31 above and Stuart Henry *The Hidden Economy* (1978).

[43] Legal processing often fails to discover its errors because it treats actual cases as exceptions which prove the rules with which it continues to operate. For an illustration see David Nelken *The Limits of the Legal Process op. cit.* n. 36 above at p. 181.

[44] Nicola Lacey *op. cit.* n. 20 above complains that Glanville Williams whilst making extensive use of his knowledge of these matters does not always offer principled justifications for these features of the criminal process.

[45] Clarkson and Keating *op. cit.* n. 1 above at pp. 579–582.

[46] *Ibid.* pp. 539–540.

[47] *Ibid.* pp. 468–469. As they put it, "in seeking to explore the crime of rape one cannot ignore its social context, not least because of the implications such a study have for the crime itself."

[48] Clarkson and Keating *ibid.* at p. 469 argue that rape is a "highly controversial and emotional" issue. They are even led to question the value of legal as opposed to sociological attempts to apportion responsibility, asserting (at p. 471) that "rape is the result of a structure of society that generally sets men up as powerful and women as victims." But it is not clear why similar comments could not be made

168   *Criminal Law and Justice*

about many other crimes (as well as the criminal label itself). It seems that they are willing to offer an analysis (partly) informed by the politics of gender but still strangely silent on matters of "class" or "race."

[49] Thus Bottomley and Pease *op. cit.* n. 4 above entitle their Chap. 6 "Criminal Statistics in Context." A good introduction to these issues is still Paul Wiles "Criminal Statistics and Sociological Explanations of Crime" in W. G. Carson and P. Wiles *Crime and Delinquency in Britain* (1971) 174–192. For an account of the problem behaviour causing concern at the time the Criminal Damage Act 1971 was passed see Stan Cohen *Folk Devils and Moral Panics* (2nd ed.) (1980). For an account of the emergence of the non-legally defined crime of "mugging" see Stuart Hall et al. *op. cit.* n. 36 above. Reflection on the meaning of criminal statistics can lead directly into an interest in the type of study represented by the law in context strategy. See J. L. Kitsuse and Aaron Cicourel "A note on the uses of official statistics" (1963) 11 Social Problems 131.

[50] These designations are not necessarily part of the self-definition of the writers I have so categorised. In particular, it should not be supposed that their prime concern is with challenging or reforming the criminal law.

[51] See William Twining, "Some Scepticism about Some Scepticisms II" *op. cit.* n. 37 above, at pp. 296–299.

[52] See Doreen McBarnet *Conviction* (1981) Chap. 7.

[53] This neglected topic is the subject of the SHHD funded *Scottish Contested Trials Project* initiated by Professor Alan Paterson and myself in Edinburgh in 1983 (the report of which is being written up by Dr. Carol Goodwin-Jones with Mr. Steven Watson at the C.C.S.P.S.L., Edinburgh Law Faculty). One of its early findings was the inclination of procurators fiscal to use their discretion to encourage contested trials where police assault was alleged (with important consequences for the possible development of the law relating to police powers). See also John Baldwin *Pre-Trial Justice* (1985).

[54] R. Bartle, *Crime and the New Magistrate* (1985).

[55] See *Caldwell* [1982] A.C. 341 H.L. discussed by Clarkson and Keating at pp. 154–157.

[56] Two of the clearest expositions of this idea are Egon Bittner "The Police on Skid-Row: A Study of Peace-Keeping," (1967) 32 Amer. Soc. Rev. 699 and David Sudnow "Normal Crimes: Sociological Features of the Penal Code in a Public Defender Office" (1965) 12 Social Problems 285. A focus on the tasks of law-enforcement agents could provide insight into the way offence categories are used in responding to complaints and maintaining order. It might allow discussion of such often neglected topics as the use of criminal law in strikes, riots, drug-control or in Northern Ireland. It could provide more vivid ways of teaching standard problems concerning theft and deception. See, *e.g.* David Telling "Trouble in Store: some thoughts on shoplifting" [1982] J.C.L. 107.

[57] See Robert Mnookin "Bargaining in the Shadow of the Law" Oxford Centre for Socio-Legal Studies (1979) (which though dealing with family law is generally applicable to criminal law wherever high levels of guilty pleas and accompanying plea negotiations are prevalent).

[58] More work is needed on the articulation of the different "logics" of enforcement, prosecution and adjudication. For one attempt see David Nelken *op. cit.* n. 36 above, Chaps. 4–6.

[59] Andrew Sanders "Some Dangers of Policy Oriented Research: The Case of Prosecutions," in this volume.

[60] W. G. Carson "White-collar Crime and the Enforcement of Factory Legislation" (1970) 10 B.J.Crim. 383.

[61] See, *e.g.* Neil Gunningham *Pollution, Social Interest and the Law* (1974),

Ingeborg Paulus *The Search for Pure Food* (1975) and Keith Hawkins *Environment and Enforcement* (1983).

[62] W. G. Carson "The conventionalisation of early factory crime" (1979) 1 Int. Journal of Soc. of Law 37–60 and "White-collar crime and the institutionalisation of ambiguity: the case of the early Factory Acts" in Gilbert Geis and Ezra Stotland (eds.) *White-collar Crime* (1980) 142–173.

[63] See *e.g.* Smith and Hogan at pp. 101–108; Glanville Williams at pp. 927–933; Elliott and Wood at pp. 151–156 (who do at least refer to some of the relevant studies) and Clarkson and Keating at pp. 174–190.

[64] Clarkson and Keating appear to accept this point when they write (at p. 194): "the law of the books should correlate with the law in action. If our whole system of criminal law is based upon an impossible premise might not the time have come to re-think the premise?" But, characteristically, they are discussing here the intelligibility of mens rea doctrine to the jury rather than any other feature of the criminal process.

[65] *e.g.*, it is debatable how far plea-negotiation in Britain is consistent with a commitment to adversarial justice. The leading empirical study in England and Wales, by John Baldwin and Mike McConville *Negotiated Justice* (1977), and the Scottish study by Jackie Toombs and Sue Moody *Prosecution in the Public Interest* (1982), are more concerned with documenting the existence of various forms of plea-negotiation than with debating its justifications. But see n. 15.

[66] See David Nelken "Law in Books v. Law in Action: Back to the Beginning in Sociology of Law" (1984) 4 L.S. 157–174.

[67] Insofar as Packer purports to be descriptive, he argues that the criminal process is characterised by "*crime-control*" not, as some later interpreters have assumed, by *due process*.

[68] Doreen McBarnet *Conviction* (1981).

[69] *Ibid.*

[70] Mike McConville and John Baldwin *Courts, Prosecution and Conviction* (1982); David Smith and Jeremy Gray *Police and People in London*: Vol. IV *The police in action* (1983) and Robert Reiner *The Politics of the Police* (1984).

[71] Sheriff G. H. Gordon "The Admissibility of Answers to Police Questioning in Scotland," in *Reshaping the Criminal Law* (1978) 317–344.

[72] See *e.g.* David Sugarman, "Law, Economy and the State in England 1750–1914: Some Major Issues"; in David Sugarman (ed.) *Legality, Ideology and the State* (1983) 213–267.

[73] Ronald Dworkin *Taking Rights Seriously* (1977).

[74] Although most of McBarnet's examples relate to procedural rather than substantive law, there is often no clear-cut separation between the two as in her illustration of the way public order offences are defined so as to facilitate police discretion in using "law as a resource."

[75] See *e.g.* William Chambliss and Robert Seidman *Law, Order and Power* (1970).

[76] Stan Cohen "Guilt, Justice and Tolerance: Some Old Concepts for a New Criminology"; in David Downes and Paul Rock (eds.) *Deviant Interpretations* (1979) 17–52.

[77] See, *e.g.* Jock Young "Left Idealism, Reformism and Beyond" In Bob Fine et al. *Capitalism and the Rule of Law* (1979) pp. 1–29; David Nelken "Capitalism and the Rule of Law: A Review Essay" in (1980) 8 Int. J. of Soc. of Law 193–200; John Lea and Jock Young *What is to be done about Law and Order* (1982).

[78] See Box *op. cit.* n. 3 above Chap. 4 for an overview.

[79] Robert Gordon "Critical Legal Histories" in (1984) 36 Stan. L.R. 57–127, *cf.* David Nelken "Beyond the Study of 'Law and Society' " (1986) 2 American Bar

170   *Criminal Law and Justice*

Foundation Research *Journal* 323–338 and "What next in the Sociology of Law" George Lurcey Lecture, Amherts U.S.A. 1986.
    [80] See Stan. L.R. *ibid.* and David Kairys *The Politics of Law* (1982).
    [81] For an example in another branch of law, it is instructive to compare Hugh Collins' recent Law in Context book *The Law of Contract* (1986) with Atiyah's earlier approach to contextualising the law of tort (see n. 3 above). Interest in the "law in action" has largely given way to examination and reformulation of the social and political theory which underlies the law. *Cf.* Hugh Collins "Contract and Legal Theory" *in* W. Twining (ed.) *Legal Theory and Common Law* (1986) 136–155.
    [82] Jerome Hall *Theft, Law and Society* (1952). For a similar recent study see A. W. B. Simpson *Cannibalism and the Common Law* (1984). Such methods could be used to provide interesting insights into recent judicial efforts to stretch the conceptual definition of deception so as to deal with credit card frauds: see *Lambie* [1982] A.C. 449.
    [83] Neither the Stanford L.R. special issue nor the Kairys volume contains an article on the substantive law of crime, although the Stanford volume does include a swingeing attack by Louis Schwartz on Kelman's earlier article. See "With Gun and Camera Through Darkest CLS-Land," 413–465 at 450 ff. and 456–461. For a wider discussion of the contribution which Critical Legal Studies can make to criminal law see David Nelken "Critical Criminal Law" in Alan Hunt and Peter Fitzpatrick (eds.) *Critical Legal Studies* (1987).
    [84] Mark Kelman "Substantive Interpretation in the Criminal Law" (1981) 33 Stan. L.R. 591–673. This is a complex article, open to varied interpretations, which my discussion makes no attempt to summarize.
    [85] See n. 33 above.
    [86] Kelman *op. cit.* at p. 592.
    [87] *Id.* at p. 600.
    [88] A more straightforward argument to this effect is found in John Griffith *The Politics of the Judiciary* (1977). Kelman does concede that judicial decisions cannot always be tied to interests of class or power, but claims that these cases can be explained by the importance of always having *some* solution, whoever benefits. For another effort to deal with this problem see Alan Stone "The Place of Law in the Marxian Structure-Superstructure Archetype" (1985) 19 Law and Soc. Rev. 39.
    [89] *Ibid.* at pp. 600–603. Curiously, however, in his article in the Kairys volume "The Origins of Crime and Criminal Violence" pp. 214–230 at p. 222, Kelman comes close to justifying strict liability on the basis that the offence of pollution "is less an act of deviance . . . than a perhaps misconceived social policy."
    [90] *Ibid.* at p. 637.
    [91] *Ibid.* at p. 612.
    [92] *Ibid.* at p. 611.
    [93] *Ibid.* at p. 613. By contrast the "compliance" methods used in dealing with strict liability offences avoid this stereotype by gearing themselves to "excuses" offered even *after* the offence has been committed. *Cf.* Bridget Hutter "An Inspector Calls" (1986) 26 B.J. Crim. 114–129.
    [94] Kelman *ibid.* pp. 610–611.
    [95] *Ibid.* p. 646.
    [96] *Ibid.* pp. 615–616.
    [97] *Ibid.* pp. 669–671.
    [98] Schwartz *op. cit.* n. 83.
    [99] Kelman, *ibid.* p. 643.
    [1] See Clarkson and Keating at pp. 248–253. In fact, judicial reasoning may embrace both determinist and neo-classical viewpoints, as in the following quotation: "If someone is forced at gunpoint either to be inactive or to do something

Criminal Law and Criminal Justice   171

positive—must the law not remember that the *instinct* and perhaps the *duty* of self-preservation is powerful and natural?" (*per* Lord Morris in *Lynch* [1975] A.C. 653 (my italics). Alan Norrie supports Kelman's view of duress in his "Freewill, Determinism and Criminal Justice," (1984) 3 L.S. 60–73 at pp. 62–65. See also Robert Musil *The Man Without Qualities* Vol. 1 (1983) at pp. 287–289.

[2] On principle see Ronald Dworkin *Taking Rights Seriously* (1977), and *Law's Empire* (1985); on policy choices see Schwartz *op. cit.* at n. 83 pp. 442–444. For an attempted reconciliation of principle and policy justifications for legal reasoning see Neil McCormick *Legal Reasoning and Legal Theory* (1978).

[3] Critical legal scholars are ambivalent about the attempt to relate types of legal doctrine to the social conditions of the time. See Gordon *op. cit.* n. 80. There seems to be some fear (I think unjustified) that showing connections between legal doctrines and social conditions is to assert the "necessity" (or even the practical advantages) of particular doctrines. An outline of an approach which avoids these problems, drawing on Fletcher's *Re-thinking Criminal Law* (1978) is offered by Bernard Jackson. He suggests that apparently inconsistent doctrinal choices in different criminal offences may be explained in terms of the historical stereotypes which accompanied the inclusion of the relevant behaviour into the criminal law. See his "Criminal Law: Analytical Concepts and Collective Images" (University of Kent Criminal Law Handout 1985).

[4] Roberto Unger "The Critical Legal Studies Movement" (1983) 96 Harv. L.R. 563.

[5] See David Trubek "Where the action is: Critical Legal Studies and Empiricism" in (1984) 36 Stan. L.R. 575–623.

[6] See, *e.g.*, Marc Galanter, "Notes on the Future of Social Research in Law" in Lawrence Friedman and Stewart Macaulay *Law and the Behavioural Sciences* (2nd ed.) (1977) at pp. 18–20.

[7] Roger Cotterrell "Law and Sociology," (1986) 13 J. of Law and Soc. pp. 9–29 at p. 16. In his view it requires some sort of "crisis" for Law to reach out to contextualising approaches. The paper as a whole is an incisive discussion of the problems raised in this section.

[8] David Nelken "Changing Paradigms in the Sociology of Law" in Gunther Teubner (ed.) *Autopoeisis in Law and Society*, EUI Florence, Italy (1987).

[9] Note the title of Nicola Lacey's paper "The *Territory* of the Criminal Law" *op. cit.* n. 20 above in which she discusses the relative merits of wider (*i.e.* including criminal justice) and narrower views of the territory of criminal law.

[10] McBarnet, *op. cit.* n. 52 above.

[11] Thus Stuart Sheingold and others point to the differences of approach between the higher and lower levels of police forces. See *The Politics of Law and Order* (1984) pp. 165–169. *Cf.* also Robert Reiner *The Politics of the Police* (1984) 87 ff.

[12] McBarnet *op. cit.* n. 66 above.

[13] Tony Bottoms and J. McClean, *Defendants in the Criminal Process* (1976).

[14] Malcolm Feeley *The Process is the Punishment* (1979).

[15] This way of formulating the question perhaps passes too quickly over what could be the more basic problem of the relation between law as *legal practice* and textbook and other commentaries on it as *legal science* (but see the end of this section where I return to this issue). For helpful discussions see Cotterrell *op. cit.* n. 7 above and Susan Silbey "Ideals and Practices in the Study of Law" [1985] The Legal Studies Forum 7–22.

[16] Both contextualising strategies discussed so far fail to address this problem. The law in context approach, because it is so busy demonstrating the law's mistaken assumptions, and critical legal scholars, because they are committed to showing that legal doctrine is a disguised form of political, economic or moral argumen-

172 *Criminal Law and Justice*

tation, both neglect to examine law as a specific form of discourse. That is to say, law's discourse may contain "wrong" assumptions, it may involve or overlap with other discourses, but may nonetheless have its own specificity.

[17] It would enlarge discussion beyond manageable bounds to consider differences in theoretical positions drawing on semiology, rhetoric, deconstruction, discourse theory, systems theory, autopoeisis, law as tradition, reflexive law etc. I consider some of these new approaches to law in other work (see n. 79 and n. 8).

[18] Clarkson and Keating 572–583; Ian Dennis *op. cit.* n. 33 above.

[19] See Clarkson and Keating p. 270 n. 51.

[20] *Kitson* (1955) 39 Cr. App. R. 66.

[21] Ronald Dworkin *Taking Rights Seriously* Chap. 2 and 4.

[22] See n. 53. Moody and Toombs, *op. cit.* n. 65 above, found that clarifying the law was one of the reasons for encouraging trial, but do not suggest it is overriding. Their evidence indicates that trial more often results from a breakdown or lack of "trust" between prosecution and defence lawyers. Paradoxically, where the outcome of trial is most uncertain either or even both sides may be *more* willing to seek a guilty plea rather than risk the uncertainty of trial.

[23] See V. Aubert "The Structure of Legal Thinking" in *Legal Essays for Frede Castberg* (1963), and V. Aubert and Sheldon Messinger "The Criminal and the Sick" in V. Aubert *The Hidden Society* (1965). Colin Campbell offered an acute discussion of these problems in "Legal Thought and Juristic Values" (1974) 1 B.J. Law & Soc. 13 but took the view that the "legal paradigm" could be challenged and displaced by alternative perspectives. Roger Cotterrell (*op. cit.* n. 7 at pp. 17–18) prefers to see various of the examples I discuss under this heading as part of the task of normative clarification. He also rightly implies that juristic thought may elaborate doctrines related to one function in ways that transcend or even undermine that function.

[24] *Dyson* [1908] K.B. 454.

[25] Clarkson and Keating at p. 315.

[26] *Ibid.* p. 226.

[27] H. L. A. Hart and A. Honore *Causation in the Law* (2nd ed. 1985); Clarkson and Keating pp. 326–350.

[28] Zenon Bankowski "The Value of Truth. Fact Scepticism Revisited" (1981) 1 L.S. 257–267 and Twining, *op. cit.* n. 2. (*Cf.* the conclusion of Francois Bailleau's Paper "Techniques Judiciaires—techniques scientifiques" (ISA Conference on Sociology of Law, Aix-en-Provence, France, August 12–15 1985) p. 29. "Un fonctionnement scientifique doit repondre a certaines regles d'objectivation et de definition d'objects qui ne sont pas conciliables avec le fonctionnement social d'une institution penale jouant un role de production normatif et organisee pratiquement pour jouer ce role."

[29] This distinction, which should be seen as suggestive rather than a hard and fast rule, is taken from Berel Berkovits, "The Man of Halakhah and the Non-Halakhic World" (547) 22 L'Eylah Journal 41–48 at p. 43.

[30] I owe this point to Robert Reiner.

[31] Jerome Frank *Courts on Trial* (1949). A recent magisterial demonstration of this theme in the realm of contract law is Patrick Atiyah's *The Rise and Fall of Freedom of Contract* (1979).

[32] Keith Bottomley *Decisions in the Penal Process* (1973).

[33] *Blaue* (1975) 61 Cr. App. R. 271.

[34] *Beard* [1920] A.C. 479; *Majewski* [1971] A.C. 443.

[35] See Clarkson and Keating at pp. 538–554 and 246–259.

[36] For example they stress the dramaturgical function of court hearings. See *e.g.*

Criminal Law and Criminal Justice   173

Pat Carlen *Magistrates' Justice* (1976) and Nils Christie "Crime Control as Drama," (1986) 13 J. Law and Soc. 1–8.
[37] See *e.g.* David Nelken *The Limits of the Legal Process* (1983) Chaps. 4–6.
[38] Norval Morris *Madness and the Criminal Law* (1982).
[39] See Niklas Luhmann *A Sociological Theory of Law* (trans. Elizabeth King and Martin Albrow) (1985) and his papers prepared for the Conference on *Autopoiesis in Law and Society*, E.U.I. 12–15th December 1985, Florence.
[40] The views of Gunther Jakobs are discussed critically by Alessandro Baratta in "La teoria della prevenzione integrazione. Una 'nuova' fondazione della pena all'interno della teoria sistematica" in (1984) 11 Dei Delitti e Delle Pene p. 5.
[41] It is important to distinguish, for example, between such unchallengeable axioms as the assumption of free will; the functional requirements of legal adjudication (as specified from within and without legal practice); and reflexive features of normative systems or communications. These may all be contrasted with illustrations of law's self-sealing circular arguments such as the distinction between crimes of "basic" and "specific" intent. (See Glanville Williams *op. cit.* n. 1 468–476, or stereotypical assumptions about types of crime.
[42] Ronald Dworkin *Law's Empire* (1985).
[43] Richard Tur *op. cit.* n. 13 above (first section) at p. 197. For a good example see *Kaur* v. *Chief Constable of Hampshire* [1981] 1 W.L.R. 578 where liability for theft turned on a recondite point of civil law.
[44] Anthony Kenny *Freedom and Responsibility* (1978) p. 142.
[45] Tur *op. cit.* n. 13 above (first section) argues that the criminal law's willingness to penalise some unintended consequences can be compared to the public's willingness to make judgments in terms of "moral luck" *Cf.* also Anthony Duff (in this volume) who thinks it important to attempt to match the public viewpoint rather than impose that of elite codifiers even though doubtful whether a public consensus exists.
[46] Celia Wells *op. cit.* n. 32. Much of this disdain is similar to the way ordinary language philosophy was more interested in the latent wisdom of ordinary language rather than those who used it. There are of course numerous empirical studies of what people actually think which could be built on for this purpose; see, for example, Leslie Sebba "Is mens rea a component of perceived offence seriousness?" (1980) 71 J. Crim. Law and Criminology 124–135.
[47] *Feely* [1973] Q.B. 530; *Ghosh* [1982] Q.B. 1053.
[48] *Camplin* [1978] A.C. 705.
[49] Sally Lloyd-Bostock "Common-sense, Reality and Accident Compensation" in David Farrington, Keith Hawkins and Sally Lloyd-Bostock (eds.) *Psychology, Law and Legal Processes* (1978) 93–111.
[50] See, for example, Clarkson and Keating p. 553 ff. on the conflicting approaches to the physiology of provocation of medicine and law. *Cf.* Alan Norrie *op. cit.* n. 98 at p. 62 "Judges may then continue to put on and off their theology as they do and doff their legal raiment with impunity content in the knowledge that when nothing is certain, anything goes."
[51] Colin Campbell and Paul Wiles "The Study of Law and Society in Britain" (1976) 10 Law and Soc. Rev. 547; David Nelken "The Gap Problem in the Sociology of Law" (1981) 1 Windsor Yearbook of Access to Justice 35–63; Jacques Commaille "La Loi et La Science: La Dialectique du Prince et de la Servante" (ISA Conference Aix en Provence France 26–31 August 1985); Austin Sarat "Legal Effectiveness and Social Studies of Law: on the unfortunate persistence of a research tradition" (1985) The Legal Studies Forum 23–31; Austin Sarat and Susan Silbey "The Pull of the Policy Audience," unpublished MSS 1986.
[52] Andrew Sanders "Some Dangers of Policy Oriented Research: The Case of

174   *Criminal Law and Justice*

Prosecutions" (in this volume) and "Two Critical Approaches to the Prosecution Process" in *Criminal Law and Criminal Justice: UCL Working Paper* 1986 (ed. David Nelken).

[53] Insofar as contextualising disciplines are employed in the formulation or reform of criminal provisions this is very often in order to *legitimate* choices taken for other reasons. This is the conclusion of an important project being undertaken at Bremen (F.D.R.) into the making of laws dealing with economic crime. See J. J. Savelsberg "Rationalities and experts in the making of Criminal Law against economic crime" (I.S.A. Conference Aix en Provence, France August 12–15 1985).

[54] Compare Eugene Kamenka and Alice Erh-Soon-Tay "Beyond Bourgeois Individualism. The Contemporary Crisis in Law and Legal Ideology" in *Feudalism, Capitalism and Beyond* (1975) (eds. E. Kamenka and R. S. Neale) and David Nelken "Is There a Crisis in Law and Legal Ideology?" (1982) 9 J. of Law and Soc. p. 177.

[55] See Ralf Dahrendorf *Law and Order* (1984).

[56] Thus, in responding to delinquency, the criminal justice process is more likely to co-operate with the positivist viewpoint implicit in "administrative criminology" than to make common cause with the view of delinquency as a choice developed in David Matza in *Delinquency and Drift* (1964). The current resurgence of a rationalist approach to adult criminal behaviour amongst criminologists is taken simply as a confirmation of law's correctness.

[57] Compare the strong reaction to Baldwin and McConville's *Negotiated Justice* (1978) with that accorded to the much more radical critique in Zenon Bankowski and Geoff Mungham *Images of Law* (1976).

[58] Michel Foucault *Power/Knowledge* (1980) (ed. Colin Gordon), Cotterrell *op. cit.* n. 7.

[59] See the preface to Smith and Hogan's textbook *op. cit.* n. 1 and Glanville Williams "The Lords and Impossible Attempts" (1986) 45 C.L.J. 33–83; Nicola Lacey *op. cit.* n. 20 (first section).

[60] Michel Foucault (trans. H. Sheridan) *Discipline and Punish* (1977); Stan Cohen *Visions of Social Control* (1985).

[61] Boaventura de Sousa Santos, "On Modes of Production of Law and Social Power" in (1985) 13 Int. J. of the Sociology of Law 249.

[62] See Peter Fitzpatrick "Law and Societies" (1984) 22 Osgoode Hall L.J. 115.

[63] Jacques Donzelot *The Policing of Families* (1979).

[64] David Garland *Punishment and Welfare* (1984) describes the growth of criminology as a response to the social crises of the 1890's in Britain. He also documents the compromises it made with legal discourse in parcelling out the administration of criminality pp. 190–225. See also Sir Leon Radzinowicz and Roger Hood *The Emergence of Penal Policy* (1986) and David Garland and Peter Young *The Power to Punish* (1982).

[65] Kelman *op. cit.* n. 84.

[66] Divergence is often more significant than conflict because it is more easily ignored by legal textbooks concerned as they are with the rationalisation and defence of the legal perspective.

[67] Legal doctrine (or legal science) is obviously less practically-oriented than judicial reasoning. Thus a typical academic criticism is that advanced by Clarkson and Keating in their comment (at p. 124) on *R. v. Steane* [1947] K.B. 997 C.C.A.: "The concept 'intention' can be expanded or restricted to meet the demands of justice in any particular case." They advance similar criticisms of the distinction between "conduct" and "result" crimes, and the way the ingredients of an offence for which full mens rea is required can vary by type of offence or even from case to case.

[68] Grant Gilmore *The Death of Contract* (1974) and *The Ages of American Law* (1977); David Sugarman "Legal Theory, the Common Law Mind and the Making of the Textbook Tradition" *in* Twining *op. cit.* n. 13, 26–62.

[69] Nicola Lacey *op. cit.* n. 20.

[70] This has important implications for the efforts of commentators to improve the consistency and coherence of the English criminal law. Insofar as the coherence possessed by the criminal law (especially on a case by case basis) depends on extralegal shared values amongst the judiciary (see A. W. B. Simpson "The Common Law and Legal Theory" in W. Twining *Legal Theory and Common Law* (1986) 25–62) confusion can result if these values are at odds with those of the commentators.

[71] Hugh Collins "Contract and Legal Theory" *in* W. L. Twining (ed.) *ibid.* 134–155.

[72] It is an open question how far other disciplines, such as psychology or economics for example, are capable of offering an interpretation of law's rationality except in their *own* terms. See, for example, Catherine Fitzmaurice and Ken Pease *The Psychology of Judicial Sentencing* (1986) and Cento Veljanovski "Economic Theorising About Tort" in [1985] C.L.P. 71 and "Legal Theory, Economic Analysis and the Law of Torts" in W. Twining *Legal Theory and Common Law* (1986) at p. 222.

[73] See Pitirim Sorokin *Sociological Theories of Today* (1966) at pp. 392–394, Gunther Teubner "After Legal Instrumentalism? Strategic Models of Regulatory Law" in G. Teubner (ed.) *Dilemmas of Law in the Welfare State* (1986) 299–327 and *cf.* the discussion in Alessandro Barrata *Criminologia critica e Critica di diritto penale* (1982) 11–14. Classical sociological ideas on forms of human relationship may have been borrowed from legal categories (for example via Ihering through Tonnies and Durkheim).

[74] Geoffrey Hawthorne *Enlightenment and Despair* (1976). In his *History of Sexuality* Vol. 1 (1979) Foucault suggests that the various (contextualising) disciplines have parcelled out personal identity between them so as to create a form of repression more penetrating than that of law.

[75] Aaron Cicourel *The Social Organisation of Juvenile Justice*, (2nd ed.) (1976).

[76] Thomas Kuhn *The Structure of Scientific Revolutions* (2nd ed.) (1970).

[77] But this may be partly a result of the same approach being applied to law as to other forms of discourse rather than attending to what is distinctive about law. Foucault, however, draws a sharp (perhaps over-sharp) contrast between law/sovereignty on the one hand and disciplines/disciplinary processes on the other.

[78] Jurgen Habermas *Knowledge and Human Interests* (trans. J. Shapiro) (1971).

[8]
The Loneliness of Law's Meta-Theory[1]

The normative question of how expert knowledge is best assessed, and how experts themselves are best evaluated and kept under a modicum of control, raises such intractable and viciously circular problems as to strangle speech' (Barnes and Edge).

1 The changing background to clashes between law and science

It is not difficult to find examples of present and past disagreements between law and science. There are long-running disputes between legal and psychiatric conceptions of insanity, and volumes of research in which psychologists and statisticians criticise legal methods of proof. More generally, many social scientists reject the use judges make of concepts such as 'market efficiency' or 'group interest'; they are baffled by judges' willingness to predict outcomes of their decisions on little scientific evidence and their disinclination to check whether the predictions are in fact sound. The line between real clashes and only apparent ones is not always easy to draw. Sometimes law and science are no more than superficially dealing with the same phenomenon. This could be said perhaps of legal and medical definitions of death. In such cases different definitions reflect different purposes and concerns rather than a genuine dispute. Sometimes law is explicit about this, as in the distinction, internal to criminal and tort law, of 'factual' and 'legal' causation. At the other extreme, legal judgments do sometimes entertain scientific impossibilities, as in decisions which have allowed a presumption of paternity even where this involved believing that a pregnancy had lasted more than a year. To an extent law may use 'doublethink' to treat its 'legal fictions' as facts. In many of the most troublesome clashes between law and science, however, the real difficulty lies precisely in deciding whether the different conceptions in play represent genuine disagreement or not.

---

1 For a longer version of this paper, which also includes some case studies of current controversies in law and science in the light of the various approaches considered here, see 'The Truth about Law's Truth', *European University Institute Working Paper* 1990/1 Florence, Italy; or 'The Truth about Law's Truth', in *European Yearbook for the Sociology of Law* 1990 (Febbrajo, Nelken and Teubner eds.) Guiffré, Milan, Italy.

A number of social and intellectual developments have led to increased questioning of the desirability and even the relevance of scientific and technical models for law. Although there are various currents and counter-currents of opinion we are beginning to see reduced enthusiasm for employing law as a method of 'social engineering', and, on the contrary, a turn toward using law as a bulwark against technocracy. This has been accompanied by important developments in the philosophical understanding of both law and science. One result of this is renewed respect for the integrity of law as a form of knowledge and practice in its own right, with potentially equal status to science. These changes represent a new challenge for critical theory. How can we avoid unreflective importation into law of competing disciplines without thereby falling back into a revisionist and one-sided exaggeration of law's independence from external influences?

2   Three ways of looking at clashes between law and science

Disagreements between law and science may be considered from a scientific perspective, a legal perspective, or from some third position. These alternatives may be entitled: the attempt to find 'the truth about law', 'law's truth'; or finally, 'the truth about law's truth'. My main concern here is with the possibilities of developing an 'third position' and the meta-theoretical strategies this may involve.

2.1   The truth about law
In keeping with the central influence of 'the idea of science' since the Enlightenment, law increasingly came to be seen as one of those subjects to which the term could properly be applied. However, it has been during this century, especially in common-law jurisdictions, that scientific and social scientific criticisms of law have reached their height and this movement has certainly not lost all its force. It would be pointless to make reference to the vast range of studies devoted to proving how certain legal rules or practices rest on mistaken pictures of the world or pursue instrumental goals in a way which a given scientific perspective deems to be misguided or ineffective. The important point for our purpose is that many of these critiques rely on a positivist conception of science as a superior, universal route to knowledge about and manipulation of the world as compared to the outmoded or imprecise guesswork embodied in the law. This viewpoint is well represented by Richard Posner, doyen of the Chicago school of 'Law and Economics', and now a Federal Court judge, in a recent address aptly entitled 'The decline of law'. For Posner, American lawyers will increasingly resort to scientific arguments before the Courts 'as an irreversible consequence of the rise of prestige and authority of scientific and other exact modes of enquiry'.[2]

From this point of view, disagreements between law and science serve mainly as opportunities to rationalize and update law's factual presuppositions and regulative techniques. However, all this begs the fundamental

2   Posner R. 'The decline of law as an autonomous discipline 1962-1987', *Harvard Law Review* (1987) 772.

question of how to tell whether a particular scientific perspective has succeeded in understanding the legal practice under criticism or has only turned the law into a pale (and inferior) imitation of itself (Samek, 1974). The 'legal point of view' disappears because it is too easy to show that the ascribed goal or function which law is failing to serve would be better accomplished by the introduction of more scientific methods. To return to the controversy stirred by Posner's earlier work, it may perhaps be a more defensible position to argue that economics has something to contribute as a check on economic assumptions or predictions made by law instead of assuming that law is itself a form of economic reasoning (Veljanovski, 1985). But it is still a problem for economics to establish how far law is bound to adhere to economic methods. For it is hard for any scientific discipline to set limits to its own applicability. If we accept the appropriateness of psychological criticisms of the reliability of witness identifications in the criminal process, why should we not accept other psychological studies whose arguments could bring us as far as replacing the accusatorial trial with a psychological tribunal? Yet this we are reluctant to do, even as we recognize the relevance of particular psychological criticisms.

There are other hidden problems involved in the importation of scientific approaches into law. Given the rivalry between scientific disciplines, and the conflicts between perspectives within them, we often face the difficulty of knowing which to adopt. These disagreements, on their face, often seem as serious as those between law and science and raise similar issues of commensurability. But law is potentially interested in the approaches of all these competing disciplines, even if it is incapable of choosing between them. In practice, law tends to incorporate ideas and methods from disciplines with which it has shared values and methods, such as economics or ordinary-language philosophy, whilst dividing jurisdiction with less assimilable knowledges such as medicine or social work. But this does not reflect a theoretically coherent strategy for learning about the world and it may reinforce law's 'blind spots' rather than compensate for them. For example, the 'methodological individualism' which is common to the 'juridical subject' of law, ordinary-language philosophy, and neo-classical economics, excludes alternative accounts of the structural sources of social behaviour found in other disciplines.

2.2 Law's truth

These problems strengthen the case for welcoming a point of view in which the sense and validity of legal rules and procedures is made independent of external scientific criteria. In this optic law's concern is with the 'institutional facts' (McCormick 1974) of the creation, maintenance and termination of normative rules rather than the 'brute facts' of the social and physical world. The connection between 'facts' and consequences is seen to pass through legal implications rather than 'cause and effect' and law may stipulate presumptions which are not recognized by science (Scoditti 1988). Above all, legal materials are to be interpreted in prescribed ways which bear on the normative features of the facts, practices and conceptions in question, rather than their physical characteristics or their relevance in terms of social engineering.

What more can be said about law's point of view? It is hard for any scientific discipline to formulate this even though the social sciences for their part would claim to have much to say about the nature and achievement of law's normative functions as well as its instrumental ones. The nearest example of a self-limiting ordinance (which just stops short of incoherence) is perhaps to be found in the conclusion reached by Arthur Leff, one of the most original, if idiosyncratic, of American 'Law and Society' scholars. In a paper devoted to the relationship between law and external disciplines Leff wrote, 'Ultimately law is not something that we know but something that we do'.[3] In more positive terms, however, social scientists have also tried to describe the contours and constraints of law's point of view as compared to that of science. Law is seen as an institution which serves distinctive social functions as compared to science, and therefore develops in different ways. Law's ostensible functions of dispute-processing and legitimation of power-holders requires it to offer certainty and reinforce common-sense expectations whereas scientific progress depends on controversy and the undermining of common-sense (Nelken 1987). The rationale of legal rules and principles under attack will therefore, in the first instance, be sought in considerations of authority, integrity, fairness, justice, acceptability, practicality and so forth which may have little or no application to science. Legal solutions will be deliberately geared to a particular time and place and to a specific community and its traditions. Likewise law's methods of fact-gathering and fact-construction will be closely connected to the adjucative process and to the problems of generating and maintaining the acceptance of those subjects to legal rules.

On this view some disagreements between law and science are to be attributed to straightforward confusion between 'institutional facts' and 'brute facts', or the difference between events in the world and their legal recognition and redefinition. Others will be interpreted in terms of such considerations as finality of decisions, the problems and requirements of doing justice on a case by case basis, or the moral and political aspects of normative regulation. Law, unlike science, has to use arbitrary cut-off points to define birth and death, the age of sexual maturity or criminal responsibility. Often it chooses not to look behind its presumptions. It will ignore the grey areas between its classifications, or its all-or-nothing adjudicative decisions, insofar as these are irrelevant to, or inconsistent with its tasks. At times functional considerations may even conflict with its usual normative principles, as in the way English criminal law deems those under the influence of drink or drugs to be nevertheless capable of 'mens rea'. But this will not always be readily admitted precisely because it represents a potential contradiction within the 'institutional fact' system itself.

The upshot of this functional account of law's specificity is that we should not expect law to parallel the internal workings or developments of science or be subject to the same tests of validity. When law calls upon science, it does so in order to extend or defend its achievement of certainty, legitimacy and so on. Science can usefully serve as a source of expertise or experience which can attest to the reliability of certain classes of fact. When it suits law's purposes, science is treated as a yardstick of positivist certainties about the world.

---

3   Leff A. 'Law and', *Yale Law Review* (1978) 87, 1011.

As Brian Wynne writes: 'Whatever it is that sustains the fact-value distinction at the heart of the legal metaphysics it is not a well-developed explicit theory of science as a special esoteric form of rational knowledge'.[4]

At other times, however, law or lawyers will have an interest in demonstrating the social contingencies of scientific claims to knowledge, such as the extent to which science treats value choices as technical problems. Acting as a sort of sociology of science, it may attack the social consensus which is required to sustain the status of particular sciences or scientists. In either case, law's conception of science tells us more about law than it does about science. .

But does this approach to law's point of view count as a method for grasping law's truth or only qualify as another attempt at a scientific description of 'the truth about law'? We can certainly find a similar functional understanding of law in works of legal theory. But how far should these works be included in the 'law-object' of our theorizing (and how far law should be considered a single or unified discourse)? A functionalist approach to legal discourse would suggest that legal statements gain their validity, at least in part, from the status and authority of those who pronounce them rather than, as in the scientific ideal, deriving their authority from their presumed closeness to the truth. But, paradoxically, this means that authoritative legal claims about law's functions can succesfully compete with those asserted by unauthorized external sources. For example, if legal actors begin to describe their role as one of truth-seeking (and if they act on this description) the phenomenon itself changes. Thus, in a recent English civil case, a judge refused a lawyer's attempt to withhold documents from the court, and denied that the civil procedure should be seen as a regulated game of conflict in which the judge served as an umpire: He insisted instead that the court was committed to learning all the truth so as to do justice (Jolowicz 1988). Whilst even the most authoritative legal statements can, of course, be shown to be legally mistaken, the issue here is whether a social scientific account of law's functions could be used to try to persuade the court that it really was involved in a game rather than the search for truth (in which case we might eventualy see opposing lawyers employing their best accusatorial techniques in arguing whether legal procedures should be understood on the analogy of a game or of science!).

One of the most difficult tasks in grasping the legal point of view is to establish the character and degree of law's interest in what scientists mean by 'truth'. The self-understanding and development of a tradition is by no means to be equated with the search for 'historical truth'. According to most leading writers on the philosophy of law it is actually mistaken to look for the 'original intent' of those who frame legal directives, which instead must be interpreted as living materials to be reconceptualized under changing conditions. But the problem is most acute in seeking to make sense of legal procedures. Thus Damaska (1986) argues that Anglo-American rules of criminal procedure give a lower priority to the attainment of truth than Continental Inquisitorial systems of fact-finding. But it is unclear how far

---

4   Wynne B. 'Establishing the rules of laws: constructing expert authority' in Smith R. & B.
    Wynne (eds.) *Expert evidence. Interpreting science in the law* (1989) London, 31.

this should be seen as truth being deliberately compromised in favour of other values such as fairness or legitimacy or whether we should rather say that what truth means for law is the result of the aplication of its own processes. In other words, is law's yardstick of correctness and justice the result of a *more* or of a *less* demanding conception of truth than that used by science? To the extent that scientific conceptions of value-free facts and the methods of obtaining them are historically and culturally specific we should not be surprised to find law adopting distinctive forms of truth-finding in other times and places (Geertz, 1983). Establishing the truth of events may depend on finding people with the appropriate reputation and authority to bear witness concerning the character of the offender rather than on discovering witnesses to the event.

On the other hand, it would be wrong to contrast law's interests and standards of truth too greatly with those we now associate with science. The weaknesses of such an approach to 'law's truth' are precisely the strong points of the previous perspective of the 'truth about law' discussed earlier. Thus Sorokin saw law as a form of proto-sociology, because its classifications of property and contract relations helped provide the impetus for Durkheim's two types of social solidarity. Likewise, the functionalist account of the way law's practical purposes condition its interest in truth should not blind us to the extent to which current legal argumentation does strive for adequacy also in terms of scientific criteria of truth. The distinctions supposedly constituting the legal point of view such as that between the 'cognitive' and the 'normative' (Luhmann, 1988), or 'principle' and 'policy' (Dworkin, 1986), are at most matters of emphasis rather than absolute contrasts. Dworkin or Luhmann both warn of the dangers which flow from judges basing their decisions on policy-calculations and the risks of linking law's validity to the instrumental success of its decisions. But, insofar as these dangers are real, they testify to the incompleteness of their own accounts of legal phenomena.

The process which German scholars describe as 'the materialization of law' means that if we restrict our attention to law's normative and symbolic aspects we would belittle the various ways it also takes an interest in predicting and manipulating social reality. The justification of legal judgements can better be read, as Summers argues, as a mixture of 'rightness' reasons and 'goal-oriented' reasons (Summers 1978). Weber's ideal-types of formal and substantive rationality were designed to allow us to examine just how far law becomes implicated in schemes of social engineering or wealth redistribution, and the degree to which its reasoning processes reached out beyond itself. Legal discourse must therefore be seen as part and parcel of wider cultural movements and changing intellectual fashions. At least some of the conceptions and practices which may be criticized from the point of view of other disciplines will have found their way into law as a result of previously accepted but superseeded versions of those same sciences. And, in current practice, other disciplinary perspectives are introduced into law via law reform, expert evidence or 'judicial notice'. It is these points which provide the justification for those perspectives which seek to show the 'truth about law'. Moreover, the application of these perspectives is self-fulfilling insofar as they become part of legal argument. Yet, by the same token, if we move too far in this direction we risk obscuring or destroying what is special about 'law's truth'. Is there then any way of discovering or deciding the degree to which respect for law's truth should condition the adoption of insights derived from other disciplines? To answer this question requires us to embark on the difficult search for a meta- theory (Beer, 1977; Hunter 1977; Lawson 1982; Quinton, 1977; Villa 1988), capable of revealing the truth about 'law's truth'.

2.3 The truth about 'law's truth'
There are many excellent studies of the rise and fall of particular types of knowledge and power and the conflicts between them (Foucault 1977; Smith 1981; Atiyah 1979; Garland 1985). But they are usually the first to admit the difficulty of deriving object lessons from these clashes (Smith 1981). On the other hand more normative approaches tend to marginalize the question of truth, to the extent that some writers see legal decision-making as distinctively engaged in handling 'practical' choices to which no theoretical 'right answers' can be discovered, as compared to what can be achieved in the realm of 'speculative disagreements' (McCormick 1978).

Both these approaches avoid attempting to provide a meta-theory of law. But there are some writers who do try to tackle this problem directly. Three responses can be distinguished. The first, which I will call the reconstructive approach, looks for meta-theoretical answers beyond the institutionalized discourses of law and science. Its problem is how to maintain this view-point in the face of post-positivist challenges to transcendent truth-claims. The second approach, following postmodern movements such as deconstruction, strongly rejects the possibility of discovering 'foundationalist' certainties. But it has to confront the obvious dangers of self-contradiction in proving its case. The third approach, which I shall call the dialogic response is the one with which I shall be particularly concerned. It reacts to the weaknesses of the other two approaches by determining to find the answer from science and law rather than elsewhere. It then has to grapple with the difficulties that are entailed in asking discourses to transcend themselves.

In the reconstructive response the search for a valid meta-theory becomes almost an end in itself, a search which maintains its momentum by showing the impossibility of abandoning it. Thus we meet arguments about the need to be 'sceptical about scepticism', the impossibility of engaging in discussion without endorsing the value of truth and the requirement of applying to our own arguments the criteria we apply to others. (Finnis, 1978; Brownsword and Beleveyld 1986; Alexy 1989). The goals of this search may be various. For some writers the aim is to interpret or recapture a transcendent source of truth and value (Finnis 1978, Habermas 1975). At the other extreme some thinkers recommend looking for a consensus at a more concrete and practical level (Waldron 1987).

The broader 'master' discourses to which law and science are usually referred include religion, morality, politics, philosophy, 'practical reason' and common sense. Such discourses often lie at the root of the 'will to truth' within law and science, as Nietzsche and Foucault have argued. It is therefore not surprising that they are again invoked when law and science find themselves facing ultimate questions – or at least the difficulty of resolving questions ultimately. The form that any such meta-theory takes will then depend on the type of argumentation and practice characteristic of the master discourse chosen, whether it be, for example the analytical techniques of philosophy, the revealed or rational truths and value-judgements of religion or morality, or the pragmatic case by case appraisals of 'practical reason'.

The second, deconstructive strategy, focusses on the limits and interdiscursivities of all arguments and 'texts'. Certainty is corroded by the endless play of 'signifier' and 'signified' and truth itself becomes an 'army of metaphors' at the command of 'the will to power'. This approach maintains its momentum in various ways. It undermines pretensions to 'totalizing' visions (Lyotard 1984), opens up attempts by legal and other texts to achieve 'closure' (Derrida, 1977; *Stanford Law Review* 1984), anticipates criticisms by self criticism (Kramer forthcoming) and ironicises all claims to truth including its own (Kennedy 1985). Some writers who follow this strategy justify their position by rejecting 'scientific' method in the name of hermeneutics. Law, history and even science are all seen to presuppose the internal grasping and application of a tradition. But the results obtained in this way are necessarily contingent to a given period and place. Gadamer, for example, rejects the possibility of a Habermasian 'ideal-speech situation' because our conceptions of what would bring us closer to it are always necessarily formulated according to prevailing cultural assumptions within a given community. Rorty, in his attacks on 'foundationalism', counterposes the hermeneutic and epistemological projects, arguing that the search for epistemological certainty must and should give way to a concern to appreciate the diversity of discourses (Rorty 1979). Rather than attempting to offer a superior, contextualised explanation of discourses (what I have categorized here as 'the truth about law' and which is explicity described in Britain as putting the 'law in context') the crucial task is to find ways of keeping the conversation between discourses going. Those who argue for a deconstructive strategy tend to say that they are trying to get away from talking about truth, rather than showing its impossibility. The nearest they come to asserting a strong thesis concerning the pointlessness of looking for a meta-theory comes in arguments derived from Kuhn and Wittgenstein on the limits to our ability to predict how discourses change. As Rorty puts it: 'The product of abnormal discourse can be anything from nonsense to intellectual revolution and there is no discipline which describes it'.[5]

Both the reconstructive route map for finding a meta-theory and the deconstructivist warnings against even setting out on the journey have their special drawbacks. The difficulty the reconstructivists face is how to avoid their resort to master disciplines from needing to be again reformulated in the discourses of either law or science. If answers are sought in the discourses of morality or practical reason, it soon transpires that asking these approaches to provide solutions on a case by case basis reproduces something very like the procedures and principles of law and therefore cannot provide any purchase for disposing of scientific challenges. Should we, on the other hand, decide that the answer to a clash is ultimately political, we will be hard put to explain what we mean without embarking on a scientific enquiry into the meanings and effects of different ways of defining the political. Are we

5   Rorty R. *Philosophy and the mirror of nature* (1979) Princeton, 320.

talking of the political sphere or of political science? Is politics to be distinguished from law and science in terms of its institutions, its functions of its characteristic discourse? Is the key point that choices between law and science are inherently matters of policy rather than principle? Or is it the need to involve ordinary people, either through representative institutions or in participatory institutions such as the jury? Even this does not exhaust the possible meaning of describing these choices as political. For some writers this could be merely a coded way of saying that what we have here are the sort of problems which lie beyond the reach of theoretical argument and are necessarily a matter of subjective evaluation or brute struggles for power.

In the unlikely event that master-discourses could provide their own unequivocal self-descriptions, and that these could be brought to bear on clashes between law and science, a number of further questions arise. At what point is it appropriate to resort to other discourses and which discourse should be used to decide this? A large part of legal discourse (and not merely constitutional law) is concerned with the question of the relationship between law and politics. Following this path would subordinate master-discourses to the decision rules of law. But there is no reason to assume that the political sphere or political discourse would define their relevance to law in the same way as law itself. Science and law may agree or disagree about the right point at which to turn to master discourses, or may have them imposed by fiat. In turn master discourses may speak without being asked or heard.

A recent study which tries to place law within the bounds of a larger discourse is that by Alexy which offers a systematic case for law as a specialized part of 'practical reason' (Alexy 1989). Alexy claims that law can be rational to the extent that it adopts the rules and canons of his ideal version of practical argumentation. Describing his work as a 'meta-discourse' on the criteria for rationality in legal argument he carefully spells out the implications of his belief that both factual assertions and value-judgements must each be tested against the criterion of the relevant 'best informed opinion'. But this approach does not really take us very far in resolving our problem of potential clashes between law and science. Alexy has some sympathy with J.L. Austin's definition of truth as 'the right and proper thing to say in these circumstances, to this audience, for these purposes, with these intentions'.[6] He concedes that law includes a variety of types of statement and that 'at any time (law) can make a transition into theoretical (empirical) discourse'.[7] Whilst accepting that normative statements cannot be tested by the methods of the empirical sciences he leaves it 'for further investigation whether normative arguments are true in exactly the same way as empirical ones'. Alexy does not deny the importance of our problem given that 'the relevance of introducing empirical knowledge of legal reasoning can hardly be overstated'.[8] But the task of specifying the rules for assessing such relevance in cases of uncertainty was too great: 'A thoroughgoing theory of empirical reasoning relevant to legal justification would have to deal with almost all the

6   Alexy R. *A Theory of legal argumentation. The theory of rational discourse as theory of legal justification* (1989) Oxford, p. 56-57.
7   Alexy R. *op. cit.* 233.
8   Alexy R. *op. cit.* 233.

problems of gaining empirical knowledge. Added to this are the problems of incorporating empirical knowledge into legal reasoning'. In the meantime 'this problem is only to be resolved by way of interdisciplinary co-operation'.[9] As we have seen, however, the question of the terms on which such co-operation should proceed is exactly the issue which needs to be solved.

If reconstructivists are tempted to travel hopefully rather than arrive, deconstructivists, for their part, find it hard to insist that they are not going anywhere. Rorty insists that there can be no 'philosophical Archimedian point' but even he writes of the possibility that the conversation amongst discourses may lead them to somehow transcend their limitations. Attempts to be consistently ironic also have difficulty in keeping this up. As Frankenburg puts it in his summary of a recent piece in this vein by David Kennedy: 'However much Kennedy wishes to get away from truth-claims, he is still constantly and implicitly asserting the truthfulness of his narrative and the authenticity of the narrator'.[10] Even with a reverse momentum, 'the postmodern skeptic, guarded by irony and advancing with all nondeliberate speed, seems unable to outrun modernity'.[11]

Both the reconstructive and deconstructive approaches will continue to find adherents. But their difficulties provide an incentive to those struggling with the prospect of a third approach. This third strategy, which could be termed 'dialogic', takes some points from each of the previous strategies, despite their apparent irreconcilability, and therefore ends up resembling neither. Like the reconstructive approach it continues the search for a positive way forward. But in common with the deconstructive approach it rejects the possibility of finding any master discourse capable of putting law and science in their proper places. Any progress that is to be made has to come from within law and science themselves. The dialogic strategy therefore seeks to juxtapose different perspectives as a spur to their self-transformation and its momentum is maintained by the dialectic of mutual interrogation. In ways which resemble calls to religious inter-faith dialogue it calls for reciprocal understanding amongst different perspectives on the presupposition that none can or should relinquish their special viewpoints. As this outline makes clear, however, the problem which confronts this approach is built into its starting premise. If perspectives must remain true to themselves how can they also hope to understand the other?

3 The loneliness of law's meta-theory

The difficulties of the dialogic approach are well set out by Febbrajo in the course of a review of the current revival of the application of 'systems theories' to law. Febbrajo poses the basic issue in a way which will by now be familiar. How, he asks, can we 'establish the degree of cognition and reflection that law can from time to time allow itself, without betraying its identity and

---

9 Alexy R. *op.cit* 233.
10 Frankenberg G. 'Down by law; irony, seriousness and reason', *Northwestern University Law Review* (1989) 83, 396.
11 Frankenberg G. *op.cit* 397.

turning itself into a different instrument of social control'.[12] Assuming that the answer must involve a search for what he calls a 'metasystem' he wonders: 'What meta-system could guarantee a mutual understanding (intersubjectivity) of the different criteria for attention, interpretation and manipulation applied by each system?'.[13] For Febbrajo the way forward in understanding the relationship between 'internal' and 'external' legal culture requires 'a mutual translation of the symbolic universes of both cultures'. But in the light of post-positivist claims concerning the mutual embeddedness of cognitive and normative arguments, any such undertaking faces 'the impossibility of establishing where one communicative channel ends, where another begins, and which of the two is tributary'.[14] Despite all these obstacles, however, Febbrajo remains committed to finding a way to ensure 'the successful reproduction of the normative-cognitive flow of information between law and society'. Although he himself does not specify how this should be done, there have been a number of interesting attempts to tackle this question. Recent efforts to reach a meta-theory through encouraging a dialogue between law and science may be placed along a continuum. At one end, the more scientific standpoints try to show how the reflexivity of science can allow it to understand even its own limitations. At the other, more legalistic approaches try to show how law's self-understanding, suitably encouraged, can find some place for all the relevant implications of external approaches. The positions towards the centre try to harness both of these reflexive strategies. By paying close attention to the arguments offered in support of these different positions we will be able to decide how successfully they deal with the problem of clashes between law and science.

I shall begin with an example at the 'scientific' end of the spectrum. In a recent discussion of the relationship between 'sociology' and 'law' Cotterrell admits at the outset that the new agenda which he must confront is the difficulty of comparing fields of intellectual endeavour because 'each constructs its own fields of knowledge and experience'.[15] He nevertheless finds an ingenious argument to show why sociology can still provide a privileged route to understanding law. This is that, uniquely, sociology is dedicated to a reflexive perspective on the development of disciplines – including itself. Law, by contrast, lacking this interest, is no more than a 'discipline-effect', whose changing knowledge-claims can therefore be best illuminated through the use of sociology (of science and knowledge). The post-positivist twist in his argument is that a 'scientific' perspective on law is here credited with a superior epistemology not because of its greater capacity for getting at 'the facts about the world' but precisely on the basis of its more sophisticated sense of the limits of disciplinary understanding. Cotterrell sees law's tendency to import the methods and findings of external disciplines as a sign of periodic crises which reveal its recognition of its disciplinary weakness and the need to resort to other perspectives in order to correct the mistaken assumptions and fictions which disfigure it.

---

12 Febbrajo A. 'From hierarchical to circular models in the sociology of law: some introductory remarks', *European Yearbook in the Sociology of Law* (Febbrajo A. ed.) (1988) Milan, 7.
13 Febbrajo A. *op.cit.* 13.
14 Febbrajo A. *op.cit.* 13.
15 Cotterrell R. 'Law and sociology', *Journal of Law and Society* (1986) 13, 11.

But can this argument provide the meta-theory we are looking for? Insofar as sociology is being put forward as the discipline capable of rising above 'competing fields of knowledge and experience' this is because law's disciplinary status had already been downgraded so that it does not represent real competition. There is some support for Cotterrell's view of law in the work of writers such as Kuhn, Rorty and Foucault, all of whom are unsure whether legal science qualifies as a 'paradigm', 'normal science', or 'episteme'. But this does not meet the point that law sees itself as a self-sufficient interpretative framework, as Dworkin would argue. If it is said that Dworkin's views are too closely identified with those of law itself, it may fairly be said that Cotterrell for his part stands too close to sociology to furnish 'the truth of law's truth'.

Even when seeking to describe its own limitations a sociological perspective cannot really transcend its own style and method of argument. Thus we find that sociological approaches to clashes between disciplines typically offer either functionalist explanations of the appropriate role of different disciplines or a conflict-oriented account of the sources of their rivalry. But this means that other disciplinary perspectives will offer alternative meta-theories which compete with that put forward by sociology. A psychological meta-theory would concentrate on the psychological aspects of disagreement between discourses and an economic approach would point to the importance of costs and benefits of the choices between different disciplines. Both of these meta-theories could also then be applied to their own evolution. Moreover law too can put forward a reflexive understanding of its own genesis and applicability which can enter into conflict with any alternatives. It does not have to work in the same way as social science to represent an epistemological equal. Whilst Cotterrell claims too much for sociology (or any scientific approach) he is surely right to highlight the particular appropriateness of the sociology of knowledge for discussing the contests between disciplines since it is hard not to draw on this approach even for criticising his arguments!

However, we may now move on to consider the less imperialistic social scientific approach to our problem which is found in the work of Ost and van de Kerchove (1987). What they offer may fairly be described as a mainstream moderate, social science viewpoint on the question. These authors admit at the outset that it is impossible to provide anything like an 'absolute' of 'unconditioned point of view'.[16] What really interests them is the extent to which it is possible or desirable to try to transcend particular disciplinary perspectives in search of a synthesis. They are well aware of the dangers of one perspective replacing rather than understanding another. This influences their central recommendations concerning the possible choices to be made between the options of what they call pluradisciplinarity, transdisciplinarity and interdisciplinarity. They reject the approach of pluradisciplinarity, by which different disciplines are joined together without any real attempt at synthesis, because this can only mean incoherence and 'scientific babel'. By transdisciplinarity, on the other hand, they mean the ideal of harmonizing this babel by creating a new common language – a sort of scien-

16 Ost F. & M. van de Kerchove, *Jalons pour une théorie critique du droit* (1987) Bruxelles, 1.

tific esperanto. But this approach is also rejected on the basis that it is utopian. Evidence for this is drawn from the deconstructive argument that any attempt to mediate between different disciplines invariably faces the difficulty of knowing how to tell whether or not a given language game had been successfully translated into another.

For Ost and van de Kerchove the only viable option is interdisciplinary. According to this, issues to be understood should be addressed through a series of different perspectives, whether sociological, psychological, psychiatric, economic, legal or whatever. There can be no hierarchical precedence amongst these various independent perspectives although, it is suggested, there may be some possibility of dialogue. Perhaps because of this hope, however, the approach of interdisciplinarity is seen as inherently unstable, leading either to attempts at transdisciplinarity or collapse into pluradisciplinarity. Ost and Van de Kerchove, unlike Cotterrell, do treat law as a fully-fledged discipline, and would presumably reject his suggestions for prioritizing social science. But, like Cotterrell, they do use a social science perspective in responding to the clash between law and social science inasmuch as they rely on the usual strategy for interdisciplinary work within science. The same attitude can be seen in the way they treat the 'internal – external distinction' in legal philosophy as if it were isomorphic with the debate between interpretative and causal approaches to explanation in the social sciences. Like Cotterrell too, they stress the value of interdisciplinarity for the purposes of critical appreciation of the limits of perspectives rather than as a route to technically improved methods of solving social problems. Efforts to actually integrate law with other perspectives are, for them, an unfailing sign of such technical or even technocratic policy concerns.

But all this begs the question whether disputes between law and social science are best handled as if they were comparable to clashes between different sciences. What Ost and Van de Kerchove's preferred approach offers is a way of seeing a problem from many different sides, including the legal one. But, for other purposes, other approaches to these clashes may be more appropriate. Pluradisciplinarity may well be a wholly unsuitable theoretical solution for interdisciplinary work. Yet this approach well describes what is often found on the ground as a consequence of the various forms of institutionalized division of labour between law and science. In the realm of law and psychiatry for example, some states in the USA adopted 'guilty but mentally ill' verdicts. This may well be 'scientific babel' but could make practical sense as an open acknowledgement of the virtues of pluradisciplinarity when these type of decisions have to be reached. Even within the scientific world, there may be something to be said for the juxtaposition of different disciplines as a heuristic device which can lead to unexpected progress. We might consider here Durkheim's use of biological terms and analogies in helping create sociology; Weber's attempt to combine historical and sociological methods, or the difficulty we have in deciding whether figures like Newton or Poincaré were primarily scientists or philosophers.

There may also be more merit in the transdisciplinary approach than is allowed for by Ost and Van de Kerchove. It may help us see how legal rules and procedures reflect attempts at synthesis, successful or otherwise, as in the way the structure of legal excuses such as provocation or duress has been said to reflect an underlying compromise between neo-classical, voluntarist, conceptions of responsibility on the one hand and more positivist, scientific, notions of determined behaviour on the other (Kelman 1981). Ost and Van de Kerchove's arguments themselves offer some encouragement for transdisciplinary work. Otherwise why should they look forward to the development of a dialogue between different disciplines or the larger picture that can be obtained by a series of disciplinary snapshots? Surely this is because the self-understanding of different disciplines is bound to be changed by a greater consciousness of the disciplinary alternatives. Moreover the familiar reflexive problem recurs here. These authors' arguments against transdisciplinarity and for interdisciplinarity have to be understood as operating at a level higher than any particular discipline if they are to count as more than just another disciplinary perspective. Thus it seems as if Ost and Van de Kerchove have taken from post-positivism the idea that truth is a matter of internal disciplinary coherence but then find it hard to stay consistent with that sort of perspectivism in making any general statements.

Moving further along the continuum takes us to an approach which still poses the problem in philosophical and scientific language but tries to find an answer which will accommodate the different demands of law and science. In a number of papers Bankowski has tried to work out the degree of force to be attributed to social science critiques of law (Bankoswki 1981, 1989), focussing in particular on attacks on legal methods of fact finding. At the outset Bankowski's comments on criticisms such as Frank's which alleged that trials failed to find 'the facts' was to reply that the law had its own 'truth-certifying procedures' which could not be challenged using criteria belonging to competing procedures. Psychological studies which purported to show the ineffectiveness of some cross-examination techniques for discovering the truth, begged the question whether they had, or could have, a proper understanding of law's criteria of truth (Bankowski 1981). At this stage, just as Cotterrell's argument can be seen as a sophisticated justification of attempts to find the 'truth about law', so Bankowski's position could be read as a defence of the inviolability of 'law's truth'. In later writings, however, he has retreated from any relativistic interpretation of the coherence theory of truth (Bankowski 1989). He now argues that it may sometimes be appropriate to take account of scientific criticisms of legal procedures, for example, of the reliability of witness identification evidence, even if at other times external critiques should be resisted.

But this of course brings us up against the meta-theoretical question of how to decide which criticisms should be accepted. Bankowski suggests, reasonably enough, that to answer this question we must 'move to a higher level' from which it may be possible to assess the appropriateness of different truthfinding procedures. He talks in functionalist language of the fit between different truth-certifying methods and the tasks they are asked to perform. Within the Anglo-American criminal justice process, for example, the police are encouraged to apprehend alleged offenders using their knowledge of previous convictions, whereas this information is kept from the court until the sentencing stage. Bankowski adds that it is ultimately the prerogative of the law to determine which type of truth-finding procedure to use at any stage of its processes. Law may choose between a more or a less restrictive approach to constructing its facts and make what use it will of lay, 'common-sense' or scientific perspectives.

Bankowski's approach demonstrates how legal procedures may make use of more than one criterion of truth. These may then be either harmonized or deliberately juxtaposed within legal procedures. But for this reason he does not offer us much help in showing how to handle genuine competition between legal and scientific perspectives. We cannot assume that police work in collecting evidence can be compared to the use of scientific methodology given the legal restraints which shape even this stage of criminal process. And the very fact that law relates its different truth-finding methods to its institutional allocation of responsibilities means that the possibility of irresolvable conflict of perspectives is avoided.

Bankowski's proposals cannot solve the problems that may be raised by external challenges when law has no settled procedures or accepted competence to use in deciding the issue. A graphic illustration of this in relation to the criminal process can be seen in the recurrent difficulties we have in deciding at which point enough evidence has accumulated to justify re-opening a case on the basis of an alleged 'miscarriage of justice'. As we know, law can deal with this, or any other question by reformulating it in terms of the kind of choice between rules or values which it typically handles. But if Bankowski is to help us appreciate when a criticism of law has sufficient cogency to be accepted he presumably wants to do more than tell us that law has to decide this for itself. Moreover, if his recommendation to think of this choice in functional terms is superficially plausible this is because both law and science sometimes use functionalist types of argumentation. But insofar as they have competing interests and priorities regarding the functions they pursue, the meaning they attach to the notion of function will be bound to differ so that the dilemma of choice returns. We therefore seem still to be left with the problem that law and science pose questions in different ways and that any possibility of commensuration is either illusory or else relies on some ambiguous measure of apparent overlap between their discourses.

Probably the most sustained engagement with the implications of this awkward conclusion is seen in the work of Teubner. For him 'epistemic authority is claimed by scientific discourse and legal discourse, and rightly so'.[17] So he sees the problem squarely as how to work out the relationship between two (or more) varieties of internal self-understanding whilst resisting any apparent short cuts or easy answers even when these are preferred by the discourses themselves. In his earlier work Teubner argued that law's constructions of the world were best seen as 'strategic' models of reality which could not be judged or impugned by drawing on social science perspectives (Teubner 1984, Blankenburg 1984, Teubner 1985). Teubner has since bolstered and developed this idea by conceptualizing law as one amongst many 'autopoietic structures' or 'epistemic subjects' each of which

17 Teubner G. *How the law thinks. Toward a constructivist epistemology of law*, EUI-working papers (1989) Firenze, 38.

operate self-referentially (Teubner 1988, 1989a, 1989b). In a recent paper entitled 'How the law thinks', Teubner reviews those arguments of Habermas, Foucault and Luhmann which may be used to develop a 'constructivist social epistemology' (Teuber 1989b). The aim is to 'de-centre' the acting subject so as to focus instead on the reproduction of discourses and structures through which this and other ideas and practices are constructed. Teubner draws on Luhmann to argue that the form of social differentiation in modern society and the functional specialization which accompanies it has led to the multiplication of independent centres of cognition each of which produce their own reality constructions. Whereas economics 'sees' the world in terms of prices, politics does so in terms of power, whilst law addresses it in terms of the distinction between legality and illegality. Teubner also adopts a strong version of the post positivist claim that the truth of disciplines depends on their internal coherence and that science does not have a privileged access to reality. Applied to our problem Teubner argues that legal communications can never succeed in satisfying the truth requirements of other discourses and should not attempt to do so. The appearance of overlap between law and science is to be understood as an example of 'interference'. By this is meant synchronic communications produced by self-referential systems which nevertheless have their own distinct referents within their own discourses. The upshot of this is that law regularly finds itself in an 'epistemic trap' insofar as its assumptions and claims are 'exposed to the test of social coherence' which in modern society is a role assigned to science, whilst it can only take account of such requirements in terms of its own discourse. It is under these conflicting pressures that law produces its 'hybrid' notions such as 'interest' or 'efficiency' which though originally borrowed from external disciplines soon take on a legal life of their own. However, 'incorporation of social science knowledge does not solve conflicts between judicial and scientific realities but adds a new reality that is neither a purely judicial construction nor a purely scientific construction, but a hybrid creature produced in the legal process with borrowed authority from the social sciences but their truth validity will be decided in the processes of legal communication'.[18] The notions developed in disciplines such as 'law and economics' are therefore stigmatized as having 'unclear epistemic status and unknown social consequences'.[19]

Teubner is at pains to deny that there can be any 'escape' from the 'epistemic trap'. He rejects the tempting solution characteristic of positivist writers, and endorsed by Luhmann amongst post-positivists, by which law renounces cognitive authority in favour of science. This is because law must serve as the ultimate forum for decision-making when scientists are in disagreement. Teubner sees it as the special role of sociology of law to show that law's cognitive constructions must prove to be unsatisfactory from a scientific point of view. He has only one positive recommendation to make. This is that instead of trying to produce cognitively satisfactory constructions of reality law should create for itself a strategic procedural role. The questions it should deal with should primarily be concerned with deciding

18 Teubner G. *op.cit.* 51.
19 Teubner G. *op.cit.* 45.

the appropriate truth-certifying procedure or forum to which to delegate any particular issue in dispute. Law's responsibility has therefore to do with the correct allocation of the burdens of risky decisions to collective actors, regulatory agencies, firms, unions, parliament etc.

Teubner's argument is probably the most original effort to date to deal with the cognitive and normative complexities raised by disagreements between law and science. But it leaves a number of important questions unclear or unsolved. These concern his conceptualization of law's claims to truth, the foundation of his own 'third position', and the merits of his 'procedural model for law'. There is a telling ambivalence in Teubner's claim concerning law's capacity to know the world. On the one hand, he wants to grant law's constructions of reality epistemic authority; on the other we are told that law is bound to lose out in competition with science because law's 'cognitive operations are secondary'.[20] This may perhaps be rationalized as an imaginative attempt to consider the problem of law's truth from both law's and science's point of view. But it does seem as if Teubner endorses scientific claims of superiority over law. Thus he writes at one point: 'social science writers are not by reason of their closer access to social reality intrinsically superior to legal conceptualizations of law in society' (Teubner 1986). If science can take us closer to 'reality', whatever that means in this context, can law really be considered an epistemic competitor except in terms of its own normative domain? It seems as if Teubner is not so far from the views of Kelsen or Luhmann by which law's epistemic autonomy is necessary tied to its distinctive, non-scientific, grasp of the world, as in Kelsen's contrast between the 'logic of imputation versus that of causality' or Luhmann's between 'the normative closedness of law as compared to its cognitive openness'. Teubner's claim often seems to amount to no more than a reworking of the familiar distinction between 'institutional' and 'brute' facts. He argues that 'empirical facts about disfunctions in organized life as a result of scientifically controlled enquiry are in no sense more 'true' than legal facts about the violation of corporate duties which are produced under the firm guidance of the rules of the law of evidence'.[21] Many writers have questioned whether there are any 'brute' facts. But Teubner chooses rather to emphasize the appropriateness of describing all 'institutional' facts as empirical since he adds '… and if these empirical facts conflict with each other there is no superiority of the scientific constructs over the legal constructs'.[22] Elsewhere too Teubner has made it explicit that for him the law deals in empirical and not only institutional facts and that he is making definite claims about law's cognitive understanding rather than merely its attribution of normative consequences. As he puts it, the point is that 'Under the pressure of normative operations (law) constructs idiosyncratic images of reality and moves them away from the world constructions of everyday life and from those of scientific discours'.[23] In sum, Teubner poses the problem as one of genuine competition between law and science even if law does not quite count as a science.

20 Teubner G. *op. cit.* 41.
21 Teubner G. *op.cit.* 38.
22 Teubner G. *op.cit.* 38.
23 Teubner G. *op.cit.* 34.

This ambivalence is directly linked to a second set of problems which concern the basis from which Teubner observes the contest between law and science. He rejects the possibility of establishing any higher level 'third position' insofar as modern social differentation has destroyed the plausibility of any overall centre of cognition. Yet here too there is an equivocation in his perspective which varies between a consistent perspectivism and a foundational confidence in the autopoietic and functionalist theories which provide the source of his arguments. Whilst he undoubtedly writes from a systems approach which allows for the 'observation of observations' he also insists that law, and any other discipline, can only understand and regulate the world by self-reflection. Thus he is more cautious than Luhmann in claiming a privileged position for sociological systems theory in explaining law (Luhmann 1985 Appendix). But there is no other obvious basis for his own argument about the relationship amongst disciplines. This, in turn, helps explain the nature of the 'solution' Teubner offers to the apparently irresolvable problem of rivalry between law and science. For Teubner there can be no cognitive resolution of the problem. He confines sociology of law to the negative task of deconstructing law's solutions because, unlike Cotterrell, he does not endow sociology with any special capacity to transcend its own vision. Instead Teubner changes tack and offers us a normative remedy for a cognitive dilemma.

But can Teubner's turn to procedure solve the difficulties of competing knowledge claims as he has posed them? The drawback of this solution from a cognitive point of view is that if law is indeed a distinctive discourse it will necessarily also have a distinctive understanding of disputes and other dispute – processing procedures. So even if its task is confined to that of procedural allocation and delegation of responsibilities amongst decision-makers this understanding may well diverge from that which other groups and forums have of themselves or that which other perspectives would reveal. Can law fulfill its allotted task without distorting the significance of the institutions which it is supposed to be servicing? If Teubner is willing to live with law's idiosyncrastic constructions in this regard we must ask why he is so uncomfortable with law's hybrid constructions of social reality, which, from law's point of view, are just as much under its control.

When examined as a normative prescription Teubner's recommendations raise even more difficulties. Procedural techniques have been proposed to increase the possibility of reaching scientific truth, as in the philosophy of science arguments of writers such as Popper. But Teubner's solution is firmly geared to the successful resolution of disputes rather than to serving as a methodological yardstick of truth. But, his shifting of the problem from the cognitive to the normative register inevitably means that his normative solution can be challenged cognitively all over again. Teubner's recommended procedural solution could be attacked, for example, for being less a compromise between competing discourses and more an endorsement of law's typical way of dealing with difficulties, as in the way it tries to avoid or narrow substantive issues down or concentrates on developing constitutional or other frameworks of responsibility. This implicit privileging of the legal point of view is therefore open to similar objections to those raised in connection with Bankowski's example of the competing truth-finding criteria within the criminal process. If these authors are not just trying to give law the better of the argument with science it remains unclear how their understanding of law can claim to improve on its self-understanding.

Although Teubner's proposals are not put forward as political recommendations there is little doubt that they do carry such implications. Although it would be wrong to apply to Teubner all the attacks levelled at Luhmann for his alleged 'false normative modesty' (Frankenberg 1989), it is plain that a preference for procedure is not politically innocent. Teubner's argument here can be seen as a development of his previous discussion of the so-called 'regulatory trilemma' (Teubner 1984). This argued that since law's comprehension of any sphere to be regulated is necessarily filtered through its own categories it can only regulate other spheres by regulating itself. For this reason law should become 'reflexive' about its own procedures and those of the spheres it seeks to regulate rather than aim directly at necessarily unpredictable substantive changes. But this argument as well as Habermas and Luhmann's surprising agreement over the virtues of law as a framework rather than as an instrument of change, runs the risk of turning evidence of failures of legal regulation into proof of the impossibility of successful regulation. In the end the choice not to risk law in schemes of social engineering is a political choice, dependent on the risks and benefits of particular interventions rather than an inherent necessity imposed by the limits of law. In the same way it is a political choice whether to attack or defend law's attemps to cloak its substantive constructions of the world in hybrid conceptual language. As Teubner himself indicates, the development of such concepts, whatever their scientific status, provides legal discourse with flexibility, openness, and the means of learning through experimentation. The clash of disciplinary perspectives, as he argues, can serve as a 'variety pool' for legal innovation, much as the range of cases brought forward by litigants provides the possibility for judges to develop the law. So why does he try to proceduralize?

There is also some inconsistency between Teubner's recommendations and his post-structuralist standpoint. According to him the choosing human agent is 'de-centred' and must be treated as one of the products of discourse itself. But it is hard then to see how Teubner's advice can find its way into the internal reproduction of law, which at present seems more than content to produce the conceptual hybrids to which he objects. More provocatively, if law's understanding of other discourses necessarily distorts their meaning how can he avoid his suggestions from suffering the same fate – even when he merely tries to tell law how to be true to itself. Thus, for all its bravura, Teubner's attempt to explain how the law thinks is either redundant or cannot avoid telling it how it ought to think.

At this stage of the argument we might be persuaded to go right to the normative end of the continuum so as to find a solution to clashes between law and science by restricting ourselves to an internal interpretation of how law normally deals with such questions. Law is often asked to resolve clashes between values such as justice and certainty or deal with conflicts of law situations which raise apparently similar issues to the one we have been considering so far. Dworkin, for example, sees law as its own meta-theory, reflexively providing its own source of authority and validity, seeking to answer the riddle of its own meaning and offer the best sense of the valued social practices to which it gives recognition (Dworkin 1986). And for him, law's best interpretation of itself necessarily includes science's best interpretation of itself. In many respects law can also be said to be a richer form of life than science.[24] It draws on various disciplines as and when required and contrasts them with robust 'common sense'. It maintains a healthy scepticism about the possibility of deriving determinate solutions from scientific arguments and reinforces this scepticism in adversarial confrontations at court (Smith 1989). Its mode of argument has been characterized as a paradigm for post-positivism (Villa 1984) and its internal development can be presented as a model of how a system can transform itself by always holding some elements immutable whilst changing others.[25]

An interesting recent attempt to develop a legal meta-theory can be found in Jackson (1988). The main purpose of his book is to further the application of Greimasian semiotics to the philosophy and sociology of law, rather than tackle problems of legal truth versus scientific truth. But Jackson's interest in truth as a species of narrative coherence means that he too has to confront many of the issues raised by post-postivist arguments in law and science. He argues that since 'truth' depends on coherence within semantic structures rather than on correspondence with external facts it is impossible to claim that law is mistaken if its claims about casual relationships or other scientific phenomena are otherwise coherent.[26] His original contribution, however, is to stress that law's truth depends on the plausibility of its story-telling structures not only in its fact-finding enquiries but even when it comes to substantive legal rules. 'Hard' cases in law are said to be those in which law has lost touch with the underlying stories which helped shape its earlier rule-making. Jackson urges the incorporation of a reflexive sensibility into legal argumentation which would oblige legal actors to justify all truth claims about their construction of legal rules and legal facts and the connection between them. An awareness of the origin of given legal rules might show that the norm had 'lost' its meaning over time, as the Erlangen School might put it (Alexy 1989), or that a norm had not been created under conditions wich would now be considered egalitarian or otherwise legitimate. We would not therefore have 'to endorse the conservative context of existing normative frameworks'.[27] The demand for normative authenticity could lead in this way to original legal arguments and the formulation of what Critical Legal Scholars call 'deviant doctrine'. (Unger 1983).

How far can Jackson help us with our problem of clashes between law and science? In his optic, law and science are not seen as monolithic rivals. Each discourse has interdiscursive connections with other forms of social communication. Law has some special forms of syntactic, semantic and pragmatic distinctiveness as compared to ordinary language in its strain towards mono-semioticity, and the special claims it makes about itself. No

---

24 Guarnieri P. L'ammazzabambini: *legge e scienzia in un processo toscano di fine ottocento* (1988) Torino, 196.
25 Hofstadter D.R. *Metamagical Themas* (1985) London, 84.
26 Jackson B. *Law, fact and narrative coherence* (1988) Liverpool, 143.
27 Jackson B. *op. cit.* 194.

doubt much the same could also be said for science. But for Jackson the question of clashes between law and science is primarily seen as the problem of being able to tell more than one story of the same event. He therefore asks 'why not enroll a panel of adjudicators from a variety of disciplines, which can look at a particular situation in all its wholeness?'.[28] But he rejects this solution, which roughly corresponds to the one put forward by Ost and van de Kerchove, as unsatisfactory on the grounds that 'we know too much about the stories of others and we habitually make comparisons'.[29] The public, we are told, expects at least the appearance of consistent treatment before the law but such expectations are bound to be disappointed in any attempt to follow this type of solution.[30] But this retreat to legal consistency leaves our problem unresolved. If this approach to law in terms of narrative coherence is to retain any critical edge over Dworkin's 'best interpretation' strategy, the enquiry into the validity of past and present legal narratives must employ a variety of disciplines, however unpredictable and inconsistent the consequences. In the end, whatever their other virtues, principles of integrity in truth-telling can tell us relatively little about the ideal mix of legal and scientific types of argumentation.

Despite the ingenuity of the arguments we have considered the results of this survey of attempts to derive law's meta-theory from a dialogue between science and law are still somewhat limited, particularly when we try to get science to get a grip on itself (Cotterrell) or to make law understand itself better (Jackson). Intermediate attempts to combine, contrast or separate the two perspectives (Bankowski, Ost and van de Kerchove, or Teubner) seem to take us further with our problem. But even they have not suggested a reliable method for reconciling questions concerning the accuracy of factual propositions, the correctness of evaluative statements and the authenticity of speakers. Rather it is these writers who have shown most clearly the difficulties which face attempts to construct a new division of labour which would parcel out such questions neatly between law and science. It remains to be seen whether it is these difficulties which provide the best insights we can obtain into the problems of developing law's meta-theory.

References

Atiyah, P. (1979) – *The rise and fall of freedom of contract*, Oxford, OUP.
Bankowski, Z. (1981) – 'The value of truth: fact scepticism revisited', *Legal Studies*, 257.
Bankowski, Z. (1989) – 'The jury and rationality' in *The jury under attack* (M. Findlay and P. Duff eds.) London, Butterworths.
Barnes, B. and Edge, D. (eds.) (1982) – *Science in context. Milton Keynes*, OUP.
Beer, S. (1977) – 'Meta-system', in A. Bullock and O. Stallybrass *The Fontana Dictionary of Modern Thought*, London, Fontana/Collins p. 386.
Blankenburg, E. (1984) – 'The poverty of evolutionism: A critique of Teubner's case for reflexive law' 18 *Law and Society Review*, 273.

28 Jackson B. *op.cit.* 194.
29 Jackson B. *op.cit.* ibidem.
30 Jackson B. *op.cit.* 144.

Brownsword, R. and Beyleveld, D. (1986) – *Law as a moral judgment*, London, Sweet and Maxwell.

Chambers, D. (1987) – 'The abuse of social science: a response to Fineman and Opie', *Wisconsin Law Review* 159.

Cohen, J. (1981) – *The probable and the provable*, Oxford, OUP.

Damaska, M. (1986) – *The faces of justice and state authority: A comparative approach to the legal process*. New Haven, Yale Univ. Press.

Derrida, J. (1977) – (trans. G. Spivack) *Of grammatology*, Baltimore, Johns Hopkins Press.

Dworkin, R. (1986) – *Law's empire*, London Penguin.

Fineman, M. and Opie, A. (1987) – 'The use of social science data in legal policymaking: Custody determinations at divorce', *Wisconsin Law Review* 107.

Finnis, J. (1980) – *Natural law and natural rights*, Oxford, OUP.

Foucault, M. (1977) – *Discipline and punish*, London, Penguin/Allen Lane.

Garland, D. (1985) – *Punishment and welfare: A history of penal strategies*, London, Gower.

Geertz, C. (1983) – *Local Knowledge: Further essays in interpretive anthropology*, New York. Basic Books.

Habermas, J. (1985) – 'Law as a medium and law as institution', in *Dilemmas of law in the welfare state*, G. Teubner (ed.) Berlin, De Gruyter.

Hunter, I. (1977) – Meta-psychology; in A. Bullock and O. Stallybrass *The Fontana Dictionary of Modern Thought*, London, Fontana/Collins.

Jolowicz, J. (1988) – 'Comparative law and the reform of civil procedure', *Legal Studies*, 1.

Kelman, S. (1981) – 'Substantive interpretation in the criminal law', *33 Stanford Law Review* 591.

Kennedy, D. (1985) – 'Spring break', *63 Texas Law Review* 1355.

Kramer, M. (forthcoming) – *Against Rhadanantos*.

Lawson, H. (1982) – *Reflexivity*. Oxford, OUP.

Luhmann, N. (1985) – *The sociological theory of law* (Trans. S. King and M. Albrow) London, RK p.

Luhmann, N. (1988) – 'The unity of the legal system', in G, Teubner (ed) *Autopoietic law: A new approach to law and society*, Berlin, De Gruyter.

Lyotard, J. (1984) – *The post-modern condition. A report on knowledge*, Minnesota, Univ. of Minnesota Press.

McCormick, D.N. (1974) – 'Law as institutional fact', *90 Law Quarterly Review*, 102.

McCormick, D.N. (1978) – *Legal reasoning and legal theory*, Oxford, OUP.

Nelken, D. (1987) – 'Criminal law and criminal justice: Some notes on their irrelation: in I. Dennis (ed.) *Criminal law and justice*, London, Sweet and Maxwell, 139.

Quinton, A. (1977) – 'Meta-theory' in A. Bullock and O. Stallybrass (eds.) *The Fontana Dictionary of Modern Thought*, London, Fontana/Collins.

Samek, R. (1974) – *The legal point of view*, N.Y. Philosophical Library.

Scoditti, E. (1988) – 'Critica e metacritica del diritto' *4-5 Democrazia e diritto*.

Smith, R. (1981) – *Trial by Medicine*, Edinburgh University Press.

Smith, R. (1989) – 'Forensic pathology, scientific expertise and the criminal law', in R. Smith and B. Wynne (eds.) *Expert evidence; interpreting science in the law*. London, Routledge, 56.

Stanford Law Review (1984) – Special issue on Critical Legal Studies.

Summers, R.S. (1978) – 'Two types of substantive reasons: the core of a theory of common law justification'. *65 Cornell Law Review* 707.

Teubner, G. (1985) – 'After legal instrumentalism.Strategic models of post-regulatory law', in G. Teubner (ed) – *Dilemmas of law in the welfare state*, Berlin, De Gruyter.

Teubner, G. and Daintith, T. (eds.) (1986) – Contract and organisation, Berlin, De Gruyter.

Teubner, G. (1988) – 'Evolution of autopoietic law' in G. Teubner ed. *Autopoietic Law: A new approach to law and society*, Berlin, De Gruyter 217.

Teubner, G. (1989a) – 'And God laughed: indeterminacy, self reference and paradox; in C. Joerges and D. Trubek (eds.) *Critical legal thought: An American-German debate.* Baden-Baden, Nomos.

Unger, R. (1983) – 'The critical legal studies movement' 96 *Harvard Law Review* 563.

Villa, V. (1988) – 'Meta-theorie' in A.J. Arnaud (ed.) *Dictionnaire Encyclopédique de théorie et de Sociologie du droit*, Paris/Bruxelles Librairie Générale/Story-scientia Editions 245-248.

Villa, V. (1984) – *Teorie della scienza giuridica e teorie delle scienza naturale*, Milan, Giuffrè.

Veljanovski, C.J. (1985) – 'Economic theorising about tort:' in *Current legal problems* (Ed. R. Rideout and J. Jowell), London, Sweet and Maxwell, 117.

Waldron, J. (1987) *Nonsense on stilts: Bentham, Burke and Marx on the rights of man*, London, Methuen.

Willock, I. (1974) – 'Getting on with sociologists', *I British Journal of Law and Society 3*.

[9]
Are Disputes between Law and Science Resolvable?

Abstract

Social scientific discussions of the acceptability of rules and procedures in the law of evidence (and elsewhere) must be certain that they have first grasped the point of what they are criticizing. What if they 'transform' the object of their enquiries in the course of interpreting them?

This paper examines the possibilities for finding the 'meta-theory' which will best allow this issue to be debated and resolved. It considers 'reconstructive' and 'deconstructive' approaches to the building of such a theory and concludes by recommending a 'dialogic' strategy in which legal and (social) scientific styles of argumentation enter into mutual interrogation.

'The normative question of how expert knowledge is best assessed, and how experts themselves are best evaluated and kept under a modicum of control, raises such intractable and viciously circular problems as to strangle speech'.[1]

Introduction

In this paper I want to discuss some issues arising from clashes or apparent clashes between legal and scientific conception of reality and methods of truth-finding.[2] The topics which will be touched on include: Can there be different truths for law and science? How can we make sense of them? Is it possible to choose between them? Without entering into the details of particular controversies here, it is not difficult to find examples of present and past disagreements between law and science. To choose only the most well-known, there are the long-running disputes between legal and psychiatric conception of insanity, and the argument of psychologists and statisticians concerning the sense and acceptability of what counts as evidence in law. More generally, many social scientists reject the judges' use of concepts such as 'market efficiency' or 'group interest'; they are baffled by 'judges' willingness to predicate the outcome of their decisions on little scientific evidence and their disinclination to check whether their conclusions are in fact sound.

It is difficult to distinguish real clashes from those that are only apparent. Sometimes law and science may only seem superficially to deal with the same phenomenon. Possible examples are the legal and medical definitions of death. In such cases different definitions reflect different purposes and concerns rather than a genuine dispute. Law is sometimes explicit about this, as in the distinction, in English criminal and tort law, between 'factual' and 'legal' causation. At the other extreme, legal judgements do sometimes entertain scientific impossibilities, as in decisions which have allowed a presumption of paternity even where the pregnancy would have lasted more than a year. To an extent law may even use 'doublethink' to treat its 'legal fictions' as facts. In many of the most troublesome clashes between law and science, however, the real difficulty lies precisely in deciding *whether* the different conceptions

---

[1] Barnes and Edge, 1982, p. 11.

[2] More extended discussion of these issues, with reference to some current controversies in law and science, will be found in my paper «The truth about law's truth» (Nelken, 1991).

in play represent genuine disagreement or not - *and in knowing how to go about answering this question.*

It may be objected that there is a ready way to resolve such disputes. To recognise the authority of law in legal contexts, such as the courtroom, and the priority of science in scientific arguments made in other contexts. Certainly, if there is an answer to our problem it would seem to involve appreciating what it means to say that truth varies in different contexts. It requires little skill to discover that the outcome of disagreements between law and sciences is different in arguments put before judges, in legal commentaries, and in multidisciplinary law reform enquiries. Once again, however, the problem at the heart of many current controversies is the difficulty of keeping the different contexts apart. Good arguments in one context carry at least a specious plausibility outside their normal context. Both science and morality, for example, tend to presume *universal* applicability of their arguments and both lay claim to law. At the same time law is often expected to adjudicate the applicability of their enterprises.

In many pressing cases of legal and scientific rivalry courts have reached an apparently practical solution. Expert witnesses in the courtroom are expected to protect the integrity of their discipline whilst at the same time serving the ends of the law. But this is often no more than a compromise rather than a solution of underlying differences. The compromise results in regular complaints about the workings of the adversarial trial, although the true source of unease lies deeper than this. One experienced English forensic expert recently complained that having to feed his scientific opinions through the adversarial process meant that the truth emerged 'bruised and mangled and possibly unrecognisable'.[3] In his view, many recent 'miscarriages of justice', could have been avoided if it had been possible to use evidence available, but not admitted, at the time of the trial. This complaint has particular force, coming as it does from a professional who specializes in the task of mediating between law and science.

The search for a meta-theory

These preliminary observations point to some of the crucial questions raised by this enquiry. Can there be a third point of view on disputes between law and science? What form would it take? Is it more a matter of searching for a new or synthetic perspective, or is it a question of prescribing guidelines for good decision-making practice when such clashes arise? Even if some questions about law are not strictly legal questions can both law and science compete in defining a legal question ? Can there be anything more to say on this matter which is not already couched *either* in terms of trying to reach a greater understanding of the nature of these disputes *or* developing a better method of deciding what to do about them? Is there any way in which such discussions (including this one) can actually stand outside the debates they attempt to transcend and avoid *competing* with the approaches they seek to understand or evaluate? In short, what sort of meta-theory should we be looking for?[4]

There are certainly many excellent social scientific studies which offer an account of the rise and fall of particular types of knowledge and power and the conflicts between them.[5] These can tell us a great deal about the reasons for the changing fortunes of different discourses - but they are usually the first to admit the difficulty of deriving object lessons from these clashes.[6] On the other hand, more normative approaches tend to marginalize the question of truth, to the

---

[3] Gee, 1987.

[4] Hunter 1977; Nelken 1991; Quinton 1977; Villa 1988.

[5] See e.g. the works by Atiyah (1979); Foucault (1977); Garland (1985); Smith (1981).

[6] See e.g. Smith 1981.

extent that some writers see legal decision-making as distinctively engaged in handling 'practical' choices to which non-theoretical 'right answers' can be discovered, as compared to what can be achieved in the realm of 'speculative disagreements'.[7]

Both these approaches therefore avoid attempting to provide a meta-theory. There are, however, some writers who do try to tackle this problem directly; who use one or more of three approaches. The first, which I will call the *reconstructive* approach, looks for meta-theoretical answers beyond the institutionalized discourses of law and science. Its problem is how to maintain this viewpoint in the face of post-positivist challenges to transcendent truth-claims. The second approach follows post-modern movements such as *the turn to deconstruction* in rejecting the possibility of discovering 'foundationalist' certainties. It must confront the obvious dangers of selfcontradiction in proving its case. The third approach, which I shall call the *dialogic* response, is the one which perhaps has most potential. It reacts to the weaknesses of the other two approaches by determining to find the answer from science and law rather than elsewhere. It then has to grapple with the consequent difficulties that are entailed in asking discourses to transcend themselves.

In the reconstructive response the search for a valid meta-theory maintains its momentum by showing the consequences of surrender. Thus it makes arguments about the need to be 'sceptical about scepticism', the impossibility of engaging in discussion without endorsing the value of truth and the requirement of applying to our own arguments the criteria we apply to others.[8] The goals of this search may be various. For some writers the aim is to interpret or recapture a transcen-dent source of truth and value.[9] At the other extreme some thinkers recommend looking for a consensus at a more concrete and practical level.[10]

The broader 'master' discourses to which those following this approach usually refer law and science include religion, morality, politics, philosophy, 'practical reason' and common sense. Such discourses often lie at the root of the 'will to truth' within law and science, as Nietzsche and Foucault have argued. It is therefore not surprising that they are again invoked when law and science find themselves facing ultimate questions – or, at least, the difficulty of ultimate resolutions of questions. The form that any such meta-theory takes will then depend on the type of argumentation and practice character-istic of the master discourse chosen, whether it be, for example, the analytical techniques of philosophy, the revealed or rational truths and value-judgements of religion or morality, or the pragmatic case-by-case appraisals of 'practical reason'.

The second, deconstructive strategy, on the other hand, focuses on the limits and inter-discursivities of all arguments and 'texts'. The endless play of 'signifier' and 'signified' corrode certainty and truth itself becomes an 'army of metaphors' at the command of 'the will to power'. This approach maintains its momentum – in spite of itself – in various ways. It purports to undermine pretentions to 'totalizing' visions;[11] open up attempts by legal and other texts to achieve 'closure';[12] anticipate criticisms by self-criticism[13] and ironicise all claims to truth including their own.[14]

Some writers who follow this strategy justify

---

[7] McCormick 1978.

[8] Alexy, 1989; Brownsword and Beyleveld, 1986; Finnis, 1978.

[9] Finnis, 1978; Habermas, 1979.
[10] Waldron, 1987.
[11] Lyotard, 1984.
[12] Derrida, 1977; *Stanford Law Review,* 1984.
[13] Kramer, 1991.
[14] Kennedy, 1985.

their position by rejecting 'scientific' method in the name of hermeneutics. They see law, history and even science as presupposing the internal grasping and application of a tradition. The results of such a tradition are necessarily contingent to a given period and place. Gadamer, for example, rejects the possibility of a Habermasian 'ideal-speech situation' because our conception of what would bring us closer to it is always necessarily formulated according to prevailing cultural assumptions within a given community. Rorty, in a series of attacks on what he terms 'foundationalism', counterposes the hermeneutic and epistemological projects, arguing that the search for epistemological certainty must and should give way to a concern to appreciate the diversity of discourses.[15] Rather than attempting to offer a superior, contextualised explanation (as in social scientific approaches which are explicitly described in Britain as 'putting the law in context') the crucial task is to find ways of keeping the conversation between discourses going.

Those who argue for a deconstructive strategy tend to say that they are trying to avoid talking about truth, rather than to show its impossibility. The nearest they come to asserting a strong thesis concerning the pointlessness of looking for a meta-theory, comes in arguments derived from Kuhn and Wittgenstein on the limits to our ability to predict changes in discourse. As Rorty puts it:
'The product of abnormal discourse can be anything from nonsense to intellectual revolution and there is no discipline which describes it'.[16]
Wittgenstein's notion of 'language games' and the 'forms of life' in which the games are embodied has been particularly influential. As one of his leading commentators explains:

'The most common form of philosophical nonsense arises when (a word) is used in a language-game other than the one appropriate to it'.[17]

Kenny goes straight on to show why Wittgenstein's ideas cannot be exploited in order to draw borderlines between different discourses in terms of 'appropriateness'.

'So it is clearly important to be able to know where one language game ends and another begins. How does one do this? Wittgenstein gives us little help here'.[18]
While it *would* be helpful to be able to distinguish cases of illegitimate crossing between language games from cases of genuine overlap, any effort to do so in a general manner becomes just another language-game. And this applies also to the use of the expression 'language-game' itself.

A somewhat neglected application of Wittgenstein's ideas by Robert Samek, designed to elucidate what he calls the 'legal point of view' illustrates some of their implications for meta-theory.[19] According to Samek, points of view can only be correct or incorrect by virtue of the criteria that led us to adopt them. Our meta-views on these points of view therefore are neither true nor false but are only evaluations of a given point of view from a particular standpoint. Samek claims that the functions of different discourses may cross-cut the point of view to which they belong and that it is our understanding of a point of view rather than the point of view itself which maps our field of interest. The upshot of this is the stringent limits on examining one language game from the vantage point of another. For example:
'the distinction between the evaluative and the assertive function of discourse is fruitful when it is used as part of an outward-looking model; when it is turned inwards and used

15 Rorty, 1979.
16 Rorty, 1979, p. 320.

17 Kenny, 1973, p. 164-5.
18 Kenny, *id.*, p. 165.
19 Samek, 1974.

reflexively it loses its thrust and becomes paradoxical'.[20]

The reconstructive route map for finding a meta-theory, and the deconstructivist warnings against even setting out on the journey each have their special drawbacks. The reconstructivists must avoid reformulating their resort to master-disciplines in the discourses of either law or science. If they seek answers in the discourses of morality or practical reason, for example, asking these approaches to provide solutions on a case-by-case basis, this soon produces something very like the procedures and principles of law; therefore it cannot provide any purchase for disposing of scientific challenges. Should we, on the other hand, decide that the answer to a clash is ultimately political, for example, we will be hard put to explain what we mean without embarking on a scientific enquiry into the meanings of defining the political. Are we talking of the political sphere or of political science? Is politics to be distinguished from law and science in terms of its institutions, its functions or its characteristic discourse? Is the key point that choices between law and science are inherently matters of policy rather than principle? Or is it the need to involve ordinary people, either through representative institutions or in participatory institutions such as the jury? Even this does not exhaust the possible meaning of describing these choices as political. For some writers, for example, references to the political could be merely a coded way to say that such problems lie beyond the reach of theoretical argument and that the answers are necessarily a result of subjective evaluation or brute struggle for power.

In the unlikely event that master-discourses could provide their own unequivocal self-descriptions which could be brought to bear on clashes between law and science, a number of further questions arise. At what point is it appropriate to resort to other discourses and which discourse should be used to decide this? For example, a large part of legal discourse (and not merely that entitled constitutional law), is concerned with the question of the relationship between law and politics. Following this path would subordinate master-discourses to the decision rules of law. But there is no reason to assume that political discourse would define its own relevance to law in the same way as law itself would delimit that role. Science and law may agree or disagree about the right point at which to turn to master discourses, or may have them imposed by another's fiat. In turn master discourses may speak without being asked or heard.

These unresolved problems in the reconstructive approach affect even the most subtle efforts to draw on broader discourses to clarify 'the truth about law's truth'. In their classic study *Causation in the Law,* Hart and Honoré, for example, examined the relationship between legal and scientific conceptions of 'causation'.[21] They argued that law's understanding of the term was, and should be, derived from ordinary, commonsense language. Illustrating their approach by a study of judicial case-law on the meaning of causation in the areas of tort and criminal law, they insisted that causation was *not* delimited by references to scientific criteria or policy-based appropriate allocations of responsibility. Instead law's approach to causation, for instance its distinction between cause and 'mere condition' as depending on the intervention of a responsible human agent, was intended to reproduce the sense of the term in ordinary speech. Thus the yardstick by which law's solutions fell to be assessed in cases of scientific challenge was its fidelity to the morally laden commonsense use of language in the attribution of responsibility. Although the authors included an analysis of the

---

[20] Samek, *ibid.,* p.324.

[21] Hart and Honoré, 1958/1985.

approach to causation in continental jurisprudence, which they felt was not inconsistent with their argument, it is clear that their remarks are most plausible in Anglo-American law which places greater store on alleged links to common-sense. But there are important criticisms to be made even in the latter context. Many would argue, for instance, that their theory is descriptively inaccurate. Judges do not conduct a careful analysis of the way words are actually used, and, more importantly, the authors' own claims regarding normal usage can often be faulted.[22] Common-sense in the courts and in ordinary language philosophy is easily taken to correspond to more local usage in Oxford. In addition, whatever law and common-sense have in common may owe as much to the influence of legal ideas of responsibility over common-sense as vice-versa.[23]

The critical issue for our purposes, however, concerns the reasons why Hart and Honoré think law must and should follow common-sense. Although this meta-level question was somewhat neglected in their original work, their response to criticism of their first edition in the preface to their second edition attempted to deal with this point. It offered a political argument asserting the advantages to be gained if law reinforced everyday beliefs about personal responsibility, regardless of their current scientific status, because this would help encourage responsible behaviour. But this claim itself needs to be tested scientifically. Nor does it exclude the possibility that for other purposes closer adherence to scientific conceptions would be more appropriate. As Martin puts it:

'There would be no reason, a priori, that a legal expert ought not to use scientific notions of cause in certain contexts. It would depend on whether certain policy considerations were furthered by the use of such notions'.[24]

Without necessarily endorsing the claim that, pace Hart and Honoré, policy must always provide the ultimate level or meta-theory by which law must be guided, it certainly sows doubts about the success of their attempt to present law as a form of common-sense beyond the reach of scientific or policy considerations.

Robert Alexy's more recent study, which tries to place law within the bounds of a larger discourse, offers a systematic case for law as a specialized part of 'practical reason'.[25] Drawing on the ideas of Perelman, Habermas and the Erlangen school, Alexy claims that law can be rational to the extent that it adopts the rules and canons of his ideal version of practical argumentation. Describing his work as a 'meta-discourse' on the criteria for rationality in legal argument, he carefully spells out the implications of his belief that factual assertions and value-judgements must each be tested against the criterion of the relevant 'best informed opinion'. This approach, however, does not really take us very far toward a resolution of the problem of potential clashes between law and science. Alexy has some sympathy with J.L. Austin's definition of truth as 'the right and proper thing to say in these circumstances, to this audience, for these purposes, with these intentions'.[26] He concedes that law includes a variety of types of statement and that 'at any time (law) can make a transition into theoretical (empirical) discourse'.[27] Whilst accepting that normative statements cannot be tested by the methods of the empirical sciences he leaves 'for further investigations whether normative arguments are true in exactly the same way as empirical ones'.[28] Alexy does not deny the importance of our problem given that 'the relevance of introducing empirical knowledge of legal

---

[22] Martin, 1987.
[23] Lloyd-Bostock, 1978:1979.
[24] Martin, 1987, p. 113.

[25] Alexy, 1989.
[26] Alexy, id., p. 56-57.
[27] Alexy, id., p. 233.
[28] Id., p. 178.

reasoning can hardly ben overstated'.[29] But the task of specifying the rules for assessing such relevance in cases of uncertainty was too great:

'A thoroughgoing theory of empirical reasoning relevant to legal justification would have to deal with almost all the problems of empirical knowledge. Added to this are the problems of incorporating empirical knowledge into legal reasoning'. In the meantime 'this problem is only to be resolved by way of interdisciplinary cooperation'.[30] As we have seen, however, the question of the terms on which such co-operation should proceed is exactly the issue which needs to be solved.

If the reconstructivist is content to travel hopefully rather than arrive, the deconstructivist, for his part, finds it hard to insist that he is not going anywhere. Rorty insists that there can be no 'philosophical Archimedean point', but even he writes of the possibility that the conversation amongst discourses may lead them to somehow transcend their limitations. Attempts to be consistently ironic also have difficulty in keeping this up. As Frankenburg puts it in his summary of a recent piece in this vein by David Kennedy:

'However much Kennedy wishes to get away from truth-claims, he is still constantly and implicitly asserting the truthfulness of his narrative and the authenticity of the narrator'.[31] Even with a reverse momentum, 'the postmodern sceptic, guarded by irony and advancing with all nondeliberate speed, seems unable to outrun modernity'.[32]

Conclusion

Although reconstructive and deconstructive approaches will each continue to find adhe-

rents, their difficulties provide incentives for those struggling to develop a third approach. This third strategy, which I have termed 'dialogic', takes some points from each of the previous strategies, despite their apparent irreconcilability, and therefore ends up reproducing neither. Like the reconstructive approach it continues the search for a solution but, like the deconstructive approach, it rejects the possibility of finding any master-discourse capable of adjudicating between law and science. Any progress that is to be made has to come from within law and science themselves. The dialogic strategy therefore seeks to juxtapose different perspectives as a spur to the self-transformation of each discipline, and its momentum is maintained by the dialectic of mutual interrogation. In ways which somewhat resemble calls to religious inter-faith dialogue, it calls for reciprocal understanding among different perspectives on the presupposition that none can or should relinquish its special viewpoint. As this outline makes clear, however, the problem which confronts this approach, and which it still has not successfully resolved, is built into its starting premise. If perspectives must remain true to themselves how far can they also hope to understand the other? Assuming that law and science are epistemological equals (which not everybody grants, even in these post-positivist times) we are obliged to model their relationship as one between two 'internal' points of view, neither of which has priority. But what then is to be the source of our models? As things stand presently, when science tries to grasp the point of a legal rule or practice it all too frequently turns law into a pale (and ineffectual) version of itself. Conversely, when law attempts to incorporate the methods or finding of science it usually ends up changing them out of all recognition in the service of its practical purposes. Some authors have therefore drawn the conclusion that any direct confrontation of the worldview and practices of law and science is best avoided. One can resolve cases of acute conflict by proceduralising a

[29] *Id.*, p. 233.
[30] Alexy, *id.*, p. 233.
[31] Frankenburg, 1989, p. 396.
[32] Frankenburg, *id.*, p. 397.

division of roles between law and science.[33]
But this strategy comes rather close to
resembling law's characteristic response to
substantive conflicts: at all costs find a
procedural solution.[34] On the other hand
recommendations for interdisciplinary dialogue[35] cannot, by their very nature, take us
beyond the intellectual search for understanding and offer little help when we are faced
with concrete choices.

To escape from this impasse it is certainly
possible to challenge the terms in which the
problem has been posed. Perhaps a meta-
theory is unnecessary. 'Law' and 'Science',
it could be said, must not be rectified. They
should rather be seen as complex discourses
and communications with fluid and overlapping boundaries. Better understanding of
conflicts between law and science would then
depend on the application of a *micro-theory*
(such as semiotics?), attentive to the different
ways communications attribute to themselves
the force and legitimacy of 'Law' and
'Science'. Nevertheless, this approach could
not, or should not, lead us to dissolve the
contrast between law and science entirely. It
is also still unclear how this strategy could
help us sort out the most stubborn examples
of disputes of which the core is whether or
not there really is a conflict. And the question of what *to do* about the problem would
in any event remain open. There is, finally,
the possible argument that there is nothing to
resolve here, or at least nothing to worry
about, because practical choices are in any
case not based on such theoretical
underpinnings.[36] But my sense is that we
would be happy to follow this 'solution' only
after we had first been convinced that disputes between law and science were intrinsically irresolvable. And to demonstrate *that*
would be about as difficult as finding a way
to resolve them.

[33] Teubner, 1989.
[34] Nelken, 1991.
[35] Ost and van de Kerchove, 1987.
[36] Fish, 1989.

References

Alexy, F., *A theory of legal argumentation:
The theory of rational discourse as theory
of legal justification* (Trans. R. Adler and
D.N. McCormick), Oxford, Clarendon
Press, 1989.
Atiyah, P., *The rise and fall of freedom of
contract*, Oxford, OUP 1979.
Barnes, B.
Edge, D., (eds.), *Science in context*, Milton
Keynes, OUP. 1982.
Brownsword, R.
Beyleveld, D., *Law as Moral judgement*,
London, Sweet and Maxwell 1986.
Derrida, J., (trans. G. Spivack), *Of Gram-
matology*, Baltimore, Johns Hopkins Press
1976.
Finnis, J., *Natural Law and Natural Rights*,
Oxford, OUP 1980.
Fish, S., *Doing what Comes Naturally*,
Oxford, Clarendon 1989.
Foucault M, M., *Discipline and Punish*,
London, Penguin/Allen Lane 1977.
Frankenburg, G., 'Down by law; irony,
seriousness and reason', 83 *Northwestern
University Law Review*, 360, 1989.
Garland, D., *Punishment and Welfare: A
History of Penal Strategies*, London,
Gower, 1985.
Gee, H., 'The expert witness in the criminal
trial', *Criminal Law Review*, 307, 1987.
Habermas, J., *Communication and the Evol-
ution of Society*, London, 1979 Heine-
mann.
Hart, H.L.A.
Honoré, A., *Causation in the Law*, Oxford,
OUP, 1985/1986.
Hunter, I., 'Meta-psychology', in A. Bullock
and O. Stallybrass, *The Fontana Diction-
ary of Modern Thought*, London,
Fontana/Collins, 1977.
Hutchinson, A., *Dwelling on the Threshold:
Critical essays in modern thought*,
Toronto, Carswell/Sweet and Maxwell,
1988.
Kennedy, D., 'Spring Break', 63, *Texas Law
Review*, 1355, 1985.
Kenny, D., *Wittgenstein*, London, Penguin
1973.

Kramer, M., *Against Rhadanantos*, OUP 1991.

Lloyd-Bostock, S., 'Common-sense reality and accident compensation', in D. Farrington et al., *Psychology, Law and Legal Processes*, 93, 1978.

Lloyd-Bostock, S., The ordinary man, and the psychology of attributing causes and responsibility', 42, *Modern law Review*, 143, 1979.

Lyotard, J., *The post-modern condition. A report on knowledge*, Minnesota, University of Minnesota Press, 1984.

Martin, R., *The legal philosophy of H.L.A. Hart: A critical appraisal*, Philadelphia, Temple University Press, 1987.

McCormick, D.N., *Legal Reasoning and Legal Theory*, Oxford, OUP 1978.

Nelken, D., *'The Truth about Law's Truth'*, European University Institute Working Paper 1990/1, Florence, Italy.

Nelken, D., 'The Loneliness of Law's Meta-Theory', In: *Plural Legalities: Critical Legal Studies in Europe* (eds. R. de Lange and K. Raes), Ars Aequi 1991.

Ost, F., Van De Kerchove M., Jalons pour une théorie critique du droit. Bruxelles, St. Louis Faculty publications, 1987.

Quinton, A., 'Meta-theory', In: A. Bullock and O. Stallybrass (eds.), *The Fontana Dictionary of Modern Thought*, London, Fontana/ Collins, 1977.

Rorty, R., *Philosophy and the mirror of nature*, Princeton, Princeton University Press, 1979.

Samek, R., *The Legal Point of View*, New York, Philosophical Library 1974.

Smith, R., *Trial by Medicine*, Edinburgh, Edinburgh University Press 1981.

Stanford Law Review, Special issue on 'Critical Legal Studies' 1984.

Teubner, G., 'How the Law Thinks; Toward a Constructivist Epistemology of Law', In: *Law and Society Review*, 23/5, p. 727. 1989.

Villa, V., 'Meta-théorie', in A.J. Arnaud (ed.), *Dictionnaire Encyclopedique de théorie et de sociologie du droit*, Paris/Bruxelles, Librairie Générale/Story-Scientia Editions 245-248, 1988

Waldron, J., *Nonsense on Stilts: Bentham, Bruke and Marx on the Rights of Man*, London, Methuen, 1987.

[10]
Can Law Learn
from Social Science?*

Introduction

In this paper I shall be discussing a fundamental problem in the relationship between law and the social sciences. Many social scientists have pointed out that the "pull of the policy audience" in legislative and administrative exercises and the confines of practical decision-making in legal settings can compromise the proper development of academic social science and blunt the edge of political critique.[1] The danger is real enough. But they have given insufficient attention to the opposite concern which will be my topic in this article. Here the charge is that the introduction of social scientific styles of reasoning can have ill effects for legal practice by threatening the integrity of legal processes and the values they embody.[2] How can social scientists be sure that they have properly understood the nature of law or the meaning and point of the legal rules, procedures, and institutions which they attempt to analyze and seek to improve? What warrant can they have that social scientific interpretation, at any level, does not end up creating law in its own image? If this is a genuine risk, what implications follow for the way law should learn from social science? I shall argue that there are no easy answers to these questions even, or especially, where law apparently welcomes contributions from social science.

* This is a revised version of a paper with the same title delivered on 19 March 2001 at the annual Drapkin Conference, Faculty of Law, The Hebrew University of Jerusalem.

1 See e.g., D. Nelken "The 'Gap Problem' in the Sociology of Law: A Theoretical Review" (1981) Windsor Yearbook of Access to Justice 35-62.
2 I have already explored this problem in a number of places. See e.g., D. Nelken, "The Truth about Law's Truth" Law Working Paper (EUI Florence 1990/1); D. Nelken, "The Truth about Law's Truth" in A. Febbrajo and D. Nelken, eds., The *European Yearbook for the Sociology of Law* (Milan, 1993) 87-163; also extracted in D. Nelken, "The Loneliness of Law's Meta-Theory" in R. de Lange and K. Raes, eds., *Plural Legalities: Critical Legal Studies in Europe* (The Hague, 1991) 172; and D. Nelken, "Are Disputes Between Law and Science Resolvable?" in J.F. Nijbour, C.R. Callen and N. Kwak, eds., *Forensic Expertise and the Law of Evidence* (Amsterdam, 1993). See also M. Constable, *The Law of the Other* (Chicago, 1994).

I should say at the outset that as a sociologist of law, I am here playing devil's advocate. It is precisely because I believe that social science does have so much to offer to the understanding of law and society that I see the need to clarify the resistance law has to learning from it. Social scientists have produced a large literature which shows that legal decision-making often rests on questionable assumptions or makes unconvincing claims about cause and effect in social life. Legislators, judges, lawyers, and others often cause harm by acting, in good or bad faith, on the basis of insufficient understanding of the social conditions and the effective possibilities of attaining the results they claim to be seeking through law. Social scientists can, do, and should provide theoretical insights and empirical findings capable of bringing all this to light. More generally, legal education typically gives disproportionate attention to analyzing the finer points of "mandarin" doctrine in the higher courts whilst neglecting the work of lower level courts and administrative decision-making and the processes of popular use and avoidance of law which loom so largely in everyday life. Here too, social scientific research can provide a valuable corrective. My words of caution about the prospects for introducing social science into law are not intended to comfort those judges or legal academics who (still) claim that legal science can be or should be a self sufficient discipline. If law is unable to learn from social science, we might, if we value social scientific methods of fact finding, choose instead to circumscribe the areas of social life in which legal modes of decision-making are applied rather than reduce social science contributions to law.

Social scientists have devoted considerable energy to showing what it is that legal actors do not, or cannot, see about the social context in which they operate. Again, nothing I have to say is intended to undermine such work on its own terms. But they study law, as they do any other phenomenon, in terms of their disciplinary projects. This means that they necessarily use concepts which emerge from and contribute to the further development of their own disciplines.[3] The issues I am

---

3   Social science insights are made possible precisely by transforming legal concepts and categories into those of the relevant social science discipline. Thus, whatever role law may have played initially in generating social science categories, sociological textbooks now reconceptualize legal phenomena in terms of issues such as social order, social control, regulation, dispute processing, governmentality, power, symbolism, and ideology, rather than respecting the doctrinal definitions of lawyers or even the relevant administrative categories.

concerned with here arise when social scientists, or others, seek to introduce social scientific ideas and findings about facts and law back into the legal system without giving sufficient consideration to the way this differs from the laboratory or the academy. This is more than a question of applied versus theoretical science. There are good practical reasons why both social scientists and lawyers should examine the "irrelations"[4] and potential incommensurabilities between their disciplines and practices if they are to make sense of and improve their everyday collaboration. But what I want to show here is that understanding and explaining the difficulties of such collaboration is itself a theoretical problem which belongs to and extends the terrain of social scientific theorizing *about* law.[5] In this article, I shall first seek to show that every way of thinking about the potential contribution of social science to law rests on a controversial philosophical and political position about the nature and role of law (and that it can hardly be otherwise.) I shall then describe three ways of understanding disagreements between law and social science and suggest how these approaches offer clues to explaining why law may have only a limited concern for (social scientific) truth.

From Legal Realism to Postmodernism

For the authors of the leading textbook dealing with what they call "social science *in* law,"[6] there is no real difficulty about ensuring that law can learn from social science. Unlike those engaged in what they characterize as "the social sciences *of* law," where the goal is the development of science for its own sake, it is enough to be clear that here, by contrast, the role of the social scientist *in* law is to offer law the benefits of existing expertise, in particular by supplying facts for courts and

---

It may happen of course that law tries to internalize concepts from the social sciences. But, on the one hand, there is a difference between learning from social science and being colonized. And, on the other, as the paper will attempt to illustrate, the crucial question is what law does with these borrowed concepts.

4   D. Nelken "Criminal Law and Criminal Justice: Some Notes on their Irrelation" in Ian Dennis, ed., *Criminal Law and Justice* (London, 1987) 139-177.

5   D. Nelken, "Blinding Insights: The Limits of a Reflexive Sociology of Law" (1998) 25(3) Journal of Law and Society 407-426.

6   J. Monahan and L. Walker, *Social Science in Law* (New York, 1985).

policy makers to consider in reaching their decisions.[7] To achieve a mutually beneficial division of labor, however, John Monahan and Laurens Walker do insist that we need to distinguish "factual" from "normative" questions. In practice, they suggest, many questions are mixed and, so, do need to be carefully picked apart. As they put it, "some questions law poses are clear and answerable, for example when the law needs to determine whether the percentage of women hired by a firm is less than their percentage in the overall labor pool." Other questions "require a great deal of rephrasing," for example, "is pornography harmful?" Still others, they suggest, are resistant to clarification through empirical research, for example, "is retribution just?"

If this division of labor is to work it is essential for lawyers and judges to know enough about social science to be able to tell the difference between sound and unsound science. Otherwise, they will be unable to tell when it is right to defer to the experts. Monahan and Walker, therefore, first of all, set out to supply guidance on how to read and understand social science arguments. Having done so, they go on to offer illustrations of the wide range of situations in which law can and does draw on social science in the course of getting its facts straight. Thus we are told about the role of social sciences in determining "the occurrence of legal acts," as in the case of alleged sex discrimination at work. We are explained its part in establishing the "identity of (future, present, and past) legal actors," for example, in decisions about who requires pre-trial detention. And we are shown its contribution to proving the "state of mind" of legal actors, as in criminal defenses based on stress syndromes. In other chapters, they discuss how social science evidence can be used to improve institutional design where the issues at stake include the ideal form of disputing procedures and the appropriate size for jury deliberation.

The examples offered by Monahan and Walker focus mainly on the use of social science expertise at court and do not begin to cover the full

---

7   *Ibid.* Monahan and Walker state: "We here view social science as an analytic tool in the law, familiarity with which will heighten the lawyer's professional effectiveness and sharpen the legal scholar's insights. The principle alternative to the insider perspective on the relation of social science to law is the "law and society" or sociology of law approach which seeks to understand the functioning of law as a social system." (p. v). It might be more accurate to say that the choice faced by each social science approach (economics, political science, sociology, psychology etc.) is whether to develop its understanding of legal phenomena according to its own idiosyncratic concepts and methods or in ways that can be internalized by law.

range of existing or potential exchanges between law and social science. But, precisely for this reason, their work provides a valuable starting point for the wider questions I wish to raise in this article concerning the fate of social science truths as they move in legal orbits. In general terms, there is nothing surprising in saying that the relevance of social science depends on the extent to which it becomes subservient to the legal. But, in my judgment, there is still much to be done in working out the implications of this idea. Monahan and Walker themselves, for instance, draw a distinction between what they call "legislative facts," the general sociological assumptions upon which law rests, and "adjudicative facts," concerned only with establishing what happened in a particular case. The contrast is important because it points to differences in the responsibilities of legislators and judges and consequently in their openness to scientific evidence. But the authors tell us less about why findings from social science literature about matters of "institutional design" tend to have different implications the closer we get to actual judicial decision-making. A well-know review by a social psychologist, for example, shows the US Supreme Court continuing to refuse to acknowledge scientifically uncontroversial findings about the link between ethnic representation on the jury and jury bias.[8] Is this mere obscurantism or does it point to law's choice to exclude certain sorts of knowledge? Within the trial process itself, even Monahan and Walker note that there are different procedural rules for prosecution and defense as far as their being allowed to lead evidence on certain excuses such as rape trauma syndrome (even if truth is by definition indivisible).

If we are to make progress in exploring these questions we will need to focus on the philosophical and political ideas about the nature and role of law which explain how these authors (and those who think like them) go about understanding and drawing the boundaries of social scientific expertise in law. Monahan and Walker, like most empirical social scientists of law, trace their inspiration to the American Legal Realists. Like them, they treat legal decision-making as a branch of social policy which requires similar methods and precision in investigating social facts and engineering outcomes. For Judge Holmes, writing not long after the beginning of the 20th Century, the lawman of the

---

8   J.A. Tanford, "The Limits of a Scientific Jurisprudence: The Supreme Court and Psychology" (1990) 66 Ind. L. J. 137.

future would need to be not merely an expert in the "black letter law"
but also in statistics and economics. Reviewing the recent period, Professor, later Judge, Richard Posner, claimed that the rise of science in
law, including the economic approach to law of which he was a pioneer,
was an "inevitable consequence of the rise of prestige and authority of
scientific and other exact models of enquiry."[9]

The Legal Realists sought to find better ways of overcoming social
problems and solving disputes. They thought of the social sciences as
crucial instruments in understanding and controlling situations along
functional lines. Even sophisticated legal scholars, such as Karl Llewellyn,
taught that law should be seen as a means to social ends, not as an end
in itself, and that it needed to be consistently examined in the light of
its purposes and effects and of their relation to each other. Once the law
is conceived in this way, and inasmuch as it is conceived in this way,
the relevance of social science for law is indisputable. In fact some
Realists thought in terms of trusting a new type of public servant rather
than the courts, though lawyers proved remarkably resilient in heading
off this challenge.[10] But increasingly courts were willing to call on social
science in support of controversial decisions, as in the famous US
Supreme Court decision in *Brown* v. *Bd. of Education*[11] concerning
racial segregation and schooling. Social scientific expertise continues to
be important as evidence before the courts, especially in criminal,
family, and commercial cases. And this will continue to be true as long
as Anglo-American (and other) legal cultures[12] justify themselves in
terms of an ideology of "pragmatic instrumentalism" according to which
law must also give consideration to the effectiveness of its interventions.

By contrast, many of the more recent developments in Anglo-American legal philosophy, including those informed by social theory, offer a

---

9   R. Posner, "The Decline of Law as an Autonomous Discipline 1962-1987" (1987) 100
    Harvard Law Review 761, at 772.
10 C. Tomlins, "Framing the Field of Law's Disciplinary Encounters: A Historical
    Narrative" (2000) 34 Law and Society Review 911-972; see also N. Duxbury, *Patterns
    of American Jurisprudence* (Oxford, 1995).
11 347 US 483, 74 S.CT 686, 98 L.Ed. 873 (1954).
12 On the concept of "legal culture" see for example D. Nelken ed., "Legal Culture,
    Diversity and Globalisation" (1995) 4 Social and Legal Studies, at 435-453; D. Nelken
    ed., *Comparing Legal Cultures* (Aldershot, 1997); D. Nelken, ed., *Contrasts in Crimi-
    nal Justice* (Aldershot, 2000); and D. Nelken and J. Feest, eds., *Adapting Legal
    Cultures* (Oxford, 2001). Anglo-American legal culture, too easily taken as self
    evident, is becoming increasingly influential largely as a result of the globalization
    of markets.

much more complex picture of law. Analogies are more likely to be drawn between law and theology or law and literary theory[13] than between law and the social and policy sciences. Increasingly, stress is placed on the importance of cultural meaning, stories, and narrative, "justice as translation," on the role of "law as communication."[14] Scholars argue that law must be seen as a form of authoritative reasoning aiming to provide a rhetorical coherence to public life.[15] They claim that matters of procedure and proof must also be treated as having a ritual character.[16] Hence the application of social science understanding risks imposing a limited and limiting set of meanings.[17] Insofar as law seeks to unfold a community's "nomos"[18] it may also need to act as a bulwark against the spread of "technical rationality" represented by enlarging the role of expertise.[19] In that case the social sciences may easily come to be treated as part of the problem rather than of the solution.[20] Likewise, critical legal theory, feminism, and critical race theory,[21] all join the ideological battle with mainstream liberal views of law but do so without in any way endorsing mainstream social science. Some post-

13   The law and literature movement goes further than standard legal theory by claiming not only that law must *use* language to fulfill its tasks but that in addition law must be treated *as* a language which constructs its own world of meaning.

14   See D. Nelken, "Law as Communication: Constituting the Field" in D. Nelken, ed., *Law as Communication* (Aldershot, 1996).

15   James Boyd White expresses considerable impatience with the social sciences approach to law, which is seen as expressive of a bureaucratic mentality which prevents us from appreciating "law as a system of discourse that the lawyer and judge must learn and use." Similarly, Richard Weisberg, the other acknowledged pioneer of the "law and literature" movement, claims that the subject he calls "poethics" is intended to occupy the void left by the failures of the economic approach to law and postmodern skepticism.

16   See the well-known article, L. Tribe, "Trial by Mathematics: Precision and Ritual in the Legal Process" (1971) 84 Harvard Law Review 1329, and the less celebrated but equally interesting article by P. Winn, "Legal Ritual" (1991) 2 Law and Critique 207.

17   D. Nelken "Can There be a Sociology of Legal Meaning?" in D. Nelken, ed., *Law as Communication* (Aldershot, 1996) 107-129.

18   See M. Minow, M. Ryan, and A. Sarat, eds., *Narrative, Violence and the Law: Essays of Robert Cover* (Ann Arbor, 1995).

19   S. Goldberg, *Culture Clash: Law and Science in America* (New York, 1994).

20   B. de Sousa Santos, *Toward a New Common Sense: Law, Science and Politics in the Paradigmatic Transition* (London, 1995).

21   See R.L. Hayman Jr. and N. Levit, *Jurisprudence: Contemporary Readings, Problems and Narratives* (St. Paul, Minnesota, 1994).

modernist writers even question the "grand narrative" of scientific reason and progress. At the micro level, sociologists of science suggest that scientific facts also require and depend on interpretation and that, much like lawyers, scientists succeed in getting their truth accepted only by adopting (changing) protocols of persuasion.

We do not have to take all these (sometimes competing) critiques on board; we could insist that there is bound to be some overlap between law and social policy and refuse to abandon the modernist paradigms for law and science. However, we still must recognize that Monahan and Walker's approach avoids a crucial (meta-theoretical) question. If law is not only a form of social policy but in addition, has different features and divergent aims, we are obliged to ask the questions: where should we draw the line between law and social science — and who should decide this? What cultural values are at stake? What about differences between the approaches adopted by different social sciences or within given social sciences? Some reflexivity about these matters has emerged in the field of law and economics,[22] which is the social science which has made the most advanced inroads into law. But the questions have been less aired in other social science disciplines.

The Politics of Expertise

All this goes to show that the role of (social) science in law is also inextricably linked to what we could call "the politics of expertise." The Legal Realists gained recognition during the New Deal period. They saw the US Supreme Court judges as using a formalist approach to law as a disguised form of conservative politics aimed at blocking necessary social interventions at the time of the Great Depression. Arguing that judicial decisions always have repercussions for the distribution of power and wealth, the Realists claimed that their recommendation to reform and apply law in terms of "fact situations" would make this process more transparent and more geared to their progressive goals.

---

22   For example, B. Ackerman in "Law, Economics and the Problem of Legal Culture" (1986) 35 Duke L.J. 929, at 931, asks whether the new system of concepts adopted by lawyer-economists will "undermine the American lawyer's capacity to express the American people's traditional principles of truth and justice. Or does it instead, enable lawyers better to express their fellow citizens' evolving understanding of the principles."

But we now know that there is nothing inherently "socially progressive" about demanding that law take more account of "scientific facts." The "law and economics" movement was in large part pioneered and sustained by those who advocated trusting more in the market place than in state intervention. Likewise, recent struggles over expert scientific evidence in mass toxic tort litigation in the USA are explicitly linked to neo- liberal politics.[23] In the realm of criminal law, on the other hand, the introduction of new excuses based on evidence of psychological syndromes has been criticized as, yet again, menacing the value of personal responsibility.[24]

The idea that legal proceedings can and should reach the same results which would be produced in other fora is often taken for granted in these debates about the proper role of expertise. Thus, when Peter Huber or others criticize judicial decisions they do so relying on what the FDA or other administrative agencies have established as scientific truth regarding the matter being litigated. As Huber puts it, "the rule of law is not half so grand as the rule of fact" and "there can be no appeal from the (higher) laws of nature," it follows that good science must be the only way of doing justice.[25] The solution to the problem of junk science is, therefore, for judges to find some better way of curbing the use of dubious experts, for example, by limiting those scientists who can be called upon to give testimony to those who have already published relevant work in reputable scientific journals. More generally, increasing the scientific knowledge of decision makers in their recourse to expertise is seen as the obvious and only answer to those instances where law seems hospitable to scientific error.

All this begs a number of important questions. How much will it help to exclude "junk science" when courts proceedings often seem to distort or transform the evidence of even reputable experts? Where the law arrives at different conclusions from that which (social) scientists would have reached, could this not be an unavoidable and even desirable result of having correctly working legal institutions? Huber insists proudly that "good science is unburdened by concerns about what is fair, just, reasonable or socially acceptable." But is that not precisely why law

---

23   R. Huber, *Gallileo's Revenge: Junk Science in the Courtroom* (New York, 1991).

24   A.M. Dershowitz, *The Abuse Excuse* (Boston, 1994); G. R. Fletcher, *With Justice for Some* (Reading, Massachusetts, 1995); D. A. Downs, *More than Victims: Battered Women, the Syndrome Society and the Law* (Chicago, 1996).

25   *Supra* n. 23, at 225.

brings other criteria to bear (for example, when the judge protects the jury from expert evidence which would be too definitive of the case.) Why not leave everything to experts or at least model law on their methods of inquiry? Is the question of how much law should correspond to science one which should be left for scientists to answer?

A temporary solution to these debates is offered by the US Supreme Court's decision in *Daubert*,[26] which instructed judges to play a larger role as gatekeepers over the admission of expert evidence (instead of delegating such matters by using the criterion of general acceptability in the relevant scientific community).[27] But, even after the *Daubert* decision, it is hard to find an overall rationale to explain which expertise courts are willing to include or exclude. We can hardly say that a concern for scientific validity lies behind the willingness to rely on handwriting experts. Why is DNA evidence accepted but Bayes Theorem resisted? Is the ready acceptance of "abuse excuses" in American courts testimony to the strength of the social sciences or more linked to the special requirements of legal defenses in United States criminal law? This certainly seems to be the key to the long acceptance of the defense based on the theory of learned helplessness in cases of killings carried out by battered women (rather than the more convincing theory based on "survival").[28] And considerations of legal politics also seem best to account for the willingness of United States courts to rely on psychiatrists ' evidence of dangerousness in order to confirm the necessity for death penalty sentences.

Attempts to mediate between the worlds of law and science often underestimate the problems involved. There is a currently popular proposal amongst some scholars in the USA to introduce a more respectful method of introducing science into law so as not to undermine but rather assist the jury in its role. This involves allowing expert witnesses to testify only as to the falsity of the "myths" on which juries may be relying as they assess the evidence. This would allow experts, for example, to counteract the belief that battered women on murder charges could, and therefore should, have left the family home rather than have retaliated with deadly force.[29] But this leaves us with the difficulty of deciding where and how the line between "facts" and "myths" should be

26   *Daubert* v. *Merrell Dow* 113 S. Ct 2786 (1993).
27   *Frye* v. *US* 293 F 1013 D.C CIR (1923).
28   Downs, *supra* n. 24.
29   *Ibid.*

drawn (in relation both to judges and juries). The task of science here could be unending and unlimited, given that its mandate is precisely to show that "lay" understanding and reasoning rests on corrigible misconception and error. And what if it is law's task to actually defend some "myths" which a community chooses to live by, not least the notion of individual responsibility?[30]

Three Approaches to Clashes between Law and Social Science[31]

As suggested by my criticism of Huber, it is reductivist simply to criticize legal proceedings for their failure to ensure that their findings correspond to scientific (including social scientific) truth. We must also ask why law and science come to diverge and whether or not any satisfactory reason can be offered to justify this. In this section, I shall describe three different approaches to this problem.

The first of these approaches, which I have called the "trial pathology approach," focuses on the alleged malfunctioning of the institutions and processes of adversarial systems. It is typical of the numerous, sometimes repetitive, discussions in law reviews, especially in the United States, of the rules of evidence regarding admissibility of expertise, the challenge of novel forms of evidence, the gate keeping role of judges, and the aftermath of the Supreme Court ruling in the *Daubert* case. At its simplest level, trial pathologies are attributed to foolish juries, lazy judges, or greedy lawyers tempted by contingency fees. But in more sophisticated versions they are seen as a result of more intractable structural features of adversarial systems. At issue here is less the status of scientific truth in general and more the particular difficulties of "science in law," including social science, conceived as one form of expert witnessing. Commentators note how experts are made to authorize conclusions they would not endorse outside the courtroom; the wrong people come to be seen as experts; judges and juries have difficulty in making sense of scientific information; and it is unreasonable to expect laymen to be able to resolve "the battle of the experts." Illustrations of suspicious expertise range from the dangers of "junk science" in the area

---

30   Note, "Feasibility and Admissibility of Mob Mentality Defenses" (1993) 108 Harvard Law Review 1111.
31   An earlier version of these approaches is set out in D. Nelken, "A Just Measure of Science" in M. Freeman and H. Reece, eds., *Science in Court* (Aldershot, 1998) at 11-36.

of mass toxic torts or the rise of new criminal defenses such as battered
wives syndrome to the complications of using so called "suppositional"
social science evidence, for example, evidence concerning psychological
traumas.[32] But most articles in legal journals take the role of expertise,
as such, for granted and many favor enlarging it, for example, by
extending the ambit of new criminal defenses.

The second "competing institutions approach" envisages law and
science as powerful and often rival institutions or "expert spaces." It is
argued that these coexist or collaborate under conditions of unstable
compromise.[33] Drawing both on the sociology of science and the sociology
of knowledge,[34] it offers both social conflict and social constructionist
accounts of the interaction between legal and scientific institutions. As
well illustrated by the sophisticated work of Jasanoff,[35] controversies
over law and technology are investigated by identifying the political and
economic interests at stake in these battles, as well as their wider public
policy ramifications. In particular we are urged to see clashes between
law and science as occasions for the negotiation of truth claims and
boundaries between different forms of authority.

This approach has a rather different take on the "problem" of legal
and scientific expertise. Rather than limit itself to the mechanisms and
aberrations of the trial process it ranges much more widely into exchanges with science in other legally-related administrative and regulatory decisions.[36] What happens in the trial is put into context in
relation to what happens before or around it. Various studies of the rise
and fall of different types of expert prestige show that science obtains
its crucial victories not so much in the courtroom as by producing
socially respected authoritative problem solvers.[37] Trials are of interest

32   D. Faigman, "To Have and Have Not: Assessing the Value of Social Science to Law
      as Science and Policy" (1989) 38 Emory Law Journal 1005.
33   For example, T. Ward, "Law, Common Sense and the Authority of Science: Expert
      Witnesses and Criminal Insanity in England, ca. 1840-1940" (1997) 6 Social and
      Legal Studies 343, suggests that the "last issue" rule of evidence law could be seen
      as law's last ditch effort to contain the inroads of triumphalist 19th century science.
34   S. Shapin, "Here and Everywhere: The Sociology of Scientific Knowledge" (1995)
      Annual Review of Sociology 289.
35   See e.g., S. Jasanoff, *Science at the Bar: Law, Science and Technology in America*
      (Cambridge, Massachusetts, 1995).
36   See e.g., W.E. Wagner, "The Science Charade in Toxic Risk Regulation" (1995) 95
      Columbia Law Review 1613.
37   See e.g., J. Donzelot, *The Policing of Families* (London, 1979); R. Smith, *Trial by
      Medicine* (Edinburgh, 1981); Ward, *supra* n. 33.

mainly because they show how each of these institutions can turn their methods on each other in the course of constructing or deconstructing each other's credibility. Unlike the first and third approaches, which each, in very different ways, tends to take the distinctiveness of law and science as their starting point, this second approach relies on the many similarities, even more than on the differences, in the way law and science produce their determinations.[38] It draws attention, in Jasanoff's words, to the way the institutions of law and science are "articulated to look as if separate."

The third way of formulating the relationship between law and science can be termed the "incompatible discourses approach." It is particularly associated with the autopoietic theories of Luhmann and Teubner,[39] though it can be formulated in a variety of other ways and draw on different strands of contemporary social and legal theory. The aim of the Luhmann/Teubner theory is to observe law and science as discourses, each of which reproduce themselves according to their own specific discursive or communicative codes. Seeking to integrate neo-functionalist, systems theory and cyberneutic concepts, those who follow this approach move from an analysis of the characteristics of law, social systems, and knowledge production in (post)modernity to an examination of legal reflexivity and the way this does or should be used to mediate the "collision of discourses" and limit the damage of consequent "fall-out."[40]

The third approach is even less interested than the second in examining the details of the adversarial system as the source of the communication difficulties which afflict the relationship of law and science. Indeed, it is often developed by theorists more familiar with Continental legal systems which rely more on inquisitorial methods and court ap-

---

38   R. Smith and B. Wynne, *Expert Evidence: Interpreting Science in the Law* (London, 1989); S. Fuchs and S. Ward, "What is Deconstruction and Where and When Does It Take Place? Making Facts in Science, Building Cases in Law" (1994) 59 American Sociological Review 481-500.

39   See, for example, N. Luhmann, "The Unity of the Legal System" in G. Teubner, ed., *Autopoietic Law: A New Approach to Law and Society* (Berlin, 1988) at 12-36 and *ibid.* "Closure and Openness: On Reality in the World of Law", at 335-348. See, for example, G. Teubner, "How the Law Thinks: Toward a Constructivist Epistemology of Law" (1989) 23 Law and Society Review 727-757; G. Teubner, *Law as an Autopoietic System* (Oxford, 1993); and G. Teubner "Altera Pars Audiatur: Law in the Collision of Discourses" in R. Rawlings, ed., *Law, Society and Economy* (Oxford, 1997).

40   Teubner, *supra* n. 39.

pointed experts. The problem, according to this approach, as Teubner puts it, is rather that law finds itself caught in an "epistemic trap."[41] On the one hand, its concepts and practices need the stamp of scientific credibility in a world where science has the legitimated monopoly of truth claims. On the other hand, its efforts to align its ideas with those of science are destined to fail as it reproduces itself according to its own code so that it only succeeds in generating "hybrid artifacts," terms "with ambiguous epistemic status and unknown sociological conse-quences."[42] Accordingly, the significance of the trial is the way it shows how the law "has enslaved science in its contexts of law offices and courts,"[43] whereas outside the courts, by contrast, law is more likely to have to give way because scientific methods of fact finding have superior credibility.

In general, it is the radicality of its social epistemology which distin-guishes the third approach from the previous "competing institutions approach." The former works with "open systems" theorizing about the relationship between law and science, each of which are treated as semi-autonomous institutions subject to reciprocal influence. For the second approach, "ideas of truth and ideas of justice are co-constructed in the context of legal proceedings,"[44] as in the mediating role of experts, such as forensic psychiatrists, or in the way litigation stimulates develop-ments in science, and vice versa. Jasanoff's aim is indeed to encourage what she calls a more "reflective alliance" between these two institu-tions in pursuit of overall public policy objectives. The "incompatible discourses approach," on the other hand, calls for a shift from theorizing in terms of the actions of human agents and institutions to that capable of understanding the reproduction of discourses and codes.

The system theory adopted by Luhmann and Teubner rejects the idea of law as a semi-autonomous institution[45] and offers instead a perspec-tive in which law is both more and less subject to influence than in the "open systems" approach. According to these theorists, law, like other social sub-systems, is simultaneously both open and closed. And it is

---

41   Teubner, *supra* n. 39, at 742-746.
42   *Ibid.*, at 747; this process starts with the very notions of science or expertise used
     by law.
43   *Ibid.*, at 745.
44   S. Jasanoff, *supra* n. 35, at xiv.
45   D. Nelken, "Changing Paradigms in the Sociology of Law" in G. Teubner, ed., *supra*
     n. 39, at 191-217.

open just because it is closed, coding the world normatively in terms of the distinction between legal and illegal as it processes other communications.[46] For this approach it makes little sense to ask discourses to be more reflective unless this takes into account the way they already constitute themselves through their own reflexivity. Discourses do not and cannot help constitute each other; each discourse only uses the inputs received from its environment by applying its own code so as to reproduce its own elements. Law and science cannot really engage in fighting over boundaries or in processes of co-construction, and any projects to improve their collaboration, including Jasanoff's, which overlook their incommensurability,[47] must be doomed. Strategies of intervention begin rather by exploring the possibility for influencing existing processes of self-organization, in relation to what Teubner[48] calls the "interference" and "structural coupling" which results from the fact that specific discourses are also part of the overall cycle of societal communication.

The systems theories of Luhmann and Teubner have in common with otherwise quite different postmodern work, such as Jean-Francois Lyotard's writing about the "differend,"[49] that they all assume a differentiation of discourses linked to the conditions of postmodern social complexity. For autopoietic theory any cognition, be it scientific or legal, is a purely internal construction of the outside world,[50] the production of "legal order from social noise." Teubner, in particular, would also like to use law to improve communication among social sub-systems and discourses. But ultimately, law can only regulate other sub-systems by regulating itself. Thus, as with other postmodern writing, rather than improving its contribution to society's search for effective technical solutions to social problems, law's (new) task must be to do justice to the "heterogeneity of discourses" aiming at least to check their various imperialisms, so as to limit the damage of fall out from "the clash of discourses."[51]

---

46   Luhmann, *supra* n. 39; Teubner, *supra* n. 39, at 749, citing D. Nelken "Beyond the Study of Law and Society" (1986) American Bar Foundation Journal 323.

47   But see C. Sunstein, "Incommensurability and Valuation in Law" (1994) 92 Michigan Law Review 779.

48   Teubner, *supra* n. 39.

49   J.F. Lyotard, *The Differend: Phrases in Dispute* (Manchester, 1988).

50   Teubner, *supra* n. 39, at 737.

51   Teubner, *supra* n. 39.

As would be expected, rather different conceptions of law and science lie behind these formulations of the problem. The first approach tends to view science as a normally reliable institution which provides true or false answers. It is represented in trials by hired experts who may turn out to be unreliable or even dishonest in single instances. It is thus the task of the law to ferret out these cases if science including social science is to make its proper contribution to law. But, though it has its uses, expertise can also be both irrelevant (as with quite a lot of social science) or improperly influential (as with psychological judgments about normal behavior) in the legal process. Moreover, there are important borderline cases where the issue faced by law is the scientific status of the expertise as such. Law reaches out to science for certainty but also has to adjudicate on the boundaries of science.

The second approach sees science more as a collective communal enterprise and stresses the point that it is the tactics which are used for reaching agreement amongst practitioners which then produce its aura of reliability. These often implicit techniques of "closure" which undergird all good science, can, with uncertain results, be imposed or exposed by lawyers in forensic contests or political struggles. The range of potential divergence between legal and scientific solutions to individual cases of harm or injustice goes well beyond the issue of "junk science." Competition between legal and scientific truth claims can be an index of differing practical interests or visions of the good life and such controversy, and uncertainty itself, can often be fruitful. Different forms or fractions of expertise fight their own turf battles, sometimes even through the courts.

The third approach assumes that the codes of law and science have different relationships to the social function of distinguishing truth and falsehood and that little is to be gained by encouraging their direct confrontation. Law's increasing attempt to provide certainty by engaging experts to tell it how to reduce social risks is only likely to exacerbate uncertainty. The way forward lies in using legal oversight to proceduralize the question of which discourse is to be given responsibility for which aspects of social regulation.

These three approaches to clashes between law and science have a variety of implications for the question of whether law can learn from social science. Perhaps the most important of these is the way they help clarify the difference between arguing that introducing social science into law is possible but would be deleterious, because law would then become more like the policy sciences, and the alternative thesis that law is unable to become more like the policy sciences, and the attempt to make it so could only lead to more uncertainty. In addition, whatever their underlying theoretical differences, it is important to see that each of these models of the law and science relationship also has specific strengths and weaknesses in shedding light on the difficulties of integrating social science into law. I shall discuss in turn how they address different actors, emphasize different aspects of law, and offer different solutions.

Each approach starts from and returns to a different angle of perspective on the legal system. Addressed respectively to the judge, the legislator, and the observer of social systems, the first approach focuses mainly on law as adjudication, the second concentrates on law as public policy, while the third treats law as a form of communicative discourse. In keeping with these standpoints, the first approach tends towards adopting an "internal" legal point of view, so as to identify pathologies for which it offers prescriptions; the second seeks to examine controversial features of interaction between law and science from an external point of view; whereas the third approach tries to model the relationship between "the two internal points of view" of legal and scientific discourses.

The trial pathology approach compels us to examine and rationalize what is special about legal procedures of evidence and proof as compared to scientific methods of discovering or testing facts. For example, it can be appropriate to suppress highly relevant facts, such as evidence of previous convictions, where this might bias juries. Likewise, limits on translating or formalizing procedural requirements where lay people are involved may be needed. Legal presumptions, fictions, and arbitrary cut off points may all be essential in organizing practical and legitimate procedures for ending disputes. The same applies to law's specialized processes for hearing and testing evidence.

The competing institutions model reminds us that, unlike science, law is also concerned with goals other than truth finding. This can explain why and when law may aim at more than truth finding and sometimes settles for less. For example, if law is to work well as a method of governance it may often need to employ ideas about cause and effect which correspond to those used by the lay public rather than those which are scientifically up to date, especially as these latter can be subject to regular change. From a functionalist perspective, law's tasks include, minimally, dispute channeling, processing, and adjudication; maintaining social order; legitimating power, expressing and unfolding community and traditional identities and values; and principled regulation of social, political, and economic behavior. The way legal goals are defined will depend on the level of abstraction we adopt: functional accounts can be offered at the level of single institutions, procedures, or rules. Different branches of law, such as the law of torts or criminal law, will also be found to be pursuing different goals. The priority given to reaching or employing "scientific" truth will vary across legal fields at different stages of the legal process and so on.

As we have seen, those who object to treating law as merely a branch of social policy insist that law has a special concern for creating and maintaining its own brand of normative coherence. It is not just that law has its reasons, but it is in some part about the meaning of authoritative materials and their implications for practical issues that arise in social life. The incompatible discourses approach takes this insight further by analyzing the differences between legal and scientific forms of argument. Unlike scientific disciplines, which are typically addressed mainly to academic peers, legal decisions are directed at other judges, lawyers, the jury, and, at least indirectly, the general public.[52] Law refuses to deal with hypotheticals, rarely spells out defeasible empirical propositions, has different ways of arguing from authority and precedent, and has special techniques of analysis such as reasoning from analogy. Lawyers and judges are involved in processing already categorized data, events which have been generated by non-academic actors, judges, litigants etc. Legal practice cannot, therefore, aspire to develop the sort of cumulative knowledge characteristic of certain scientific disciplines. But nor does it aspire to. As compared to scientific reasoning, law is more prescriptive than explanatory, concerned in the main with evaluating social behavior in the light of rules, principles, and values.

The "solutions" offered by each of these approaches correspond, as we would expect, to their rather different diagnosis of "the problem." For the first model the question is how collaboration between fact finding in law and science should best be organized in the course of well adjusted legal proceedings. For the second the issue is how and when periods of open disagreement can serve healthy functions for the body politic. For the third the challenge has to do with the clashing of discourses. The first approach, therefore, helps us in thinking about what uses of science are compatible with the integrity of the trial process. The second prompts us to examine what considerations are relevant to assessing whether and

---

52   See E. Rubin, "Law and the Methodology of Law" (1997) Wisconsin Law Review 19.

when legal oversight can help to improve the standards of social science and vice versa. The third causes us to reflect on the overall role of law and legal regulation in relation to other self-referential discourses in the complex interchanges of modern society.

Social Science Is Not Only for Social Policy

In conclusion, it may be useful to see where the argument has taken us regarding the need for law to learn from social science. The main point which should have emerged from this paper is that we do not have to think of social science only as handmaiden to a scientistic style of social policy. Indeed, some of the main critiques of and resistance to bureaucratic knowledge have come from social scientists. If anything, it is those responsible for law-making and decision-making, such as politicians, administrators, and judges, who try to preserve positivist social science in aspic, because it suits the division of labor on which they rely. Whatever law can or cannot learn from social science experts in framing legislation, improving administration, or holding trials, social scientists can also contribute to reflections on what it means to respect the specificity of the "legal" as it applies, in various ways, to all these activities.

It should be equally evident that social science cannot go it alone in trying to deal with the range of meta-theoretical questions thrown up by its relationship with law. The social sciences can interrogate the conditions of their existence (the sociology of knowledge tries to do just this). But there is always a limit to such reflexivity.[53] Even if the problem is (wrongly) posed as simply one of distinguishing facts and values, law and the social sciences will have different ways of grasping this dilemma (is it a factual or normative question?). One obvious disciplinary partner which should be of help in examining the questions discussed in this paper is legal philosophy. But it has to be said that there is still little serious engagement over this issue between philosophers of law and social scientists.

In a recent paper,[54] Jeremy Waldron, a leading philosopher of law, (and a former colleague at Edinburgh University) revisits a famous polemic ("Transcendental Nonsense and the Heaven of Legal Concepts") by Felix Cohen, a prominent Legal Realist. Cohen claimed that legal

---

53   D. Nelken, *supra* n. 5.
54   J. Waldron, "Transcendental Nonsense and System in the Law" (Jan., 2000) I Columbia L.R. 16-55.

concepts such as "property" or "causation" were "transcendental non-sense," without clear empirical referents and manipulable at will. Waldron replies that such concepts are not to be treated as camouflage for something else: theology, political preferences, or the political and economic views of a previous generation. Legal rules do not serve, as the Realists supposedly taught, only as predictions of what the courts will do in particular disputes, and legal concepts cannot and should not deal only with the "brute facts" of such disputes. It would be quite wrong for courts to seek, as the Realists proposed, to substitute these concepts with ones better geared to producing the best policy outcomes for each of the factual situations facing them. For if they were to do this, the courts would risk substituting themselves for policy makers rather than respecting the separation of powers. Rather, says Waldron, legal concepts necessarily abstract from particular cases and form part of a self referential system whose meaning is to be sought in relation to the (changing) sense of other legal concepts, producing what he calls "a mutual accommodation matrix." Their very lack of precision also allows law to keep track of very different factual situations within general rubrics and to encompass competing and changing political and policy preferences.

Waldron's understanding of legal concepts is a theoretical advance on the set of assumptions taken over from the Realists which are employed by Monahan and Walker (though we have already noted that in practice courts and administrative agencies actually prefer expertise which treats legal concepts as if they were concerned with brute facts). What is disappointing, however, is the way Waldron makes no reference to social scientific thinking such as that developed by writers such as Luhmann and Teubner, who, as we have seen, have put forward very similar but more detailed claims about the importance of law as a self-referring autopoietic system.[55] Moreover we cannot leave matters where Waldron does. If we agree, at least for the sake of argument, that the point of legal concepts is to serve as a "mutual accommodation matrix" we then need to investigate how and where they serve this specific purpose or "function," rather than the pragmatic purposes envisaged by the Realists. We may even want to test whether this function is being adequately performed. And to do this, in the end, law and legal theorists will need to learn from social science.

55 Compare Teubner's provocative claims in his 1989 paper "How the Law Thinks" in which he writes "there is no way to challenge cognitive constructions of law neither by social realities themselves nor by common sense nor by socially controllable observation."

[11]
Can there be a Sociology
of Legal Meaning?

The 'law and society' tradition is an attempt to break open the legal box of
secrets ... It exposes law to intense beams of light that flow in from outside;
once you observe law in this light it can never seem the same again. (Friedman,
1994: 130)

To give meaning, however, is not a neutral activity, something disappears at the
same time. (Josipovici, 1990: 49)

Working in the sociology of law has yet to come fully to terms with the
challenge of approaching law as communication. The past few years have
seen the founding of a number of new journals which have pioneered the
application of semiotic, literary and various forms of critical social theory to
the discussion of 'law as communication' (in the UK, see, for example, the
International Journal of Semiotics of Law and *Law and Critique*: in the
USA, the *Cardozo Journal of Law and Literature* and the *Yale Journal of the
Law and Humanities*). Even the generalist American law journals have
hosted numerous special symposia devoted to the relationship between 'law
and literature' (see, for example, amongst others less well known, the collections in *Texas Law Review*, 1982, and *Michigan Law Review*, 1982,
1989). In addition to influential monographs which explore law and literature or law as literature (for example, White, 1973, 1984, 1985, 1990;
Weisberg, 1992), many of the central debates between leading social theorists have increasingly come to concern the special characteristics of 'law as
communication' (Deflem, 1994; Lenoble, 1994). But discussion of these
developments still remains marginal to mainstream sociology of law journals such as the *Law and Society Review*; the *Journal of Law and Society*;
Social and Legal Studies; or the *International Journal of the Sociology of
Law*). Likewise, the leading English-language textbooks, such as Lempert

and Sanders (1986) or Cotterrell (1992), continue to adopt a theoretical framework in which law 'interacts' with society rather than highlighting the extent to which this relationship is one mediated by or even constituted by language itself.

This chapter looks more closely at some of the implications of asking the sociology of law to move from the study of 'law and society' to a focus on 'law as communication'. First we indicate how this new direction is related to those developments associated with the 'linguistic turn' which have made considerable inroads into the social sciences more generally. We then go on to argue that what is involved here is not just a change of *topic* for sociology of law but rather its need to face new problems of reflexive and postmodern theorizing which call its own foundations into question. In particular the question whether it is plausible to conduct a sociological search for legal meaning is discussed.

SOCIOLOGY OF LAW AND 'THE LINGUISTIC TURN'

For much of the twentieth century sociologists of law (like other social scientists) assumed that the justification for bringing their insights to the investigation and reform of law processes was that this would allow us to see what law could not or would not appreciate about the limits of its attempts to know and control the social world. This project did not of course go uncriticized. Concern was regularly expressed about allowing the progress of sociology of law to be determined by problems of assisting or criticizing the formulation of legal and social policy, as in the many studies which set out to demonstrate 'the gap' between legal norms and ideals and their actual effects (Nelken, 1981, 1983). But the worry here was that sociology of law would thereby be distracted from pursuing its own disciplinary agendas. These criticisms therefore reflected, if anything, *more* rather than less scepticism regarding the intrinsic reliability of legal communications, since these were considered hardly worthy even of being dismissed. More recently, however, there has been increasing dissatisfaction with many of the central features of the 'law and society' paradigm (Nelken, 1986, 1987b). Although some leading scholars still adhere strongly to the former mandate in which sociology was valued as providing special access to law's 'box of secrets' (Friedman, 1994), others concede that almost every element of the former paradigm is now 'up for grabs' (Simon, 1994: 952).

Here we can do no more than mention a few of the arguments which are helping to undermine what has been described as the earlier 'imperial' (Trubek, 1990) confidence which underlay social scientists' claims to understand law better than it knew itself. The original framework of 'law and society' may never have been intended to be more than an eclectically defined 'space' within which to locate a variety of social scientific studies of the law, but it was based nonetheless on concealed assumptions about the relationship between law, sociology and society (Nelken, 1987b) which can be called into question. It was soon seen, for example, that the connection between 'law' and 'society' was an 'internal' one rather than a relationship between two independent entities (Nelken, 1985). Critical Legal Scholars argued that it would be more fruitful to examine the way law 'constituted' society rather than fulfilling determined functions within it (for example, Gordon, 1984) and the 'constitutive' perspective was then extended and re-elaborated by scholars within the field of sociology of law (Hunt, 1993; Sarat and Kearns, 1993b). From Continental social theory came the criticism that English-language sociology of law too easily reduced itself to being 'a sociology of courts and lawyers' rather than the study of the reproduction of law itself (Luhmann, 1985). Further development of Luhmann-inspired autopoietic theory then focused attention on the way law communicated according to its own code (Nelken, 1987b; Teubner, 1988, 1989, 1993).

More generally, however, debates within the sociology of law are themselves being shaped by the wider rise of non-positivist and anti-positivist epistemologies and methods. The older truth claims of the social sciences are challenged as attention shifts from description to narrative and from explanation to persuasion and rhetoric. (See, for example, Brown, 1987; Clifford, 1988; Clifford and Marcus, 1986; Mumby, 1993; Rabinow and Sullivan, 1979; Simons, 1989; Somers, 1994). What has been described as the 'linguistic turn' in the social and human sciences has pushed the question of language and processes of communication more and more to the centre of social theorizing. Many earlier sociological approaches, such as symbolic interactionism, social constructionism and ethnomethodology, also emphasized the centrality of symbols and meaning to social life. But what is new about the linguistic turn and much related postmodernist writing is the account it offers of the way selves and societies are constructed and reconstructed through rhetorical practices. Society thus becomes a text to be interpreted and, for some writers, signs take on a life of their own, referring not to underlying social relations but to their own reality. Applied to social thinking about law this means that law comes to be seen less as a technical means to an end and more as a story we tell about ourselves. Renewed interest in the politics of interpretation, in the processes of writing and reading and in the way texts persuade pervades fields as different as anthropology, psychology and the sociology of science (see, for example, Woolgar, 1988; Nelken, 1994). Legal scholarship has been influenced by these trends through the importation of literary theory (see Dworkin, 1986), social theory and postmodern writings (Douzinas and Warrington, 1990).

110   Law as Communication

In addition, as always, factors beyond the academy have also played an important part in changing the focus of scholarly debates. The political loss of faith in the welfare state has tarnished the ideal of the sociologist of law serving as the handmaid of social engineering by legislation in the service of a fairer or more efficient society (Trubek, 1990). The role attributed to law is now more likely to be that of serving as a bulwark against technocracy, as Habermas might put it, so as to help defend the 'life world' against colonization by the logic of administrative systems. Even those who are more sceptical about the possibilities of the public sphere also question law's role as social engineering and ask it rather to help the 'structural coupling' of autonomous sub-systems of society (Teubner, 1993).

Within the sociology of law the new focus on communication leads both to the breaking down of previous guiding conceptual distinctions and to the opening up of new approaches which might previously have been spurned as insufficiently 'scientific'. Instead of seeking to relate law to its context, as in classical 'law and society' work, or even deciding to read texts to see how they contain context, as the Critical Legal Scholars do (Nelken, 1987a), it is now the contrast between text and context which is being called into question.[1] As Stanley Fish argues, the distinction between text and context is impossible to maintain because there can be no such thing as non-contextual sense. A context is not an entity but a bundle of tacit assumptions that organize the world and change in response to its reorganizing work in materials. It is never possible to focus on 'meaning independently of background of "supplemental" considerations' (Fish, 1989: 329). Similarly, if older work in the sociology of law was concerned to study both how actions communicate and how communication works as symbolic action, what is now being argued is the need to transcend the distinction between action and communication:[2] texts communicate about culture and culture is itself a text.[3] Enquiries are directed to showing how communications and discourses reproduce themselves, and the way the same institution may appear simultaneously in different discourses (as 'contract' is a figure both of economics and of law). Instead of sociology being given an external, privileged position in understanding law's communications, the relationship between law and sociology becomes a search for mutual comprehension between two 'internal' points of view' (Nelken, 1990/93).

All this also has implications for the way empirical investigations are carried out within the discipline The earlier wave of 'law and society' studies concerned with the influence (or 'impact') of law often took legislation as their object of interest. More importantly, however, they also took the statute as their implicit model of law. Current scholarship is less interested in exploring how law 'effects' society. Instead it typically places emphasis on judicial decisions and the images of culture and community that these mobilize and the way legal communications reinforce identifications and activate memories.[4] If older work sought to borrow its explanatory tools from social sciences such as sociology, economics or political science, new styles of argument are borrowed from intellectual heroes who straddle the boundaries of social and literary theory (such as the writings of Derrida or Fish). Some of the studies published by members of the 'Amherst School' and, in particular, the interesting recent collections of papers edited by Sarat and Kearns (1991, 1992, 1993, 1994) are the best illustrations (though by no means the only ones[5]) of the new style of work which combines sociological and literary sensibility.

On the other hand, the temptation to take the 'linguistic turn' within the sociology of law has not gone without criticism. For some it represents just too convenient a flight from context to text. Just as the work of Critical Legal Scholars was accused of avoiding the hard grind of empirical work required to establish the practical reach and complexities of legal ideology (Trubek, 1984) so the new sociological concern with texts risks placing exaggerated emphasis on judges' opinions (or other artefacts of what Trubek calls 'mandarin culture') in societies which, it is urged, are influenced far more by statutory and administrative regulation than by judicial decision making. For Boyd White, perhaps the leading figure in the 'law and litera-ture' movement, the judge's opinion is the paradigm case of law because it is centrally concerned with the problem of meaning, whilst other legal behaviour, such as legal advice or the application of statutes, is done in its shadow. But this presupposes rather than demonstrates the central social significance of the moment of legal interpretation.

It is also argued that adopting a constitutive view of law risks seeing society too much through the eyes of legal decision makers or policy makers. Unless it is backed up by painstaking ethnographic investigations, writing about stories in and about legal texts tends to assume rather than actually show their importance in everyday life.[6] Older approaches in the sociology of law may have placed too much stress on law as an instrument, but the approaches which are best suited to exploring 'law as communication' may themselves be ill-equipped to tell us about the instrumental influence of law. In general, given that the search for meaning is already central to legal doctrine and legal philosophy asking that social theorizing about law go the same way can be seen as a return to interpretation which risks losing, as Friedman (1994) complains, exactly that difference of perspective which social analysis brings to law. On this view the 'linguistic turn' would be likely to lead sociology of law to concentrate its energies too much on a competitive search for legal meaning. We would do better to avoid what Maureen Cain has recently described as 'the absurd choice between prioritising text or prioritising con-text in an attempt at understanding' (Cain, 1995: 71).

SOCIOLOGICAL SENSE AND LEGAL MEANING

For those influenced by the 'linguistic turn' any move towards a focus on 'law as communication' inevitably requires thinking about the relationship between law's way of communicating and our way of communicating about law. On the one hand, claims about texts, stories or the rhetorical character of writing, reading and interpretation in law can all be applied to the scholarly communications which themselves use these ideas. On the other hand, there may be features of our own way of communicating which interfere with our ability to grasp other types of communication. As far as the sociology of law is concerned, we need to ask whether there can be a sociology of legal meaning which does not merely impose sociological sense on its object of enquiry (Nelken, 1990/1993). Although this question will be discussed at a somewhat general level it is obvious that it carries enormous implications for the more concrete efforts of sociologists to explain and interpret legal behaviour. In short, have the social sciences up to now merely been creating law in their own image?

The claim that sociology (or any other scientific discipline) is unable to provide an authentic interpretation of legal meaning is not new. In particular it has regularly been put forward by legal theorists from Kelsen to Dworkin. A contrast is made between an 'internal' and 'external' perspective on law; only the internal perspective, which involves correctly following the approved processes of normative deduction or participating in the appropriate place and manner in the debate over what law means, is allowed to provide authentic insight into law. The alternative, 'external' approach is said to be able to offer only (causal) explanation of *how* law comes to its decisions, or a generalized scepticism concerning the possibility of determinate communication (Dworkin, 1986).

Sociologists, for their part, have been equally ready with their replies. It is obvious that sociological interpretations of law do not count as legal statements unless and until they are adopted by players within the legal system. But legal theorists, it is said, make too rigid a distinction between what is 'external' and 'internal' to law, given that judges themselves often and necessarily resort to 'external' forms of knowledge in some of their decision making. Moreover the meaning of the distinction is itself slippery. Legal theorists may find it convenient to operate with a positivistic definition of sociological methodology based on 'external' styles of explanation, but this leaves right out of account the more interpretative and hermeneutic strands of social investigation. It is more convincing to argue that both law and sociology necessarily operate with their own 'internal' distinctions – in terms shaped by their own disciplines – between what they each deem to be external and internal to law (Nelken, 1990/1993).

More recently, however, similar criticisms of social science to those levelled by legal philosophers have been made by a variety of literary and
postmodernist approaches to legal communication. The radical claim, put
forward for example by scholars of the 'law and literature' movement, is
that the social sciences are inherently incapable of making sense of law.
They must recognize that law is itself a competing discourse and a different
way of imagining the world. In so far as these arguments can be distinguished from those advanced by legal philosophers, how should sociology
of law respond to this new challenge?

The most straightforward response the sociologist can make to defend the
mainstream paradigm of sociology of law is to say that it sets out deliberately to transmute legal meaning into sociological sense. Its contribution
lies, for example, in taking such legal categories as civil or criminal proceedings and reformulating them under the more general rubric of 'disputes'. Thus sociological interpretations of law can and should only reproduce sociology. The quickest way for a scholarly discipline to go wrong is
to fail to develop its own concepts and methods or to seek to account for or
explain matters which its concepts do not permit it to grasp (Grace and
Wilkinson, 1979). There is no point even in posing the question whether
sociological accounts also count as good interpretations of law; if it were to
follow law's criteria its arguments would in turn not be acceptable to sociology. Sociology of law must maintain sufficient distance from the categories
used by legal actors and legal theory because these are unable to offer an
adequate cognition of social reality (Pennisi, 1991). The proper role for
sociology is thus to be true to its own way of posing problems – whatever
reformulation of legal meanings this requires. Sociologists who take this
line offer accounts of legal communication which can and do seek to illuminate the interpretative work of legal and other actors as they communicate in
and about the law. But their (social) communications are assumed to be
wholly transparent to sociology and no special epistemological status is
given to the categories and concepts used by these actors themselves.

A variant on this approach is more willing to treat law as possessing its
own code of meaning rather than subsume it in the study of individual
communications by social actors. For Niklas Luhmann and his collabora-
tors, law does indeed have its own way of communicating with the environment, based on its own founding distinction of legal/illegal. To this extent,
then, law does represent an epistemological equal. But sociology, as part of
the science sub-system, can nonetheless provide an account of the way law
communicates, just as it can even offer an explanation of what these theorists call 'legal closure'. The call for a sociology of legal meaning can only
mean that sociology should do its best to clarify its accounts of the differences it sees between legal and other communicative codes. No sub-system

can overcome the paradox which founds its own code of meaning. The important point is not to confuse law's own communications with scientific communications about law, the danger which Teubner (1989) characterizes as 'the epistemic trap'.

But how exactly should we formulate the relationship between sociological sense and legal meaning? What is it that sociology can offer and where can it mislead us? Let us consider at greater length here the arguments of those theorists who are less insistent on simply presupposing the distinction between sociological sense and legal communications but rather struggle with the problem of showing either why sociology *can* offer a better interpretation of law than law itself or, conversely, why it must *fail* to do so. As an example of the claim that sociology of law can make better sense of law than law is able to make of itself, we will consider some of the recent writings of Roger Cotterrell, amongst the most respected and subtle of contemporary sociologists of law. As an illustration of the argument concerning the limits of sociology we will discuss some points made by James Boyd White, an acknowledged leader of the American 'law and literature' movement.[7] It will be argued that neither of their alternative positions (in some ways each the mirror image of the other) is ultimately persuasive, but that, for this reason, the possibility of producing a sociology of legal meaning remains an open question.[8]

Cotterrell has returned to the issue of sociology's claim to know better than law in a number of different publications. Although his arguments were initially developed as a critique of the claim by legal dogmatics and legal theory to exclusive rights to the interpretation of legal communication, he has further developed his views in the face of talk about 'legal closure' which would appear to rule sociology out of play. The terms of the question, as Cotterrell sees them, are well set out in one of the earliest of these papers (Cotterrell, 1986). When sociologists write about law, he argues, they cannot avoid confronting the difficulty of comparing sociology and law as fields of intellectual endeavour because 'each constructs its own fields of knowledge and experience' (Cotterrell, 1986: 11). He nevertheless finds an ingenious argument to show why sociology can still provide a privileged route to understanding law. This is because only sociology is dedicated to a *reflexive* perspective on the development of disciplines – including itself – its fundamentally reflexive self-conscious, self-contextualising character makes it unlike the political-intellectual practices of law and capable, by its nature, of examining the social foundations of legal knowledges and practices' (Cotterrell, 1986: 189). Law, by contrast, lacking this interest, is no more than a 'discipline-effect', whose changing knowledge-claims need to be illuminated through the use of sociology (of science and knowledge). Indeed Cotterrell sees law's periodic tendency to import the methods and findings of 'external' disciplines as a sign of crises which reveal its recognition of its own disciplinary weakness and the consequent need to resort to other perspectives in order to correct the mistaken assumptions and fictions which disfigure it.

Rather than treat this merely as a restatement of sociology's claim to be more 'scientific' than law, we should note that Cotterrell introduces an interesting post-positivist twist in his argument. A social scientific perspective on law, he argues, should be credited with a superior epistemology, not because of its greater capacity for getting at 'the facts about the world', but precisely on the basis of its more sophisticated sense of the *limits* of all disciplinary understanding. Thus, even though law *sees itself* as a self-sufficient interpretative framework, sociology is capable of understanding law's limits better than law does itself. On the other hand, it remains the case that Cotterrell's argument succeeds only if we allow him to downgrade law's disciplinary status so that it does not represent real competition. The problem of course is that the same argument can be applied to sociology. Can it – any more than law – really see its own limits? Can it transcend its own style and method of argument (without ceasing to be sociology)? If sociology typically offers either functionalist or conflict-oriented accounts of law's operations, does this not reveal more about sociological models than it does about legal meaning? Cotterrell's solution is much less convincing if, instead of privileging social science, we follow the view of those, such as some leading anthropologists, who claim that law and social science must be understood as competing types of 'local knowledge' (Geertz, 1983).

More recently Cotterrell has again defended sociology's ability to throw light on law in relation to various assertions of 'legal closure' (Cotterrell, 1993). Cotterrell is deeply sceptical of 'the multifaceted but ubiquitous idea that law is, in some way, radically autonomous, self-reproducing or self-validating in relation to an environment defined as "extra-legal"' (1993: 175). He rejects the claim that law is 'self-standing and irreducible, or has an independent integrity which is normally unproblematic, natural or self-generated, and not dependent on contingent links with an extra-legal environment of knowledge or practice'. At one level his intention in all this is only the apparently modest one of showing the utility of a *sociological* perspective or set of perspectives on legal closure. 'My aim', he says, 'is not to show that conceptions of normative or discursive legal closure are misguided in the particular contexts in which these conceptions have been developed, but that they can be reconsidered in a broader sociological perspective' (Cotterrell, 1993: 175). But, as we will attempt to illustrate, his own logic leads him inexorably to attempt to demonstrate the value of sociological insight as a remedy for law's inability to understand itself.

Cotterrell first distinguishes normative from discursive closure. He has no difficulty in showing that normative closure is always only a matter of

116   *Law as Communication*

degree and that there is no absolute separation between legal and other rules; the fact that empirical social conditions are always shaping and re-shaping legal rules means that even the extent of law's relative autonomy is itself a result of changing historical contingencies. More pertinent for our problem is his discussion of *discursive closure*. This Cotterrell (1993: 183) defines as the claim that law 'is a distinct discourse possessing its own integrity, its own criteria of significance and validation, its own means of cognition and of constituting the objects of which it speaks'. Typically, as he rightly says, this goes along with the argument that discourses are incom-mensurable, that truth or validity criteria, established by discourse, function within it without reference to the status of criteria outside that discourse; that there are no meta-discourses which make it possible to adjudicate on the relative merits or validity claims of different discourses (see, for exam-ple, Nelken 1990/1993). The upshot of this reasoning – *and it is this conclu-sion which he refuses* – would be that a sociological perspective on legal closure would be unable to address the significance of legal closure for *law*: that is, for the discourse of law.

If we are to avoid arriving at such a result, says Cotterrell, it will be necessary to show 'first, that a sociological discourse about law is possible if law is, itself, a distinct discourse', and 'secondly, that a sociological characterisation of legal closure is relevant to participants in any such legal discourse' (1993: 183). The way to achieve this is to seek to understand the significance of claims of legal closure without necessarily taking them at face value. Thus, 'viewed sociologically, legal closure can be treated primar-ily as a means by which various forms of legal or political practice attempt to enhance their own legitimacy. Ideas of legal closure are part of the means by which an appeal to the legal 'provides legitimacy in a variety of empiri-cal settings'. On the other hand, 'such a perspective ultimately denies that law is adequately understood as a "closed" system, knowledge field, intel-lectual discipline or discourse. But it recognises the social conditions that may make law so appear, or which seem to impel the "legal" to seek to achieve "closure" in a variety of ways'. He convincingly rejects arguments which insist that the legal sociologist is forced either to participate in legal discourse or to remain outside, condemned 'to inhabit an external discourse, unrelated to and unable to embrace, invade or interact with law'. Because law consists of diverse, loosely and contingently related rhetorics and rationalities drawn from *realpolitik*, moral conviction, arguments of eco-nomic efficiency, techniques of textual interpretation and criticism, and many other sources (Cotterrell, 1993: 185), there is every reason to think that the sociologist can engage with and contribute to refurbishing these resources of legal communication. It is again up to sociology to help law's reflexivity.

But has Cotterrell now finally succeeded in showing that sociology of law can make other than good sociological sense of law? Cotterrell is careful to deny that he is proposing sociology as a meta-theory or even as a unified disciplinary perspective. Yet we are now told that a sociological account is superior to a merely legal perspective, not only because it occupies a 'higher' epistemological status (by being more reflexive) but also because it offers a 'broader' perspective. For him 'a sociological perspective can be more inclusive and illuminating than that of a legal participant because it embraces particular participant perspectives but goes beyond them, recognising their diversity, interpreting and preserving them within a widening vision of law in society'. He admits that there is no 'true or complete view to be gained by such means, only the possibility of more comprehending and comprehensive ones – capable of incorporating without denying or trivialising, more specific participant perspectives' (Cotterrell, 1993: 190). But, as the title of his piece clearly indicates, his argument cannot do more than offer a *sociological* perspective on legal closure if the criteria of what constitute 'higher' or 'broader' truths about law are to be supplied by sociology itself. It is hardly surprising that sociology is unwilling to confirm the validity of law's own understanding of its closure if this would foreclose its own perspective, and it is difficult to imagine how it could consistently do so. But even if sociology could just about make such an argument (for example, by defining itself as the most reflexive of disciplines whilst specifying law's task as that of producing closure), as Cotterrell's own argument shows, we could not really claim that law was closed if it was left to sociology to demonstrate that closure.

On the other hand, it seems that Cotterrell still retains a lingering suspicion that there may be something about law which escapes sociology's ken. In his chapter in the present volume, for example, he notes that 'many recent enquiries about symbolism in law are concerned to recognize the indefinitely wide ramifications of the ambiguity of symbols, and to emphasize the rich overlay of symbolic references that provide the "irrational", contradictory or mystificatory foundations of modern legal rationality'. Acknowledging that the law operates through the creation of *infinitely suggestive ambiguities* (emphasis in original), Cotterrell sees the move to the study of the symbolic as partly 'a response to gaps or inadequacies in the established paradigms of sociological inquiry about the social significance of legal ideas' (see, for example, Winn, 1991). He acknowledges, at the same time, that sociology, for its part, tends to confine and 'tame' the symbolic ambiguity or indeterminacy of rule systems by specifying their functional place in a rationally explained legal order. But this is then justified as the only way to avoid conceding so many (local) meanings that it would become impossible to be systematic. What is interesting, however, is the way this is described as

118   *Law as Communication*

a strategy rather than a demonstrable 'truth', as a means of avoiding what he
calls 'the heavy cost' of otherwise allowing the investigation of symbols to
remain indeterminate and unlimited. Even his concession that our investigations can never *exhaust* the significance of legal symbols glosses over the
more basic difficulty of how to know whether we have got it right at all. The
weakness of Cotterrell's approach remains the difficulty he has in showing
us that sociology of law can overcome not only legal closure but also
sociological blindness. Otherwise we might be more persuaded by Fish's
provocative remark that there can be no 'broader', but only 'different',
truths.

The opposite line of argument, developed by representatives of the 'law
and literature' movement such as James Boyd White, makes much of just
such blindness. White's strong thesis is that the social sciences not only fail
to offer a satisfactory route to grasping law's meaning but that, on the
contrary, they can actually represent an obstacle to such understanding. In
part White buys into the distinction, so stressed by legal theorists, between
an internal and external point of view.[9] But his argument goes much further
than this. For him, social science commits 'the radical intellectual vice of
our day' which is 'to insist that everything can be translated into one's own
terms, instead of seeing itself as one amongst many languages' (White,
1990: 259). The question of reflexivity is as central for him as it is for
Cotterrell, but, according to White, it is law which, as an element and
expression of a society's reflexivity, helps constitute and transform a community's culture. It is therefore law, rather than sociology, which is the only
discourse which can listen to and translate all the others in society. This
means that his argument against the social sciences ends up taking a similar
form to that advanced in their favour by Cotterrell. If we were to attempt to
work out what should be the weight given to social scientific reasoning in
law, as compared to other aspects of culture, such an enquiry could not itself
be carried out in terms of scientific reasoning but only by rhetorical methods
of persuasion. The sociology of sociology is of little value here. Social
science reasoning cannot serve as its own justification.

For the 'law and literature' movement law must be approached as a
language of its own, a special way of reading and writing and speaking. It is
not a procedure of scientific reasoning but rather a resource of argument. It
invites agreement with its conclusions through a rhetorical and literary
process which 'works' by persuasion and 'contains' rather than resolves
contradictions as does a poem. By contrast, a social science approach to law,
and economics in particular, imposes a bureaucratic means–ends policy-
oriented discourse onto law which fails to appreciate and impoverishes
law's way of communicating. For such scholars 'the principal question for
the lawyer or student of law is what policies should be adopted, that is, what

value choices should be made and how they should be put into effect, given our various constraints. Once a choice of value is made, law is simply a system of implementation. Laws are rules that work, or don't work; the main issue is compliance, and here is the role for legal expertise, namely how to secure it, or how to evade it. Lawyers are either architects or engineers for a social machine' (White, 1994: 34). In principle White does of course concede that the social sciences do represent at least one way of understanding law and thus form part of law's 'many-sided conversation'. But this concession is more apparent than real. For what he repeatedly seeks to demonstrate is the wrongheadedness of the starting-point adopted by the social sciences and the incompatibility of their discourse with that attributed to the law.

White offers a number of specific criticisms of such wrongheadedness. He accuses the social sciences of systematically misinterpreting law by concentrating only on the 'outcomes' of rules or decisions. For social scientists to look through a judicial opinion to the 'reality' behind the facade is, by definition, 'to declare that there is, or ought to be, no discourse that is distinctively legal, no distinctively legal questions, methods or institutions' (White, 1990: 95). This prevents them from appreciating that the point of legal communication is ultimately 'the keeping alive of texts, the primary activity of legal actors the interpretation and composition of authoritative texts' (ibid.). In the life of the law communication is itself a form of action rather than a means to any other end. For him, 'talking we create a character for ourselves and a relation to others, we offer to constitute a community of a certain kind, for good and ill, and this is often the most important part of what we do' (ibid.).

Social scientists, White argues, are obliged by their own protocols to adopt an impoverished view of legal discourse. On the one hand, they tend to concentrate on the way legal language conveys information and regularly attempt to separate the form from the substance of its messages. On the other hand, they fail to see that the language they themselves use is not simply a neutral tool of exploration but is itself rather the bearer of a certain culture. In this way they fail to recognize the possible disjunctures between their own type of communications and those of law. By ignoring the constraints which shape judicial or other legal communications they obscure the questions which are central to the understanding of legal discourse, such as: 'Who is speaking? From what position? Within what division of powers? And to what audiences?' (White, 1984: 266ff). According to White there is no way these questions could be raised within social science. If the social scientist were to seek to interpret the meaning of such constraints then he would be 'no longer engaging in his own discipline, whatever that is, but in law' (White, 1990: 97).

120   *Law as Communication*

The problems produced when legal communications are transformed into the sort of propositions that social scientists are used to handling can be well seen if we contrast the different roles of the 'expert' and the judge. Because they take their role as experts for granted, social scientists miss the point that what is distinctive about legal judgements is 'that they are not simply policy judgements, made by actors with despotic powers, but judgements made by actors with limited authority, an authority that is governed by texts external to themselves to which they must look to determine both the proper scope of their power and the standards by which it is to be exercised' (White, 1990: 95). The judge can never ask what is best without at the same time asking who should have power to decide this question and within what limits. The policy advisor, on the other hand, assumes that he has despotic powers to create the 'best results' for the parties and society as a whole, whether this is defined in terms of solving a problem, of maximizing utility, or of defending rights and liberties. The only question is, what is the best result? This question can be asked in general terms or particular ones, it can exclude or include questions of institutional competence, expected rates of voluntary compliance, and so forth. It can be a complex investigation that includes an abstract enquiry as to the standards by which the 'best' should be determined. But in all such cases, this kind of expert conversation takes place on a plane removed from institutional life, without any sense of obligation to texts or choices made by others, among a 'we' who are not defined only by our commitment to this sort of talk (White, 1990: 96).

On the other hand, the law, according to White, works in quite another way. It provides a set of speaking places where real differences of view and interest can be defined and addressed; it is continuous with ordinary language and politics and thus necessarily respects the culture it acts upon and out of. Its methods of reasoning are not linear but multidimensional and its conversations take place among a plurality of voices. Law is inherently idealizing, taking as its constant subject what we ought to do, who we ought to be. In sum, the task of law is to provide a place and a set of institutions and methods where this conversational process can go on.

What sort of response can sociologists make to these arguments? Since attack is often the best form of defence we should not be surprised to find that social scientists have levelled important criticisms at the work of authors in the 'law and literature' movement. We may discount those generalized complaints which simply reassert the validity of the model of the social sciences, as when Posner (1988) accuses the 'law and literature' movement of having 'no proper methodology or project'. But social scientists are on stronger ground when they argue that members of the 'law and literature' movement cannot, even if they wanted to, avoid making social scientific assumptions about law. A sociological approach would want to test Weisberg arguments for the persuasiveness of Cardozo's memorable phrases (Weisberg, 1992) by asking whether, and under what conditions, such communications owe their success to their imprecision. It would also claim a role in the process of appreciating the power of narratives and the factors which influence judges in such choices. Explaining which stories are available in a given stock and why stories diverge also necessarily brings you back to social science.

The writings of James Boyd White have been particularly singled out for paying insufficient attention to the social and political context of literature, the social role of law and the ideological dimension of language. By underplaying the social and moral differences in society he conceals the extent to which agreement has come about only through conflict (the constitutive understandings of American life, says Levinson, have been written in blood). Who is Boyd White's ideal reader and can such a person be assumed (Douzinas and Warrington, 1994)? White's approach, it is argued, makes it impossible to see how the language of law translates social reality into its own terms in order to control it (Mann, 1989: 159). His authorial style has been criticized for the way it silences other academic voices. If legal discourse operates in a similar way, White may have succeeded in mirroring law, but he cannot then also maintain his claim that it is a discourse which enables conversation. He himself admits that the discourse of law has its own dangers; he notes especially the way the intellectual and social form we call 'the rule' can reduce people and events to caricature, and the legal formulas which disguise exercises of power that are essentially authoritarian in nature (White, 1990: 79). And he includes amongst these dangers the tendency of law to think it is the only language. But all this then begs the question why he systematically seeks to minimize the insights social science interpretations of law can bring, when these are often helpful precisely to protect against the dangers he identifies. Without addressing such problems it is difficult to credit Boyd White's hopes that a community's problems can be successfully resolved through (legal) conversation or that the ideal criminal process should be one which allows the convicted criminal to consent to his punishment.

Most importantly, perhaps, the arguments which 'law and literature' writers make against the social sciences, concerning the potential differences between the assumptions and models of the social sciences and those of law, can equally well be applied to humanistic and literary approaches themselves. The mere attractiveness of the literary analogy for legal theorists or judges, and the way this can be exploited for the purposes of interpreting and reproducing law, does not in itself prove that the ways of literature are those of the law – any more than the fact that judges and legislators also sometimes draw on the social sciences. The parallel between law and litera-

122   *Law as Communication*

ture has to be argued for (making sociological claims where necessary) and is far from perfect. On the one hand, the social contexts of literary and legal productions are very different: most importantly, the process of legal judgement, it is argued, takes place in a 'field of violence'. The problems of legitimation are greater in the case of law, and this explains the difference in the role of precedents (or influences) in the two activities (Yoshino, 1994). Similarly, there are functional differences between literary and legal communications. Law, and not literature, is attributed the social function of deciding disputes. Where literature flourishes through its ambiguity, law is supposed to be clear and predictable. Unlike literature, interpretation in law is subject to a system of appeal courts and to binding final decisions. As compared to literature, law's functioning makes it necessary to choose between stories, and sometimes also to set limits to which stories are admitted (Massaro, 1989). On the other hand, resort to the social sciences may also lend unexpected support to the literary analogy. By refusing to take the law's commitment to avoid ambiguity at face value, social scientists can show how judicial formulations, founding constitutions and legal rituals may all gain by being ambiguous. Likewise, in the everyday practice of law, lawyers may deliberately multiply possible readings of a document at the appropriate stage of their negotiations. Here the insights and methods of the social sciences can be used to show that legal and literary texts and communications have more in common than might seem at first sight.

The essential point to emerge is that it is not only the social scientist who must ask herself how (far) her ways of communicating allow her to enter into a dialogue with the law. We may just as much query whether law should be influenced by debates in the field of literary theory. Is the interdeterminacy of meaning demonstrated by literary theorists a similar problem for law as it is for the interpretation of literature (Graff, 1982; Levinson, 1982)? Why are only certain forms of literary criticism, such as the reader response theory, embraced by Dworkin's legal theory? We could well imagine the different consequences for legal theory which would follow from adopting the view of those post-structuralists who argue that neither reader nor writer can control the meaning of the text. (It is this, in the first instance, rather than political differences which divides Dworkin from many of the Critical Legal Scholars.) More fundamentally it has been asserted that it can never be defensible to elect only one literary theory and present it as having definite consequences for the law (Mann, 1989). Law's attempt to consecrate only certain versions of another discipline is indeed a common feature of the way it preys on other knowledges, but it reveals as much about law's need for legitimation as it does about the applicability of the theory alleged to be applicable. By now the approach of 'law as literature' itself includes debates over the relevance or otherwise of the parallel to literature (there are at least four rival positions, according to Thurschwell, 1994). Some of the most interesting recent contributions to the field of law and literature are concerned with this very problem (Cole, 1988; *Texas Law Review*, 1993; Posner, 1988, 1990; Yoshino, 1994). Yoshino, for example, highlights the two opposite dangers, as he says, of forcing the two fields of law and literature too close together or driving them further apart than they actually are (1994: 479).

But could it be possible in principle to rely only on the resources of literary theory (without resort to the social sciences) to examine the extent to which the parallel between law and literature can be taken? Let us take as an example the thesis argued for by Stanley Fish, probably the most sophisticated scholar writing in this interdisciplinary field. For him, the problem of finding legal meaning is absorbed in the more general issue of the limits of theorizing law as a practice. He insists that there is no pre-existing legal meaning which could be respected by our interpretations. Law is an impossible attempt to fix meaning: it is we ourselves – in our interpretive communities – who put in place the constraints that provide meaning. Fish, perhaps surprisingly, admits that debates in literary theory are at present irrelevant to the concerns of law, but he argues that this merely reflects current modes of argumentation in law and literature rather than any inherent sociological or other facts about law. According to him, 'the difference then between science and law, on the one hand, and literary criticism, on the other, is not the difference between rhetoric (or style) and something else, but between the different rhetorics that are powerful in the precincts of different disciplines' (Fish, 1989: 298). Thus 'the reason that literary criticism has little to offer to the interpretation of statues and constitutions is not a result of the essential nature of the two disciplines but of the interpretive accounts presently but not inevitably in force' (Fish, 1989: 303).

So far Fish can be taken to be arguing that we cannot theorise law as having any necessary properties outside those of our interpretive accounts. The most we can do (as with the attempt to define the Divine only by negative attributes) is to reject any form of theorizing that creates law in its own image. He is firmly critical, for example, of the idea that legal decision making can be grasped by legal philosophy or by any other form of academic theorizing – as can be seen in his famous exchanges with Dworkin (Fish, 1989) or the more recent comments on Goodrich (Fish, 1991). But even Fish resorts to (questionable) sociological claims about the essential features of law as a practice in attacking other scholars' efforts to interpret law. In order to mount his attacks on legal theorists he makes a series of sociological assumptions about law's operations and functions that he seems to want us to accept as being more than the result of rhetorical arguments currently in place. Law is said to be about deciding, judging and crafting opinions so as to end disputes and so not open to the luxury of endless theorizing (Fish, 1989: 522). Law has no real autonomy but has to pretend to autonomy because 'its function would be put in danger if exposed to unorthodox interpretation' (Fish, 1991: 159). Such sociological assumptions are not only debatable: more serious for a theorist such as Fish, they are also banal. It is enough to contrast the ideas of a social theorist such as Luhmann, who claims that, rather than see law as a dispute solver, we should treat disputes as serving law's need to reproduce itself. In the end Fish's approach to interpretation is also more of a parochial expression of what would be expected of a literary theorist than he himself acknowledges. His notion of 'interpretive community' (Fish, 1980) strongly conjures up the world of literary theory's warring schools, and excludes for example the equally if not more plausible analogy of religious texts and communities of faith (Sherwin, 1988).

None of this proves that the 'law and literature' movement must allow its arguments to be measured by social scientific criteria, any more than social scientists (despite the influence of the 'linguistic turn') should accept seeing their explanations reduced to no more than 'rhetorical tropes'. What we are arguing is that the comparison of law to literature must justify itself heuristically just as much as is the case for social scientific approaches to law. It cannot itself provide an answer to the question of how far to take the literary parallel and therefore those who call on literary theory as a model are not necessarily better placed than social scientists. They too must choose which literary theory to adopt and face the risk that the analogy to literature obscures as well as reveals. Writers such as Boyd White often do write as if 'law' and 'literature' are interchangeable terms, just as we also encounter the claim that law *is* narrative (Luban, 1989). But if we disregard some of the stronger claims of some of its spokesmen (or of recent philosophical fellow-travellers such as Dworkin) it could be more fairly argued that the law and literature movement succeeds in highlighting the literary features of legal communication rather than showing us that this is all there is to law.

We can now therefore return to our starting-point concerning the possibility of a sociology of legal meaning. At one level we have queried the basis of Cotterrell's claim that sociology as at present constituted can understand law better than law understands itself. At the very least, sociology of law must pay much more attention to the problem of possible differences between sociological and legal communications in carrying out its investigations. Only if it is able to do this will it vindicate Cotterrell's argument that sociology is peculiarly well suited to calling its own claims into question. It has also been suggested above that, in approaching this task, there is much that the social sciences can learn from the 'law and literature' movement. We do not need to accept extreme claims that the social sciences are necessarily condemned to see law in instrumental terms. And, as we have tried to show, the very possibility of debating the applicability of social science in law, or assessing the superiority of rival humanistic conceptions, itself presupposes a sociology of legal processes and communications. But the arguments examined in this chapter do remind us of the extent to which disciplinary approaches impose as much as find the sense of what they interpret. If sociological interpretations are persuasive they may end up changing, for better or worse, what they set out to understand.

NOTES

1   These arguments also have important implications for the approach to legal education described in Britain and elsewhere as using the social and human sciences so as to put 'law in context'. Apart from the difficulty of separating text from context, this approach often only succeeds in getting law 'out of context', because any serious effort to examine law in its context would actually require us to show how and why law's reproduction requires it *not* to be aware of its context (cf. Nelken, 1990/93).

2   See, for example, Sarat and Kearns (1992b: 103–5) discussing the transformation of law's violence into legitimate force as a matter of language and rhetoric.

3   Garland, for example, in a highly influential re-examination of the sociology of punishment, stresses the need to study penality as a 'cultural text' which communicates meaning. He argues that punishment communicates 'not just about crime and punishment but also about power, authority, legitimacy, normality, morality, personhood, social relations, and a host of other tangential matters' (Garland, 1990: 152).

4   Thus Cotterrell (in this volume) describes how 'constitutional thought evokes, reinforces or proclaims certain cultural characteristics of that society'.

5   See, for example, the importance given to literary approaches by Scheppele in her recent review of legal and social theory for the *Annual Review of Sociology* (1994).

6   For elaboration of the distinction between 'instrumental' and 'constitutive' theories of law, see Sarat and Kearns (1993b). Marcus suggests that we think about everyday life 'not literally as "the social" that the law penetrates, but rather as the main figure or trope that constructs the essence of the social in the imagination of overlapping sociological and legal discourses' (Marcus, 1993: 242–3).

7   I shall concentrate mainly on White's *Justice as Translation* (1990) which is widely seen as summarizing most of the points made in earlier works, such as White (1973, 1984, 1985, 1994).

8   The artificial juxtaposition of arguments taken from Cotterrell and Boyd White which I offer in this chapter is justified only for present purposes. The writings of Cotterrell I draw on are not concerned with the arguments of the 'law and literature' school. Likewise, as explained in Chapter 1, Boyd White, like other members of the 'law and literature' movement, is less interested in spelling out conceptual arguments for or against the usefulness of sociology of law than in offering us new ways of experiencing and engaging with legal texts.

9   White says he wants to resist 'the impulse, quite common in our culture, to see the law from the outside as a kind of intellectual and social bureaucracy; rather I am interested in seeing it from the inside, as it appears to one who is practicing or teaching it' (White, 1994: 29).

126   *Law as Communication*

REFERENCES

Brown, R.H. (1987), *Society as Text: Essays in Rhetoric, Reason and Reality*, Chicago, University of Chicago Press.

Cain, M. (1995), 'Horatio's Mistake: Notes on Some Spaces in an Old Text', *Journal of Law and Society*, **22**, 68.

Clifford, J. (1988), *The Predicament of Culture: Twentieth Century Ethnography, Literature and Art*, Cambridge, Mass., Harvard University Press.

Clifford, J. and G. Marcus (1986), *Writing Culture: The Poetics and Politics of Ethnography*, Berkeley, University of California Press.

Cole, D. (1988), 'Against Literalism', *Stanford Law Review*, **40**, 545.

Cotterrell, R. (1986), 'Law and Sociology', *Journal of Law and Society*, **13**, 9.

Cotterrell, R. (1992), *The Sociology of Law*, 2nd edn, London, Butterworths.

Cotterrell, R. (1993), 'Sociological perspectives on legal closure', in A. Norrie (ed.), *Closure or Critique: New Directions in Legal Theory*, Edinburgh, Edinburgh University Press, 175–93.

Deflem, M. (ed.) (1994), *Special Issue: Habermas, Modernity and the Law: Philosophy and Social Criticism*, **20**, (4).

Douzinas, C. and R. Warrington (1990), *Postmodern Jurisprudence*, London, Routledge.

Douzinas, C. and R. Warrington (1994), *Justice Miscarried: Ethics, Aesthetics and the Law*, London, Harvester Wheatsheaf.

Dworkin, R. (1986), *Law's Empire*, London, Fontana.

Fish, S. (1980), *Is there a Text in this Class? The Authority of Interpretive Communities*, Cambridge, Mass., Harvard University Press.

Fish, S. (1989), *Doing What Comes Naturally: Change, Rhetoric and the Practice of Theory in Literature and Legal Studies*, Oxford, Clarendon Press.

Fish, S. (1991), 'The Law Wishes to Have a Formal Existence', in A. Sarat and T. Kearns (eds), *The Fate of Law*, Ann Arbor, University of Michigan Press, 159–209.

Friedman, L. (1994), 'Is there a Modern Legal Culture', *Ratio Juris*, **7**, (2), 117–32.

Garland, D. (1990), *Punishment and Modern Society*, Oxford, Oxford University Press.

Geertz, C. (1983), *Local Knowledge: Further Essays in Interpretive Anthropology*, New York, Basic Books.

Gordon, R. (1984), 'Critical Legal Histories', *Stanford Law Review*, **36**.

Grace, C. and P. Wilkinson (1979), *Legal Phenomena and Sociological Theory*, London, Macmillan.

Graff, G. (1982), '"Keep of the Grass", "Drop dead" and other indeterminacies: A response to Sanford Levinson', *Texas Law Review*, **60**, 405.

Hunt, A. (1993), *The Constitutive Theory of Law*, London, Routledge.

Josipovici, G. (1990), *The Book of God*, New Haven, Yale University Press.

Lempert, R. and J. Sanders (1986), *An Invitation to Law and Social Science*, London, Longman.

Lenoble, J. (1994), *Droit et Communication*, Paris, Editions du Cerf.

Levinson, S. (1982), 'Law as Literature', *Texas Law Review*, **60**, 373–403.

Luban, D. (1989), 'Difference made legal; The court and Mr King', *Michigan Law Review*, **87**, 2152.

Luhmann, N. (1985), *A Sociological Theory of Law*, London, Routledge.

Mann, S. (1989), 'The Universe and the Library: A Critique of James Boyd White as Writer and Reader', *Stanford Law Review*, **41**, 959.

Marcus, G. (1993), 'Mass toxic torts and the end of everyday life', in A. Sarat and T.R. Kearns (eds), *Law and Everyday Life*, Ann Arbor, University of Michigan Press, 237–74.

Massaro, T. (1989), 'Empathy, legal storytelling and the rule of law: New words, old wounds', *Michigan Law Review*, **87**, 2099.

Mumby, D. (ed.) (1993), *Narrative as Social Control*, London, Sage.

Nelken, D. (1981), 'The "Gap Problem" in the Sociology of Law: A Theoretical Review', *Windsor Yearbook of Access to Justice*, 35–62.

Nelken, D. (1983), *The Limits of the Legal Process: A Study of Landlords, Law and Crime*, London, Academic Press.

Nelken, D. (1985), 'Legislation and its Constraints: A Case-Study of the British 1965 Rent Act', in D. Khosla, C. Whelan and A. Podgorecki (eds), *Legal Systems and Social Systems*, London: Croom Helm, 70–87.

Nelken, D. (1986), 'Beyond the Study of "Law and Society": A Review Essay', *American Bar Foundation Journal*, 323–38.

Nelken, D. (1987a), 'Criminal Law and Criminal Justice: Some Notes on their Irrelation' in Ian Dennis (ed.), *Criminal Law and Justice*, Sweet & Maxwell, 139–77.

Nelken, D. (1987b), 'Changing Paradigms in the Sociology of Law', in G. Teubner (ed.), *Autopoietic Law: A New Approach to Law and Society*, Berlin, De Gruyter, 191–217.

Nelken, D. (1990/1993), *The Truth about Law's Truth*, E.U.I. Working Paper, E.U.I. Law Department, Florence, 1990, reprinted in A. Febbrajo and D. Nelken (eds), *European Yearbook of Sociology of Law*, 1993, Milan, Giuffrè, 87–163.

Nelken, D. (1994), 'Reflexive Criminology?', in D. Nelken (ed.), *The Futures of Criminology*, London, Sage, 7–42.

Pennisi, C. (1991), *La Costruzione Sociologica del Fenomeno Giuridico*, Milan, Giuffrè.

Posner, R. (1988), *Law and Literature: A Misunderstood Relation*, Cambridge, Mass., Harvard University Press.

Posner, R. (1990), *The Problems of Jurisprudence*, Cambridge, Mass., Harvard University Press.

Rabinow, P. and W. Sullivan (eds) (1979), *Interpretive Social Science: A Reader*, Berkeley, California University Press.

Sarat, A. and T.R. Kearns (eds) (1991), *The Fate of Law*, Ann Arbor, University of Michigan Press.

Sarat, A. and T.R. Kearns (eds) (1992a), *Law's Violence*, Ann Arbor, University of Michigan Press.

Sarat, A. and T.R. Kearns (1992b), 'A journey through forgetting: toward a juris-

128   *Law as Communication*

prudence of violence', in A. Sarat and T.R. Kearns (eds), *Law's Violence*, Ann Arbor, University of Michigan Press.

Sarat, A. and T.R. Kearns (eds) (1993a), *Law in Everyday Life*, Ann Arbor, University of Michigan Press.

Sarat, A. and T.R. Kearns (1993b), 'Beyond the Great Divide: Forms of Legal Scholarship and Everyday Life', in A. Sarat and T.R. Kearns (eds), *Law in Everyday Life*, 21–63.

Sarat, A. and T.R. Kearns (eds) (1994), *The Rhetoric of Law*, Ann Arbor, University of Michigan Press.

Scheppele, K. (1994), 'Legal Theory and Social Theory', *Annual Review of Sociology*, **20**, 383–406.

Sherwin, K. (1988), 'A matter of voice and plot. Belief and suspicion in legal storytelling', *Michigan Law Review*, **87**, 543.

Simon, J. (1994), 'Between Power and Knowledge: Habermas, Foucault and the Future of Legal Studies', *Law and Society Review*, **28**, (4), 947–61.

Simons, H. (1989), *Rhetoric in the Human Sciences*, London, Sage.

Somers, M. (1994), 'The narrative constitution of identity: a relational and network approach', *Theory and Society*, **23**, 605–49.

Teubner, G. (ed.) (1988), *Autopoietic Law: A New Approach to Law and Society*, Berlin, De Gruyter.

Teubner, G. (1989), 'How the Law Thinks: Towards a Constructivist Epistemology of Law', *Law and Society Review*, **23**, (5), 727–56.

Teubner, G. (1993), *Law as an Autopoietic System*, Oxford, Blackwell.

Texas Law Review (1993), 'Note: Reading Literature/Reading Law: Is there a Literary Jurisprudence?', **72**, 132.

Thurschwell, A. (1994), 'Reading the Law', in A. Sarat and T.R. Kearns (eds), *The Rhetoric of Law*, Ann Arbor, University of Michigan Press, 275–332.

Trubek, D. (1984), 'Where the Action is: Critical Legal Studies and Empiricism', *Stanford Law Review*, **36**, 575.

Trubek, D. (1990), 'Back to the Future: The Short Happy Life of The Law and Society Movement', *Florida State University Law Review*, **18**, 1.

Weisberg, R. (1992), *Poethics and Other Strategies of Law and Literature*, New York, Columbia University Press.

White, J. Boyd (1973), *The Legal Imagination*, Chicago, University of Chicago Press.

White, J. Boyd (1984), *When Words Lose their Meaning*, Chicago, University of Chicago Press.

White, J. Boyd (1985), *Heracles' Bow*, Madison, University of Wisconsin Press.

White, J. Boyd (1990), *Justice as Translation*, Chicago, University of Chicago Press.

White, J. Boyd (1994), 'Imagining the Law', in A. Sarat and T.R. Kearns (eds), *The Rhetoric of Law*, Ann Arbor, University of Michigan Press, 29–55.

Winn, P. (1991), 'Legal Ritual', *Law and Critique*, **11**, (2), 207.

Woolgar, S. (ed.) (1988), *Knowledge and Reflexivity*, London, Sage.

Yoshino, K. (1994), 'What's Past is Prologue: Precedent in Literature and Law', *Yale Law Journal*, **104**, (2), 471.

[12]
Blinding Insights?
The Limits of a
Reflexive Sociology of Law

Is there a danger that sociological approaches to law end up creating law in their own image? Can they set their own limits? Could they help further rather than hinder the process by which law becomes more technocratic? Continuing a debate with Roger Cotterrell, this paper offers an examination of Cotterrell's suggestion, in the last issue, that these dangers can be avoided provided that sociological interpretation of legal ideas recognizes an allegiance to law rather than to academic sociology. By contrast, I propose a reflexive strategy intended to invite sociology to examine the ways in which its discourses and practices are both similar to but also different from those of law.

'Sociology was born in a state of hostility to law.'

N.S. Timashev

'A little sociology leads away from the law, much sociology leads back to it.'

M. Hauriou

What is law for sociology? And what is sociology to law? Above all, what is sociology of law – and more generally any other study of 'law and' – good for? From its emergence as a topic of academic enquiry there has been division and sometimes competition between those approaches to the sociological understanding of law whose main aim is to reveal what law is unable (or unwilling) to see, and those whose goal is to help law see more clearly. The first approach relates law to its wider historical and social environment, and to competing and overlapping disciplines and practices, and has little difficulty in showing how legal actors often have little grasp

I should like to thank my friend Roger Cotterrell for providing me with a pre-publication draft of his paper in the last issue and encouraging the continuation in these pages of the many stimulating discussions we used to have as fellow teachers on the London University LLM Law and Social Theory course.

David Nelken

of the factors which shape the 'inputs' and 'outcomes' of their decisions. The second presupposes most of these constraints and seeks to improve the quality of decision making in terms which can be used by legal actors. Where the first type of scholarship deliberately transforms legal definitions into sociological categories[1] the second seeks to translate sociological insights into legal concepts.[2]

How do these approaches relate? Is there a way of combining them? More precisely, how far can the methods useful for showing the limits of law's sociological understanding of the world also be used for helping law to overcome those limits? Whereas we should expect there to be much common ground[3] there have always also been scholars who have argued that a synthesis is neither possible nor desirable. Typically the concern of many sociologists of law has been that the 'pull of the policy audience',[4] or the limitations of practical decision making in legal settings, would compromise the proper development of academic social science or blunt the edge of political critique. But there is also an opposite worry – and it is this which will be my topic in this paper. Here the charge is that the introduction of different styles of reasoning can have ill effects for legal practice by misunderstanding and thus threatening the integrity of legal processes or the values they embody.[5] In particular, the introduction of 'social scientism' will either succeed all too easily in making law more of a policy science than is really good for it, as is claimed by many adhering to the 'law and literature' movement,[6] or else, even in failing, will produce a 'hybrid' monstrosity which is neither law or social science, as asserted by autopoieticists such as Gunther Teubner.[7]

1 All the major textbooks, including Roger Cotterrell's magisterial synthesis of the field, reconceptualize legal phenomena in terms of issues such as social order, social control, regulation, dispute processing, governmentality, desert, distribution, power, symbolism, ideology, or rationality, rather than the doctrinal definitions of lawyers or administrative categories.

2 This classification is put forward by John Monahan and Laurens Walker in their leading United States casebook, *Social Science in Law* (1994): 'we here view social science as an analytic tool in the law, familiarity with which will heighten the lawyer's professional effectiveness and sharpen the legal scholar's insights. The principal alternative to the insider perspective on the relation of social science to law is the "law and society" or sociology of law approach which seeks to understand the functioning of law as a social system.' Variations on this distinction are captured in other classifications such as sociology of law versus sociolegal studies, 'law and society' versus sociological jurisprudence, and so on.

3 This is occupied in Britain by the deliberately ecumenical socio-legal association, or the 'law in context' series of textbooks which is dedicated to 'broadening the study of law from within'.

4 A. Sarat and S. Silbey, 'The Pull of the Policy Audience' (1988) 10 *Law and Policy* 97.

5 L. Tribe, 'Trial by Mathematics: Precision and Ritual in the Legal Process' (1971) 84 *Harvard Law Rev.* 1329; M. Constable, *The Law of the Other* (1994); D. Nelken 'A just measure of science' in *Science at Court*, eds. M. Freeman and H. Reece (1998).

6 See, for example, J. Boyd White, *When Words Lose their Meaning* (1984).

7 G. Teubner, 'How the Law Thinks: Toward a Constructivist Epistemology of Law' (1989) 23 *Law and Society Rev.* 727; when law 'enslaves' science it produces hybrid creatures having 'unclear epistemic status and unknown social consequences'.

This type of warning is likely to seem a distraction (or worse) in the midst of the continuing struggle by socio-legal scholars to broaden and open out legal education in opposition to 'black-letter' methods of imparting legal doctrine, and an often politically conservative refusal to see the social embeddedness or implications of the legal.[8] But though awkward to deal with, the questions raised are important ones. There are lots of good reasons to encourage students and practitioners to think about law with the help of other disciplinary perspectives. But is it going too far to call law 'a parasitic discipline'?[9] As I have asked elsewhere, does this carry the implication that law should open up ever further to the findings and methods of other disciplines? (and what if different disciplines pull in different directions)? Is there any point at which this process should stop?[10] If every way of seeing, as Kenneth Burke put it, is also a way of non-seeing, must this not also apply to sociology itself? Could sociology of law thus be blinded by its own insights?[11] Might the attempt to use sociological interpretations to help law become more reflexive threaten important features of law's way of acting in the world? If it is increasingly law's difficult task to resist the spread of merely technocratic decision making, is a sociological approach to law part of the problem or part of the solution?[12]

It is with these questions in mind that I want to respond to a characteristically lucid and profound paper by Roger Cotterrell in the last issue of this journal,[13] which, in part, deals with previous ways on which I have tried to focus on such issues.[14] Cotterrell insists on the centrality of sociology of law for legal education and legal practice. Legal ideas, he says, *must* be interpreted through employing social insights because this allows 'the deliberate extension in carefully specified directions of the diverse ways in which legal participants themselves think about the social world in legal terms'[15] and is a 'necessary means of broadening legal understanding taken as the systematic and empirical understanding of a certain aspect of social life which is recognized as "legal".'[16] But this forthright reply does not mean that he is insensitive to the danger that, in trying to understand law better than it understands itself, sociological interpretation could end up creating law in its own image. Quite the contrary. Cotterrell insists that we adopt a sociological approach

8 See the papers in A. Bradney and F. Cownie (eds.), *Transformative Visions of Legal Education* (1998), also published as special issue (1998) 25 *J. of Law and Society.*

9 The title of Bradney's paper in the above collection.

10 D. Nelken, 'Getting the Law "out of Context"' (1996) 19 *Socio-Legal Newsletter* 12.

11 Sociologists have no difficulty in accepting that the economic approach to law runs such risks but have not applied the argument to themselves

12 See S. Jasanoff, *Science at the Bar* (1995); Nelken, op. cit., n. 5.

13 R. Cotterrell, 'Why Must Legal Ideas be Interpreted Sociologically?' (1998) 25 *J. of Law and Society* 171.

14 D. Nelken, 'Can there be a sociology of legal meaning?' in *Law as Communication*, ed. D. Nelken (1996) 107.

15 Cotterrell, op. cit., n. 13, p. 190.

16 id., p. 191.

which does not in fact involve any such imposition on law of what he calls an 'alien or colonizing methodology'.[17] His 'transdisciplinary' conception of the sociology of law is one in which 'the use of the word sociological does not imply adherence to the distinct methods, theories or outlook of the academic discipline called sociology' or that of 'any other specific social science or other discipline'.[18] For him, 'if sociological inquiries about law have an intellectual or moral allegiance then this is to law itself'.[19]

In so disposing of what he at times calls a 'false problem' Cotterrell, it seems to me, risks creating new ones. What is to be the shape of this kind of sociology of law? Has he really succeeded in showing that law *must* be interpreted sociologically, and what is the force of this *must*? Can he even make such a claim within the terms of his discipline or, to take him at his own word, has he handed over the power to make this decision to broader legal discourses? Although he does not say so in so many words, Cotterrell's arguments could be taken as an attempt to justify and revive what used to be called 'sociological jurisprudence'. Where once the boast of social studies of law was the proud (if never fully explicated) slogan that 'law is a social science', we are now told that if sociology of law has any allegiance, it is to law itself.

Is all this a step forward or backward? In examining Cotterrell's arguments I shall both seek to place them within the scheme of overall changes in the development of his thinking and to contrast his proposals for the future direction of the field with my own somewhat different reflexive strategy. As against Cotterrell's recommendation to loosen sociology of law from its disciplinary moorings, I shall argue that the attempt to deploy social insights so as to help law's reflexivity requires us to pay *more* rather than less attention to their disciplinary and discursive connections. I shall discuss in turn sociology of law's role as a sub-discipline of sociology, the need to theorize the relationship between sociology and law, and the dilemmas of integrating academic theorizing into social practices such as legal decision making.

THE STRENGTH OF WEAK TIES?

In a recent retrospective of his own work, Cotterrell explains that when he first 'nailed his flag to the mast of social science' his goal was to discover 'new', more 'objective' and 'realistic' ways of observing and interpreting law.[20] However later on he came to advocate a 'critical, analytical view of the scientific quest itself and a reflexive attitude to the faith in science on

---

17 id.
18 id., p. 182.
19 id., p. 187. Since he goes on to say that this allegiance is to enriching the perspectives of participants in legal processes, it could be said that sociology actually retains allegiance to itself.
20 R. Cotterrell, *Law's Community* (1995) 15 ff.

which it is founded',[21] in particular, rejecting the boundaries of sociology as a limit to the aspirations of social studies of law. Increasingly concerned 'to go beyond attempts to justify a particular vision of science', his current work is thus less motivated by the search for 'a scientific means of revealing facets of law often hidden from sight',[22] and more by the desire to formulate a coherent 'moral vision' with the help of which law can and must be made to serve new social purposes.[23]

Work in the first stage, up to and including the first edition of his textbook, rests on the premise that 'the aim of empirical legal theory (is) that law is always viewed "from the outside" from the perspective of an observer of legal institutions, doctrines and behaviour, rather than that of a partic-ipant'.[24] In what is still the mainstream rationale of the subject, sociology's strength is here seen a function of law's weakness: 'sociological analysis of law has as its sole unifying objective the attempt to remedy the assumed inadequacy of lawyer's doctrinal analysis of law'. As Tamanaha notes, legal doctrine is here seen as inadequate in two senses: that there is more to know about law in society than can be found in legal doctrine alone; and secondly, and more controversially, that legal doctrine mystifies reality so that legal and other actors do not understand their own activities.[25]

In the second stage of his thinking (from around 1986), Cotterrell began to focus on the problem that academic sociology might itself be subject to limits. He envisaged sociology and law as different discourses, each with its own conditions of existence, in which 'each constructs its own fields of knowledge and experience'.[26] But he nevertheless finds an ingenious argu-ment to show why sociology can still provide a privileged route to under-standing law because it is dedicated to a *reflexive* perspective on the development of disciplines – including itself. Law, by contrast, lacking this interest, is no more than a 'discipline-effect'.[27] Thus, 'paradoxically', it is sociology's weakness which constitutes its strength. Sociology's weakness is shown by the fact that it has not managed to become a successful form of power/knowledge, that it is contested both by general common sense and

21 id., p. 16.
22 id.
23 See, for example, R. Cotterrell, 'Law and Community: A New Relationship' (1998) *Current Legal Problems* forthcoming.
24 R. Cotterrell, 'The sociological concept of law' (1983) 10 *Brit. J. of Law and Society* 241, at 242. This does not exclude, says Cotterrell, exploring the perspectives of insiders as long as it is clear that it is not the role of the sociologists to take on their perspective.
25 B. Tamanaha, *Realistic Socio-legal Theory* (1997) 191. Tamanaha criticizes Cotterrell, argu-ing that he and other sociologists of law soon became 'insiders' because 'the self-reflective quality of theoretical practices have a relentless ability to absorb whatever begins as external to the practice when first introduced'. This is now apparently also Cotterrell's view. I would be less certain that most legal discourses count 'as theoretical practices'.
26 R. Cotterrell, 'Law and Sociology' (1986) 13 *J. of Law and Society* 11.
27 Cotterrell, op. cit., n. 20, p. 109. I am much in sympathy with this approach, except for the important difference that I do not assume that reflexivity can save sociology from reproduc-ing itself rather than law.

by more specialized disciplines, and that its lack of rigorousness makes it an 'easy target for intellectual sharpshooters'.[28] But rather than any of this constituting an impediment, it is exactly these weaknesses which allow the sociological imagination to play such a positive role in shaping legal discourse. In fact, as he argues now, through this most 'practical'[29] view of legal ideas, sociological insights can help legal discourses reach interpretative solutions to puzzles which would otherwise be impossible to resolve.

Cotterrell's recent paper contains some novel arguments, in particular, regarding the commensurability of legal discourses and sociological methods and the utility of sociological insights in legal processes. But it is best understood as the strongest statement yet of his new-found conviction that the social study of law can contribute most to the understanding of law by weakening its own ties to sociology.

Is this new account useful as a description or even as an aspiration for anything which could plausibly still be described as sociology of law? Cotterrell is not greatly concerned about this label. But a more important difficulty that is raised is the basis for defining what count as sociological insights (since Cotterrell speaks of gathering them wherever they may be found) and how to measure success in understanding the social aspects of law once we have broken free of 'any particular academic discipline'.[30] Reflexivity in the sense of self-criticism, the recognition that truths are partial and that there is still far to go, will not be enough to establish if any progress is being made.

But, in any case, it is not so easy to become un-disciplined. The 'paradox' of sociology's weakness constituting its strength means that it is not even that clear whether in what he now prefers to call 'a sociological perspective on legal theory' Cotterrell is really asking us to abandon sociology or still seeking to make ever stronger claims on its behalf. It would indeed be paradoxical if the author of the leading British textbook in the sub-discipline, a textbook actually criticized for being over-concerned with professional sociological respectability,[31] turned his back on all that he had achieved.[32] In fact, Cotterrell continues to make explicit reference to the sociological perspective and to mobilize a working idea of what constitutes social insight which is firmly situated within the boundaries of academic sociology. Many times his argument comes close to the near tautology of

---

28 id., pp. 65 ff.
29 Cotterrell, op. cit., n. 13, p. 178.
30 id., p. 177.
31 S.S. Silbey, 'Loyalty and Betrayal: Cotterrell's Discovery and Reproduction of Legal Ideology' (1991) 16 *Law and Social Inquiry* 80.
32 Near the beginning of his recent article (op. cit., n. 13), Cotterrell says that existing types of sociological studies of the 'law in action' remain of central importance. Apparently we are not forced to choose between the approaches represented by the two stages of his thinking despite their different implicit assessments of sociology's disciplinary strengths or their different ideas of appropriate methodologies for producing social insight.

claiming that only sociology can satisfactorily explain the way law is constituted by and reconstitutes social ideas, even though the larger case he is advancing is that it is legal discourses *as such* which are and must be concerned with such insights when deciding cases or otherwise intervening in social life.[33] Other disciplinary approaches, such as law and literature, are swiftly, and not entirely convincingly, despatched as self-evidently poor competitors to sociology,[34] just as he has criticized other recent approaches to legal discourse for being insufficiently concrete about the specifics of place, authors, and empirical evidence.[35] Most significant, his arguments in favour of law's need for social insight often rely exactly on the external understanding of law produced by disciplinary protocols rather than partic-ipants' experiences; thus he rejects Dworkin's idea of law as an ongoing conversation about integrity because, he argues, justice must primarily be treated as the result of a discussion shaped by the constraints of power.[36] Nor is his call for sociology of law to swear intellectual allegiance to law assumed to be in any way inconsistent with a continuing requirement to 'radically extend' lawyers' views[37] or to 'transform legal ideas by reinter-preting them'.[38]

My reservations about some aspects of the way Cotterrell has reformu-lated the task of a social study of law must, however, be understood against the background of overwhelming agreement with most of what he is trying to do (indeed, he generously cites some of my recent work). I also worry about the dangers of false dichotomies such as that between merely 'taking problems' as defined by law or policy makers and 'making problems' to fit an academic discipline.[39] I too am convinced that sociology of 'law' needs to deal with legal doctrine and not limit itself to providing a 'sociology of courts and lawyers', and I have used the overworked phrase 'changing paradigms' to point to new developments capable of redirecting studies into law and society.[40] Like Cotterrell, and at about the same time, I concluded that legal and sociological discourses needed to be

---

33 Cotterrell, op. cit., n. 13, pp. 177, 181. He avoids tautology by asserting that sociology can also help legal discourses to extend and systematize their implicit social insights. But this begs the question why they need to go in this rather than another direction.

34 id., p. 183.

35 R. Cotterrell, *The Sociology of Law* (1992, 2nd ed.) at 308–9.

36 Cotterrell, op. cit., n. 13, pp. 180–1.

37 id., p. 191.

38 id., p. 190.

39 D. Nelken. 'The "Gap Problem" in the Sociology of Law: A Theoretical Review' in *Windsor Yearbook of Access to Justice* (1981) 35; and 'Law in Action or Living Law? Back to the Beginning in Sociology of Law' (1984) 4 *Legal Studies* 152.

40 D. Nelken, 'Beyond the Study of Law and Society' (1986) *Am. Bar Foundation J.* 323; and 'Changing Paradigms in the Sociology of Law' in *Autopoietic Law: A New Approach to Law and Society*, ed. G. Teubner (1987) 191.

confronted.[41] We both think that the notion of reflexivity may be the key to further progress in understanding the relationship between law and sociology, but are cautious about embracing autopoietic ideas of self-referential recursivity.

Yet it is over the question of reflexivity where we also most differ (at least in terms of what we now choose to emphasize). Cotterrell increasingly stresses the need to free social insights from the limits of academic sociology so as to help law reflexively overcome its blind spots; I think we should worry just as much about how to further sociology's own reflexivity.[42] The programme I have proposed for what I call the second generation of 'law in context' work is, therefore:

> to seek an account of law which contextualises the bounded and practical rationalities of legal and other actors and the process of legal reproduction *without assuming that they could or should have adopted the place, point of view or practice of the discipline which produces this account.* Even for social scientists, law's lack of awareness, or selective awareness of its context, must be treated as an intrinsic, if changing, feature of its social reproduction, rather than as simply the origin of corrigible errors to be excised by the expert or political activist.[43]

In the rest of this paper I shall therefore try to clarify what may be at stake in these different ways to employ the idea of reflexivity. Deliberately oversimplifying, we could say that where Cotterrell presently seeks the aim of increasing legal reflexivity by requiring sociology to go beyond its limits as an academic subject, I suggest that sociology of law should try better to understand its limits as a way of seeing. Where he argues that sociology has the capacity to transform legal discourses despite their claims to autonomy, I am more interested in noting the way law (necessarily) transforms other discourses. Finally (and as a consequence) we disagree over how easy it is to use 'social insights' in deciding what solutions are appropriate in legal disputes.

SUBVERTING THE DISCIPLINE

Many writers think that the task of sociology of law is simply to concern itself with larger sociological issues such as social order, social action

---

41 D. Nelken 'Criminal law and criminal justice; some notes on their irrelation' in *Criminal law and Justice*, ed. I. H. Dennis (1987) 139. I first came to see the need to give attention to what I called 'irrelation' as I reviewed the difficulties of synthesizing insights about crime and criminal justice into criminal law. I have tried to produce more wide-ranging analyses (in D. Nelken, 'The truth about Law's Truth' in *European Yearbook for the Sociology of Law*, eds. A. Febbrajo and D. Nelken (1990) 87–163; 'The Loneliness of Law's Meta-Theory' in *Plural Legalities: Critical Legal Studies in Europe*, eds. R.de Lange and K. Raes (1991) 172; 'Are disputes between Law and Science resolvable?' in *Proceedings of the Bologna International Conference on Sociology of Law*, ed. V. Ferrari (1991); Nelken, op. cit., n. 10; and Nelken, op. cit., n. 5.
42 For a fuller discussion of five kinds of reflexivity, see D. Nelken, 'Reflexive Criminology?' in *The Futures of Criminology*, ed. D. Nelken (1994) 7.
43 Nelken, op. cit., n. 10.

or social change, avoiding a non-sociological concern with 'relevance'.[44] Cotterrell, as we have seen, increasingly argues that the social study of law needs to break the hold of academic sociology. I too have argued that unreflexive dedication to sociology could end up making us lose touch with what is distinctive about law – all the more so if law sees itself as more central to social order than sociology would make it appear.[45] But if we are to bring sociology of law up against its limits, we still have to recognize, rather than simply deny, its dependence on sociology. Much of the work on 'courts and lawyers' in the United States-inspired 'Law and Society' tradition – and much of that synthesized in Cotterrell's textbook, despite his declared commitment to a definition of law as 'institutionalized doctrine' – does in fact often assimilate the study of law to the approaches used in other sociological sub-disciplines such as the sociology of organizations or professions. And it is this which gives a basis to the accusation by some critics that sociology tends to treat law as a type of policy science.

If we are to build a reflexive sociology of law there may therefore be more to be gained from comparing its problems to some of those posed in other sub-disciplines, all of which might belong with Gurvitch's classification of the sociology of law as part of 'the sociology of the human spirit',[46] like the sociology of religion, the sociology of art, the sociology of knowledge, and the sociology of science. Internal developments in these sub-disciplines have much in common with sociology of law as a result of wider intellectual/political developments and fashions in and outside sociology. Thus, the sociology of science has had to face a challenge to the established Mertonian school which focuses on the social organization of science and of scientists and the way science is shaped by and shapes the wider society; instead, critics argued, it was necessary to ask what is science and how its credibility is accomplished.

Closer examination of these other sub-disciplines soon shows that what are sometimes presented as unique problems of sociology of law are also found in these other subjects. Each can claim – with good reason – to be concerned with more than one relatively distinct sector of social life.[47] Albeit for different reasons, law, science, religion, and art all claim to have some 'autonomous' features which are not reducible simply to 'the social'.[48] In various ways each also faces the issue of constituting or dissolving the distinction between subject and object (and 'society' and 'sociology' more

44 A particularly strongly argued version of this view is C. Grace and P. Wilkinson, *Sociological Inquiry and Legal Phenomena* (1978). Sociology of law here has much in common with other sub-disciplines caught in the tensions of a relationship between theoretical and applied knowledge such as sociology of medicine, sociology of industry, sociology of the family or the sociology of education.

45 I owe this point to my colleague Carlo Pennisi

46 G. Gurvitch, *Sociology of Law* (1947).

47 Religion is 'at the core of all understanding of social cohesion and much social change' (M. Hill, *The Sociology of Religion* (1973) vii).

48 'The appearance of autonomy is essential to the work of art' (A. Hauser, *The sociology of art*, tr. K.J. Northcott (1982) 317).

generally).[49] All have to face the question of their capacity to interpret other discourses and the danger of transforming the very object of study.[50]

Unlike current writing in the sociology of law,[51] work in the sociology of religion, for example, openly struggles with the question 'is the sociology of religion possible?'[52] or more specific puzzles such as how can the sacred be grasped, or why do believers apparently believe untrue propositions?[53] The familiar question whether you have to be a participant or should rather take a stance of 'methodological atheism', is also central. As Yinger puts it, 'can you see a stained glass window from the outside?'[54] The advantages of an external approach are that we are not distracted by the total effect and can see the construction of the window better. But, at the same time, we may in this way fail to understand the experience of those on the inside.

To avoid misunderstanding I should stress that I am not suggesting that sociology of law should simply be *equated* with any of these other sub-disciplines, nor that it should just borrow its ideas from them; differences between the objects of these sub-disciplines may be as important as similarities. But paying more attention to the way sociology deals with other areas of culture may still yield important lessons. There is, for example, an all-too-familiar division within the sociology of religion between those who describe themselves as pursuing religious sociology and the scientific sociology of religion (and some evidence that this does lead to different ways of pursuing the discipline). But it has not been suggested that the correct measure of a sociologist of religion's ability to understand the sacred should be the extent to which she is able to influence religious developments.

If anything, it is Cotterrell himself who at times seems to be advocating that we abandon sociology of law for the sociology of (legal) knowledge as a sort of 'ideology critique'. If so, we would need to ask hard questions about the limits of the sort of sociology of knowledge advocated by Karl Mannheim (which seems to shape Cotterrell's approach). The idea of reflexivity is, of course, all-important to Mannheim because he needs to be able to justify his claim to be able to deconstruct other people's ideologies. For Mannheim, intellectuals were able to take a more comprehensive – and thus privileged – view of social life because of their marginal place in the class structure and their (alleged) relative immunity to the utopianism, conformism, and ethnocentrism of common sense. But what if these intellectual vices are essential components of the vision which animates legal practice? What implications does this have for ideology critique and the incorporation of social insights

49 'The concepts of science and society collapse into each other' (S. Woolgar, *Science: the very idea* (1988) 13).
50 Thus Hauser, op. cit., n. 48, asks if there can be objectivization of the subjective experience of art.
51 For an exception, see P. Winn, 'Legal Ritual' (1991) 11 *Law and Critique* 207.
52 Hill, op. cit., n. 47, p. 4.
53 P. Hamilton, *The Sociology of Religion: Theoretical and Comparative perspectives* (1995) 6.
54 J.M. Yinger, *The Sociological Study of Religion* (1970) 2.

into law? Things have also moved on since Mannheim. The so-called strong programme in science[55] tries to show that *both* 'true' and 'false' scientific discoveries are symmetrically subject to social conditioning. By contrast, in the sociology of law and in critical legal studies, attempts are still being made to delegitimize those legal institutions or laws that are politically disliked merely on the basis that they are socially conditioned.

LEGAL CLOSURE AND SOCIOLOGICAL REFLEXIVITY: A NEW AGENDA

If sociology of law is (necessarily) tied to sociology as a discipline we therefore need to examine more carefully how its reflexivity and that of law relate. Cotterrell attacks this problem by arguing that dichotomies such as that between 'internal' and 'external' approaches to law need to be transcended. Because law (understood sociologically) is *social, systematic,* and *empirical,* it is readily assimilable to sociology. As others have argued, law was a sort of proto-sociology, just as sociological insights are the 'ghosts of jurisprudence past'. Cotterrell praises the adoption of social insights because they make it possible 'to systematize law's perspective beyond the needs of particular participants'[56] in the legal process. But the suspicion remains that the criterion he is using is more appropriate to sociology than law. While science may progress in this way, why should an ever 'broader' view necessarily help law? It may be going too far to say that there are never 'broader' but only 'different' interpretative strategies.[57] But it is certainly plausible to claim that law needs to concentrate in its own way on individual cases in all their particularity.

How far will Cotterrell's account of the continuity between law and sociology get us? Even if we concede, for argument's sake, that legal discourses are all social, systematic, and empirical, this would not guarantee a smooth matching of the discourses of law and sociology.[58] We should note, further, that what this characterization leaves out – for example, the idea of law as also a hermeneutical search for correct and coherent textual meaning – could be even more significant for any discussion of the commensurability of these discourses. Most fundamentally, however, it would be unwise to assume that law is – by definition – concerned with systematic, empirical knowledge of the social world. Surely this is exactly what is in question, It is the *variability* in the extent to which legal discourses (or legal systems) express these features which distinguish them from sociology – and it is the study of this variability

55 See, for example, D. Bloor, *Knowledge and Social Imagery* (1976).
56 Cotterrell, op. cit., n. 13, p. 191.
57 S. Fish, *Doing what Comes Naturally* (1989).
58 After all, even within the social sciences, there are considerable differences between, say, psychology, history or economics, and we are far from the possibility of a unified interpretation of the social world.

which forms the subject matter of sociology.[59] Cotterrell admits all this and even explains that two of law's essential features can come into conflict because law (but presumably not sociology) is caught in the tension between systematic knowledge and 'the wilderness of single instances'. His argument that legal ideas must be interpreted sociologically thus presupposes but does not demonstrate that law must necessarily be interested in the *maximum* extent of systematic empirical knowledge of the social world. Moreover, it is the extent to which law does not correspond to this model which he himself relies on in explaining the need for sociology.

Perhaps the problem of sociology's commensurability with law (as I raised it) needs to be specified more carefully. It would be a fallacy to assume that sociology can only understand that which is similar to it. If that were so, there would be no possibility of developing, say, a sociology of sport or of literature. But becoming part of what is being studied is another matter altogether. The sociology of literature does not have to be literature, the sociology of ritual does not itself have to be a form of ritual, and so on. To argue that law 'maintains social solidarity' obviously does not mean that sociology itself has this function or can help in achieving it (arguably it could at times even be a threat). On the other hand, it is just because sociology *can* provide a sociological account of such a variety of phenomena that there is a real danger of taking the part for the whole and allowing sociology to create law or other objects in its own image. And the only prophylactic is for sociology to search as much as possible to provide insights regarding its *differences from*, as much as its similarities to, that which it is trying to understand. Cotterrell rightly cites Weber as an authority for the possibility of a sociology of legal ideas and doctrine (and not only a sociology of the 'law in action'). But it was Weber himself (and not just Kelsen) who insisted on the sharp difference between the sociological and juristic point of view,[60] a distinction which – significantly for our purposes – Weber based largely on the claim that the juridical view 'takes empirical validity for granted' and is not interested in what 'actually happens in a community'.

My main problem with Cotterrell's new arguments about encouraging legal reflexivity, however, have to do with his continuing focus on the idea of 'legal closure' as a self-serving ideological claim. His conception (like that of most mainstream sociologists of law) still seems too influenced by the zero-sum idea of 'relative autonomy', popular in the 1970s, as compared to

59 Is law 'wholly' concerned with the life of individuals in groups? What about those religious legal systems that purport to be concerned with regulating the relationship with the transcendental? The claim that law is empirical – because it deals with actual rather than idealized social conditions – is even more controversial. Some legal systems, and many single institutions, rules, and procedures, can be seen as describing, evoking or seeking to impose idealized conditions without necessarily tackling the empirical questions of how to realize or reconcile the ideals being celebrated. In his *Social Systems and Cultural Dynamics* (1937, 3 vols.), P. Sorokin explores the variablity of law when it forms part of ideational, sensate, and idealistic cultures.

60 M. Rheinstein, *Max Weber on Law in Economy and Society* (1966).

those approaches which concentrate on the way law incorporates and responds to outside factors as part of its own reproduction.[61] Put bluntly, legal practice (and, even more, legal scholarship) is certainly open to external inputs and it may even seek or require them. But what is important is what it does with or to them.

This starting point explains why Cotterrell treats internal-external, insider-outsider, observer and participant, and other similar distinctions as no more than powerful constructions intended to close law off as a more or less self contained world of thought and practice, even if he does also admit that these dichotomies do have more than ideological substance. Cotterrell cites me as supporting the proposition that the internal-external distinction is not to be taken seriously for sociological purposes because it is internal to the legal construction of the world.[62] But what I actually argued was that *each discourse* constructs 'inside' and 'outside', and so on, in its own way as an internal distinction, not that the distinction had no meaning. What followed, I claimed, was the necessity to model the relationship between law and sociology *in terms of two 'internal' points of view.*[63]

In contrast to the features of law which he identifies, Cotterrell argues that other supposed 'indicators' of law's truth: the legal/illegal code, its probabilistic and particularistic logic in adjudication, its resort to cut-off points, its presuppositions, its concern for 'institutional facts', and in general its character as 'practical reasoning' come nowhere near establishing law's claim to constituting an independent discourse. But, as we have seen, the issue is not so much disproving law's pretence to closure but, rather, seeing how far we can provide a sociology of this process as a practical accomplishment – and it is in this sense that these indicators may serve as valuable clues to law's peculiarities as a social practice even if they do not demonstrate its disciplinary independence.

The differences between social science and law would then not be taken so much as a sign of the inadequacy of the latter discourse but of differences in their objectives. Unlike science, law, especially the common law, aims at a rapprochement with rather than a revision of 'common sense' so that people can understand the rules which they are supposed to follow and that judging can take place in terms of widely accepted and relatively certain standards. Sociology can indeed see more than law. Yet, as Tim Murphy puts it, in terms which go to the heart of what I have been arguing so far, 'the law can see everything but has no desire to see'.[64]

61 Some years ago I commented on Cotterrell's summary of Luhmann's approach which said that 'legal discourse protects itself, perhaps is immune to interference from external knowledge fields' saying that 'much depends on noticing that law's autonomy lies not in its freedom from being influenced by external causes and influences but in the way in which it incorporates and responds to them.' Nelken, op. cit. (1987), n. 29, p. 155 ; the passage was quoted in approval by Teubner in his classical 'How the Law Thinks' (op. cit., n. 6, p. 749), though the cite is missing.
62 Cotterrell, op. cit., n. 13, p. 188.
63 Nelken, op. cit. (1990), n. 41, p. 112.
64 W.T. Murphy, *The Oldest Social Science* (1997) 114.

A range of interesting recent writing in legal and social theory tries to analyse the differences, as well as the similarities, between sociological reflexivity and legal closure so as to explore what it is that law 'has no desire to see'. Although there are, of course, important differences between these theories, they provide the best starting points for mapping out the future of a reflexive approach to the sociology of law. Some authors do perhaps over-emphasize the distinctiveness of legal discourse. Thus, postmodern writers such as Jean-Francois Lyotard concentrate on the incommensurabilities of different discourses – the 'phrases in difference' – which have resulted from the alleged collapse of metanarratives of truth or justice.[65] And Niklas Luhmann's theory of autopoiesis, which relates law as a sub-system to other sub-systems of economics, politics or science, claims that law is 'cognitively open' to inputs from science (including sociology) but 'normatively closed'.[66] But even sociological theories which appear to suggest a sharp line between law and other discourses do so as part of their overall scheme which does explain how discourses interrelate in modern or postmodern social systems.

Other approaches, perhaps because they are less theoretically ambitious, are even more useful. Ed Rubin, for example, stresses law's specificity as a 'prescriptive discipline' which is relatively unconcerned with cumulating accurate accounts/explanations of the social world. He shows how, in contrast to the sciences, law relies on data created by others and has a different, more 'reactive' and 'involved' relationship with external social forces.[67] Peter Shuck argues that science, law, and politics belong to different and largely competing cultures. For him, the cultures' divergences are more striking than their commonalities:

> . . . They are not merely unique ways of living and thinking but also represent radically different modes of legitimating public decisions . . . Each then invokes a distinctive conception of truth, or less grandly, of how to achieve the good.[68]

Finally, Murphy himself offers an original account of what it could mean to say that 'law is a way of being not an instrument of manipulation'.[69] Whereas law was once a form of proto-sociology (as Cotterrell argues), it has now been by-passed by other methods of governing society which regulate on the basis of statistics and the constructions of social categories in terms of averages and risk. Law's gaze relies fundamentally on personal experience and the 'trained eye'; it fosters immediacy and connection of objects by textual analogy and metaphor. As such, it no longer has any significant affinity with modern social science: 'to claim that law is a social science is to conflate distinctive epistemic styles'.

---

65 J.F. Lyotard, *The Differend: Phrases in Dispute*, tr. G Abbeele (1988).

66 N. Luhmann, 'Operational Closure and Structural Coupling: The Differentiation of the Legal System' (1991) 13 *Cardozo Law Rev.* 1419.

67 E. Rubin, '"Law and" and the Methodology of Law' (1997) *Wisconsin Law Rev.* 521.

68 P.H. Schuck, 'Multiculturalism Redux: Science, Law and Politics' (1993) 11 *Yale Law and Policy Rev.* at 4–5.

69 Murphy, op. cit., n. 64, p. 101.

Writers in the 'law and literature' school have a different way of empha-
sizing the flaw in conceptualizing law as essentially a form of social regulation. Law should be seen as an authoritative search for meaning, as an
activity of justification, says Boyd White, because it is always about a set
of speaking places, about conversation and authority, authorizing who says
what, when, and why.[70] Rather than focus on outcomes, attention turns to
language and form (and literary parallels such as plays and poems); as a
mode of persuasion, law involves methods of close reading 'designed to keep
alive texts or create character'. Other theorists, less tempted by the analogy
between law and literature, also emphasize how successful argument must
correspond with certain persuasive modalities, in which social and empirical
considerations have only limited and unpredictable weight.[71]

For all these approaches, nothing could be more mistaken, as Cotterrell
correctly points out, than making 'law's truth an abstract site of understanding removed from particular kinds of locations'.[72] In fact, law itself has lots
to say about the variations in procedure and substance in its different
locations (and in some of these the style of social science investigation and
argument is obviously much more relevant than in others). But, in all their
locations, legal discourses are constituted by a complex interplay between
what they can, cannot, and should not see. Legal actors work within
hierarchies and follow procedures designed to ensure that some actors have
more or different 'insights' than others at different stages. In all modern
criminal processes, for example, the police are not supposed to double guess
beyond a certain point what will happen to the cases they report: to do so
would nullify the purpose of the following stages of the legal process. In
accusatorial systems, the defence is allowed to plan strategy on the basis of
sociological predictions while this would be frowned on for the prosecution.
To the extent that legal processes are constructed as strategic games, knowledge is not an end in itself; when and which information is 'discovered' is
guided by other criteria.[73]

JURISTIC PROBLEMS AND SOCIAL SOLUTIONS

Those who see sociology's task as revealing what law cannot or will not see
have the relatively straightforward though important job of showing how
legal solutions frequently fail to grasp social problems. But Cotterrell wants
us to go further. His goal is to reveal and systematize law's proto-social
ideas so as ensure that legal solutions are better shaped by social insights.
By treating legal ideas 'as an aspect of social ideas in development' so as to
clarify the socio-political contexts and implications of past and present

70 J. Boyd White, *Justice as Translation* (1990).
71 D. Patterson, *Law and Truth* (1995); D. Bobbitt, *Constitutional Interpretation* (1991).
72 Cotterrell, op. cit., n. 13, p. 180.
73 See Nelken, op. cit. (1990), n. 41.

decision making',[74] Cotterrell believes that sociologically inspired resolutions can be crafted even, or especially, where legal doctrine faces only conflicting precedents (as in his example of the confused status of private-purpose trusts in English law). Perhaps. But what if, as I have been arguing, the introduction of social insights also has the potential to distort or at least change legal practices rather than simply help them to sort out self induced muddles?

Once again, the problems I am raising have nothing to do with the untenable claim that law is free of outside influence (whether cognitive or normative). The differences between the ways law reaches closure and sociology advances its own reflexivity does not mean that social insights, ideas or facts do not or cannot enter the reproduction of legal cognition. In different settings, such as the university, courts, tribunals, or regulatory policy-making bodies, and at various stages of legal and administrative processes, those who take or influence decisions may have their ideas changed by education, policy discussions, political action or activism, legal advocacy, lobbying or media reports. Present or future legal and other decision makers may be informed by, presuppose or actually seek out assistance in obtaining such insights.

In this sense, Cotterrell is obviously right to argue that social insights do and should influence the crafting of legal solutions to social issues. We are indeed all legal realists now; Anglo-American legal scholarship regularly produces a sort of interdisciplinary bricolage. No serious discussion of the present and future of, say, public law, negligence or family law could be carried on in Britain without some reference to social considerations.[75] The puzzle that concerns us here, however, is whether there is a way of guiding this process which could tell us when and in what way social insights *must* shape legal decision making and the likely effect of introducing such insights. Our undoubted ability to describe and perhaps even explain the rise and fall of different forms of social knowledge in legal processes works well enough after the event, but does not provide us with a metric or even a rule of thumb for deciding what to do in particular cases. In general, social insights seem to function differently when they serve to open up legal closure than when they are used to provide closure. Can we ensure social insights get into law in a way which reflects their sociological sense but also respects the differences and integrity of different discourses and practices?[76]

Until quite recently Cotterrell admitted that 'it is still very much an open question how far any productive dialogue or integration of normative legal theory with empirical legal theory is possible'[77] even though he went on to

74 Cotterrell, op. cit., n. 13, pp. 190–1.
75 See the chapters by D. Oliver, B. Hepple, and M. Freeman in *Law and Opinion at the End of the Twentieth Century*, ed. M. Freeman (1997).
76 For an important illustration of such difficulties, see the discussion of the use of 'battered women's syndrome' as a method of displacing law's 'myths' about wife battering in A. Downs, *More than Victims: Battered Women, the Syndrome Society and the Law* (1996).
77 R. Cotterrell, *The Politics of Jurisprudence* (1989) 232. I have been arguing that we need to draw a sharper distinction than Cotterrell does between 'dialogue' and 'integration'.

insist that a synthesis was essential because legal doctrine itself cannot explain legal change or grasp the social reality it needs to handle. More recently he explained that 'in one sense law and sociology as forms of professional practice are similar in scope yet wholly opposed in method and aims'.[78] Faced with these differences, some authors propose that we uproot social science insights from the methods which generate them,[79] but this, of course, begs the question of what happens when we separate an approach from its methodology. Cotterrell's new arguments about the similarities between law and sociology, on the other hand, seems to be suggesting that their methods are not after all that different:

> The sociological understanding of legal ideas reflects methodologically law's own fragmented and varied methodological characteristics as understood by those who participate in or are affected by legal practices.[80]

But is this convincing? An alternative view would suggest, on the contrary, that for social insight to be effective in shaping legal discourses (for better or worse) it is neither *necessary nor sufficient* for them to have much in common. Donald Black, for example, has repeatedly claimed that his rigorously external behaviourist interpretation of legal behaviour (like the long-standing tradition of behaviourist prediction of judicial decision making) may be highly useful to lawyers in planning their litigation strategies. Indeed, he predicts the evolution of what he calls 'sociological law', as lawyers reflexively internalize the finding that sociology provides the best guide to legal outcomes.[81] Conversely, even if we were to concede that the interpretative search for social insight is, as Cotterrell claims, more like law (and vice versa) than the methodology pursued by any other discipline, this does not guarantee that social insights can therefore be well-integrated; indeed it may be an explanation of their relative *lack* of integration. In many legal processes, what law calls for is precisely forms of knowledge/power which are in fact *different* and thus supplemental to its own.

Cotterrell himself has repeatedly argued that 'law' seeks to borrow from other disciplines mainly when it is undergoing crises in which it is unable to maintain at least the appearance of discursive self-sufficiency.[82] But how is this claim to be reconciled with his more voluntaristic vision of the possibility of bringing social insights at will to help law achieve better understanding of its tasks? He suggests that the adoption of sociological insights is the most 'practical' of approaches for participants in legal processes – but we must, of course, ask: most practical for whom, and why? It is no doubt

---

78 Cotterrell, op. cit., n. 35, p. 5. At p. 6 he added 'law is a practical craft of systematic control of social relations and institutions. Sociology is a scientific enterprise that seeks systematic knowledge of them', though, once again, he went on to suggest that these dividing lines would have to give way eventually.

79 Rubin, op. cit., n. 67.

80 Cotterrell, op. cit., n. 13, p. 189.

81 D. Black, *Sociological Justice* (1989) 102.

82 Cotterrell, op. cit., n. 20, p. 55.

possible to provide a sociological analysis of the significance of the different precedents concerning the status of private-purpose trusts which relates this to deeper social conflicts and contradictions. But can any proposal to resolve these clashes be anything other than a political choice to close down some alternative interpretations in favour of others?

What is really involved in going from dialogue to integration? How can context become pretext? What happens when we switch from explaining the 'truth about law' to co-producing 'law's truth'?[83] Why choose law?[84] What if the Rortian project of changing moral vocabularies[85] is better carried on in other spheres?[86] For George Gurvitch – no simple-minded believer in the separate worlds of 'is' and 'ought' – it was, none the less, essential to differentiate between the 'art' of sociological jurisprudence and the 'scientific' project of sociology of law.[87] Part of the difficulty here has to do with the relationship between theory and practice, or, rather, between, on the one hand, the practices of academic explanation and critique and, on the other, those of legal decision making, myth making, rule following, and participation in rituals.[88] The attempts by Stanley Fish to prove that theory is irrelevant to practice are probably exaggerated[89] (much depends on how far anyone really believes that theory can 'guide' practice). But Pierre Bourdieu has shown convincingly how easy it is for free-ranging theorizing to misconstrue the temporal and constrained logic of practical reason and everyday decision making.[90] Certainly, a sociological perspective also reveals similarities in the way that both sociology and law warrant their truth claims and make them stick.[91] But if we follow Cotterrell's call to integrate social insights into law, we must at least accept that interpretation in practical contexts is itself already 'application' (and thus a species of 'violence').[92] The successful adoption of our interpretations necessarily depends on and becomes part of law's

---

83 Nelken, op. cit. (1990), n. 41.

84 Not everybody (for example, second- and third-wave feminists) would necessarily welcome law becoming more effective in its grasp of reality.

85 R. Rorty, *Contingency, Irony and Solidarity* (1989).

86 Compare the careful discussion of the interrelationship but also necessary differences between the projects of critique, utopianism, and reform in N. Lacey, 'Normative Reconstruction in Socio-Legal Theory' (1996) 5 *Social and Legal Studies* 131.

87 Gurvitch's caution on the 'necessity of detaching the sociology of law from the teleogical art of jurisprudence' (Gurvitch, op. cit., n. 46, p. 134) is all the more significant because his ambitions for sociology of law are otherwise so much in line with those of Cotterrell.

88 Compare Cotterrell, op. cit., n. 35: 'some of the myths and mysteries of law must be carried with us as we try to subject it to the questioning gaze of science' (1st ed., p. 331).

89 See, for example, M. Rosenfeld, *Just Interpretations* (1998) at 34–45.

90 P. Bourdieu, *The Logic Of Practice* (1990).

91 S. Fuchs and S.Ward, 'What is Deconstruction and where and when does it take place? Making Facts in Science, Building Cases in Law' (1994) 59 *Am. Sociological Rev.* 481.

92 A. Sarat and T.R. Kearns, *Law's Violence* (1992).

legitimation – because only law is allowed to give binding interpretations.[93] But this is not what Cotterrell means by talking about allegiance to law.

It seems to me that Cotterrell's latest formulation of its task well illustrate how a reflexive sociology of law has to struggle with three interrelated dilemmas. The first is the choice between *techne* and *physis* or, as he puts it, between 'sociology as engineering' and 'sociology as enlightenment'. Cotterrell says he has now definitely opted for the latter, and this probably explains the repeated use of the word 'insight'. But while he argues that 'science' is only an aspiration, it is still *this* which is the aspiration. Despite some gestures towards the postmodern,[94] he continues to be attached to the power of sociology's truth to resolve problems which befuddle legal doctrine by helping law overcome 'partial perspectives'. But where does this power come from? Sociology of law's guiding paradigm assumes that a better understanding of social 'context' can provide the clue to the 'fit' law has had and should have in the future.[95] But Cotterrell (like Roberto Unger before him[96]) increasingly wants to transcend the impression of 'false necessity' which can be the legacy of social science in pursuit of a vision of how law could help create a new social and communal order: law as a *transformer* of context.

One person's vision can be another's nightmare. Where does Cotterrell's vision come from and what grounds it? The second dilemma faced by sociology of law is that between criticism and completion of law's work. Cotterrell is uninterested in merely deconstructing law – and, equally, law would have little to gain by borrowing a deconstructed method from sociology.[97] Does this mean that social insights are to be brought in to help provide the determinacy which law is unable to achieve by itself? The source of Cotterrell's vision, however, is more an ideal of what law should become in the future than what it is now: social theory and social insight, therefore, are to play their role as part of 'internal' or 'immanent' critique. But if allegiance is to an ideal of law not to law as it is now, how far can a process of critique and of broadening law's understanding also provide the means for legal closure?

Perhaps law is itself only one part of a larger project of social change. On whose terms? The final dilemma is that between the responsibilities of expertise, and the duty, rather, to give 'voice' to the experiences and wishes of social participants, especially those whose voices law ignores. This issue

93 Monahan and Walker (op. cit., n. 2) would have judges instruct juries as to established social scientific facts in the same way as they now instruct them with respect to binding principles of law.
94 Cotterrell, op. cit., n. 35, at p. 310 argues that we should 'not be constrained even by visions of truth'.
95 Nelken, op. cit. (1986), n. 40.
96 R. M Unger, *What Should Legal Analysis Become?* (1996).
97 D. E. Litowitz *Postmodern Philosophy and Law* (1997).

was brought to the fore by Susan Silbey's review of Cotterrell's textbook,[98] but is an increasingly favoured methodological trend within the United States 'law and society' and critical legal scholars' movements. Cotterrell (but not only Cotterrell) has difficulty in identifying the specific 'historical subject' whose interests could provide him with his standpoint and yardstick for change; he offers instead a role for the expert as mediator of knowledge claims. On the one hand. Cotterrell invites us to respect 'local, partial perspectives' rather than replace them. The broader perspective which seeks to interpret these knowledges must itself be 'grounded in, enriched and validated by them'.[99] On the other hand, he recognizes that 'social knowledge' about law is shaped by ideology but argues that sociology of law can help unmake ideology by revealing law's fragilities and strengths.[100] The danger, of course, is that if 'particular narratives which cannot be generalized'[101] are first obliged to satisfy the protocols of sociological understanding, we risk (as much as law) betraying the lived experience of individuals who have declining faith in experts and yet cannot manage without them.[102]

Both sociology and law risk becoming technocratic and imposing their truth on social actors; each also claims to have the potential to resist these trends. Is law or sociology better equipped to be the bulwark against the further spread of technocratic means-end rationality? Is law or sociology more suited to protecting the local and the pluralist? Which is more in touch with the common sense of social actors? In the end, I may only be offering a further note of caution concerning the dangers which Cotterrell warns about when discussing the blinkers of academic sociology. Sociology of law is obliged to pay allegiance (if we must use this language) to both law *and* sociology. Law's style as a social practice, even perhaps its social function, is to blur the dilemmas it faces. But sociology's insights may also obscure even as they reveal. Sociology of law has as its primary task to expose law's dilemmas, but also – as far as it can – to recognize its own.

98 Silbey, op. cit., n. 31.
99 Cotterrell, op. cit., n. 35, at pp. 310.
100 id., pp. 311–12.
101 Cotterrell, op. cit., n. 13, p. 191.
102 Z. Bauman, *Legislators and Interpreters* (1987).

[13]
Comparatists and Transferability

Introduction

Law is on the move. Social engineering through law, for all that it is some-what out of fashion 'at home' in many industrially developed societies, is increasingly practised abroad. The range of societies currently caught up in what many still describe as 'legal transplants', but which I shall be calling 'legal transfers', is not confined to those in the developing world, though even this covers places as different as China, south-east Asia or Latin America. It also includes almost all of the ex-communist countries and, in many respects, even the countries seeking to harmonize their laws within the European Union. Indeed, the developments associated with the globalization of markets and communication mean that few, if any, places are now immune. If the 'law-and-development' movement is thus in its second (some say third) wave, the question has been raised of how to avoid repeating the 'mistakes' made the first time round.[1] A selective overview of some of the debates concerning the possibility and appropriateness of legal transfers may perhaps make a contribution to this task.

Three sets of interrelated issues will need be considered. How far is it possible to understand other peoples' law? What can be done to ensure that only that law is transferred which 'fits' into its new setting? Finally, in what ways are current wider political, economic and social developments affecting processes of legal transfer? I shall try to explore these questions with special reference to the possibilities of closer collaboration between sociologists of law and comparatists.[2] There are good reasons for trying to encourage such cooperation. Even if the extent of mutual citation is still

---

[1] See Armin Hoeland, 'Evolution du droit en Europe centrale et orientale: assiste-t-on à une renaissance du "*Law and Development*"?', Droit et société, 1993, No. 25, p. 467.

[2] See also Roger Cotterrell's contribution to this book.

438

regrettably poor, it would often be difficult to draw a useful line between these two bodies of scholarship. Both these academic endeavours are interested in understanding the way legal transfers are affected by interests, mentalities and institutions. Each is struggling to make sense of developments such as Europeanization and globalization which are producing new configurations of the legal, the economic and the political spheres. Sociologists can gain much from comparatists' often first-hand descriptions of efforts at legal transfers and reflections on the obstacles encountered.[3] Some comparatists, for their part, look to the social sciences (with exaggerated expectations) for a 'theory' which could explain and predict the likely result of legal transfers. Faced with strategic or tactical questions in transferring law, comparatists need to consult the existing social science literature so as to learn the lessons of past efforts at social change through law. Comparatists, in turn, have something to teach sociologists about the dangers of ethnocentrism when moving law from one culture to another.

Despite these potential gains, comparatists and sociologists often prefer to ignore or criticize each other's work rather than engage with it.[4] Sociologists typically accuse comparatists of focusing too narrowly on legal doctrine and 'law in the books' and of neglecting the way law operates in practice in its relation to the wider social structure. For their part, comparatists accuse sociologists of neglecting legal doctrine and intellectual history. In contrast to the normative thrust of much comparative work, most sociologists of law tend to have a more explicit commitment to scientific theory-building, testing and experimentation. But the modernist paradigm is under siege and confidence in the possibilities of social engineering may well need to be tempered by the wisdom coming from comparative work more rooted in the humanities. In practice, moreover, some comparatists involved in recommending legal transfers demonstrate an equally blind faith in legal know-how and do-it-yourself social science. And even social scientists often mix the explanatory and normative registers, as I shall seek to show with reference to their efforts to establish the likely or past 'success' of legal transfers.

---

[3] For example, see Thomas W. Waelde and James L. Gunderson, 'Legislative Reform in Transitional Economies: Western Transplants – A Short-Cut to Social Market Economy Status?', (1994) 43 Int. & Comp. L.Q. 347; Gianmaria Ajani, 'By Chance and Prestige: Legal Transplants in Russia and Eastern Europe', (1995) 43 Am. J. Comp. L. 93.

[4] But see David Nelken and Johannes Feest (eds.), *Adapting Legal Cultures* (Oxford: Hart, 2001).

Even if there are important differences between these approaches, it could be argued that it is just these differences which provide the starting-point for collaboration.[5] But any proposed division of labour must also take account of internal differences within each camp. Thus, while some comparatists seek a common core in the laws of different societies,[6] others stress the distinctiveness of legal cultures.[7] Many sociologists seek positivist or functionalist explanations of patterns of legal life,[8] but some insist on the need to interpret their inner meanings.[9] Some – even if perhaps not most – comparatists continue to raise fundamental doubts about the contribution that social scientists can make to the understanding of legal transfers. The assumptions and models of sociology of law may even be seen as more a part of the problem than the solution. On one view, social scientists easily underestimate how profoundly law is embedded in its environing culture. They need to realize that they can never put themselves in a position to grasp other people's law as they themselves understand it – and that this is a *sine qua non* of effective transplantation. On another view, the problem is the opposite. Here, sociologists are described as greatly exaggerating the degree to which law needs to 'fit' the society in which it is currently found. They fail to recognize the very existence of legal transplants as something which undermines any attempt to construct a sociology of law.

It is tempting for sociologists to ignore what may seem extreme and, therefore, unconvincing objections to their work.[10] But this would be a mistake. Certainly, these arguments cannot be accepted in the form in which they are presented. But they do contain partial and complementary insights into the problems involved in seeking to understand the possibilities and limits of legal borrowing. In the following effort to rethink legal transfers, I

---

[5] See David Nelken, 'Puzzling Out Legal Culture: A Comment on Blankenburg', in *id.* (ed.), *Comparing Legal Cultures* (Aldershot: Dartmouth, 1997), pp. 58–88.

[6] For example, see B. S. Markesinis (ed.), *The Gradual Convergence* (Oxford: Oxford University Press, 1994).

[7] For example, see Pierre Legrand, 'European Legal Systems Are Not Converging', (1996) 45 Int. & Comp. L.Q. 52.

[8] For example, see Erhard Blankenburg, 'Civil Litigation Rates as Indicators for Legal Culture', in Nelken, *supra*, note 5, pp. 41–68.

[9] For example, see David Nelken, 'Studying Criminal Justice Comparatively', in Mike Maguire, Rod Morgan and Robert Reiner (eds.), *The Oxford Handbook of Criminology*, 2d ed. (Oxford: Oxford University Press, 1997), pp. 559–76.

[10] For example, see Lawrence Friedman, 'Some Comments on Cotterrell and Legal Transplants', in Nelken and Feest, *supra*, note 4, pp. 93–8.

440

shall begin by trying to extract the important elements of truth contained in these critiques.[11] I shall seek to demonstrate that even if these criticisms point to the errors of some sociological approaches, they also prove the need for such inquiry. This is because little progress can be made by continuing to argue *whether or not* law should be treated as an inextricable part of the wider society and culture. Instead, we need to look for the best route to capturing the way law both does, and does not, 'fit' society and culture and identify the way this is changing under current conditions. As Gunther Teubner has argued, the study of legal transfers thus offers an ideal opportunity 'to get beyond dichotomies which juxtapose cultural dependency and legal insulation or social context and legal autonomy'.[12]

Does respecting difference rule out a social science of legal transfers?

How well must we understand another society before being in a position to bring about legal transfers? Pierre Legrand, in a succession of learned articles, has warned of the difficulties that face the scholar who wishes to understand the law of other legal cultures, especially if he or she wants to grasp it in the way it is understood by the natives of that culture.[13] Once we understand law in its richest sense,[14] the best that can be achieved is to give people a taste of 'otherness' – what it would be like, for example, to be part of French or German legal culture.

---

[11] In counterposing the writings of Pierre Legrand and Alan Watson as competing critiques of functionalist sociology (see *infra*), I do not intend to suggest any other symmetry in their work. Watson purports to be using historical facts (as well as some comparative work) to show the impossibility of existing sociological theorizing about law. For his part, Legrand is more concerned with the impossibility of transplants whoever advocates them. While Legrand actively argues against legal transplants, it is not clear how far Watson would actually want to encourage them rather than merely insist on their inevitability. Legrand is even more critical of Watson than of sociology, though both might agree about the constitutive role for legal culture of what are not merely technical-legal distinctions.

[12] Gunther Teubner, 'Legal Irritants: Good Faith in British Law or How Unifying Law Ends up in New Divergences', (1998) 61 Modern L.R. 11, p. 17.

[13] For example, see Legrand, *supra*, note 7; *id.*, 'Against a European Civil Code', (1997) 60 Modern L.R. 44; *id.*, 'What "Legal Transplants"?', in Nelken and Feest, *supra*, note 4, pp. 55–69 [hereinafter 'What "Legal Transplants"?'].

[14] For Legrand, 'What "Legal Transplants"?', *supra*, note 13, p. 60, comparative law is more than the study of legal rules and institutions: 'The comparatist must adopt a view of law as a polysemic signifier which connotes *inter alia* cultural, political, sociological, historical, anthropological, linguistic, psychological and economic referents.'

But if the scholar cannot fully understand another culture, still less is this possible for a judge or lawyer. Legrand severely criticizes the work of those of his comparatist colleagues who seek to demonstrate or produce legal convergence, to reveal an underlying 'common core' of principles and so forth. Any attempt to interpret and apply a 'borrowed' law or institution is bound to be different from the interpretation which would be made of it by those participating in a different 'legal *epistémè*'. Hence his radical conclusion that 'legal transplants' are, strictly speaking, impossible. Meaning cannot survive the journey: 'there could only occur a meaningful "legal transplant" when both the propositional statement as such and its invested meaning – which jointly constitute the rule – are transported from one culture to another. Given that the meaning invested into the rule is itself culture-specific, it is difficult to conceive, however, how this transfer could ever happen.'[15] Attempts at harmonization are, therefore, bound to fail and even to cause harm. Legrand thus connects the appropriate strategy to adopt in understanding another culture to the assumption that difference is something we should treasure and protect. For both theoretical and practical reasons, we should 'prioritize' difference.[16]

Much of Legrand's argument is valuable and timely. He is surely correct to warn of the theoretical errors and political dangers of any functionalist approach, which assumes that all societies face the same 'social problems' – to which law can and must provide a solution. Variation in how 'problems' are conceived, and even whether given situations are treated as problems, is the very stuff of cultural analysis. He is also right to remind us how much law is bound up with meaning, identity and the sense of community and tradition. Some social science approaches do tend to underestimate these factors. Moreover, social science cannot claim any certainties in interpreting 'other' cultures. Indeed, there are leading anthropologists, like Clifford Geertz,[17] whose celebration of 'local knowledge' forms part of an attack on the conventional methods of social scientific disciplines, such as the anthropology of law.[18] But these considerations do not stop Geertz, any more than Legrand himself, from attempting to offer accounts of other societies.

[15] *Ibid.* [16] See Pierre Legrand's contribution to this book.
[17] See Clifford Geertz, *Local Knowledge* (New York: Basic Books, 1983).
[18] Post-modern anthropologists such as James Clifford and George Marcus, of course, go even further in questioning the possibility of objective accounts of other cultures. See James Clifford and George Marcus (eds.), *Writing Culture: The Poetics and Politics of Ethnography* (Berkeley: University of California Press, 1986); James Clifford, *The Predicament of Culture* (Cambridge, Mass.: Harvard University Press, 1988).

442

And the call to privilege difference would make no sense if comparison was actually impossible. Yet, it is far from obvious how far Legrand wishes his arguments to be taken. On the one hand, some might argue that they do not go far enough. What about the belief that particular cultures are *sui generis*, as with the debates over Japanese 'uniqueness' or the insistence that certain religious traditions can only be understood from within? How about those versions of 'perspectivism' according to which certain truths can be grasped only from a specific standpoint such as that provided by membership of categories like women, the working class or intellectuals? On the other hand, does Legrand stop short of relativism and does he want to?[19] Is it plausible to believe that modern cultures are so distinct as to be incommensurable? Why not say the same of differences between sub-cultures? How can we understand the past?

Legrand does seem to place exaggerated stress on the study of difference rather than similarity. Reflection on our own (contrasting) cultural 'starting-point' is always of crucial importance in any comparison and should be taken very seriously when planning legal transfers.[20] But whether or not it is better to concentrate on showing the existence of differences rather than similarities depends on the context and purpose of comparison. Many societies are only too aware of being perceived as different! Academic work which shows surprising and unexpected similarities between these and other societies may be of as much value as that which demonstrates difference and may carry important implications for the possibility of legal transfers. More generally, it is hard to imagine any process of identifying differences which does not require the capacity to distinguish them from similarities. The same applies to the process of deciding which differences count. If difference is 'inexhaustible', how do we decide what differences are important? When is a difference a difference?

Much the same applies to the conclusions Legrand draws for the practice of legal transplants. Taken at its strongest, Legrand's thesis is incontrovertible, but also unhelpful. If by 'legal transplants' we mean the attempt to use laws and legal institutions to reproduce identical meanings and effects in different cultures, then this is indeed impossible. But is there anyone who argues that this is in fact possible? Certainly not Alan Watson, who

---

[19] See Luke Nottage, *Convergence, Divergence, and the Middle Way in Unifying or Harmonising Private Law*, European University Institute Law Department Working Paper 2000/1 (2001).

[20] See David Nelken, 'Telling Difference: Of Crime and Criminal Justice in Italy', in *id.* (ed.), *Contrasting Criminal Justice* (Aldershot: Dartmouth, 2000), pp. 233–64.

COMPARATISTS AND TRANSFERABILITY   443

popularized the term and who is the direct target of Legrand's criticisms. Who says that what is wanted is an exact transplant? So everything depends on what we mean or wish to mean by 'transplants' and how seriously we take this metaphor.[21] It can hardly be gainsaid that legal transfers are possible, are taking place, have taken place and will take place. What exactly is happening or is likely to happen in such transfers is another story.

In his most recent work, Legrand sets out to clarify – and also perhaps modify – his earlier claims.[22] He admits that it would be a contradiction for us to assert that cultures are totally incommensurable and their communications untranslatable. He concedes that it is possible to go a long way in understanding 'the other' – indeed, that our possibility to dialogue with others presupposes likeness. He even suggests that to assert difference is not to argue for a dichotomy but for a relationship. When it comes actually to carrying out comparative research, he acknowledges that we need to identify some similarities in an institution or practice before we can even talk of differences. Furthermore, he admits that assertions of given 'difference' are culturally contested and that the observer constructs differences in the course of trying to identify them (given that re-presentation is as much prescriptive as descriptive). But none of these concessions are allowed to do much to modify his overall stance. Legrand still insists on what he calls 'radical epistemological diversity'[23] and the impossibility of ever comprehending others as they understand themselves. Whatever similarities we may presuppose or find, '[our] responsibility [is] to characterize, articulate and justify [the ineliminability of difference].'[24]

A puzzling feature of Legrand's argument is his assumption that the goal of the comparatist must always be to try to see foreign law as 'the native' does. It is no small matter to decide which native should serve as the measure of our successful understanding of another culture. But, more than this, depending on our purposes, we may be seeking more or less understanding than that which the native possesses. Not only may the outsider sometimes see more than the native does,[25] but the natives themselves may be more interested than Legrand admits in what they can learn from the

---

[21] See *id.*, 'Beyond the Metaphor of Legal Transplants? Consequences of Autopoietic Theory for the Study of Cross-Cultural Legal Adaptation', in Jiri Priban and *id.* (eds.), *Law's New Boundaries: The Consequences of Autopoiesis* (Aldershot: Dartmouth, 2001), pp. 265–302.

[22] For example, see Pierre Legrand's contribution to this book.   [23] *Ibid.*   [24] *Ibid.*

[25] Legrand talks of natives having a '(perhaps unelucidated) attachment to a familiar legal tradition': *ibid.* But this makes it clear that we cannot assume that all natives know their own tradition or use this knowledge as the criterion by which a tradition is defined.

444

relatively external perspective of the foreign lawyer or social scientist (and this seems especially true where policy-driven legal transfers are being considered). Legrand's argument should probably, therefore, not to be taken as a recommendation concerning comparative methodology *tout court*. In the context of legal transplants, the issue is less the 'scientific' validity of our interpretation of law than the need to understand (and predict) how the 'native' lawyer or judge or scholar will act upon 'reception' of a foreign law. Legrand's demonstration of our inability to put ourselves in the place of the native is then to be understood as a warning to the outsider to respect the integrity and independence of the tradition which it is the task of insiders to unfold.[26]

But if the reason to stress difference is as much political as it is intellectual, this raises a new set of questions. Is it always politically sound to privilege difference? Is this what natives always want to do? Legrand denies that his position has anything to do with nationalism or cultural fundamentalism. His is rather a defensive move intended to counterbalance those comparatists who, he claims, see particularity as epiphemenonal and treat difference as an evil to be overcome at all costs. But many contemporary legal transfers are bound up with deliberate transitions from apartheid, Fascism or communism. If we were to concentrate here mainly on how best to preserve existing differences, we would surely be missing the point.

Though couched in general terms, it might be said, however, that Legrand intends his arguments to be limited to contexts similar to the current attempts at greater harmonization of law within the European Union (stigmatized by him as 'an instrumental re-invention of Europeanism dictated by the ethos of capital and technology').[27] But the reflections of a comparatist about the importance of preserving cultural differences are unlikely in themselves to provide enough of a guide for resolving complex issues of socio-legal policy-making. Surely all depends on the purpose, reach and likely effects of a given legal transfer? The link between the descriptive and the prescriptive parts of Legrand's argument is, in any case, somewhat forced. He objects in principle to legal transfers whose explicit aim is to try to make societies more alike rather than encouraging them to develop the distinctiveness of their own traditions. The fear is of what would be lost if 'success' in such enterprises actually resulted in the smoothing out of

---

[26] Legrand speaks of traditions as 'epistemic peers, serving equally well by catering to their respective communities' specific historical needs': *ibid*.

[27] *Ibid*.

differences. But, at the same time, Legrand also believes that underlying differences in legal *epistémès* mean that such efforts are, in any case, bound to fail – even ending up, as he says, by accentuating differences.[28] But, if this is so, why the fear about the loss of distinctiveness? Why oppose efforts toward European Union harmonization in the name of protecting diversity if we can be confident that transferred law will actually lead to more divergence?

Legrand's arguments are at their most persuasive if we take them to show only that existing differences do sometimes need to be defended. But we need to be sure that we know exactly what we are trying to protect. Legrand writes mainly about the need to preserve the distinctive legal traditions of common law and civil law. What is the relationship, however, between the intellectual concept of 'legal *epistémè*' which he employs and the socio-political entity represented by the integrity of a legal culture or a legal tradition – and how far are these ethnocentric concepts which themselves belong to a specific legal-cultural context? Do such categories coincide with, or transcend, nation states, pointing us toward rejecting or toward respecting national differences? What of regional and local differences within nation states? It is difficult to be consistently in favour of difference because this would lead to insisting on the existence of evermore micro-differences even within the same tradition. But where does the right to difference stop?

We also need to ask how a tradition maintains its distinctiveness. The meaning and boundaries of traditions are not unchangeable. What defines the boundaries of a tradition and what falls outside it? And who has the power to formulate this definition? The constitutive role of those engaged in arguing about and constructing tradition seems all-important here, a point Legrand accepts. Indeed, if the achievement of tradition is to make 'the past live in the present', no hard and fast line between invented and reworked tradition is possible.[29] Some apparently long-standing 'traditions' are relatively recent 'inventions',[30] others pertain to 'imagined communities'.[31] Moreover, all traditions are in some sense hybrids, even if many bearers of tradition do their best to deny this. Traditions do not evolve only in

---

[28] Legrand, *supra*, note 7, p. 69: 'a common European law, far from eradicating the *summa differentia* between the two legal traditions, would exacerbate it by sharpening its contours.'

[29] See Martin Krygier, 'Law as Tradition', (1986) 5 L. & Phil. 237.

[30] See generally Eric Hobsbawm and Terence Ranger (eds.), *The Invention of Tradition* (Cambridge: Cambridge University Press, 1983).

[31] See Benedict Anderson, *Imagined Communities* (London: Verso, 1983).

446

accordance with some underlying or evolutionary logic but are frequently transformed as a result of voluntary or forced engagement with other cultures whereby something new emerges. Hence the appropriateness and assimilability of proposed legal transfers is itself an essential element of such internal disagreement over the boundaries of tradition.[32]

A hermeneutic approach such as that recommended by Legrand could help us identify some of the factors (even if not all of them) which are appreciated by the social actors concerned, which serve to make their tradition coherent. But the external observer should not necessarily endorse any given vision, least of all the idea that difference – and the rejection of foreign models – is in itself a value. By taking a stand in favour of some differences rather than others, there is a risk that the observer could end up imposing hegemonic claims of similarity and coherence made by some interpreters of the tradition at the expense of others. Opposing larger-scale changes, the observer may unwillingly offer comfort and assistance to those attacking lower-level or other internal differences within their tradition – and the groups or minorities bearing such ideas and practices. In this way, Legrand's ideal comparatist would become just as much a participant in claims about the need or possibility of seeking to take ideas from elsewhere as those purporting to promote transfer or harmonization. But – according to his own argument – they would be participants without the capacity to understand fully the tradition they would be seeking to defend.

Is there any point in asking whether legal transfers will fit the societies in which they are adopted?

The upshot of the argument so far is that, despite the strictures of Legrand, there will sometimes be situations in which natives and others will want to consider when and how to transfer law. But evidence of the continuing importance of the issues raised by Legrand can be seen in the way those engaged in such exercises themselves often ask how they can best ensure that the transferred law will 'fit' well into its new environment. But it is exactly this sort of inquiry which other writers insist is, in many respects, both unnecessary and useless. In particular, the view regularly proposed and re-proposed by Alan Watson is that legal transplants just happen and

---

[32] For an illustration, see Antoine Garapon's description of the tensions within present-day French legal culture: 'French Legal Culture and the Shock of "Globalization"', (1995) 4 Soc. & Leg. Stud. 493.

that they happen all the time, quite irrespective of whether they have any broad socio-economic or other 'fit' with the society for which they are suggested or in which they are adopted.[33] Social scientists stand accused not, as with Legrand, of advocating impossible legal transplants, but of failing to recognize the significance for their understanding of law of the very ease and inevitability with which legal transfers take place.

Watson's argument (which was also directed against some styles of work in comparative law as much as to sociology of law) is that a large proportion of law in any society is a direct result of 'legal transplants' and thus owes its form and content to its origins in other times and places. Rules of private law, in particular, are often out of step for long periods with the needs and aspirations of society or any particular group or class within it. This includes bodies of law having a great impact on practical life, such as contract law or land law. Other major branches of law, such as conflict of laws, also develop with no input at all from society. Watson denies that such law is shaped by the purposes of politics, arguing that '[o]ver most of the field of law, and especially of private law, in most political and economic circumstances, political rulers need have no interest in determining what the rules of law are or should be (provided always, of course, that revenues roll in and that the public peace is kept)'.[34] 'It follows', says Watson, 'that usually legal rules are not peculiarly devised for the particular society in which they now operate and also that this is not a matter for great concern'.[35]

Other comparatists, such as William Ewald,[36] follow Watson's lead in arguing that the frequency of legal transplants demonstrates the fallacy of attempting to produce a sociology of law. These comparatists describe the sociological view they reject as the 'mirror theor[y] of law' and attribute this idea somewhat indifferently to all sociologists of law.[37] While an interest in the problem of how law relates to society is certainly a defining characteristic of their work, evidence that all sociologists rely on such a crude theory

---

[33] For example, see Alan Watson, *Legal Transplants*, 2d ed. (Athens, Georgia: University of Georgia Press, 1993) [hereinafter *Legal Transplants*]; *id.*, *Social and Legal Change* (Edinburgh: Scottish Academic Press, 1977); *id.*, *Law Out of Context* (Athens, Georgia: University of Georgia Press, 2000) [hereinafter *Law Out of Context*].

[34] *Id.*, *Roman Law and Comparative Law* (Athens, Georgia: University of Georgia Press, 1991), p. 97.

[35] *Id.*, *Legal Transplants*, *supra*, note 33, p. 96.

[36] See William Ewald, 'Comparative Jurisprudence (II): The Logic of Legal Transplants', (1995) 43 Am. J. Comp. L. 489.

[37] *Id.*, p. 492.

448

(or metaphor) is certainly exaggerated. It would be enough to consider
the historical sociology of Max Weber. It is true that, at the outset of his
career, Emile Durkheim did argue that law could be treated as an 'index'
or mirror of society.[38] But his concern was less with what shaped law than
with how law could be used to map long-term changes in types of social
solidarity.[39] Moreover, Durkheim saw law as playing a key role in reproducing and not merely reflecting society. Yet, the key point here is that
Durkheim's claims have been criticized by virtually all later sociologists.[40]
In fact, he himself soon modified his arguments, for example, by finding an
independent role for the political as well as by rethinking the relationship
between ideas and social practices.[41]

The larger charge that sociologists of law always reduce law to an
epiphenomenon of society is also misleading. Thus, Ewald cites Lawrence
Friedman as an illustration of the way contemporary sociologists treat law as
overly dependent on society.[42] But Friedman's thesis, that 'law is reshaped by
change, that nothing is historical accident, nothing is autonomous, everything is moulded by economics and society',[43] is no more and no less than the
claim that, taking the longer view, law changes over time in response to social
developments. Can this be doubted?[44] It is enough, as Friedman suggests,
to compare the similarities in the form and substance of law in all modern
industrial societies with their own previous pre-industrial legal regimes.[45]
In addition, throughout his writings, Friedman has sought to stress how law
is an instrument and the result of group conflict, both of which are aspects
of law incompatible with the 'mirror' metaphor. Comparatists often fail to

---

[38] See Emile Durkheim, *The Division of Labour in Society*, transl. by W. D. Halls (London:
Macmillan, 1984) [1892].

[39] See Roger Cotterrell, *Emile Durkheim: Law in a Moral Domain* (Edinburgh: Edinburgh University
Press, 1999), pp. 70–4.

[40] In the words of Cotterrell, 'the index thesis, as [Durkheim] explains it, seems to show the worst
aspects of the positivist orientation of his sociology': *id.*, p. 33.

[41] See Emile Durkheim, 'Two Laws of Penal Evolution', in Mike Gane (ed.), *The Radical Sociology
of Durkheim and Mauss* (London: Routledge, 1992), pp. 21–49 [1901]. The translation is by
T. Anthony Jones and Andrew T. Scull.

[42] Ewald, *supra*, note 36, p. 492, referring to Lawrence M. Friedman, *History of American Law*, 2d
ed. (New York: Simon & Schuster, 1985).

[43] Friedman, *supra*, note 42, p. 595.

[44] Strictly speaking, though, Friedman's claim is overargued. Why should law be exempted from
the effects of 'historical accident'?

[45] See Lawrence M. Friedman, 'Comments on Applebaum and Nottage', in Johannes Feest and
Volkmar Gessner (eds.), *Proceedings of the Second Oñati Workshop on Changing Legal Cultures*
(Oñati: International Institute for the Sociology of Law, 1998), pp. 139–49.

distinguish the functionalist claim, that law matches the 'needs' of something we call 'society', from the pluralist or conflict-theory argument, that law serves as part of the strategies of certain groups in society and that the 'law in the books' and, even more, the 'law in action' reflect the changing balance of forces in society. Friedman is a follower of the second of these theories. And such an approach in no way commits him or anyone else to the idea that law must always arise from within the society concerned, rather than be borrowed from abroad or even imposed from the outside.

Watson makes much of the fact that which legal rule is transferred depends on the accident of which foreign university lawyers attended, chance encounters between scholars or chains of mistaken interpretations of ancient texts. But his own theory (or refusal of theory), which claims that law serves no one's interests because it so often has foreign roots and is just the special province of lawyers, is highly implausible. To show Watson's claim to be accurate, more needs to be done than illustrate the survival of socially irrelevant legal distinctions and doctrines or provide examples of the contingent, the unforeseen, and the apparent 'inertia' of law. What would be required would be exactly that careful sociological investigation of the relationship between different branches of law and their social significance which Watson wants to reject a priori.

Paradoxically, whatever his actual claims about the ease of legal transplants, Watson's chosen metaphor strongly suggests that transplanting laws is, and should be, an arduous affair.[46] Certainly, medical transplants are highly planned and not something one undergoes lightly! And botanical transplants too are often carefully programmed. In practice, even Watson sometimes admits that what happens *after law has been transferred* depends on exactly those matters of social context which law-and-society scholars take to be central. He admits the possibility of barbarization or failure and the fact that law can be influential even when totally misunderstood. And he points out that the impact of legal transplants in a new setting will typically be very different from that in their society of origin: 'The insertion of an alien rule into another complex system may cause it to operate in a fresh way.'[47] He observes further that '[t]he whole context of the rule or concept has to be studied to understand the extent of the transformation.'[48] These are arguments which bring his approach very close to those espoused by sociologists.

---

[46] See generally Nelken, *supra*, note 21.
[47] Watson, *Legal Transplants, supra*, note 33, p. 116.   [48] *Ibid.*

450

The real importance of Watson's claims do not lie in their capacity to undermine a mirror theory of law, which has few, if any, adherents. Rather, the evidence of incongruity between legal rules and social life which he offers can be used to challenge and enrich our understanding of the various and varying forms taken by the relationship between law and society. And it is exactly that problem – the shared concern for how law connects to or 'fits' society – which represents the mainstream paradigm of sociology of law.[49] Such a paradigm allows for – indeed, presupposes – considerable disagreement over what is meant by 'law', what is meant by 'society' and what is meant by 'fit'.[50] For example, very different conclusions will be reached if law is seen as governmental order, as an aspect of social control, as the institutionalization of community norms, as cultural *epistémè* (as Legrand would favour) or as an aspect of the ideology of lawyers as a professional group or sacred clique (as Watson would prefer). Few of these starting-points have much to do with the idea of law as a mirror of society. If law as 'governmental social control' begins where community ends, it clearly cannot mirror social norms.

Empirical investigation of law's relation to society covers a wide range of what fits with what, how it fits, when it fits and which is the best way to study such fit. Theory and research may focus on macro-social change, such as the transition from 'status to contract' (and back again?) or on Durkheim's (flawed) arguments about the change from mechanical to organic solidarity or on Niklas Luhmann's examination of the relationships between the legal and other sub-systems, which maintain the high level of complexity achieved in the transition from modern to late-modern society. The macro-fit between modern law and modern society can be sought in the idea of 'equivalence' generated within the capitalist mode of production (as identified by Pashukanis)[51] or in the needs and problems created by advanced technology and the accompanying culture of expressive individualism.[52]

---

[49] See Robert Kidder, *Connecting Law and Society* (Englewood Cliffs, New Jersey: Prentice-Hall, 1983).

[50] As a policy inquiry, the question of 'fit' also connects with the famous 'gap' problem in social studies of law, which focuses on the question whether laws achieve the goals they are supposed to be fulfilling. See David Nelken, 'The "Gap Problem" in the Sociology of Law: A Theoretical Review', (1981) 1 Windsor Yearbook of Access to Justice 35. The relevance of this question for debates over legal transfers hardly needs to be spelled out.

[51] See Evgeny B. Pashukanis, *Law and Marxism: A General Theory*, transl. by Barbara Einhorn (London: Ink Links, 1978) [1924].

[52] See Lawrence M. Friedman, *The Republic of Choice* (Cambridge, Mass.: Harvard University Press, 1990).

Alternatively, attention may be given to more micro-social connections between law, social norms and social action, as in the attempt to discover how the norms of contract law actually influence business relationships, or to the degree of interdependence between legal norms and other sources of order.[53]

All of these inquiries, and others, can provide valuable insights into the potential problems involved in transferring law from one socio-economic and cultural context to another. At the same time, however, sociologists of law have long been aware that law does not always fit society. As the discussion of Legrand and Watson suggests, the relationship may, on the one hand, be so close that the question of fit does not even arise. On the other hand, it may be out of phase with social change, whether it is behind or ahead of other developments, or, more subtly, it may allow social change by not itself changing.[54] Law can 'belong' not only to other places, but also to the past, to a previous social and economic order, to tradition and to history, as much as to the present. Or it can aim at the future, acting as an index of *desired* social, political and economic change, of what society would like to become (or *should* like to become).

Over the last few years especially, attention has increasingly been directed at theorizing exactly these aspects of law.[55] Such attempts to rethink the 'law-and-society' relationship have, in some respects, gone in directions parallel to the opposing comparative critiques we have been discussing. Arguments for an identification between law and social life have been strengthened by research into 'law as ideology', 'law in everyday life' or, as some writers would have it, law as 'constitutive' of society.[56] Work emanating from the 'law-as-literature' movement, or the study of 'law as communication' more generally,[57] also supports Legrand's warning about the importance of seeing law as a way in which society transmits and reinterprets its myths,

---

[53] See Robert C. Ellickson, *Order Without Law: How Neighbours Settle Disputes* (Cambridge, Mass.: Harvard University Press, 1991).

[54] See Karl Renner, *The Private Institutions of Private Law and their Social Functions*, ed. by Otto Kahn-Freund and transl. by Agnes Schwarzschild (London: Routledge & Kegan Paul, 1949).

[55] For example, see David Nelken, 'Beyond the Study of "Law and Society"?', [1986] Am. Bar Found. Research J. 323; *id.*, 'Changing Paradigms in the Sociology of Law', in Gunther Teubner (ed.), *Autopoietic Law: A New Approach to Law and Society* (Berlin: Walter de Gruyter, 1987), pp. 191–217.

[56] For example, see Alan Hunt, *Explorations in Law and Society: Towards a Constitutive Theory of Law* (London: Routledge, 1993).

[57] See generally David Nelken (ed.), *Law as Communication* (Aldershot: Dartmouth, 1996).

452

rather than treating it merely as an instrument used for the purpose of achieving regulatory goals.

But social theorists have also stressed the need to overcome the idea that there is any necessary link between a given social context and a given form of law. Some stress law's capacity to transcend and transform social contexts.[58] Others debate the nature and implications of law's autonomy from other social discourses and the way this relates to the autonomy of art, religion or science.[59] Autopoietic theorists, for their part, put forward a sophisticated account of the way that legal operations are linked to other legal operations rather than directly to other sub-systems of modern society.[60] In short, law not only has a social context, but it also makes its context.[61] A future task for sociology of law (and not only for sociology of law) is to reconcile these competing understandings of law. At stake, among other things, is the prospect of getting a better grip on what is involved in deliberate efforts at legal transfer.

Can we make a success of legal transfers?

Watson may be right that legal transfers often just happen but he tends to belittle the importance of cases where transfers occur either by direct imposition or as part of larger socio-legal changes. The conclusions he draws from his historical examples are also of little help if we are called upon to take a part in promoting or assessing such transfers. To be told that the details of such legal transfers are of interest only to lawyers and scholars while business people just want the greatest posssible harmonization so as to get on with their affairs seems altogether too slim and skewed a basis for policy-making. We will need to think more systematically if we wish to explain why some laws remain a dead letter while others are transformed out of recognition. This will require us to pay attention to the way the

---

[58] For example, see Roberto Mangabeira Unger, *False Necessity: Anti-Necessitarian Social Theory in the Service of Radical Democracy* (Cambridge: Cambridge University Press, 1987).

[59] For example, see Roger Cotterrell, 'Why Must Legal Ideas Be Interpreted Sociologically?', (1998) 25 J. L. & Society 171; David Nelken, 'Blinding Insights? The Limits of a Reflexive Sociology of Law', (1998) 25 J. L. & Society 407.

[60] See Gunther Teubner, *Autopoietic Law* (Oxford: Blackwell, 1993).

[61] For a reflection on getting the law 'out of context', see David Nelken, 'Getting the Law "Out of Context"', (1996) 19 Socio-Legal Newsletter 12. Watson's volume by the same title (*Law Out of Context, supra*, note 33) is disappointing because it does not mark any real progress toward this goal.

relationship or 'fit' between law and society varies culturally and thus overcome ethnocentric ideas about how law must fit society.

One way of taking such matters further is to examine debates over 'success' and 'failure' in writing about transnational legal transfers. For it is in this 'mixed discourse', which combines aspects of technocractic and normative evaluation, that sociology of law and comparative law are most likely to cross paths. Talking about a successful transfer always invokes evaluations, even when the term is used by social scientists. At the extreme, it could sometimes be more appropriate to describe 'resistance' to legal transfer as success. But even those most opposed to a social-engineering approach to law find it difficult to avoid recourse to descriptive claims about what is likely or not likely to happen when they argue in favour or against given projects of legal transfer. But the conceptual and empirical difficulties that face any inquiry into the potential success of legal transfers do not end here.[62] We shall need to distinguish three sets of problems. What do we mean by 'success'? What are the conditions which make legal transfers more or less successful? Finally, and most importantly for present purposes, how far are problems in assessing success bound up with cultural variability in the way people think, or should think, about the fit between law and society? I shall discuss these matters in turn.

There is no consensus about how to define success, nor about the way it should be measured. Should we view the type of legal pluralism that characterizes areas such as south-east Asia, which has played host to a series of legal transfers,[63] as an example of success or failure? Apparent success at one level can conceal underlying failure at another. The introduction of modern law in Japan is technically a success. But, according to some insiders, it has left a feeling of inauthenticity linked to the idea that if modernity had to be imported, Japan is not really Modern.[64] We can even ask if success is always good. The introduction of new legal rules can either stabilize or unsettle existing normative practices, just as it can consolidate or

---

[62] See David Nelken, 'The Meaning of Success in Transnational Legal Transfers', (2001) 20 Windsor Yearbook of Access to Justice 349 [hereinafter 'The Meaning of Success']; *id.*, 'Towards a Sociology of Legal Adaptation', in *id.* and Feest, *supra*, note 4, pp. 7–54.

[63] See Andrew Harding, 'Comparative Law and Legal Transplantation in South East Asia: Making Sense of the "Nomic Din"', in Nelken and Feest, *supra*, note 4, pp. 199–222.

[64] See Takao Tanase, 'The Empty Space of the Modern in Japanese Law Discourse', in Nelken and Feest, *supra*, note 4, pp. 187–98. This interpretation of Japanese experience, albeit controversial, lends some support to Legrand's argument about the impossibility of legal transplants ('What "Legal Transplants"?', *supra*, note 13).

undermine competing expertises.[65] Legal innovations – whether at home or abroad – may sometimes be considered 'too successful' if they 'colonize' or displace other established normative or technical patterns of regulating social relationships without the use of law, leading to 'juridification'.

Other conceptual problems have to do with who has (and who should have) the power to define success. Put differently, whose goals count? Those of the country 'exporting' its law or those of the country receiving it? What about the differences among competing economic interests, among members of governmental and non-governmental organizations (NGOs), parliamentarians, judges, lawyers and other professionals as well as all the other groups likely to be most affected by the law? Should success be judged in terms of an outside observer's assessment of results and effects or in terms of the views of the insiders promoting or being affected by the transfer? How do the criteria used by outsiders and insiders relate to each other? Are we interested more in the experience of politicians, policy-makers, judges, scholars, lawyers, business people, ordinary working people or immigrants and those on the margins of society?[66] What if members of the receiving society want different or even contradictory things? Is success a matter of actually achieving the right fit between law and society or rather the capacity to have one's claims about this accepted?

A second set of issues concerns the conditions for success. The sociology of law textbooks tell us that the likelihood of successful social change through law in *national* contexts depends on what is being transferred, by which source, the way the transfer is introduced, the number of social groups involved, as well as a potentially unlimited number of wider background factors and previous historical experiences.[67] Many of these considerations, such as the authoritativeness of the source of law or the mediating role of institutions, will also be applicable to transfers between countries.[68] But some postulated conditions only beg the question. What does it mean, for example, to say that '[l]aw must appear compatible with cultural assumptions'?[69] Other claims in this literature border on the ethnocentric: the alleged special

---

[65] See John Flood, 'The Vultures Fly East: The Creation and Globalisation of the Distressed Debt Market', in Nelken and Feest, *supra*, note 4, pp. 257–78.

[66] See Eve Darian-Smith, 'Structural Inequalities in the Global System', (2000) 34 L. & Society R. 809.

[67] For example, see Roger Cotterrell, *The Sociology of Law*, 2d ed. (London: Butterworths, 1992), pp. 44–65.

[68] See *id.*, 'Is There a Logic of Legal Transplants?', in Nelken and Feest, *supra*, note 4, pp. 70–92.

[69] *Id.*, *supra*, note 67, p. 59 [discussing the views of William M. Evan].

difficulties of regulating family life or the need to present projects of legal change in ways that do not make them seem utopian are problems which are perceived very differently in different legal cultures.[70] As importantly, proposing legal transfers to other societies raises distinctive questions. In a national law-reform setting, law will often do no more than accompany or register long-standing processes of social change. In transnational legal transfers, however, it is *typical* for law to be asked to jump-start the wider process of social change and leap-frog over long-standing social and cultural obstacles.

How far are the 'conditions' of success beyond our control? It can be helpful to distinguish between what we might call the 'objective' and 'subjective' aspects of this question. As an example of objective condition, we might consider the debate over whether legal change in newly developing or in ex-communist countries has to proceed following the same stages as taken in the west. Is the existence of a certain type of legal profession a pre-condition for certain types of social change? Societies going through a post-communist transition also face the problem whether the extension of competition and the 'free market' should precede, accompany or follow the construction of effective multi-party democracy. Some studies of democratic transitions from Fascist and communist regimes emphasize the need to resolve the problem of creating democratic politics before tackling the construction of free-market capitalism.[71] But the Japanese experience seems to show that successful modernization can equally well be brought about by effective collaboration between a relatively authoritarian government bureaucracy and private industry.[72]

Yet the success of legal transfers depends not only on past or present objective circumstances but also on how far social actors decide to treat these as if they were unchangeable and beyond their control. Martin Krygier argues that we should distinguish between 'pessimistic' and 'optimistic' approaches to legal transplants.[73] Such attitudes regarding the feasibility of changing established institutions or the possibility of overcoming cultural obstacles to change are often manifested with reference to the question of

---

[70] *Id.*, p. 60.

[71] For example, see Juan J. Linz and Alfred Stepan, *Problems of Democratic Transition and Consolidation* (Baltimore: Johns Hopkins University Press, 1996).

[72] See Tanase, *supra*, note 64.

[73] Martin Krygier, 'Is There Constitutionalism After Communism? Institutional Optimism, Cultural Pessimism, and the Rule of Law', (1996–7) 26 Int. J. Sociology L . 17.

456

how far back in history it is necessary to go in seeking an explanation for the present problems to which a transplanted remedy is being proposed.

What, finally, of the connection between arguments about success and ideas of 'fit'? Many issues concerning legal transfers are discussed as if they are only a matter of appropriate pre-conditions, of getting the 'timing' right. But they also go to the heart of the theoretical question of the 'fit' between law and society. Is it a mistake to deregulate prices before implementing competition law? (Can things be done the other way round?) At what stage should a society opt for more market and when for more regulation? Do markets produce rules or rules markets? Must stable institutions precede rules? Should we characterize the nexus between law and the market in capitalist societies as a system of unstable predictability or predictable instability? All these matters rely on implicit ideas about how law does, and how it should, relate to other aspects of society and culture. Sometimes, these are made explicit. In considering whether the 'developmental state' must follow the model of law-and-capitalism in the first capitalist societies, Tom Ginsburg asks: 'How does a system based on personalistic social relations and close ties between business and government move toward a more open and transparent system governed by generally applicable rules? What configuration of political interests are required to initiate and sustain such a transformation?'[74]

Many insightful scholars return from trips abroad where they have been asked to give advice about potential transfers convinced more than ever of the way legal reforms depend on culturally specific presuppositions about the appropriate fit between law and society. Thus, Edward Rubin tells us that his experience in China confirmed him in the view that the type of administrative law used in the United States depends on the presence of a litigious culture and the presumption that party involvement by numerous interest groups can be relied upon to comment on, and improve upon, bureaucratic regulations. Hence, it would not be currently appropriate in China. Rubin's conclusions are worth reporting in full: 'by a sort of double reflection, the characterization of American law that China's distance illuminates becomes a way of perceiving what the underlying characterization of a Chinese law would be. That law draws upon the hierarchy, centralization and governmental prestige in the Chinese system. It would

---

[74] Tom Ginsburg, 'Does Law Matter for Economic Development? Evidence from East Asia', (2000) 34 L. & Society R. 829, p. 851.

create governmental supervisory agencies, independent of other agencies, but possessing the full power and prestige of government, to enforce statutorily required procedures. The ultimate lesson is that little can be borrowed, but much can be learned, from foreign law.'[75] On which, one might comment that often, for better or worse, borrowing is also a way of learning.

However, it would be a fundamental mistake to confine discussions of legal transfers to questions of how new rules, ideas or institutions 'fit' *what already exists*. Legal transfers are frequently – perhaps predominantly – geared to fitting an imagined *future*. Most legal transfers are imposed, invited or otherwise adopted because the society, or at least some groups or elites within that society, seek to use law for the purposes of *change*. The goal is not to fit law to what exists but to reshape what exists through the introduction of something *different*. Hence ex-communist countries try to become more like selected examples of the more successful market societies or South Africa models its new constitution on the best that western regimes have to offer rather than on constitutional arrangements found in its nearer neighbours in Africa. Thus, rather than aiming to reproduce past or present conditions or ideals, law aims to overcome these. The hope is that law may be a means of resolving current problems by transforming society into something more like the source of the borrowed law. In this way, a legal transfer is part of the effort to become more democratic, more economically successful, more secular (or more religious). In what is almost a species of sympathetic magic, borrowed law is deemed capable of bringing about the same conditions allowing for a flourishing economy or a healthy civil society that are found in the social context from which the borrowed law has been taken.[76] In some cases, such as in the modernization of Japan or in Italy, after the recent collapse of the ruling political parties,[77] the search, more modestly, may be for institutions which will make societies more 'normal'. But even this quest for achieved normality can easily be self-defeating.

---

[75] Edward Rubin, 'Administrative Law and the Complexity of Culture', in Anne Seidman, Robert Seidman and Janice Payne (eds.), *Legislative Drafting for Market Reform: Some Lessons from China* (London: Macmillan, 2000), p. 108.

[76] See Julie Mertus, 'The Liberal State vs. the National Soul: Mapping Civil Society Transplants', (1999) 8 Soc. & Leg. Stud. 121.

[77] See David Nelken, 'A Legal Revolution? The Judges and Tangentopoly', in Stephen Gundle and Simon Parker (eds.), *The New Italian Republic: From the Fall of the Berlin Wall to Berlusconi* (London: Routledge, 1995), pp. 191–206.

458

The search for dissimilar legal models is perhaps most likely where the legal transfer is imposed by third parties as part of a colonial project and/or insisted upon as a condition of trade, aid, alliance or diplomatic recognition. But it also characterizes the efforts of international organizations, such as the International Monetary Fund (IMF), when they seek to reshape societies according to a supposedly universal pattern of political and financial integrity. And it may be requested or agreed upon mainly as a way of marking a willingness to accept the 'rules of the game' of the wider global economy. This explains the adhesion to the intellectual property or anti-trust provisions of the World Trade Organization by countries which have few ways of enforcing such rules or little need to do so.

All of this complicates any attempt to use the criterion of 'fit' as a way of measuring success in introducing new law. Is the appropriate fit that which corresponds to the understanding or working of the law or institution in its society of origin? Or is it that which results when it is successfully 'reworked' for the society in which it now has to operate? Without prior research, we should also not assume that we actually know how law worked even in its original context. The study of legal transfers presents us with a challenge to document the considerable socio-cultural variation in the extent to which law actually conditions social action, both in the society of origin and in that of arrival. But we also need to consider differences in whether *it is thought to need to do so*. This has important implications for assessing typical claims that transplanted law must 'fit' the society to which it is introduced if it is to be 'effective' – and it also helps us predict when and where such claims are likely to be made.

Future empirical research is likely to illustrate the point that what is actually being exported in the present round of legal transfers, along with any given legal institution or procedure, is a culturally specific ideology. The legal philosophy which underpins current law-and-development activity is broadly describable as that of 'pragmatic legal instrumentalism'. It promotes *the very idea that law is something which does or should 'work'*, together with the claim that this is something that can or should be assessed in ways which are separable from wider political debates. Time will tell, for example, how far NAFTA will succeed in altering a legal culture such as Mexico's where, we are told, 'law institutes without regulating'.[78] But it will often be difficult to draw a clear line between economic and political change, on

---

[78] Sergio López-Ayylon, 'Notes on Mexican Legal Culture', (1995) 4 Soc. & Leg. Stud. 477, p. 479.

the one hand, and cultural change on the other. In either case, in Pierre Legrand's terms, legal transfers may be more a means of changing local narratives, rather than continuing them.

Legal transfers in changing contexts: an agenda for research

Every instance of legal transfer has its own history and needs to be examined in its own right. The idea that 'theory' can provide us with a means of predicting what will, or must, happen to legal transfers will usually prove misplaced or at least elusive; 'thick' description may be the best that we can achieve.[79] But the social scientist should also try to say something about the larger context in which these transfers take place. In particular, in order to make progress in rethinking legal transfers, we shall have both to clarify what is special about current developments and also ask whether existing models of legal transfer offer appropriate and comprehensive frameworks for understanding them.

In seeking to classify the kinds of legal transfers which are currently taking place, we may want to distinguish *different* processes of legal transfer happening at the same time. Take, for example, the following types of transfer (which do not begin to exhaust all the possible ways of distinguishing different mechanisms and processes of legal change):

1. Cases where one country borrows or submits to new laws introduced from another society (though there are likely to be very important differences between cases where this takes place as part of colonial imposition or as a result of other forms of influence).
2. Processes involving the spread of standards, regulations or 'soft law', for instance, through attempts at harmonization of private law within the European Union; conventions on biodiversity, genetic engineering or the internet; labour regulations by the International Labour Organization or international taxation agreements.
3. Cases where 'third cultures', such as arbitration fora in Paris or Zurich, reflect and further processes of globalization of law.

But we may also be interested in examining what *unites* present initiatives. For example, we may choose to explore the way transnational activities of legal transfer are linked to national, international and transnational

[79] Clifford Geertz, *The Interpretation of Cultures* (London: Fontana, 1973), p. 7.

460

actors – and how NGOs, such as the IMF or large charitable foundations, intersect or reconstitute these boundaries. We will need to bear in
mind not only such central legal activities as those connected to legislation
and standard-setting, adjudication, regulation, mediation and dispute set-
tlement, but also mutual exchange and networking as with international
meetings of judges, lawyers, academics, police or customs officers, as well
as efforts to create new legal, economic, political, social and educational
institutions.

It is tempting to summarize present developments as all, in one way
or another, illustrating the globalization of law. But it is important not
to make one-sided assumptions about what is meant by 'globalization' or
the way it affects law.[80] Globalization is a process which has multiple and
often contradictory aspects (social, cultural, economic, political, technical,
etc.). There are major changes taking place in world trade and communication. But their effects are neither uniform nor easily predictable. The label
is often used to cover developments which could be understood in other
terms; and it would be wrong to attribute to globalization what are simply
parallel but indigenous processes. Most importantly, globalization does not
mean that the world is necessarily becoming more homogeneous or harmonized. Much of the economic and financial integration which characterizes
globalized markets of production and consumption also presupposes, and
produces, divergence and difference or inclusion and exclusion.[81] Sometimes, globalization actually strengthens the local.[82] If globalization often
marginalizes the local, it is in part through its ability to define others as
'merely' local. For some observers, globalization should even be seen as no
more than a temporary vogue for neo-liberal policy choices dressed up in
the language of economic inevitability.[83]

Law can act as the bearer of globalization but it can also form part of the
resistance to it. To say that legal innovations are usually part and parcel of

---

[80] See Wolf Heydebrand, 'From Globalization of Law to Law under Globalization', in Nelken
and Feest, *supra*, note 4, pp. 117–37; *id.*, 'Globalization and the Rule of Law at the End of
the Twentieth Century', in Alberto Febbrajo, David Nelken and Vittorio Olgiati (eds.), *Social
Processes and Patterns of Legal Control: European Yearbook of Sociology of Law 2000* (Milan:
Giuffrè, 2001), pp. 25–127 [hereinafter 'Globalization and the Rule of Law'].

[81] For example, see David Nelken, 'The Globalization of Crime and Criminal Justice: Prospects
and Problems', in Michael Freeman (ed.), *Law and Opinion at the End of the Twentieth Century*
(Oxford: Oxford University Press, 1997), pp. 251–79.

[82] See Francis Snyder, 'Governing Economic Globalization: Global Legal Pluralism and European
Law', (1999) Eur. L.J. 334, p. 336.

[83] For example, see Allan Scott, 'Globalization: Social Process or Political Rhetoric?', in *id.* (ed.),
The Limits of Globalization: Cases and Arguments (London: Routledge, 1997), pp. 1–24.

longer-term social changes does not mean that law can be reduced to an inevitable concomitant or expression of such larger trends of convergence or globalization.[84] A weak feature of such a 'convergence thesis' is that it fails to explain how far, when and why law, or some components of law or any particular model of law, becomes a necessary part of doing things as compared to other forms of securing market certainty, political legitimacy or whatever.

If we are to take a stand for or against the globalization of law (for example, in the name of protecting diversity), we need to take care not to get any one aspect of these developments out of focus. For example, in his stringent criticisms of efforts geared to harmonization of law within the European Union, Pierre Legrand suggests that the law-making and law-enforcing activities of Europe's central agencies risk imposing the style and substance of civil-law at the expense of common-law legal culture.[85] By contrast, Maria Rosaria Ferrarese sees the globalization of law as essentially a process by which Anglo-American legal culture is systematically overpowering its civil-law competition by facilitating and promoting 'marketization'. Ferrarese points to the way corporations are becoming the new crucial legal actors as law comes to be linked to the needs of business rather than to national jurisdictions. She illustrates her argument with examples of many telling changes, ranging from the redefinition of the 'public' and the 'private' to the increasing use of oral proceedings.[86] No doubt there is evidence of both trends but it is important to recognize that matters are not one-sided.

Globalization of private and public law involves legislative, judicial or other efforts to extend cross-frontier trade and communication including e-commerce, the melding of 'private' and 'public' in international trade litigation and the creation or regulation of 'third spaces'. Although this is claimed to be in the general interest of free trade, we would be wrong to assume that all trading nations or all types of businesses gain equally. As an example of the globalization of criminal law, we can take the creation of international war tribunals or measures to permit the pursuit of crimes across national boundaries. Many initiatives aim to curb what are said to be common social problems, such as organized crime, money laundering, corruption, paedophilia, unauthorized immigration, environmental pollution, unregulated scientific experimentation, breach of copyright, counterfeiting or computer hacking. Sometimes, these measures also involve proposed

---

[84] See Lawrence M. Friedman, 'Is There a Modern Legal Culture?', (1994) 7 Ratio Juris 117.

[85] See Pierre Legrand, 'Against a European Civil Code', (1997) 60 Modern L.R. 44.

[86] See Maria Rosaria Ferrarese, *Le istituzioni della globalizzazione* (Bologna: Il Mulino, 2000).

462

solutions, as with the extension of transnational ethics in pharmaceutical research or common rules on asylum for refugees. But, again, whether, and how far, such problems are really the same in all the societies concerned and who benefits most from the struggle against them remains moot. Another important example of the globalization of law is found in the effort to spread human rights, as seen, for example, in international campaigns against wife-beating or female circumcision. Here, the success of globalization can be measured in the ability to deny that gains for victim groups are being bought at the expense of loss of cultural diversity.

Our theories of legal transfer are also likely to be affected by these social changes. Some writers make perhaps overstrong claims arguing that the interdependencies created by globalization require us to re-examine the whole comparative project. Wolf Heydebrand, for example, talks of the 'tension between the more or less static and interpretative comparative project and the dynamic longitudinal project imposed by the resumption of globalization'.[87] For her part, Maureen Cain suggests that where there are common causes and concerns, old-style comparison no longer has a point and risks ending up as either 'occidentalism' or 'orientalism'.[88] The assumptions which lie behind officially sponsored moves to legal transfer also change over time and place. Tom Ginsburg tells us that the new law-and-development movement is characterized by a focus on the techniques appropriate for transferring legal and political institutions, as if these can be abstracted from culture and from wider social change: 'today's development policy assumes that a country must adapt the proper institutions to facilitate growth and that institutions can be transferred across borders.'[89]

The theoretical models we use must make allowance for the variety of ways in which legal transfers can take place. Lawrence Friedman suggests that we should distinguish between processes of borrowing, diffusion or imposition.[90] Writers who draw on autopoietic theory likewise propose distinguishing between *ad hoc* contacts, systemic linkages and

---

[87] Heydebrand, 'Globalization and the Rule of Law', *supra*, note 80, p. 110.

[88] Maureen Cain, 'Orientalism, Occidentalism and the Sociology of Crime', (2000) 40 Brit. J. Criminology 239.

[89] Ginsburg, *supra*, note 74, p. 833. See also Wojciech Sadurski, 'On the Relevance of Institutions and the Centrality of Constitutions in Post-communist Transitions', in Jan Zielonka (ed.), *Democratic Consolidation in Eastern Europe*, vol. I: *Institutional Engineering* (Oxford: Oxford University Press, 2001), pp. 455–74.

[90] See Lawrence M. Friedman, 'Borders: On the Emerging Sociology of Transnational Law', (1996) 32 Stanford J. Int. L. 65.

co-evolution.[91] This also suggests the need to think more carefully about the relationship between such different processes and the commonly used metaphor of 'legal transplants'. Despite its continuing popularity, this metaphor seems ill-equipped to bring out such differences. Even with reference to straightforward attempts to introduce new legal institutions, the metaphor can easily prove misleading. In biological or botanical adaptation, success may indeed be a matter of 'survive or perish'. But, in the case of adapting legal systems, a far wider range of outcomes is possible – and, indeed, likely – and it will often not be clear whether survival refers to the legal system (or a given institution within it) or to the larger society itself.

It would be a mistake to see the problem here as simply requiring us to avoid resorting to metaphors. The use of 'living' or 'dead' metaphors is an intrinsic and unavoidable element of all our analogies and explanations. Rather, we need to become more aware of the implications of different metaphors. For example, what is illuminated and what is obscured by the alternative metaphor of 'palace wars', which Yves Dezalay and Bryant Garth suggest as the key to understanding the way legal ideas are now fought over by social elites at home and abroad?[92] Even the anodyne term 'legal transfers', which I chose for its very inoffensiveness, conjures up a sense of geographic mobility of law that could be misleading with respect to some processes by which law comes to be imitated abroad.

In line with my general argument, it is important to appreciate how different metaphors mobilize and favour different ideas about how law fits society. 'Mechanical' metaphors of legal transfer, for example, are those which use the language of borrowing, export, diffusion, circulation or imposition. They tend to accompany talking about law in the language of 'impact' and 'penetration' and reflect a vision of law as a working institution, as an instrument and as a technique of social engineering. Organic metaphors, however, speak about 'grafts', 'viruses' and 'contamination' and, of course, 'transplants' (whether medical or botanical). Legal transfers, when they succeed, thus 'set root' or 'blossom' and are described as 'fertile'. The use of these metaphors is likely to belong to a functionalist model of law as an interdependent part of a larger whole. Thus, to talk of 'legal adaptation' is to

---

[91] See John Paterson and Gunther Teubner, 'Changing Maps: Empirical Legal Autopoiesis', (1998) 7 Soc. & Leg. Stud. 451. See also Gunther Teubner, 'Global Bukowina: Legal Pluralism in the World Society', in id. (ed.), Global Law Without a State (Aldershot: Dartmouth, 1997), pp. 3–38.

[92] Yves Dezalay and Bryant Garth, 'The Import and Export of Law and Legal Institutions: International Strategies in National Palace Wars', in Nelken and Feest, supra, note 4, pp. 241–56.

464

use a metaphor derived from the language of functionalist survival. Finally, discursive metaphors apprehend law as communication, as narrative and as myth. Transferring law, on this approach, is to be understood mainly as a matter of translating and reformulating explicit and implicit meanings.

Law can be treated as an instrumentality, as part of a functioning whole or as communication. Depending on the purposes of our research into legal transfers, we may wish to privilege the exploration of one or more of these aspects of law. In replacing the metaphor of 'legal transplants', we should be careful to ensure that we are able to address all these aspects as and when relevant. Gunther Teubner's proposal to substitute the metaphor of 'legal irritants' does touch on all these three aspects of law. His work is also important because of the way it shows how theorizing about the possibility of legal transfers must be, and can be, linked to the understanding of new legal and social developments. In elaborating his critical account of judicial efforts to bring about legal harmonization in Europe, Teubner draws on Luhmann's social-systems theory and, in particular, on his idea of legal autopoiesis so as to show the way in which the binding arrangements between law and society have changed in conditions of late modernity.[93]

However, Teubner's arguments are not free of ambiguities.[94] His proposed new metaphor is unlikely to solve all our problems in understanding legal transfers. Thus, Teubner argues that legal transfers tend to lead to the 'creation of new cleavages in the interdependence of operationally closed social discourses'.[95] Because this unpredictability suggests the need for caution in undertaking legal transfers, Teubner's ideas have been quickly embraced for political-normative reasons rather than for theoretical-explanatory purposes. But some scholars who cite his work have no real interest in, or sympathy for, the theory which provides the framework for his argument. They fail to note that an insistence on the need for hermeneutic and interpretive exploration of legal culture and legal meaning would be quite incompatible with Teubner's attempts to apply Luhmann's observer-based systems theory. Nor is the idea of distinct legal *epistémès* consistent with Luhmann's 'scientific' attempt to postulate a universalistic definition of law. Finally, Teubner himself is by no means as pessimistic about the possibility of legal transfers as he is sometimes made to seem.[96]

---

[93] See Teubner, *supra*, note 12.   [94] See Nelken, 'The Meaning of Success', *supra*, note 62.
[95] Teubner, *supra*, note 12, pp. 31–2.
[96] His actual argument is that 'legal irritants' force the specific *epistémè* of domestic law to a reconstitution in the network of its distinctions and also provoke the social discourse to which law is closely tied to a reconstruction of its own. See Teubner, *supra*, note 12.

From the perspective of the sociology of law, a defect of much comparative work, both in theory and in practice, is the failure to engage in sufficient empirical research into what else is happening in the societies promoting or receiving legal transfers. There would seem to be little point in seeking to protect legal distinctiveness if other things in the society or culture concerned were already changing so as to achieve harmonization even without resort to law. Take, once again, the debates over harmonization within the European Union. There is currently considerable legal discussion over the appropriateness or otherwise of introducing harmonized European criminal proceedings as a means of tackling the considerable problem of frauds against the European Union budget.[97] But no one engaged in this controversy seems in the least worried about the well-established common auditing methods used by agencies such as the European Court of Auditors! To take a different example, many of the governmental and international agencies which promote legal change in developing countries focus on formal as opposed to informal institutions. These are easier to identify, analyse and engineer in ways that can produce the measurable results by which such bureaucracies justify their existence. Yet, there are likely to be informal institutions, less amenable to change by external interventions, which already carry out many of the tasks of the formal institutions whose performance the agencies are seeking to improve.[98]

Much the same applies to what may *not* be happening in receiving societies as compared to those doing the exporting of legal institutions or ideals. In considering current (renewed) efforts to export the 'rule of law', both to former communist countries or to emerging economies, careful attention needs to be given to the differential pace of technological revolutions and other social developments. William Scheuerman has put forward a schematic but provocative analysis of the effects of technical change on business life under late-modern forms of capitalism, arguing that the political and legal infrastructure of globalization bears little resemblance to the liberal model of the rule of law.[99] The rule of law was particularly useful to business people when it met their aspirations to make time and space manageable so as to reduce uncertainty based on distance and duration of commercial exchange. Now, however, the compression of time and space

---

[97] For example, see House of Lords Select Committee on the European Community, 'Prosecuting Fraud on the Communities Finances – The Corpus Juris', 62d session, 9th Report (1998–9).

[98] See Ginsburg, *supra*, note 74, p. 850.

[99] William E. Scheuerman, 'Globalization and the Fate of Law', in David Dyzenhaus (ed.), *Recrafting the Rule of Law: The Limits of Legal Order* (Oxford: Hart, 1999), pp. 243–66.

466

which characterizes globalization means that there is less of an elective affinity between capitalism and the rule of law. The risks the rule of law helped reduce are now, Scheuerman argues, better dealt with by the time-space compression made possible by modern technology: communication via computer is much quicker than creating and enforcing legal agreements. Against this background of social change, law increasingly loses its autonomy and becomes porous and open-ended. Flexibility is now all-important and business people have less need of standard and consistent norms. They thrive instead on the opportunities provided by difference between legal regimes. Arbitration is treated as the best option in cases of dispute.

No less importantly, the rule of law used to be valued because it protected business transactions from arbitrary interference by the state. But now, argues Scheuerman, at least as far as multinational business is concerned, companies often have the same rights as states themselves (as with NAFTA). The fact that poorer states need the investment which these businesses bring them means that the balance of power is no longer to their advantage. There follows a competition to reduce legal safeguards and there is, by now, considerable evidence that economic globalization flourishes where lower standards in protecting labour, health and the environment are exploited by powerful companies.[100] It would be misleading to ignore these or other similar factors when assessing the likely outcomes of introducing the type of separation between the state and the market identified with the classical (but now somewhat dated) idea of the 'rule of law'.

---

[100] See Fiona Haines, 'Towards Understanding Globalization and Corporate Harm: A Preliminary Criminological Analysis', paper presented at the Law and Society Association annual conference, Chicago, 2 June 1999, on file with the author.

[14]
The Meaning of Success in Transnational Legal Transfers

In an article published some while ago in the *Windsor Yearbook of Access to Justice* (Nelken 1981)[1] I sought to show that it was possible to examine the "gap" between aim and outcome in domestic legal interventions in ways that were valuable both for socio-legal theory and legal policy. On this occasion I want to return to this question in respect of the increasingly common incidence of cross national forms of legal transfer and borrowing.

For many writers these transfers raise crucial issues of legal policy which are in many ways parallel to the concerns about successful domestic social engineering in the 1960's and 1970's. A good example is provided by the following which is taken from a current grant submission to the National Science Foundation on the part of leading members of the USA "Law and Society" community.

Do legal transplants work? When do transplants succeed, as in Poland; when do they fail, as so far in Russia? There are now well-established "rule of law" programs in numerous organizations and agencies of funding and assistance, including U.S.AID, the World Bank, the Asian Development Bank, and the Inter-American Development Bank. Evaluations of efforts to strengthen judicial institutions have so far not been very optimistic. Nevertheless, such efforts continue as the centerpiece of programs to promote business investment and the protection of human rights.

These nationally targeted programs in support of the rule of law are only a part of the phenomenon that must be studied. There are also many examples of transnational institutions created to create quasi-judicial fora for the resolution of transnational disputes or the promotion of accountability for human rights violations. Examples include International Criminal Tribunals for War Crimes, the World Trade Organisation's dispute resolution machinery, NAFTA's dispute resolution processes, and other more or less formalized institutions such as international commercial arbitration or transnational efforts to control drug trafficking.

Developments in one area or institutional setting are closely related to developments in other areas and settings. The processes that produced the

This paper derives from a series of workshops organised at the Onati Institute of Sociology of Law 1997-1999 which were financed by the Volkswagen Foundation. The workshops were jointly planned and run by Erhard Blankenburg, Johannes Feest (then Director of the Institute), Volkmar Gessner and myself. This paper is particularly concerned with the issues raised in the third workshop, "Adapting Legal Cultures", the collected papers of which (edited by Nelken & Feest) are forthcoming.

1 D. Nelken, "The 'Gap Problem' in the Sociology of Law: A Theoretical Review" (1981) 1 *Windsor Y.B. Access Just.* 35-61.

NAFTA and that NAFTA has produced, for example, are having a strong impact on the role of lawyers and the position of law in Mexico and, to a lesser extent perhaps, in the United States and Canada' (Law and Society 2000).

On the other hand, there is certainly something paradoxical about this interest in sponsoring social engineering abroad at a time when in the domestic context efforts to achieve social policy and welfare aims through law have lost much of their support. Some of those deeply engaged in earlier rounds of trying to increase access to law do offer somewhat cynical accounts of the "palace wars" which lie behind many current initiatives to export and import law (Dezalay & Garth 1996,1997, 2001). And there is no lack of sophisticated theorists waiting to tell us why efforts to transfer law from one society to another are doomed to create confusion (Legrand 1996,1997; Teubner 1998).

One way of focusing these issues is to ask about the meaning of success in transnational legal transfers (and how far these transfers raise problems which go beyond those found in the domestic context). Students of legal transfers often write as if it is possible to determine what makes for success or failure. Indeed this is implicit in the widespread use of the metaphor of legal transplants with its reference to deliberate attempts to graft foreign bodies from one place to another. But the apparently straightforward idea of success in cases of botanical or medical transplants is much more problematic in the case of adapting legal systems. In this paper I shall do no more than touch on some of these problems, suggesting, as in my earlier article, that they themselves should be placed at the centre of enquiry into the effects of legal intervention.

The Meaning of Success

Can we, should we, talk of success and what could this mean in the case of legal adaptation? The first problem here has to do with the sort of exercise we are engaged in. The use of the term success has strong evaluative overtones, it gives the impression of endorsing one outcome rather than another, and easily ends up mixing together normative and explanatory enquiries. On the other hand, studies which claim to be determinedly descriptive and realistic (such as Dezalay & Garth, 2001) do not and cannot easily get away from evaluations of what they describe. In particular the distinction between the instrumental and merely symbolic or ornamental effects of law often runs up against the problem of generalizing across different legal cultures in which the place occupied by law may be quite different. In many societies it is exactly the ability to capture the symbolic which is all important. Such writers also risk reducing the range of ideal and material interests which shape legal transfers to no more than the search for power and prestige (whereas motives in human affairs are almost always more complicated).

We could, in theory, speak about the success of a transfer whilst being opposed to it, or feeling unhappy about the result. This will often have been the case in the past for countries under colonial control, and in the present period could apply to those seeking to resist the effects of such trends as globalization, Americanization or Europeanization. Even within a society legal interventions can be considered "too successful" when they "colonize" or displace other established normative patterns of regulating social relationships without the use of law (leading to what has been described as "juridification").[2] In practice, the introduction of new legal rules can either stabilize or unsettle existing normative practices, and the same applies to the role of law in relation to competing expertises (see Garth and Dezalay, 2001, and Flood, 2001). Success from one point of view does not necessarily entail success from another. What we witness, when legal change does lead to social change, is a radiating set of intended and unintended outcomes.

Some authors start the other way round. The likelihood of "failure" is mobilized as an argument against the credibility of deliberately pursuing legal transfers. Legrand (1996, 1997, 2001) for example, shifts rather quickly from claims about the difficulty of attaining certain outcomes to impassioned warnings against even trying. There is some risk of incoherence here. If transplants are "impossible", why insist on the negative effects of efforts to achieve harmonization? Teubner (1998) also sets out to convince us that attempts at convergence through law can only end up in creating greater divergence because of the way law can only be "structurally coupled" to other discourses. But he, too, pleads in favour of doing all that is possible to maintain diversity. We may be left wondering whether these authors really do believe that it is impossible to achieve greater harmonization and convergence or whether they fear that it is all too possible—but undesirable.[3] What remains uncertain is how far it can ever be possible to distinguish the descriptive from the judgmental in describing the possibilities and outcomes of legal transfers. Would talking about "effects", rather than success and failure, help us keep the two issues apart, or would it only lead to more obscurity?

The next difficulty has to do with the sort of legal adaptation which is under examination. There would certainly seem to be important differences to be borne in mind when dealing with imposed, invited, or unplanned examples of legal transfer. There is something to be said for limiting discussions of success to cases of deliberate attempts at legal adaptation, such as when a country seeks to borrow from another, or a legal institution attempts to impose common standards. While it makes sense to judge the success of such deliberate attempts at legal transfer in terms of the goals of the various parties involved, the matter becomes much more complicated when we come to deal with a phenomenon such as globalization which, by definition, is a phenomenon beyond (or out of) control (Nelken 1997). It would beg the question to assume that the various actors involved in and effected by globalization have common goals. But, on the other hand, it could be argued

---

2 Transplants can be more successful abroad than at home as in the way tulips succeeded better in Holland than in Prague from where they were imported. Some transplants, such as the introduction of rabbits into Australia, can be "too successful"!

3 The problem posed by Legrand (1995) – all too plausibly—is the danger that common law patterns of legal culture and reasoning will lose out to those of Continental law in any European wide harmonization.

that we cannot afford to leave out of consideration the many ways in which laws adapt other than as a result of deliberate choice. Surely there is all the more reason to want to find ways of talking about the successful or unsuccessful results of these other processes and developments, even if these are not well formulated in terms of goals and achievements?[4]

What makes a transfer a success? Scholars use very different criteria. It might be thought that the best evidence of success of a legal transfer would be its complete absorption into the legal and political culture which has imported it. Krygier (1997) in fact uses the example of the introduction of the institution of the ombudsman in Poland as his illustration of the possibility of successful transplantation even in Eastern Europe. But Friedman (1998) argues that the world-wide spread of the ombudsman is a sign of indigenous needs and offers no proof of Scandinavian influence. More than this. Sometimes the success of a transplant may actually depend on its origins being forgotten. Jettinghoff (2001) points out that labour exchanges in Holland are a forgotten legacy of the German occupation, and that such institutions were actually abandoned in post-war Germany. Tanase (2001, in describing the Japanese experience, draws our attention to a paradox. The very need to import law from outside can create a sense of in-authenticity. Many people in Japan wonder whether they are really part of a "modern" country because they still recognize the foreign origins of the legal institutions which they have "successfully" adopted.

The way success is conceived also determines whether or not legal transfers are thought to be generally feasible. Watson, in his many writings about legal transplants, and Friedman in his important contributions to sociology of law (*e.g.,* Friedman 2001), are both sanguine about the possibility of transfers. But they are confident for quite different reasons. Watson is mainly concerned to show that law travels easily between very different contexts—whatever happens to it afterwards. Friedman thinks transplants generally succeed because larger social circumstances eventually reshape or bypass paper rules.

At the same time, ambiguity over the meaning of success regularly leads to the slaying of straw men. Harding sees the history of legal transplants in East Asia as largely successful "if one judges by the criterion of whether the law has stuck or come unstuck" (Harding, 2001; see also, Nottage 2001). Such commentators are impressed by the way laws are imported into often very different social contexts in which they do then get used. But they accept, perhaps too easily, that transplanted laws are bound in some respects to work differently in the countries in which they are imported. On the other hand, Bradley, writing about the extent of convergence of family law in Europe, argues that: "contrary to predictions in the transplants thesis, construction of a unitary legal system in this area of private law will not be entirely trouble free" (Bradley 1999:132). But who claims that success

---

4 Some theoretical approaches to legal transfers would in any case avoid talking of group and individual goals in favour of such units as "self-steering systems" and "discourses" (see *e.g.,* Paterson & Teubner 1998).

is trouble free? Even Watson would never have supported such predictions if this is Bradley's criterion of success.

At one extreme, Legrand (1996,1997,2001) argues that harmonization of law can never be achieved because the meaning of law in different cultures can never be the same – "meaning cannot survive the journey". On the other hand Prosser (2001) suggests that harmonization of law is actually easier than it is made to seem. He argues that we should not make too much of differences in legal culture, which often serve mainly to conceal effective similarities.

It is surely insufficient merely to note that foreign legal rules or institutions have been legally adopted without asking whether or not they have actually been put into effect. But it is more difficult to decide what baseline we should use for determining whether a transfer has or has not been successful. Friedman (1998) rightly notes that it is foolish to speak of (transplanted) law "failing" if we do not know the extent to which a particular law or practice ever "penetrated" the society to which it is assumed to belong. Is it safe to assume that the goal of legal transfer is to produce greater harmonization of social behaviour (and whose behaviour matters?) and not just harmonization of rules and decisions? Must the rules or institutions transferred fulfil the same aims and achieve the same results in their society of adoption as in their society of origin? Is it even plausible to expect them to? What if working in the same way they produce different outcomes? What if they have to work differently to achieve "the same" results?

According to Watson subsequent development of a legal rule in a way that does not parallel developments in its original society should not be confused with rejection. If it is successful a transplant grows in the new body and becomes part of that body – as it would have continued to grow in the parent system (Watson 1974: 27). But, according to Dezalay and Garth (2001), those who seek to apply borrowed law have to justify deviance from the original model in terms that resonate with the centre – otherwise the transplant will not be considered the genuine article. The increasing ease and speed of communication between centre and periphery means that it is more difficult now than in the past to sustain and justify such "deviance".

As this shows, it is important to notice that the question of success can arise in more than one stage of the transfer of legal rules and institutions. We may be concerned with how a legal adaptation *emerges* – the choice of law – or with the way it exerts its influence – the *results* of a given transfer. Our way of explaining the first of these matters may well be different from the second, likewise our assessment of what "success" means in each case. The time-frame being used plays an important role in explaining and judging success. There may be some matters which are crucial when we focus on shorter periods – such as the legal technicalities of borrowing, or the often highly contingent political circumstances which accompany legal transfers. On the longer view, technique may be taken as a constant and the significance of historical contingencies "smoothed out". The metaphor of legal transplants may also create some awkwardness in addressing the question of success in certain situations (Nelken 2001). What of multilateral legal trans-fers? What about the effects in terms of battles for power and prestige of legal transfers on the countries exporting such law (Dezalay and Garth, 2001). How should we judge the overall outcome of a series of transfers from different (incompatible) donors? Does the not uncommon situation of complex "legal pluralism" – the result of successive waves of transfers (Harding, 2001) show the success or rather the failure of transplants?[5]

The Conditions of Success

Assuming for the purpose of argument that we can or must talk of suc-cess what does the success of a legal transfer depend on? What variables must we examine in seeking to assess or explain success and failure? How far does transferring law abroad depend on the same factors which affect the success of legal interventions at home? We must be prepared to find that the conditions for success will depend on what is being transferred, by which source, to which receiving society, the way the transfer is intro-duced, and a potentially unlimited number of wider background factors and previous historical experiences. It will also be necessary to reflect on how far the variables in question represent a matter of objective circumstance and how much they depend on there being treated subjectively "as if" they were unchangeable or must not be changed.

Faced with either strategic or tactical questions of how to bring about social change through law there would seem much to be learned from the existing social science literature which has attempted to distil the lessons of past efforts at social engineering. The approach to law which has been described as "pragmatic instrumentalism" characterizes many examples of modern uses of law in the home contexts of modern Western societies. Sociology of law textbooks thus contain ample discussions of domestic efforts at social change through law. These discussions should have at least some relevance also for efforts to implement law across societal bound-aries. They can help us understand what are the prerequisites and what are the likely outcomes of legal change. Such issues should include the ques-tion: Is the existence of a certain type of legal profession a precondition for certain types of social change? How does legally initiated change involve wider groups in society?

But we must also consider the question, how far a pragmatic instrumen-tal approach to law can itself be taken for granted in other legal cultures.

Cotterrell (2001), in discussing the possibility of legal transplants between societies, claims that lawyers can engineer massive change as long as what is imported is seen as an "organic development appealing to tradi-tional understandings of legal excellence, appropriateness, justice or practi-cality". As would be expected, this argument is consistent with his discussion of the limits of law as an instrument of social change in domes-

---

5 Orucu (1995) offers an original non-evaluative typology of the results of legal transfers (using culinary metaphors) in which she emphasizes the different outcomes of legal trans-fers in cases where the societies concerned started from conditions in which they already enjoyed either or both legal or cultural affinities.

tic contexts, as set out in his textbook of sociology of law (Cotterrell 1984). His summary of the literature there indicates that the first condition for effectiveness is that the source of law must be authoritative and prestigious and that it has to be shown to be congruent with aspects of the society's heritage. The success of legal interventions depends also on the type of law being transferred, and on the parties being affected. A crucial role is played by the agencies responsible for implementing the law that must be able to employ positive sanctions as well as other methods of persuasion to ensure compliance. Often the problem of effective change comes down to how to transform institutions rather than influence individuals.

This said, there are also likely to be extra difficulties in making law effective in situations of legal transfer. Some of these derive from the wider circumstances in which legal transfers take place. Cotterrell points to the difficulty of measuring the effectiveness of law even in domestic contexts given that other factors are changing at the same time. Typically, legal innovations are part and parcel of longer term social changes, such as the relative improvement of safety standards at work and in food hygiene over the past century. When law is transferred to new social contexts this embeddedness of legal change in social change may often not hold true; here, it is typically law which is being asked to jump start the wider process of social change or leapfrog over long standing cultural obstacles. Cotterrell explains that the instrumentalist role of law, the way law comes to depend less on its congruence with popular mores and begins to be capable of transforming them, emerges (in particular places) only at a particular stage of legal development. But this means that it will always be relevant to ask whether the role of law in the countries in which law is being transferred is at the same stage of development as that from which the law is taken.

There are different opinions about the general role of time in affecting the success of legal transfers (and this may also depend on the type of legal transfer under consideration). In discussing legal change in Latin America Dezalay and Garth (2001) suggest that time is needed for a transplant to take effect and that this depends, on their approach, on the process by which a cosmopolitan elite transforms its symbolic capital over the generations. In commenting on ex-communist transitions, however, Sadurski (2000) is agnostic about whether it is better to move quickly or more cautiously towards a new Constitution. For him "the right timing is a context-dependent matter, and is usually known only with the benefit of hindsight." Discussing the same region, Cotterrell (2001) describes how the problem of conferring legitimacy on emerging political legal arrangements depends on what he sees as the delicate balance between action in the shorter term and in the longer term as different social actors wait to see whether others will obey or not.

A linked question frequently raised by those seeking to bring about successful legal transfers is whether there is a temporal order which must be respected. For example, societies going through a post-communist transition face the problem whether the extension of competition and the "free market" should precede, accompany, or follow the construction of effective multi-party democracy.[6] Linz and Stepan (1996), in their study of democratic transitions from both fascist and communist regimes, emphasize the need to resolve the problem of creating democratic politics before tackling the construction of free market capitalism. But the Japanese experience seems to show that successful modernization can equally well be brought about by effective collaboration between a relatively authoritarian government bureaucracy and private industry (Tanase, 2001).

Other problems in the applicability of the larger literature on "the limits of law" derive less from what may be special about the conditions under which legal transfers are made and more from the ethnocentrism of allegedly universal propositions about what it is that makes law effective. Anglo-American writers make much of the need to give people incentives to set law in motion, but the extent to which legal cultures deem it appropriate to leave law to be initiated by private parties, rather than by representatives of the state, varies considerably as between different societies (Ferrarese 1997).

In considering the prospects for legal transfer it is crucial to give attention to *the types of law* it is intended to transplant (see Cotterrell, 2001). But because the meaning and significance of different types of law are culturally variable it is increasingly difficult to make generalizations about which type of law transfers most smoothly. It used to be thought that it was easier to transfer law dealing with economic matters as compared to those bearing on the private or religious spheres (Massell, 1968). But more recent scholarship has complicated the picture by showing the possibility of using law to transform such spheres (Starr, 1992). Cotterrell (2001) notes that business communities (such as Turkish money lenders) can have economic interests for resisting legal change, and how, on the other hand, changes in family law may be pushed through as part of struggles for women's emancipation. But even Cotterrell may not go far enough. In his textbook he cites Pound's comments (in relation to the domestic context) on the ill-advisedness of using law to interfere too much in regulating family affairs. Cotterell himself (2001) argues for similar caution in using law in such spheres when he discusses the relationship between law and different forms of "strong" and "weak" community. Yet there are wide differences in the way different legal and religious cultures treat family relations; some see family matters as the very first priority in terms of the need for detailed legal regulation! And even in our own type of society family life is increasingly being regulated.

More could be said also about the variation amongst different national, legal and religious cultures with regards to the aim of making people good through law. In some cultures law itself represents a form of morality, in others it is supposed to respect and back up morality, in others, such as Japan, law is assumed to undermine morality (see Tanase, 2001). Whereas

---

6 Given the present vogue for neo-liberal economic solutions to social and political problems it is easy to forget that transplants may concern schemes for greater regulation as much as for greater deregulation or privatisation.

for some common law countries it may be true that law "must not seem utopian" (Cotterrell, 1984: 59-60), in some cultures in Continental Europe law gains allegiance precisely by its ability to present "counterfactual ideals" (Van Swanningen, 1999), even if adhesion to law in the short term is then often more symbolic than real.

Much has been written about the variables that are especially relevant to the choice of society from which legal transfers are taken. It is frequently argued that the main factor here has to do with the prestige of the nation or legal system from which law is taken. But in order to avoid this being a tautology we would need to be able to unpack this idea. How far can this explain the current influence of American models of common law at a time of globalization? Do economic power and legal prestige always go together? Comparative lawyers have often noted that England's greatest period of economic and political power did not lead to the adoption of common law on the Continent. What, if anything, has changed? If law and economic goods circulate in the same circuits–why are Japanese goods so welcome but not their law?

One standard starting point for the analysis of legal transfers is the pre-existing relationship of past contacts and similarity, and difference between the society which is the source of law and the society interested in importing. Intimacy, duration and intensity of previous contact are all said to be crucial. It is argued that the more similar the two societies, or at least the more similar the institution being borrowed, the more likely a transfer is to be successful. The success of the institution of ombudsman in some former Communist countries for example could in this way be attributed to the fact that such societies already had experience of being encouraged to bring complaints about middle level bureaucracy. Often lawyers will explicitly say they are seeking models from what they claim are similar or compatible societies. They will choose to reject laws which come from countries they do not want to come to resemble, as in the reaction in the ex-Soviet Union to legislative proposals that are seen to be modeled on the United States (Waelde and Gundersonde 1994: 374-5; Ajani 1995).

On the other hand and under some circumstances, for example because of educational or other historical connections, lawyers and politicians may look rather to very different sorts of society as the source of the prestigious law they wish to import. Moreover, and this is a point often overlooked, those actively encouraging transplants in periods of political transition often consciously choose to borrow law from a very different kind of society. In this way they hope to use law as a means of overcoming current problems by transforming their society into one more like the source of such borrowed law. The aims here can include the effort to become more democratic, more economically successful, more secular, or more religious. For some societies, such as modernizing Japan (see Tanase, 2001), or Italy, after the recent collapse of its ruling political parties (Nelken, 1996b, 2000), the search may simply (or not so simply) be for institutions which will make them more "normal", even if this search for normality is often doomed to be self contradictory (see Tanase, 2001). The transfer of dissimilar models is of course even more likely where the legal transfer is imposed by third parties as part of a colonial project. But it also character-izes the efforts of international organizations, such as the International Monetary Fund, when they seek to reshape societies according to a suppos-edly universal pattern of political and financial integrity.

So far, we have discussed the conditions for successful legal transfer as if these were objective matters of calculable engineering. But the potential success of legal transfers cannot merely be read out of the historical record (or the social science literature).[7] How that record is read itself influences what is done and what can be done. Harding (2001), for example, is broadly optimistic about the possibilities of further development towards Western models of law in South East Asia despite culture differences and current problems linked to political corruption, the banking system and environmental pollution. For an optimist, even scandals can be taken not so much as evidence of deep underlying problems but as a sign that the soci-ety concerned is (at last) recognizing the need to do something about a problem.

For some writers this element of subjectivity in the way scholars and others choose to describe and act in the light of alleged constraints on legal transfers is all-important. Commenting on scholarly debates over the possi-bilities of change in Russia and other former communist countries of East-ern Europe, Krygier (1997) argues that we should distinguish between pessimistic and optimistic approaches to legal transplants. Scholars can vary as to whether they are hopeful or otherwise either about the feasibility of changing institutions or about the possibility of overcoming cultural obstacles to change. Such attitudes will often be manifested with reference to the question of how far back in history it is necessary to go in seeking an explanation for the present problems to which a transplanted remedy is being proposed. Explanations can either be sought in deep underlying aspects of culture, or in more recent aspects of social structure. In the case of some former communist countries there is debate over whether recep-tiveness to Western legal institutions depends on the way they were shaped during the period of Communism or on longer lying historical differences in politics, religion and legal culture. For other countries looking to import foreign models of law, disagreement concerns the weight to be attributed to the recent influence of colonization as compared to previous experience or otherwise of self-government or political unity.

Logically speaking, our views about the possibilities of understanding another culture, and hence our capacity to model the process involved in successful transfer and regulation, will influence our confidence in recom-mending legal transfers. Concerned that the complexities of introducing change should not lead to paralysis, Krygier argues that there is no reason to assume that history, by itself, demonstrates the possibility, or impossibil-ity of change, in a given situation. In practice, he argues much depends on

---

7 Some theories try to build such uncertainty into their arguments, as when autopoietic theo-rists argue that prediction is impossible unless one is dealing with "a trivial machine" (Paterson & Teubner 1998).

the "will" of those engaged in transfers not to be trapped by history. The same ambivalence between objective constraint and subjective will characterizes discussion of the problem of "missing" institutions in the pursuit of legal and social change. The existence and vitality of specific kinds of legal and political institutions does make a difference. As Sadurski argues, when reviewing a series of accounts of the varying fates of various ex-communist transitions:

> [I]f there is one single conclusion that can be drawn from the impressive variety of arguments, reports and theories included in this book, it must be that institutions matter...institutions matter in the sense that they are not neutral; they do not merely channel and organise pre-political forms of collective life. Rather, they crucially affect, influence and change the way politics develop...even when this is not always obvious to participants in the events (Sadurski 2000).

But institutions can be created and do not necessarily depend on predetermined conditions. As Sadurski again puts it:

> these outcomes do not reflect previous aspects of culture or economy of the countries concerned...any attempt to attribute a particular difference in institutional patterns to a relevant difference in the tradition, forms of civil society, economic development, or any other non-institutional factor within any of the countries – would be extremely risky (Sadurski 2000).

It would seem plausible to assume that those who are optimistic about the possibility of change are politically progressive (or at least see themselves as such) whereas those who are pessimistic tend to be conservative (and see themselves as such). But this will not always be so. Some of those who espouse "Asian values", or urge a return to Muslim "fundamentalist" values, can be among the most optimistic social engineers (transplanting as it were from the past). Likewise, Legrand (2001), who, in Krygier's terms, could be described as a cultural pessimist, actually presents himself as politically progressive. He is critical of the arguments of those who favour a European harmonization of law claiming that it is their unwillingness to recognize differences in tradition and culture which is basically conservative. For him they "trivialize the political so as to meet the regulatory needs of liberal capitalism". Meanwhile, those committed to selling law abroad tend just to get on with it, paying little heed to those who warn that they fail to acknowledge the problems posed by difference, or that they risk eliminating valuable aspects of legal and political diversity (Legrand 1999b, 2001; Teubner 1998). It is usually sufficient to present the change as one that is of value in itself and/or corresponding to that being sought by those asking for such transfers.

As this example illustrates, the possibilities and dangers of self-fulfilling prophecies are not limited to debates over Eastern Europe. In some of their writings authors like Friedman treat convergence as "inevitable". Others, like Teubner, see the production of increasing divergence as what is unavoidable. Talking in this way can itself help encourage a trend or help to ward it off. It can be particularly interesting to ask why scholars or activists who were pessimistic in one generation then become pessimistic in another or vice versa. Dezalay and Garth (2001) discuss post-war attempts by USA agencies to influence legal developments in Latin America. They ask why the "law and development" movement is widely described as a failure whereas current more *ad hoc* influences are seen as having more success. Their account shows that it is very difficult to decide how far our judgements of success depend on the results obtained or on changes in our expectations given the other changes which have taken place. Above all, however, what they emphasize is the extent to which judgements of whether legal transfers have been a success (as well as judgements of whether they are likely to be a success) are a result of competition over social definitions. According to them it is important to investigate the form such competition takes, not only in the country to which the law is being transferred, but just as much in the country doing the exporting.

Measuring Success and Claiming Victory

How can we measure the success of a legal transfer? There are enough problems in assessing the outcome of technical innovations: no one would say that the telephone is not a success even if it is used much more as a means of communication between those who live nearby, than, as had been anticipated, between people living at long distance. Assessing social innovation is even more complex. It is not just that proposing or introducing legal reforms, such as mediation or court management, in the name of greater working "efficiency", also forms part of political strategies and carries political implications. In many societies questions of legal organization are political "all the way down". The idea of "success" assumes that law has goals which can be measured (a task to be fulfilled by legal policy and social science.) And there is no doubt that many of those involved in the business of legal transfer do claim to have some instrumental goals in mind. But the engineering approach to law varies greatly in its relevance as between types of law, as well as between one legal culture and another. As Cotterrell (2001) puts it, "the way law is conceptualized – for example as rules, as ideas embedded in legal culture, as a part of culture in some wider sense, or as an instrument for particular purposes – colours the way that the success (indeed, the very possibility) of legal borrowing is judged".

Recent theories, such as Luhmann and Teubner's auto-poietic approach to law, by revising our ideas of legal engineering, would lead us to be more cautious about the sort of success we should be looking for. "Legal irritants", says Teubner "cannot be domesticated; they are not transferred from something alien into something familiar, not adapted to a new cultural context, rather they will unleash an evolutionary dynamic in which the external rule's meaning will be reconstructed and the internal context will undergo fundamental change" (Teubner 98:12). But, even within societies with a history of using law for social engineering, law cannot always be thought about only in terms of measurable goals. The increasing use of "soft law" and of open-ended standards complicates the process of assessing outcomes (see *e.g.*, Joerges, Schepeland & Vos 1999, on the increasing resort to standards in the European Union context). Some law is explicitly facilitative and is intended to give opportunities for private negotiation rather than to achieve specific outcomes. But how are we to assess success if the use of law does not have to satisfy regulatory goals and there is no prescribed "end state"?

There is an even more basic issue here. Consider the difference between considering law as an "instrument" or treating it as a "narrative" (Nelken 1996a). One of Legrand's chief arguments against the possibility of legal transplants is that it too easily assumes that law is an enterprise in social engineering. He insists that we need to see law as an integral part of the way a society sustains its reigning myths and narratives. Deciding whether a reinterpretation or translation of a text is more or less successful takes a very different course than investigating the outcome of social engineering. What makes a good translation is its faithfulness to different worlds rather than its effects or consequences.

The notion of success is normally linked to showing how the transferred law (also) fits its new environment. But what if societies have different ideas of what that "fit" needs to be? In assessing success should we be using the criterion of "fit" customary in the exporting or in the importing legal culture? Greater sensitivity to cultural variability as to the place which law occupies in different societies may suggest that often what is being transplanted along with a particular legal institution or procedure is the ideology of "legal instrumentalism"– the very idea that law is something which does or should "work" (together with the claim that this is something which can or should be assessed in ways which are separable from wider political debates.) This opens up room for an important set of research questions about the ideological effects of legal transfers. For example: how does the NAFTA Treaty affect a legal culture such as Mexico where, we are told, "law institutes without regulating"? (Lopez-Ayylon 1995). The drive towards legal instrumentalism may not be without its costs in terms of normative pluralism and flexibility. Some of the same societies which are so reluctant to apply (managerial) ideas of efficiency to law are at the same time places where "practical" skills in using or avoiding State law, in obedience to other normative expectations, are highly developed.

Even assuming we can decide what constitutes success there is no reason to assume that success will be an all or nothing affair, rather than a mixed bag. In the first place, we may be dealing with a legal transfer which explicitly sets out to be selective but then has the result that the importing country gets more, or less, than it bargained for. Note, for example, Harding's claim (2001) that Malaysia and other countries in South East Asia have made considerable strides in the direction of importing many kinds of Western Law even if their governments prefer to hold on to their indigenous versions of internal security and labour law. Likewise, once law is transferred, people may choose to use only part of what is available, as in the way those in Malaysia, Saudi Arabia, Russia or Turkey tend to use only parts of imported family law or commercial law. Most commonly, success is partial. Garth & Dezalay (2001) contrast the continuing failure to create American-type law schools in Latin America with the important role in debt restructuring played by Latin American corporate lawyers who first came to America to study, and then collaborated with U.S. firms. But they also emphasize how in Latin America it is less important to be a successful lawyer than to be able to convert such symbolic legal capital into political capital at the right moment.

The same change can also have both "good" and "bad" effects. According to Sadurski this is true of the way higher courts in ex-Communist countries of Eastern Europe have helped "constitutionalize politics" (Sadurski 2000). An adaptation can have contradictory effects, or an adaptation may work at one level but fail or cause problems at another level. In Italy, unlike Anglo-American cultures, the police tend to be trusted by the community the more they are seen to be free from its influence ñ this is true especially, but not only, in the South of the country where organized crime is so powerful (Nelken 1994). But, under the influence of Anglo-American models, the idea of "community policing", of police responsive to their local community, is spreading and has already led to changes at the level of the municipal police (Nelken 2000). How, if at all, this will affect policing at the national level has yet to be seen.

The problems of judging success in legal transfers between societies are certainly no less than those which confront us in the appraisal of domestic socio-legal interventions. A classical difficulty here concerns the way we determine the goals of legal transfers (Nelken 1981). Starting with legislative outcomes we cannot assume that any given initiative in transferring law has only one goal, that it represents the goal of any particular group, or even that it has a clear and achievable goal. What those transferring law are trying to do will vary across time and place. At one extreme we could place the lawyer who writes a new code and then leaves "the natives" to get on with it, and at the other, there are stories of administrators and missionaries who are determined to shape subjects into legal bearers of rights and duties (Comaroff & Comaroff 1995). In studying transnational legal transfers it will not even be enough to consider whether the new law functions in practice if the reason that it was imported was only as a means to a further end. Often the point of introducing new law is the hope that it will (magically?) bring about the conditions – a flourishing economy or a healthy civil society – found in the wider context in which the borrowed law flourishes (see Mertus 1998).

Whose goals count? Is success to be judged from the perspective of those promoting or those receiving the transfer? What should we do if, as is likely, they are in disagreement? Does the meaning to be given to success depend on the aims of the intentions and interests of those promoting an adaptation, and those who then do (or do not) make use of new opportunities, or submit to new controls or requirements (or resist and avoid them)? Or, is it something for the scholar to assess in terms of external criteria, taking into account perhaps also those factors and unintended outcomes which could not have been known to the social actors concerned, such as the way a given change is affected by the differentiating and integrating effects of globalization?

In all but the most technical of legal transfers there are likely to be conflicting interests at stake, involving different governments or different economic interests, or among members of governmental and non-
governmental organizations, parliamentarians, judges, lawyers other professionals – as well as the various parties likely to be most affected by the
law. Businessmen may encourage resort to one or other type of legal forum
because of the benefits to their organization, politicians may promote the
adoption of new criminal procedures or civil legal remedies because of the
implications for the groups which support them, judges gain recognition by
introducing mediation schemes in their courts, experts of one kind or
another suggest that they can offer the needed services. The alleged (convergent) "functional necessities" of modern societies are achieved through
hard fought battles and subject to a large degree of contingency.

As this suggests, the most fundamental question from which there is no
escape is who gets to determine what is meant by success. What some
observers and participants will see as success, others may well see as failure. Conversely, what some may describe as "failure" may be lauded by
others, from either the political left or right, as (successful) "resistance".
This applies whether we are talking about borrowing a foreign law,
attempts at harmonization, or the effects of globalization and deregulation
on "free trade" (as the recent protests since Seattle at WTO talks have dra-
matized). It concerns not only the transfer of instrumental laws such as
rules about product liability, but also, arguably even more, the attempt to
transfer general principles. For example, against the background of Chinese tradition, what some see as the welcome spread of "the rule of law"
can be criticized as the marginalization of the importance of "*quing*", or
appeal to others feelings, versus "*li*" or reasonableness. (Man & Wai 1999).
And even if a transfer is viewed positively, what often matters most for
political groups, for their allies in different places, for cosmopolitans and
locals, and for different groups of professionals (in both importing and
exporting countries), is who gets the credit and the benefit.

As with controversial domestic legal interventions the "goal" of any
legal transfer will often be fought over by groups or individuals–its "meaning" will unfold over time. Success will then turn on the ability of one
group to impose its interpretation of the outcome of a particular transfer or
adaptation and to tell a convincing story of what has occurred. More subtly,
it may also depend on the ability to impose a particular interpretation of
what success means or the way it should be measured. Dezalay and Garth
(2001) describe those actors who promote transfers as "double agents"
because at the same time as participating in the process of exportation they
help define the criteria according to which the success of transplant is to be
defined.

On the other hand, just as we need to avoid assuming that the definition
of success is self-evident we also need to avoid romanticizing the idea of
"resistance". This may be represented not only by popular movements,
labour organizations, local peasants or craft workers but also by a host of
other subjects including local Mafias, national and local politicians and
businessmen, landowners with vested interests, Catholic or other religious

hierarchies, or Islamic or other radicals. What were once "counter hege-monic" social movements (Santos 1995) can change (or fail to change) their role or strategies as conditions change. Sometimes, as in present day Argentina or Chile, "cause lawyers" may be heavily involved in testing the limits and applicability of new statutes passed under international pressure to protect the rights of racial and ethnic minorities, workers and consumers, or the environment. Their effort may be to use foreign borrowed law to serve the interests of non-elite groups in the face of a politically condi-tioned judiciary. Nor should we underestimate the power of local actors to make selective use of what is being offered, or their ability to craft accounts of their goals which mediate between what they expect and what is expected of them. As Mertus puts it in writing about the way social actors in former Yugoslavia construct acceptable stories which address the competing ideologies of liberalism and nationalism, they "whisper nation-alism even as talking what intervenors want to hear" (Mertus 1998).

References

Ajani, G. (1995) "By Chance and Prestige: Legal Transplants in Russia and Eastern Europe," 43 *Am. J. Comp. L.*: 93-117.

Bradley, D. (1999) "Convergence in Family Law: Mirrors, Transplants and Political Economy," 6 *Maastricht J. European and Comp. L.*: 127-150.

Comaroff, J. and Comaroff, J. (1995) "The Discourse of Rights in Colonial South Africa: Subjectivity, Sovereignty, Modernity" in A. Sarat & T.R. Kearns, eds., *Identities, Politics and Rights*, University of Michigan Press: 193-238.

Cotterrell, R. [2001] "Is There a Logic of Legal Transplants?" in D. Nelken and J. Feest, eds., *Adapting Legal Cultures*, Hart Publishing.

Cotterrell, R. (1984) *The Sociology of Law* (2d edition), Butterworths.

Dezalay,Y. and Garth, B. (1996) *Dealing in Virtue*, University of Chicago Press.

Dezalay,Y. and Garth, B. (1997) "Law, Lawyers and Social Capital: 'Rule of Law' versus Relational Capitalism", *Social and Legal Studies*, 6: 109-43.

Dezalay,Y. and Garth, B. [2001] "The Import and Export of Law and Legal Institu-tions: International Strategies in National Palace Wars" in D. Nelken & J. Feest, eds., *Adapting Legal Cultures*, Hart Publishing.

Ferrarese, M.R. (1997) "An Entrepeneurial Conception of the Law? The American Model Through Italian Eyes" in D. Nelken, ed., *Comparing Legal Cultures*, Dartmouth: 157-182.

Flood, J. [2001] "The Vultures Fly East: The Creation and Globalization of the Dis-tressed Debt Market" in D. Nelken & J. Feest, eds., *Adapting Legal Cultures*, Hart Publishing.

Friedman, L. (1998) "Comments on Applebaum and Nottage" in J. Feest & V. Gessner, eds., *Proceedings of the 2nd Onati Workshop on Changing Legal Cul-tures*, Onati: 139-149.

Friedman, L. [2001] "Comments on Cotterrell and Legal Culture" in D. Nelken & J. Feest, eds., *Adapting Legal Cultures*, Hart Publishing.

Harding, A. [2001] "Comparative Law and Legal Transplantation in South East Asia" in D. Nelken & J. Feest, eds., *Adapting Legal Cultures*, Hart Publishing.

Joerges, C, Schepeland, J, & Vos, E. (1999) "The Law's problems with the involve-ment of Non-Governmental Actors in Europe's Legislative Processes: The Case of Standardisation Under the 'New Approach'" 1999/9 Law Working Papers, European University Institute.

Krygier, M. (1997) "Is There Constitutionalism After Communism? Institutional Optimism, Cultural Pessimism, and the Rule of Law" in *Int'l J. Sociology* 26, 4,1996-1997: 17-47.

Law and Society Association (2000), Newsletter.

Legrand, P. (1996) "European Legal Systems are not Converging" in 45 *I.C.L.Q.*: 52.

Legrand, P. (1997) "Against a European Civil Code" in 60 *Modern L. Rev.*: 44-63.

Legrand, P. [2001] "What Legal Transplants?" in D. Nelken & J. Feest, eds., *Adapting Legal Cultures*, Hart Publishing.

Linz, L. & Stepan, A. (1996) *Problems of Democratic Transition and Consolidation*, John Hopkins University Press.

Lopez-Ayylon, S. (1995) "Notes on Mexican Legal Culture" in D. Nelken, ed., *Social and Legal Studies*: Special Issue on Legal Culture, Diversity and Globalization 4 ,4: 477-492.

Man, S.W. & Wai, C.Y (1999) "Whose Rule of Law? Rethinking (Post-) Colonial Legal Culture in Hong Kong", *Social and Legal Studies* 8:147-170.

Massell, G. (1968) "Law as an Instrument of Revolutionary Change in a Traditional Milieu: The Case of Soviet Central Asia", *Law and Society Rev.* 2:179.

Mertus, J. (1999) "The Liberal State vs. the National Soul: Mapping Civil Society Transplants", *Social and Legal Studies* 8:121

Nelken, D. (1981) "The 'Gap Problem' in the Sociology of Law: A Theoretical Review" in 1 *Windsor Y.B. Access to Just.* 1981:35-61.

Nelken, D. (1994) "Whom Can you Trust? The Future of Comparative Criminology" in D. Nelken, ed., *The Futures of Criminology*, Sage:220-244.

Nelken, D. (1996a) "Law as Communication: Setting the Field" in D. Nelken, ed., *Law As Communication*, Dartmouth, 3-25.

Nelken, D. (1996b) "Judicial Politics and Corruption in Italy" in M. Levi & D. Nelken, eds., The Corruption of Politics and the Politics of Corruption: Special Issue of the *Journal of Law and Society*, Blackwell, 95-113.

Nelken,D. (1997) "The Globalization of Crime and Criminal Justice: Prospects and Problems" in M. Freeman, ed., *Law and Opinion at the End of the 20th Century*, Oxford University Press, 251-279.

Nelken, D. (2000) "Telling Difference: Of Crime and Criminal Justice in Italy" in D. Nelken, ed., *Contrasting Criminal Justice*, Dartmouth.

Nelken, D. (2001) "Beyond the Metaphor of Legal Transplants? Consequences of Autopoietic Theory for the study of Cross-Cultural Legal Adaptation" in J. Priban & D. Nelken eds., *Consequences of Autopoiesis*, Dartmouth.

Nottage, L. [2001] "The Still-Birth and Re-Birth of Product Liability in Japan" in D. Nelken & J. Feest, eds., *Adapting Legal Cultures*, Hart Publishing.

Orucu, E. (1995) "A Theoretical Framework for Transfrontier Mobility of Law" in R. Jagtenberg, E. Orucu & A. de Roo, eds., *Transfrontier Mobility of Law*: 4.

Paterson, J. & Teubner, G. (1998) "Changing Maps: Empirical Legal Autopsies", *Social and Legal Studies,* 7: 451-486.

Prosser,T. [2001] "Marketisation, Public Service and Universal Service" in D. Nelken & J. Feest, eds., *Adapting Legal Cultures*, Hart Publishing.

Sadurski, W. (2000) "Conclusions: On the Relevance of Institutions and the Cen-

trality of Constitutions in Post-Communist Transitions" in J. Zielonka, ed., Democratic Consolidation in Eastern Europe, vol. I: Institutional Engineering, Oxford
University Press.

Santos, B. de Sousa (1995) *Towards a New Common Sense*, Routledge.

Starr, J. (1992) *Law as Metaphor: From Islamic Courts to the Palace of Justice*,
SUNY Press.

Tanase, T. [2001] "The Empty Space of the Modern in Japanese Law Discourse" in
D. Nelken & J. Feest, eds., *Adapting Legal Cultures*, Hart Publishing.

Teubner, G. (1998) "Legal Irritants: Good Faith in British Law or How Unifying
Law Ends up in New Divergences" in *Modern Law Review* 61.1:11-32.

Van Swaaningen, R. (1999) "Reclaiming Critical Criminology: Social Justice and
the European Tradition" in *Theoretical Criminology* 3,1:5-29.

Waelde, T.W. & Gunderson, J.L. (1994) "Legislative Reform in Transitional Economies: Western Transplants: A Short Cut to Social Market Economy Status?", 43
I.C.L.Q.:347-378.

Watson, A. (1974) *Legal Transplants: An Approach to Comparative Law*, Scottish
Academic Press.

[15]
An e-mail from Global Bukowina[1]

Abstract

This paper uses Teubner's reinterpretation of Ehrlich's idea of 'living law' in his paper on 'Global Bukowina' as a test case of what is involved in making a classical author speak to current issues. It argues that interpretation is a form of appropriation and that the process of re-contextualising ideas involves an unstable compromise between establishing what an author meant and what an author means.

Why do we still study classical authors? In particular, how can we find a balance between seeking to establish what they actually said – and making them mean something for us today? This paper forms part of a larger study of the influence of Eugen Ehrlich, a professor of Roman law in the city of Czernowitz, in the province of Bukowina, at the outskirts of the Austro-Hungarian Empire.[2] Ehrlich, whose main works were written before the First World War, is generally considered the founder of the sociology of law. So an examination of the way his work has been re-read in the later history of the discipline can provide a good illustration of our theme. I shall be concentrating especially on a well-known paper by Gunther Teubner, provocatively called 'Global Bukowina' (Teubner, 1997). which, as its title suggests, seeks to apply Ehrlich's insights to the changed world in which we live today.

What is the relationship – if any – between Global Bukowina and the province where Ehrlich lived and worked? In the course of searching for references to Ehrlich, I came across the website 'Bukovina Society of the Americas', which caters for those nostalgic about their roots in historical Bukowina. As well as acting as a venue for those seeking to share news or find out more about their ancestors, this well-organised site also includes information on features of life there in the past. Most of these descriptions concern the histories of ethnic Germans living in the province. As far as I have been able to determine, the site has nothing to say about Ehrlich, even if, for sociologists of law, he is one of the intellectual glories of real-life Bukowina. But, curiously, as footnote 1 to this paper shows, someone has actually written in from Brazil to say that they have become interested in Bukowina through Teubner's paper and to thank the creators of the site for rescuing its history! The imposition of the textually constituted 'Global Bukowina' onto the real Bukowina thus seems to reflect something of what Baudrillard was getting at in his analyses of the interaction of virtual and real worlds (see e.g. Baudrillard, 1994). Teubner's Ehrlich, as the progenitor of Global Bukowina, is more 'real' than the historical Ehrlich, and Ehrlich or 'Ehrlich' lives on through Teubner's appropriation of his work. This paper will be concerned with the techniques and implications of such appropriation.

---

1 These reflections were stimulated by an e-mail sent to the guest book of the site 'Bukovina Society of the Americas' (www.bukovinasociety.org/guestbook.html). Thursday, 11 January 2007; 09:05:23 – 0800. 'Prezados Senhores, Me interessei pelo tema depois da leitura do texto de Gunther Teubner – "Global Bukowina: Legal Pluralism in the World Society". Parabéns pelo interesse no resgate da história da Bukowina. Abraços Leonardo Arquimimo de Carvalho (São Paulo, Brazil).'

2 Much of this paper will be incorporated in a much longer chapter that will appear in Hertogh (forthcoming).

190

Contextualisation, de-contextualisation and re-contextualisation

Why should we still be interested in Ehrlich's controversial philosophical, historical, psychological or sociological propositions? There are many reasons to be concerned with the work of great writers of the past. But for our purposes it is helpful to contrast the aim of seeking to get *a writer's ideas right* with that of trying to decide whether the ideas themselves *were right*. These certainly seem like relatively distinct exercises. The first of these approaches could be said to aim at adding to the footnotes on Ehrlich, the second focuses more on the way Ehrlich figures as a footnote in the work of later writers.

The importance of context varies for the two enquiries. For the first approach it is essential to understand Ehrlich 'in the context' of his time and place. We might, for example, try to explain how a scholar of Roman law could have come to make this sort of breakthrough to sociological fieldwork, or set out to trace similarities and differences between his idea of living law and the ideas about 'social law' in the work of writers such as Savigny or Tönnies. In the second type of enquiry, however, our interest would focus more on what has been made of a scholar's ideas – and on what can still be made of them. So the point would be more the need to get Ehrlich 'out of context' in the sense of describing how his work has been (or can be) made to transcend his setting in Bukowina at the beginning of the twentieth century.[3] If in the one case we would engage in careful exegesis in order to grasp what Ehrlich *meant*, in the other we would be more concerned with showing what Ehrlich *means* for us today.

In practice, however, though there are important differences in emphasis, these enquiries cannot entirely be kept apart. Even if our research is focused on the way Ehrlich's work influenced later authors, we will still need to engage in some exegesis of what he actually said (Nelken, 2008). It would be question-begging to speak of *Ehrlich's* influence unless we can be sure that the ideas others are using are those *actually* espoused by Ehrlich. In fact, writers who try to get Ehrlich right are frequently motivated by the desire to show that the way other commentators have got him wrong is not merely a matter of mere antiquarian interest. Thus, in an earlier paper, I devoted considerable attention to distinguishing Ehrlich's ideas from the ways in which they had been re-presented by Roscoe Pound (Nelken, 1984). But at the same time I also argued that Pound's summary of his views obscured the way Ehrlich's contribution could still be of value. Clearing up the misconceptions about what Ehrlich was wrongly supposed to have argued was a prerequisite to going on to reveal the relevance of what he actually said to current debates. And, as I shall seek to show here, a return to the text not only typically accompanies the claim to have uncovered the 'true' or 'real' historical Ehrlich, but can also figure as part of the search for new meaning in older texts in the light of the later perspectives they are taken to prefigure.

Our interest in relating Ehrlich to his context will also depend on our conception of how the sociology of law progresses. On one (scientistic?) view of sociology of law as a 'science' our prime task is to subject Ehrlich's de-contextualised hypotheses to empirical testing. To contextualise him involves making an imaginative leap back before not only the birth of the discipline of sociology of law but also before there were studies of 'law and psychology' or 'law and economics'. Ehrlich's contribution would then have to be considered as of mainly historical interest on a par with other writings in the sciences of his period. If the sociology of law can 'progress' scientifically, or rather, just because it can progress, we should not expect the founder of the discipline to do more than set out directions to follow. We can learn from Ehrlich only by leaving him behind.

---

3   This is oversimplifying. It could be argued – it *has* been argued – that it was the marginality of Ehrlich's context – 'on the periphery' of the Austro-Habsburg empire – that enabled him to see 'more' than his contemporaries.

But most writers (including major textbook writers such as Treves or Cotterrell) see the sociology of law as less assimilable to this idea of scientific progress (Friedman, 1986). They would encourage us to return to Ehrlich, as to other founding fathers, such as Durkheim, Weber or Marx, less because of the empirical validity of their specific claims and more because of the continuing relevance of the fundamental issues they dealt with and the way they dealt with them. On this view, Ehrlich's arguments, as also the criticisms made of them at the time, may be as relevant today as they were then. The earliest reviewers of his work wondered about the relationship between legal sociology and legal history (Vinogradoff, 1920) – but the issue of disciplinary boundaries is as problematic now as it was then. Critics complained about Ehrlich using the term 'law' in talking of living law – most notably in Kelsen's controversial attack on what he saw as Ehrlich's failure to defend the rights of citizens as declared by state law. And there are still heated debates about the normative implications, if any, of claiming that societies are characterised by regimes of legal pluralism.

Even where Ehrlich gets things 'wrong', this can be instructive. Many of the early comments, both on the original German edition and of the later American translation, echo those still being made today. Max Rheinstein, a hard though not unsympathetic critic, applauded Ehrlich for opening jurists' eyes to the relations that actually exist between family members, the way wealth is actually transferred from the dead to the living, and how people actually buy and sell. But he also accused him of peddling half truths. He considered it a (politically motivated!) mistake to describe custom as law; social behaviour patterns do not always coincide with what people really believe are the right values. It was important to see that law does make space for other normative systems, which it may then incorporate. But this should not be taken as a general rule. Ehrlich's arguments applied mainly, Rheinstein claimed, to what can be called 'stop gap law', the rules people make for themselves in private transactions. In terms of legal practice, he argued, it was misleading to reduce legal science to sociology. Whilst legal sociology can be of assistance to judges, questions of justice involve matters of political prudence which do not and often should not coincide with popular sentiment (Rheinstein, 1938).

The philosopher and jurist Morris Cohen, for his part, thought Ehrlich was overreacting against the historical school (Cohen, 1912–1914, pp. 535–7). He too insisted that law should not be confused with custom. The practice of tipping waiters, he pointed out, is custom not law, and there is nothing gained by calling it law. By contrast, the arcane details of wills are law and not custom. Businesses may make their own agreements irrespective of the law, but they always act (in his prescient words) in its shadow. The state may not dictate everyday life, but its importance should never be under-estimated. It would otherwise be hard to understand why such hard battles are fought over who should control the government (Cohen, 1936, p. 684.)

The fact that many of the issues raised by his work still do not seem to have found agreed solutions shows how far Ehrlich's ideas do transcend their original context. Nonetheless, it is important to see that any 'return' to Ehrlich also involves a process of re-contextualisation. Later writers give *new* meaning to older authors as they 'appropriate' classical texts so as to make them speak to and for present purposes. And it is this use which makes them classics in the same way that 'traditions' enable 'the past to live in the present' (Krygier, 1986). Even if we were to set out only to repeat exactly what Ehrlich is thought to have said, introducing his ideas can have different 'meaning' depending on the changing context in which he is quoted. They would, for example, likely have a different impact at a time when there is concern about too much state intervention or 'juridification', as compared to a period or extensive privatisation. But most returns to classical authors in any case, to a greater or lesser extent, also involve explicit attempts at (re)interpretations. Since any interpretation of what a past writer has written is contestable, however, other commentators may allege that the new interpretation represents a departure from the correct meaning – and it is through such debates that traditions develop and earlier scholars' arguments are given new life.

As this suggests, a given response to Ehrlich will therefore often tell us as much if not more about the interpreter than it does about what is being interpreted. On the one hand, Rheinstein thought Ehrlich's arguments were vitiated by their political sub-text. Science disguised as the desire to legitimate only that law that was popularly accepted – what he described as the 'postulate of complete and homogenous democracy'. For him, 'Ehrlich's basic proposition that the norms of law are nothing but the actual customs and habits of the people does not withstand the scrutiny of methodological analysis. It is the statement not of a scientific truth but of a political postulate. Nevertheless, Ehrlich's work occupies 'a high rank in legal sociology' (Rheinstein, 1938, pp. 238–9). By contrast, Maoist writers in China (first introduced to his sociology of law by Pound) wrote of 'the reactionary essence of Ehrlich's sociology of law' (Dong, 1989, p. 904). As we shall see, Ehrlich's ideas have been pressed into service both within a framework of Pound's common-law cultural presuppositions and projects, and in terms of Luhmann's continental and civil law assumptions.

This raises the question of what yardstick to use in order to decide whether the work of an older writer has been so (mis)interpreted so as not to deserve to count as an example of his or her influence. It would have been possible, as in my earlier discussion of Pound on Ehrlich, to write this paper too in the form of a protest at the way Ehrlich continues to be 'appropriated' by later scholars in ways that often pay scant attention to what he really said. As we shall have cause to note, there is indeed more than a little special pleading in the more recent accounts of Ehrlich offered by leading authors such as Alex Ziegert (again), or Gunther Teubner. But my main purpose in this revisiting of Ehrlich is *not* to try, yet again, to 'save' Ehrlich from his interpreters by offering a better reading of his text. If we are concerned with the usefulness of Ehrlich's contribution to the discipline we need also to ask questions about which interpretations have more heuristic value. But once we do this, to insist we are only interested in setting the record 'straight' about what Ehrlich actually said sounds somewhat pedantic if not actually misleading.

If the meaning of an author is inevitably subject to different interpretations, in the search for the most useful interpretation there may often be only a fine line between misinterpretation and creative reinterpretation. Questions about interpretation can arise not only where scholars claim to be explaining what Ehrlich really meant, but also where they argue that he got things wrong. And they, of course, also apply to our efforts to interpret Ehrlich's interpreters 'correctly'. So we need always to ask how any given interpretation *becomes* authoritative. This does not mean, of course, that any interpretation of Ehrlich is as good as any other. There must be some limits to how far we are entitled to rewrite past thinkers in the light of current concerns. But we do need to acknowledge that the value of any interpretations may change from one context of time and place to another.

I may have been justified in trying to prise Ehrlich away from the embrace of Pound's socio-legal engineering *if, at the time I wrote, such an interpretation of his work was as serving as a block on the development of sociology of law.* But that still leaves open the question whether Pound may have made 'good' use of Ehrlich in his own time. Under current conditions, it is arguable that attempts to re-read Ehrlich in the light of a major sociological theorist of the range and sophistication of Niklas Luhmann should not be rejected *tout court*, even if, again, these interpretations do require some straining of Ehrlich's prose. In other words, we also need to ask if reading Ehrlich's work in the light of autopoietic theory of law as a communicative sub-system of society may be helpful in advancing the discipline.

In discussing Teubner's interpretation of Ehrlich's ideas in Global Bukowina, I shall seek to show that he does somewhat mischaracterise what Ehrlich meant at the time he wrote. But I shall also suggest that his paper represents a highly creative effort to apply Ehrlich's ideas to new challenges in the light of new ways of theorising social change. Moreover, as we shall see when discussing his arguments in detail, the question of how we should respond even to his presentation of Ehrlich's work becomes even more complicated when we find ourselves dealing with an interpreter who *admits* that he or she is also changing or developing the ideas they have borrowed from him. As I shall try to demonstrate, such efforts at re-contextualisation produce an unstable compromise between the aims of contextualisation and de-contextualisation – between getting Ehrlich right and claiming that he is right.[4]

From 'law in action' to legal autopoiesis

For a long time there was a tendency (especially, but not only, in English-language discussions) to assimilate Ehrlich's arguments to Anglo-American ways of talking about 'law in society'. This certainly facilitated drawing on him in dealing with socio-legal problems as they are posed in common law jurisdictions. This is most clearly seen in Pound's original introduction to the first translation of Ehrlich's *Grundlegung* (Pound, 1936/1962) and endorsed by Ziegert (Ziegert, 1979). But what we are now witnessing is in some respects an opposite trend, one which treats Ehrlich's work as belonging to the world view of Continental legal systems and adopts him as a forerunner of the one of the most advanced schools of continental sociology of law, that associated with Niklas Luhmann. Curiously, this too is expounded in the introduction to the (new) English translation of Ehrlich's magnum opus (Ziegert, 2001). In this novel framing of Ehrlich's ideas, we are told that Ehrlich represents an approach for which Luhmann's sociology of law is 'the continuation' (Ziegert, 2001, p. xxxi), if not the sociological culmination. All this, even though Luhmann himself does not even refer to Ehrlich!

When I last wrote about Ehrlich, more than twenty years ago, my main goal was to set out the differences between his ideas and those of Pound. Ziegert (one of the few to appreciate the continuing relevance of this then half-forgotten pioneer) had argued that Pound's distinctions between 'law in books' and 'law in action' 'could only be' that put forward by Ehrlich (Ziegert, 1979). In my article I claimed that, on the contrary, the ideas were different. In fact, even Pound himself, in a retrospective towards the end of his career admitted that he had (as he put it) 'developed' living law into the somewhat different concept of 'law in action' (Pound, 1938).[5] Whilst acknowledging that there was some overlap between the concepts of 'law in action' and 'living law', I set out to show that Ehrlich's original idea of living law should be considered a more promising and richer starting point for an approach more open to mainstream sociological concerns and less geared to the problem of legal effectiveness.

I was convinced then of the overriding importance of correcting Pound's misinterpretations: getting Ehrlich 'right' was the only way that his valuable insights could be recovered. I would still argue that Pound's use of Ehrlich limits the potential contribution of the idea of living law. But, whilst it is good that more scholars (including Ziegert) have come to agree that it is important to recognise the differences between these authors, I would now add that simply claiming that Pound got Ehrlich 'wrong' oversimplifies the issue of how classical authors are made relevant to contemporary problems. To a great extent it is impossible to read a past author except through current lenses (Gadamer, 1975). What Pound took from Ehrlich can be seen as having special relevance for his own time – and may be an interpretation that could still be salient in other times and places. Equally, alternative 'readings' have to 'prove' their superiority, now and in the future.

Ziegert's new interpretation in his introduction aims both to present a faithful picture of Ehrlich and also to show him as a forerunner of Luhmannian thinking. This can sometimes lead to

---

4   My paper on Ehrlich was no exception. In the final footnote (in Nelken, 1984), I proposed drawing on Ehrlich to construct a more 'ecological' approach to law reform (something which Gunther Teubner later asked me to elaborate on).

5   In his introduction to Ehrlich's book, he had already complained that 'Europeans had a phobia of the state'. But he was living in the new deal USA of the 1930s, not in Europe.

surprising reformulations of his ideas. We are told that Ehrlich is the founder of the 'genuine social level apart from the individual'. For Ehrlich, like Luhmann, in thinking about law, 'expectations not sanctions matter'. What Ehrlich was trying to say in speaking of living law was that:

> 'the norm structure in inner order of associations is what individuals need as reference point to construct themselves as behaving individuals and expect from others what they can reasonably expect from themselves . . . this reflexive domain is the domain of law and has nothing to do with the state governance [sic] or sovereignty.'   (Ziegert, 2001, p. xii)

Likewise, the account of Ehrlich's policy sympathies though put in unfamiliar language is not implausible. He is said to be against the self aggrandisement of lawyers and state functionaries, but to believe that 'society' will keep these in check. Ehrlich, we are told, shows law's 'blind spot' which results from the fact that law 'is a trade', and lawyers refer back only to legal practice and so do not see what else is happening. In a few cases, Ziegert's interpretations seem particularly forced ones. For Ehrlich, we are told, the 'evolution of legal decision-making legal practice conditions the social order for further evolution and specialises the court based decision making system as the effective hub of the living law'. But, whilst it is fair to say that Ehrlich did admire the common law and the (somewhat idealised) way he assumed it operated, describing what courts do as 'the hub of the living law' seems a strange way of re-presenting a book that (pace Luhmann) sought to describe how living law was actually rooted in the everyday life of associations.

Arguably, Ziegert's reformulations of Ehrlich also do a disservice to Luhmann by blurring the way his approach to socio-legal theorising involved a 'paradigm' shift from 'open system' to 'closed system' theorising about law in society (Nelken, 1987). On this point, Ziegert explains that 'Ehrlich does not deny the need the fact of legal specialisation and differentiation'. But 'non denial' is hardly the equivalent of the theoretical breakthrough which Luhmann builds on the back of his radical differentiation of legal and other communicative systems. Ziegert goes on to say that, for Ehrlich, '[w]hat makes legal propositions legal is not a higher normativity but the specialised differentiated performance of a subject of social operations responding to pressures of uncertainty' (Ziegert, 2001, p. xxiii). Here, too, it would seem more correct to say that, unlike Luhmann, Ehrlich mixes discussions of law and morals at the level of social pressures but seeks to distinguish them in terms of the psychology of the individuals deciding whether to recognise their legitimacy.

The same applies when Ziegert tells us that, '[l]ike Luhmann, Ehrlich is a scientific observer of law in its social context' (Ziegert, 2001, p. xv). Again, it would seem more appropriate to recognise that 'context' has more of a technical meaning for Luhmann, at least as explained by Teubner, his leading interpreter in legal sociology. Law *makes* its own context – and there are a series of contexts depending on what subsystem we start from. Likewise, when Ziegert affirms that, for Ehrlich, 'Law can never control the factual order itself' we need to avoid confusing two senses of 'control'. Ehrlich thinks that only a better informed form of legal decision making could – and should – do justice to the facts of the living law (this was his legacy to the American Legal Realists). But, for Luhmann, order comes from, or is imposed on the 'noise' of the outside world, and law's role includes maintaining normative expectations by 'not learning' from the antinomian facts of social life. If Ehrlich's message is that we must stop buying into jurists' way of seeing the world, for Luhmann 'scientists' must make a 'second-order' assessment of law's way of observing the world – or as Teubner puts it of 'how the law thinks' (Teubner, 1989).

Though we should appreciate the effort to make Ehrlich speak to present concerns we should also, I think, be cautious about assimilating him to conventional wisdom rather than using him to gain a perspective on it. Whereas Ziegert once told us that Ehrlich's work could provide a valuable resource for improving efforts at social engineering (Ziegert, 1979), he now tells us that Ehrlich, like Luhmann, is sceptical about such efforts and that time has shown the sense of this scepticism (Ziegert, 2001). However, the current period is different from the early 1980s. An obsession with the limits of 'legal effectiveness' can easily become a theoretical dead end in a period where everyone assumes an instrumentalist role for law and exaggerates its ability to produce social change. But matters may be different at a time where there is too much cynicism about law's ability to deliver social progress. The same applies to the closely related research obsession with the so called 'gap' between law's promise and achievement (Nelken, 1981). What is a tired approach within pragmatic, technically oriented, Anglo-American legal cultures may be much more heuristically useful in places, such as some continental European jurisdictions, where the 'gap' between legal promise and implementation is typically so wide that it is just taken for granted (Nelken, 2001a). In such societies, filtering Ehrlich's message through Luhmann's formulas may be less innovative than it might otherwise seem.

But all depends on what is done with these ideas. In this respect, it is interesting to contrast Ziegert's re-presentation of Ehrlich with Gunther Teubner's argument about 'Global Bukowina' (Teubner, 1997). Teubner, like Ziegert, is engaged in a rewriting of Ehrlich in Luhmannian terminology. But whereas, for Ziegert, Ehrlich's ideas were right when they were first put forward and (when properly reformulated) are still valuable now, Teubner, more surprisingly, argues that Ehrlich was actually wrong in his own time and only really comes into his own now at a time of globalisation. In addition, whereas both Ziegert and Teubner treat Ehrlich as a forerunner of the Luhmannian doxa, Teubner is explicit about the need also to change and 'update ' Ehrlich's arguments.

These differences are linked to the topics which these authors use Ehrlich to address. Ziegert is concerned with his relevance to law in the nation state, the context Ehrlich was originally writing about. Teubner, on the other hand, in developing a highly original autopoietic excursus on global law explores Ehrlich's relevance in examining the role of law in the international arena in exchanges mainly involving private actors – matters about which Ehrlich said little in his *Grundlegung*. According to Ziegert, Ehrlich is not to be understood primarily as concerned with legal pluralism. Indeed, he uses Luhmannian language to show how different elements of Ehrlich's scheme of thought such as living law and norms for decisions are integrally related. Teubner does take Ehrlich to be a forerunner in the study of legal pluralism, but gives this a very different meaning when re-examined in the light of the Luhmannian theory of autopoiesis.

Ziegert wants us to accept that Luhmannian insights can help get us to the heart of what Ehrlich was really trying to say. In assessing his interpretation, the question we need to ask ourselves is the relatively straightforward one whether we find his reading Ehrlich convincing and suggestive. But, with Teubner, it is difficult to know how seriously he wants us to take his argument as actually an interpretation of Ehrlich. Does his use of the term 'Global Bukowina' represent a genuine effort to apply Ehrlich's ideas to the new global context? Or is it no more (and no less) than a playful – and paradoxical – metaphor. After all, if everywhere is now a periphery, where is the centre? (Can there be only periphery?) What, if anything, is there in common between Ehrlich's Bukowina and the world being remodelled by globalisation? Between a province waiting for ethnic nationalism and a world in which state borders lose meaning? Teubner's audacious proposal that Bukowina has now gone global lays a direct challenge to those who say Ehrlich's ideas necessarily relate to specific space and time conditions of a province in the defunct Austro-Hapsburg empire. But, at the same time, the use of this phrase itself perpetuates the misconception that Ehrlich's ideas get their sense from the (relative) lack of state presence in Bukowina. Ehrlich is seen as able to be relevant now (only) because we have a new situation of normative life again being formed *beyond* the reach of state. Yet it seems more faithful to Ehrlich to say that his arguments concerned the possibilities of normative life being formed *outside* of the state, even if not necessarily *beyond* its jurisdiction.

In any case, Teubner is also quite explicit about what he sees as the need to correct and 'develop' Ehrlich's ideas if we are to grasp the new form of global law beyond the state. This makes it difficult to decide how far Teubner's 'updating' is intended to be true to what Ehrlich might himself have said if asked to theorise *lex mercatoria*. What evidence there is on this point does not go in Teubner's favour.[6] What is more clear is that Teubner finds Ehrlich convincing on some points even if he also sees the need for revisions. Thus, he agrees with Ehrlich that the basis of law is in society and not in legal dogmatics – placing Ehrlich's formulation of this truth as the headnote of his paper. He also sees merit in the fact that, as he puts it, Ehrlich 'asks where are norms actually produced and treats politics and social on equal footing' (Teubner, 1997, p. 11). There are also happy parallels in their endeavours. Where Ehrlich's idea of living law, as he says, 'breaks a taboo' that law must be identified with the state so too does the idea that there can be a *lex mercatoria* independent from all nation states.

But, as with Ziegert, the process of translating Ehrlich's ideas into the theoretical language of Luhmannian autopoietic theory can also make it difficult to know where Ehrlich ends and Luhmann begins. Most important, the source of living law for Teubner is not that hypothesised by Ehrlich. Teubner does not anchor this in the order of associations as such (except in so far as he sees law as 'closely coupled' with economic processes). Rather, he relies on the autopoietic theory of law which takes law to be one of a number of self-referring discursive sub-systems each constructing their own environment. But, as we noted when discussing Ziegert's recent work, this Luhmannian idea has no real trace in Ehrlich. Nor was Ehrlich, unlike Teubner, trying to explain how law in general or contract law in particular succeeds in keeping the paradoxes of its self-validation latent. If anything, he observed a lack of wider social validity of much state law.

Teubner talks about law being produced 'at the boundary with economic and technological processes'. He tells us that, likewise, according to Ehrlich, 'living law is produced in the periphery of the legal system in close contact with the external social process of rule formation'. It is true that Ehrlich too suggested that economic development has and will transform law from within (the theme taken up later by Karl Renner, see Renner, 1949). But it is far from obvious that Ehrlich sees the distinction between the centre and the periphery as Teubner does. For example, his definition of living law included lawyers' contracts, which would have been a productive source of law even in Imperial Vienna. What is more, the notion of periphery, as employed by Teubner, is ambiguous as between, on the one hand, Ehrlich's location in the province of Bukowina on the edges of the Austro-Hapsburg empire, and, on the other, everyday life which is *everywhere* peripheral to what goes on in the courts.

Teubner's focus is on the legal regimes created by and for global non-state actors by invisible social networks and invisible professional communities which transcend territorial boundaries. He sees these new forms of global law as growing up in a world characterised by a highly globalised economy and a weakly globalised politics. Even if Ehrlich's own examples were domestic ones, many of the regimes Teubner wishes to analyse do come near to what Ehrlich meant by living law. Transnational contracting, arbitration and the other processes of *lex mercatoria* could be so characterised, as could 'intra organisational regulation in multinational companies'. It would also seem fair to assume that Ehrlich's concept can be applied to 'all forms of rule making by private governments' and 'professional rule production', though it should also be noted that Ehrlich's interest was less in rule making as such and more the way such rule systems are actually applied in practice.

On the other hand, Teubner's example of 'technical standardisation' as an instance of living law has a more dubious pedigree. The whole phenomena of so-called 'bureaucratic administrative law' (Nelken, 1982) seems far from Ehrlich's concerns, and his account of living law gives little indication that he realised that a form of normativity based on technical standards and conventions would become so important. Even Teubner's example of human rights law is not a straightforward case of

---

6   Michaels (2005) quotes a little known paper by Ehrlich concerning the history of private international law from which it seems likely that he would then have denied the status of law to lex mercatoria. On the other hand, we do not know what Ehrlich would say now and, on our interpretation, it is that which interests Teubner more than what Ehrlich actually said then.

living law. Much human rights is actually promoted or underwritten by state law or international law. Even if non-state actors such as NGOs, etc., play a crucial activist role it still seems crucial to recognise the extent to which these associations are making rules for others (Nelken, 2006), not, as in Ehrlich's account, only for their own members. As far as these two key elements of global law are concerned, the idea of living law may obscure more than it reveals about them.

Why, then, bring Ehrlich into it, given that he had little to say about such transnational legal regimes? Teubner arrives there by a process of elimination. We cannot, he says, understand legal globalisation via political theories, there is no world constitution to 'structurally couple ' law and politics: these legal regimes are governed less by international courts or worldwide legislation than by multinational law firms. So Ehrlich's 'living law' is the best candidate for describing how the globalisation of law 'creates a multitude of de-centred law making processes in various sectors of civil society independently of national states' (Teubner, 1997, p. xiii). On the other hand, the way Ehrlich himself characterised living law in Bukowina will not as such suffice for understanding these new forms of global living law. Teubner therefore draws a strong contrast between the sense of Ehrlich's arguments in their time and place, and the updating of his ideas for today's world.

As against Ehrlich's idea of living law, Teubner advises, law is 'not drawing its strength now from ethnic communities as the old living law was supposed to do'.[7] 'Ehrlich', Teubner goes on, 'was of course romanticising the law creating role of customs, habits and practices in small scale rural communities'. The global world, by contrast, relies on 'cold technical processes not on warm communal bonds'. But the assumption that Ehrlich is putting forward a thesis of legal pluralism rooted in ethnic communities – even if Teubner is certainly not the only commentator to take such a line – rests on a tendentious interpretation which has poor support in the text itself. This way of reading Ehrlich also displays the genetic fallacy by confusing factors that may have helped give rise to his argument, with the substance and validity of his ideas themselves. In fact, Ehrlich's claims were intended to be potentially universalisable ones, applicable well beyond Bukowina, and had less to do with ethnic differences than with the way law – like norms are created through the life of 'associations', whether peasants' holdings or behaviour of banks and other commercial enterprises in deciding whether to sue their debtors. This helps explain why the question of ethnic pluralism was not the main issue for early critics of Ehrlich such as Kelsen, whose objection was more to Ehrlich linking law to the actual normative practices of groups even when these were inconsistent with the Austrian code.

Teubner's revisions go much further however. For him the problem with applying Ehrlich's ideas is not merely the non-universability of the contingencies of ethnic pluralism in Bukowina. It is the link between the law and people's social experiences which needs to be broken if we are to understand how law reproduces itself. We must recognise that 'the lifeworld of different groups and communities is not the principal source of global law'. Instead, he argues, we should shift:

'from groups and communities to discourses and communicative networks, the proto law of specialised organisational and functional networks nourished not by stores of tradition but from the ongoing self-reproduction of highly specialised and often formally organised and rather narrowly defined global networks of an economic, cultural, academic or technological nature.'

---

7   The formulation of this sentence is somewhat ambiguous and it is therefore not entirely clear whether Teubner himself totally endorses this account of Ehrlich's ideas. Does 'supposed to do' here mean 'as commonly thought'? But, then, if Teubner knows better, why does he makes it seem as if this does represent Ehrlich's views? Or does 'supposed to do' mean what living law 'should' reflect the different laws of ethnic communities? This would be a different claim having less to do with where law comes from than with the need to recognise cultural diversity.

198

Teubner inserts Ehrlich's ideas into what he (unlike Ziegert) acknowledges to be a new and unfamiliar framework. We must, he argues, replace:

'rule, sanction and social control with speech acts, coding transformation of differences and paradox. It is not rules but communicative events that should be our focus and it is the self-organising process of rules that is important in understanding the symbolic reality of legal validity, not the possibility of imposing sanctions.'   (Teubner, 1997, p. 13)

But, at the same time, he suggests that it is only if we make this move towards autopoiesis theory that we can come to discover how, in some respects, Ehrlich's approach is now *more valid* than it was in the past. As he puts it, 'although Eugen Ehrlich's theory turned out to be wrong for the national law of Austria, I believe that it will turn out to be right, both empirically and normatively, for the newly emerging global law' (Teubner, 1997, p. 3).

Once again, however, such striking arguments need to be carefully unpacked. In what sense does the truth of Ehrlich's (many) ideas depend on what happened in the past or on what the future brings? Should scientific claims be judged in the light of historical events? What exactly is Teubner referring to when he asserts that Ehrlich 'turned out' to be 'wrong'? This cannot, for example, include his claims about the centre of gravity of law being in society, since Teubner takes this as his starting point. Have Ehrlich's ideas about living law been discredited? Must we really go beyond the boundaries of state law in order to find merit in Ehrlich's theses? When exactly did Ehrlich's theory 'turn out to be wrong'? When the First World War caused the Austrian empire to collapse? Or when he was forced to teach in Romanian in the last years of his life (before the Nazis and communists then tried to cancel his memory)? Arguably, the rise of ethnic nationalism could actually prove Ehrlich's point about the importance of more local loyalties rather than those to the imperial state (and it is strange for Teubner to call the law of the Austro-Hungarian empire 'the national law of Austria').

What evidence, on the other hand, does Teubner have that Ehrlich will eventually turn out to be right? Even if we choose to look beyond state law it is not obvious why the growth of *lex mercatoria* proves Ehrlich to be 'right'. It certainly shows that there can be forms of normative ordering that some call law, even though they are not based on state recognition. But Ehrlich was not mainly concerned with whether normative orderings were (already) actually called law, but with whether scientific observers had reasons to call them law. And there are, of course, pace Teubner, still many who argue that *lex mercatoria* is not really law whatever it is called. And although Teubner thinks Ehrlich has been proven right through having 'predicted' the rise of non-state global law, he himself asserts that it is only a question of time before these new forms of global law will be, as he says, 're-politicised' (although admittedly he considers that this will not take place through traditional political institutions but via 'structural coupling' with specialised discourses). Once this takes place, would this mean that Ehrlich will again have 'turned out' to be wrong? Is his a thesis that only works for periods of transition-interstitial times as well as places?

Conclusion: interpretation as appropriation

In this review of some recent re-presentations of Ehrlich's ideas we have shown the difficulty of maintaining any simple distinction between efforts to place a writer's work in its context and attempts to get it out of its context. A degree of 'rewriting' forms an important part of re-contextualising projects whether these be carried out by Pound, Ziegert or Teubner. Once we accept that interpretation is a form of appropriation it becomes harder (though not impossible) to distinguish between the appropriation and misappropriation of a previous writer's ideas.

For our purposes it makes sense to ask how far Teubner is faithful to Ehrlich. But we should not be surprised if Teubner's account of what is right and wrong about Ehrlich's arguments tells us at least as much about Teubner – and his desire to show the value of the autopoietic approach to law and society – as it does about Ehrlich. Any discussion of Teubner on Ehrlich which is only interested in Ehrlich is therefore going to miss the point of what Teubner is doing. We are dealing with an author who has openly chosen to 'use' Ehrlich as a pretext to introduce a series of papers about non-state law. So the more appropriate question is how far Teubner's reading of Ehrlich's work has helped him throw new light on *lex mercatoria*.

Teubner begins his paper by contrasting a top-down political global order based on American policing (he refers to Clinton's 'humanitarian' peacekeeping) to one constructed by means of an Ehrlich-type bottom-up 'peaceful' legal order. The latter, which he sees as more important, he equates with a range of developments in global non-state law. As it happens, after 9/11 things have 'turned out' differently with respect of the extent of American military engagements than Teubner or anyone else could have anticipated. But the more important issue is whether Global Bukowina really represents the alternative to the imposed Pax Americana that Teubner claims it does. Is *lex mercatoria*, for example, actually emancipated from politics – or is it precisely political by pretending not to be so? It is after all the genius of the common law that it 'appears' to be more geared to bottom up economic necessities than top-down political projects. Hence the growth of *lex mercatoria* can be seen as helping promote American ideas about the relationship between state and market and spread ways of doing law which privilege the symbolic capital of their professional elites (Dezalay and Garth, 1996).

Questions can also be asked about the political implications of Teubner's rewriting of Ehrlich. As is not uncommon in his writings Teubner deliberately blurs the line between describing and advocating (Nelken, 2001b). Here he argues that *lex mercatoria* should be legally recognised for what it is, the prototype of non-state law that is inevitably replacing that of the nation state. As against this, Ralf Michaels, for example, has recently insisted that:

> 'instead of moving the state to the periphery of our analyses and thereby ignoring its importance for our problems, we should move it into the centre of our analysis, so we can critique its role in globalisation.'

According to him:

> 'if we want to emancipate non-state law vis-à-vis the state, then it is not enough to look at the requirements on the side of non-state law. We must also look at what is necessary on the side of the state to make such emancipation possible. And we must ask what kind of emancipation this will be.'

For Michaels:

> 'The simple idea that because globalisation brings about a plurality of legal orders the state should recognise all these orders as law is either too radical or not radical enough. The idea is too radical if it expects the state to do things that run counter to what the state, as it exists right now, is about. In a nutshell, the state will always react as state to the challenges of globalisation, including the challenge from non-state communities and their laws. The idea is not radical enough if it believes that such a change could be brought about without changing the role of the state. In order to overcome the state-focus of conflict of laws, we must, ultimately, overcome the state itself. Ultimately, by acknowledging the right of everyone to make law, we accept that no one has the right to make law anymore. If everyone is able to claim jurisdiction, no one will have a superior position to mediate between conflicting regulations of conflicting communities anymore, at least not from a superior basis.' (Michaels, 2005)

If Teubner is entitled to appropriate Ehrlich for his purposes, the same applies to those who have in turn been stimulated by Teubner's ideas. Some of these writers have in fact gone on to develop his creative 'reworking' of Ehrlich in unexpected directions. Whilst Teubner himself counterposed Global Bukowina to the idea of a global political government, Thomas Mathiesen, for example, takes Teubner's idea and uses it to chart the recent growth of a global control system, what he describes as a frightening '*lex vigilatoria*' of surveillance removed from the political control of individual nation-states (Mathiesen, 2005). According to Mathiesen, the signs of this global control without a state may be seen in the ties between, for example, the SIRENE exchange, Eurodac, communication control through retention and tapping of telecommunications traffic data, the spy system Echelon and so on. Mathiesen's account shares with Teubner's a focus on the way legal regimes becoming increasingly untied or 'de-coupled' (to use Teubner's term) from nation-states, but the idea of imposed normative order represented here is a far cry from that described by Teubner – or for that matter by Ehrlich.

As we see, Mathiesen cites Teubner on Global Bukowina in order to make an argument that he would probably not recognise. But other authors offer even more contestable interpretations of Teubner on Ehrlich. In an original discussion of the spread of transgenic technologies through 'timespace', Paul Street draws on the disciplinary resources of critical human geography, post-structuralism and actor network theory. His aim in large part is to show how new developments are challenging the boundaries of existing academic disciplines. Thus he describes modes of ordering that weave together legal and other normative systems through what are made to seem inanimate material technologies. For these technologies to flourish, he argues, a range of interrela-tionships must occur that cut across social and legal boundaries and mobilise farmers, government departments, texts, individuals, international organisations, corporations, non-governmental orga-nisations and lawyers, as well as the seeds themselves and a host of other 'actants' (as Latour describes them). Law in the form of intellectual property rights plays a special role in bringing dispersed actors together in polymorphic social networks and maintaining the meaning of bio-technologies through time and space so as to enrol farmers into social networks necessary for the purposes of producers.

In the course of developing his argument, Street takes aim at Luhmann who, he alleges, denies that 'law comes out of the social'. He likewise criticises Teubner for his 'attempt to give law an autonomy beyond society' (Street, 2003, p. 9). His case-study, he says, shows rather that all law is always social and that there is no 'global law'. Specific companies invent genetically modified seeds, and use texts, objects, private policing and copyright law with the help of state to enforce their vision of facts about seeds and their claims to exploit their property rights. In the end, even (even?) Ehrlich is seen to have got things wrong. Street concludes his article saying that 'only through examining the particular practices and processes can we glimpse the performative power not of law itself, but of those networks that successfully manage to mobilise law. For law to be successful, it must in one sense be living law. It must be a law that exists beyond the proclama-tions and practices of lawyers and the state. But this is not Ehrlich's conception of living law. While it is a law that dominates life itself it is a law that lives within, and a law that leads to convergent habitual behaviour, but only for so long as it continues to be mobilised' (Street, 2003, p. 28).

Unlike Teubner, therefore, who tries to anchor his concept of Global Bukowina in Ehrlich's pioneering scholarship, Street prefers to emphasise how new developments require a radical new way of thinking, starting from scratch. It is not entirely clear what Street finds lacking in Ehrlich's approach – his exegesis of what Ehrlich wrote is even more tangential to the real point of his paper than Teubner's use of him. But let us assume that Street is right to say that what he is describing does not correspond to what Ehrlich was talking about when he introduced the concept of living law. It would be all too easy to explain this by saying that Ehrlich did not really anticipate the developments Street describes. *Pace* Ziegert and Teubner we could also wonder why anyone should have expected him to. On the other hand, matters are different if, like them, we are interested not only in what Ehrlich once meant but also what Ehrlich now means. In that case we could argue that his legacy includes all that his work has inspired – including efforts to go beyond him.

References

BAUDRILLARD, Jean (1994) *Simulacra and Simulation.* Ann Arbor: University of Michigan Press.

COHEN, Morris Raphael (1912–1914) 'Recent philosophical – legal literature in French, German, and Italian', *International Journal of Ethics* 26: 528–46.

COHEN, Morris Raphael (1936) 'On Absolutisms in Legal Thought', *University of Pennsylvania Law Review* 84: 681–715.

DEZALAY, Yves and GARTH, Bryant (1996) *Dealing in Virtue.* Chicago: University of Chicago Press.

DONG, Ji Wei (1989) 'Sociology of Law in China: Overview and Trends', *Law and Society Review* 23(5): 903–14.

FRIEDMAN, Lawrence (1986) 'The Law and Society Movement', *Stanford Law Review* 763–80.

GADAMER, Hans George, (1975) *Truth and Method.* New York: Seabury Press.

HERTOGH, M. (ed.) (forthcoming) *Re-Discovering Ehrlich.* Oxford: Hart Publishing.

KRYGIER, Martin (1986) 'Law as Tradition', *Law and Philosophy* 5: 237–62.

MICHAELS, Ralf (2005) 'The Re-Statement of Non-State Law: The State, Choice of Law, and the Challenge from Global Legal Pluralism', *Wayne Law Review* 51: 1209.

MATHIESEN, Thomas (2005) 'Lex Vigilatoria – Towards a control system without a state?', Essays for civil liberties and democracy, European Civil Liberties Network, available at www.ecln.org/essays/essay-7.pdf.

NELKEN, David (1981) 'The Gap Problem in the Sociology of Law', *Windsor Yearbook of Aceess to Justice* 35–62.

NELKEN, David (1982) 'Is there a crisis in law and legal ideology?', *British Journal of Law and Society* 9: 177–89.

NELKEN, David (1984) 'Law in Action or Living Law? Back to the Beginning in Sociology of Law', *Legal Studies* 4: 157.

NELKEN, David, (1987) 'Changing Paradigms in the Sociology of Law', in G. Teubner (ed.), *Autopoietic Law: A New Approach to Law and Society.* Berlin: De Gruyter, pp. 191–217.

NELKEN, David (2001a) 'Law's Embrace', *Social and Legal Studies* 3: 444–60.

NELKEN, David (2001b) 'Beyond the Metaphor of Legal Transplants?: Consequences of Autopoietic Theory for the Study of Cross – Cultural Legal Adaptation', in J. Priban and D. Nelken (eds.), *Law's New Boundaries: The Consequences of Legal Autopoiesis.* Aldershot: Dartmouth, pp. 265–302.

NELKEN, David (2006) 'Signaling Conformity: Changing Norms in Japan and China', *Michigan Journal of International Law* 27: 933–72.

NELKEN, David (2008) 'Eugen Ehrlich, Living Law, and Plural Legalities', *Theoretical Inquiries in Law* 9: 2.

POUND, Roscoe (1936/1962) 'Introduction' to E. Ehrlich, *Fundamental Principles of the Sociology of Law* (W. L. Moll, trans.). New York: Russell and Russell.

POUND, Roscoe (1938) 'Fifty Years of Jurisprudence', *Harvard Law Review* 51: 777–812.

RENNER, Karl (1949) *The Institutions of Private Law and their Social Function.* London: Routledge & Kegan Paul.

RHEINSTEIN, Max, (1938) 'Sociology of Law, Apropos Moll's translation of Eugen Ehrlich's Grundlegung der soziologie des Rechts', *Journal of Ethics* 48: 232–9.

STREET, Paul (2003) 'Stabilizing flows in the legal field: Illusions of permanence, intellectual property rights and the transnationalisation of law', *Global Networks* 3: 7–28.

TEUBNER, Gunther (1989) 'How the Law Thinks', *Law and Society Review* 23: 727–57.

202

TEUBNER, Gunther (1997) 'Global Bukowina: Legal Pluralism in the World Society', in G. Teubner (ed.), *Global Law without a State.* Aldershot: Dartmouth, pp. 3–28.

VINOGRADOFF, Paul (1920) 'The Crisis of Modern Jurisprudence', *Yale Law Journal* 29: 312–20.

ZIEGERT, Kurt Alex (1979) 'The Sociology behind Eugen Ehrlich's Sociology of Law', *International Journal of the Sociology of Law* 7: 225.

ZIEGERT, Kurt Alex (2001) 'Introduction', to Eugen Ehrlich, *The Fundamental Principles of Sociology of Law.* New Brunswick: Transaction Publishers: 19–44.

Index